A TEXTBOOK OF HUMAN RESOURCE MANAGEMENT

(For BMS, BBA and Other Management Courses)

Late Dr. C.B. MAMORIA
Ex. Prof. and Head of Department,
Faculty of Commerce and Management Studies,
University of Udaipur,
Udaipur.

S.V. GANKAR
Management Consultant Human Resources
and Visiting Faculty in
Management Institutes.

Himalaya Publishing House

ISO 9001 : 2015 CERTIFIED

First Edition	:	**2001**
Second Revised Edition	:	**2003**
Third Edition	:	**2004**
Fourth Edition	:	**2005**
Fifth Edition	:	**2006**
Sixth Edition	:	**2007**
Seventh Edition	:	**2008**
Edition	:	**2009, 2010, 2011, 2013, 2014**
Reprint	:	**2017, 2018, 2022**
Reprint	:	**2025**

Published by : Mrs. Meena Pandey
for **HIMALAYA PUBLISHING HOUSE PVT. LTD.,**
"Ramdoot", Dr. Bhalerao Marg, Girgaon, Mumbai - 400 004.
Phone: 022-23860170, 23863863; **Fax:** 022-23877178
E-mail: himpub@bharatmail.co.in; **Website:** www.himpub.com

Branch Offices :

New Delhi : "Pooja Apartments", 4-B, Murari Lal Street, Ansari Road, Darya Ganj, New Delhi - 110 002. Phone: 011-23270392, 23278631; Fax: 011-23256286

Nagpur : Kundanlal Chandak Industrial Estate, Ghat Road, Nagpur - 440 018. Mobile: 09325409992, 09325908881

Bengaluru : Plot No. 91-33, 2nd Main Road, Seshadripuram, Behind Nataraja Theatre, Bengaluru - 560 020. Phone: 080-41138821; Mobile: 09379847017, 09379847005

Hyderabad : No. 3-4-184, Lingampally, Besides Raghavendra Swamy Matham, Kachiguda, Hyderabad - 500 027. Phone: 040-27560041, 27550139

Chennai : No. 34/44, Motilal Street, T. Nagar, Chennai - 600 017. Mobile: 09380460419

Pune : "Laksha" Apartment, First Floor, No. 527, Mehunpura, Shaniwarpeth (Near Prabhat Theatre), Pune - 411 030. Phone: 020-24496323, 24496333; Mobile: 09370579333

Cuttack : Plot No. 5F-755/4, Sector-9, CDA Markat Nagar, Cuttack - 753 014, Odisha. Mobile: 09338746007

Kolkata : 3, S.M. Bose Road, Near Gate No. 5, Agarpara Railway Station, North 24 Parganas, West Bengal - 700 109. Mobile: 09674536325

DTP by : Sanhita

Printed at : Geetanjali Press Pvt. Ltd., Nagpur. On behalf of HPH.

PREFACE

The Indian Business Scenario has vastly changed due to Government's Policy of Liberalisation and Globalisation. There have been vast changes in Management of corporate business companies. The demand for professionally qualified executives have also increased.

The Universities and Management Education Institutes have introduced various courses in management education to suit the needs of the business world. The post-graduate level management courses in Indian Universities and Management Institutes have established their work in quality of education and as a result of this, there has been a rise for providing the young executives in all spheres of business, trade and commerce.

Human Resource Management as a subject in the management education has already occupied a place as an important core subject.

This book has been written for students at Graduate level degree courses in the Indian Universities. The material included covers the basic need of understanding the fundamentals in Human Resource Management. We do hope the book will be found useful to the students as well as the teachers at graduate level.

The revised edition contains the recent trends that are taking place in Human Resource Management in India and briefly abroad.

The authors shall be pleased to welcome all suggestions which could improve the contents in the future edition.

CONTENTS

SECTION I

SECTION II

SECTION - I

1. Introduction to Human Resource — Personnel Management
2. Functions of Personnel Management
3. Personnel Management in India
4. Human Resource Planning
5. Job Analysis, Job Design — Job Evaluation
6. Recruitment and Selection Process

1

Introduction to Human Resource — Personnel Management

ORGANISATION AND PERSONNEL MANAGEMENT

Organised work in the Society started much before the industrial revolution and establishment of industrial organisation. The Egyptians, Greeks, Mughals had created monuments like Pyramids of Egypt, Cathedral of Milan. St. Paul's in London St. Peter's in Rome, Taj Mahal in India. These monuments were built using management techniques and tools. The creators of these, had managerial insights like, Planning, Organising, directing, executing and controlling. Earliest organised work can be found in the Army — whose job was to protect the Kingdoms and territories. These are examples of organised work. However the factory — which is a productive system where organised work activities take place started in the middle of Seventeenth Century. In the factory system a large scale employment takes place, employing manpower and capital. Factory is an example an organisation engaged in activity useful to mankind. Similarly, other organisations where organised work with help of Human Resources takes place were developed to fulfil the needs of human beings.

The characteristics of an organisation are:

(a) An organisation is an institution, created by society to undertake a set of tasks. It existence can be temporary or permanent.

(b) There are more than one person in an organisation to perform the tasks. They may be partners or employees.

(c) The relationship between these employees are defined and structured.

(d) The relationship will produce interaction between these employees over a period of time and this will sustain a process for carrying out the given task.

(e) Hence organisation is a hierarchically structured process whose employees work together to achieve the organisational goals.

An organisation may be a manufacturing firm, a business concern, an insurance company, a governmental agency, social organisations, hospital, a university, a public school system, or a religious trust, cause-oriented groups and even families. It may be small or large, simple or complex. An organisation is a human grouping in which work is done for the accomplishment of some specific goals, or missions. For example, the goal of a manufacturing concern might be to produce and supply the goods and services to satisfy the demands of a market. A hospital may provide preventive and curative health services to the people of the area; or the business's goal might by not only to earn profit but also to survive in the competitive market for long. However, the goals of the organisations will not all be the same but an organisation has its own objectives, which may remain relatively constant, but they are likely to be modified over a period of time, as per the changing needs and circumstances. Organisational objectives are most likely to be multiple, as the organisation try to achieve several goals and to serve a number of different category of people. In order to achieve the goals, a well-run organisation works out a set of rules sometimes called policies, programmes, regulations, procedures or guidelines and sanctions. These are designed not to restrict creativity but to assist its members in accomplishment of the organisational goals.

MANAGER'S JOB

There are five basic functions, which all managers have to perform: (1) Planning (2) Organising (3) Staffing (4) Leading and Motivating and (5) Controlling. The specific activities included in these functions are:

1. *Planning:* Establish goals, develop rules and procedures, prepare plans, forecast, predict or project some future occurrence.
2. *Organising:* Giving each subordinate a specific job or task, establish departments, delegate authority to subordinates, establish channels of authority and communication, coordinate work of subordinates.
3. *Staffing:* Decide what type of employees are to be recruited, selective prospective employees, set performance standards, compensate the employees, evaluate their performance, training, developing and counselling them.
4. *Leading and Motivating:* Getting others to do their jobs, motivating, maintaining morale amongst employees.
5. *Controlling:* Set standards, e.g., sales targets, quality standards, production schedules, levels, compare actual performance with standards set, take corrective actions as needed.

To look after the various functions set for the organisation, adequate resources in men and materials have to be arranged by individuals who serve as managers within organisations. Such people have to make things happen to aid in the achievement of the organisational objectives, to co-ordinate the resources of the organisation – 4 important Ms, *viz., money, material* (raw or semi-manufactured), *machinery* (or fixed assets and plants), and *men* (or human resources). It is an effective combination and dovetailing of these factors on which the success or failure of the organisation depends. The resources by themselves will not help the organisation to accomplish the objective, unless there is an effective co-ordination and utilisation of these human and non-human resources.

While the human resources available to management in an organisation are only one part of resources which must be co-ordinated, it is through the combined efforts of the people that monetary and material resources are utilized for organisational objectives. Without human efforts, organisations cannot accomplish their objectives. Rensis Likert rightly observes, "All the activities of any enterprise are initiated and determined by the persons who make up that institution, plants, offices, computers, automated equipment, and all else that make a modern firm uses are unproductive except for human effort and direction of all the tasks of management, managing the human component is the central and most important task, because all else depends on how well it is done."

Consequently, the managers have a central responsibility not only for the behavior and performance of other people but also of their own behaviour. Managers are appointed at various levels to organise and co-ordinate the activities of the team members or fellow work associates. This constitutes a hierarchy of management, where individuals perform different roles: some are at the top level management, others are at the intermediate and lower levels of the management group. Those at the lower levels are responsible to persons at a higher organisational level. The greater the commitment of the members to organisational objectives, the greater is the degree of effectiveness with which the organisation works.

PEOPLE AT WORK

The principal component of an organisation is its 'human resources' or 'people at work.' Human resources have been defined as "*from the national point of view,* the knowledge skills, creative abilities, talents and aptitudes obtained in the population; whereas *from the viewpoint of the individual enterprise,* they represent the total of the inherent abilities, acquired knowledge and skills as exemplified in the talents and aptitudes of its employees." Jucius calls these resources, 'human factors,' which refer to "a whole consisting of inter-related, inter-dependent and inter-acting physiological, psychological, sociological and ethical components."

It is the human resource which is of paramount importance in the success of any organisation, because most of the problems in organisational settings are human and social rather than physical, technical or economic. Failure to recognise this fact causes immense loss to the nation, enterprise and the individual. In the words of Oliver Sheldon, "No industry can be rendered efficient so long as the basic fact remains unrecognized that it is principally human. It is not a mass of machines and technical processes, but a body of men. It is not a complex of matter, but a complex of humanity. It fulfils its function not by virtue of some impersonal force, but a human energy. Its body is not an intricate maze of mechanical devices but a magnified nervous system."

'People at Work' comprise a large number of individuals of different sex, age, socio-religious group and different educational or literacy standards. These individuals in the work place exhibit not only similar behaviour patterns and characteristics to a certain degree, but they also show many dissimilarities. Each individual who works has his own set of needs, drives, goals, and experiences. Each has his own physical and psychological traits. Each human being is not only a product of his biological inheritance but also a result of interactions with his environment. Family relationships, religious influences, racial or caste backgrounds, educational accomplishment, the application of technological innovations, and many other environmental-experimental influences affect the individual as he works. Among the environmental factors that influence work behaviour are various organisational elements (authority relationships; organisational goals, procedures, rules and policies: informal group relationship, the type and manner of supervision received by the employee, etc.) People come to work with certain specific motives to earn money, to get employment, to have better prospect in future, to be treated as a human being while at the place of work. They sell their labour for reasonable wage/salary and other benefits. It is these people who provide the knowledge and much of the energy through which organisational objectives are accomplished.

The management must, therefore, be aware not only of the organisational but also employee needs. None of these can be ignored. The achievements for the organisations of the 'people at work,' 'the people who manage them' (*i.e.,* managers themselves), and other groups of the public (such as the consumers, shareholders, the entrepreneurs, the governments, the suppliers, etc.) are possible through a concerted effort. The employee develops four dimensional relationships: *(i)* those between management and workers; *(ii)* those among the workers themselves; *(iii)* those among the managerial personnel; and *(iv)* those among different members of the organisation and the community. In other words, he develops "human relations" the purpose of which is *not* to enable him to discover clever techniques for winning friends and influencing people through personality development; *nor* to enable him to manipulate people as though they are puppets, *but* to assist him in working more effectively with other people in organisation."

MANAGEMENT OF MEN IS A CHALLENGING JOB

"The Management of Man" is a very important and challenging job; important because it is a job, not of managing 'men,' but of administering a social system. The management of men is a challenging task because of the dynamic nature of the people. No two persons are similar in mental abilities, traditions, sentiments, and behaviour; they differ widely also as groups, and are subject to many and varied influences. People are responsive; they feel, think, and act; therefore, they cannot be operated like a machine or shifted and altered like a template in a room layout. They, therefore, need a tactful handling by management personnel. If manpower is properly utilised, it may prove a dynamic motive force for running an enterprise at its optimum results and also work as an elixir for maximum individual and group satisfaction in relation to the work performed.

Manpower management is a most crucial job because "managing people is the heart and essence of being a manager." It is concerned with any activity relating to human elements or relations in organisation. Material elements, however, are beyond its domain. This view has been rightly summed up by J. M. Dietz (of Chicago). He observes: "A business or an industry can be thought of as an inter-weaving of human elements and material elements, with the human elements as the warp; while inter-locking and inter-weaving with this element are the material elements — the woof of the fabric. The warp of the fabric is the human element appearing and reappearing, the strength giving element holding the entire fabric together, and giving it life and a character of continuity." A business cannot succeed if this human element is neglected.

IMPORTANCE OF HUMAN RESOURCE MANAGEMENT

The importance of human resource management can be discussed, after Yodder, Heneman and others, from three standpoints, *viz.*, social, professional and individual enterprise.

(a) Social Significance: Proper management of personnel, enhances their dignity by satisfying their social needs. This it does by: *(i)* maintaining a balance between the jobs available and the jobseekers, according to the qualifications and needs; *(ii)* Providing suitable and most productive employment, which might bring them psychological satisfaction; *(iii)* making maximum utilization of the resource in an effective manner and paying the employee a reasonable compensation in proportion to the contribution made by him; *(iv)* eliminating waste or improper use of human resource, through conservation of their normal energy and health; and *(v)* by helping people make their own decisions, that are in their interests.

(b) Professional Significance: By providing a healthy working environment it promotes team work in the employees. This it does by: *(i)* maintaining the dignity of the employee as a 'human-being'; *(ii)* providing maximum opportunities for personal development; *(iii)* providing healthy relationship between different work groups so that work is effectively performed; *(iv)* improving the employees' working skill and cpacity; *(v)* correcting the errors of wrong postings and proper reallocation work.

(c) Significance for Individual Enterprise: It can help the organisation in accomplishing its goals by: *(i)* creating right attitude among the employees through effective motivation; *(ii)* utilising effectively the available human resources; and *(iii)* securing willing co-operation of the employees for achieving goals of the enterprise and fulfilling their own social and other psychological needs of recognition, love, affection, belongingness, esteem and self-actualisation.

Dynamic and growth-oriented organisation do require effective management of people in a fast-changing environment. Organisations flourish only through the efforts and competencies of their human resources. Employee capabilities must continuously be acquired, sharpened, and used. Any organisation will have proper human resource management *(i)* to improve the capabilities of an individual; *(ii)* to develop team spirit of an individual and the department; and *(iii)* to obtain necessary co-operation from the employees to promote organisational effectiveness.

DEFINITION OF PERSONNEL MANAGEMENT

We produce below a few standard definitions given by experts of personnel management, which will give an idea of what it means.

"It is that phase of management which deals with the effective control and use of manpower as distinguished from other sources of power."

"Its objective is to understand what has happened and is happening and to be prepared for what will happen in the area of working relationships between the managers and the managed."

If an analysis is made of these definitions it will be seen that personnel (or manpower) management involves procedures and practices through which human resources are managed (*i.e.,* organised and directed) towards the attainment of the individual, social and organisational goals. By controlling and effectively using manpower resources, management tries to produce goods and services for the society.

Prof. Jucius has defined personnel management as: "The field of management which has to do with planning, organising, directing and controlling various operative functions of procuring, developing, maintaining and utilising a labour force, such that the: *(a)* objectives, for which the company is established are attained economically and effectively; *(b)* objectives of all levels of personnel are served to the highest possible degree; and *(c)* objectives of the community are duly considered and served."

According to this definition, personnel management is concerned with the *managerial* (planning, organising, directing and controlling) and *operative* (procurement, development, maintenance and utilisation) *functions*, with a view to attaining the organisational goals economically and effectively and meeting the individual and social goals.

Edwin Flippo states: "Personnel Management is the planning, organising, directing and controlling of the procurement, development, compensation, integration, maintenance and separation of human resources to the end that individual, organisational and social objectives are accomplished."

This definition is a comprehensive one and covers both the management functions and the operative functions. The purpose of all these functions is to assist in the accomplishment of basic objectives.

According to French, "Personnel Management is the recruitment, selection, development, utilization of and accommodation of human resources by organisations. The human resources of an organisation consist of all individuals regardless of their role, who are engaged in any of the organisation's activities."

Personnel management, has been defined by Scott and others thus:

"It is that branch of management which is responsible, on a staff basis for concentrating on those aspects of operations which are primarily concerned with the relationship of management to employees and employees to employees and with the development of the individual and group. The objective is to attain maximum individual development, desirable working relationship between employers and employees and employees and employees, and effective moulding of human resources as contrasted with physical resources."

The Institute of Personnel Management, London, formulated an official definition of personnel management after the Second World War and modified it in 1965 to incorporate progressive trends and professional developments in the U.K. The two definitions are reproduced below:

"Personnel Management is that part of the management function which is primarily concerned with the human relationships within an organisation. Its objective is the maintenance of those relationships on a basis which, by consideration of the well-being of the individual, enables all those engaged in the undertaking to make their maximum personal contribution to the effective working of that undertaking."(1945)

"Personnel Management is that part of management concerned with people at work and with their relationship within an organisation. Its aim is to bring together and develop into an effective organisation the men and women who make up an enterprise and having regard for the well-being of the individual and of working groups, to enable them to make their best contribution to its success."(1965)

The essence of the definitions is that Personnel Management is concerned with *men at work;* and with *their group relationship,* with a view to achieve the objectives of the organisation through their maximum personal contribution towards the work-goal achievement. The new definition places emphasis on the 'group aspect.' In this definition three objectives are explicit: *(a)* to maintain good relationships within an organisation, *(b)* to enable each person to make his maximum personal contribution to the organisation as a member of the working group, and *(c)* to achieve these things through respect for human personality and the well-being of the individual.

The National Institute of Personnel Management India defines Personnel Management thus:

"Personnel Management, Labour Management or Staff Management means quite simply the task of dealing with human relationships within an organisation. Academically the three aspects of Personnel Management are: *(i) the welfare function* concerned with working conditions and amenties such as canteens, creches, housing, personal problems of workers, schools, and recreation; *(ii)* the *personnel function* concerned with recruitment, placement of employees, remuneration, promotion, incentives, productivity etc. *(iii)* the *industrial relations functions* concerned with trade union negotiation, settlement of industrial disputes, joint consultation and collective bargaining. All these aspects are concerned with human element in industry as distinct from the mechanical."

Lawrence Appley, former President of the American Management Association, has perhaps given the best possible definition of Personnel Management. According to him, "It is a function of guiding human resources into a dynamic organisation that attains its objectives with a high degree of morale and to the satisfaction of those concerned. It is concerned with getting results through people." According to him, "all management is personnel management as it deals with human beings, its development can best be discussed in terms of human development, philosophical, psychological, spiritual and physical." The development and utilisation of human resources is not by any means an ancillary activity but a central element in the operation of a business.

CONCEPT OF PERSONNEL MANAGEMENT

On the basis of the various definitions given above, a few basic facts and characteristics may be noted about Personnel Management.

First, Personnel Management is concerned with managing people to "at work. Such people or personnel do not simply refer to "rank and file employees" or "unionized labour" but also include "higher personnel" and "non-unionized labour." In other words, it covers all levels of personnel, including blue-collared employees (craftsmen, foremen, operatives and labourers), and white-collared employees (professional, technical workers, managers, officials and proprietors, clerical workers and sales workers). The shape and form that personnel administrative activity takes, however, may differ greatly from company to company; and, to be effective, it must be tailored to fit the individual needs of each organisation.

Second, it is concerned with employees, both as individuals as well as a group, the aim being to get better results with their collaboration and active involvement in the organisation's activities, *i.e.,* it is a function or process or activity aiding and directing individuals in maximising their personal contribution.

Third, personnel management is concerned with helping the employees to develop their potentialities and capacities to the maximum possible extent, so that they may derive great satisfaction from their job. This task takes into consideration four basic elements, namely, the capacities, interests, opportunities and personality of the employees.

> *Capacities* — refering to those abilities or attainments, inherited or acquired, that a employee has, is capable of and must to a certain degree exercise in his work.
>
> *Interests* — not only an individual's desires and ambitions, but also his instinctive impulsive tendencies, vague yearnings, and ill-defined cravings that may or may not stir him to his fullest action in performing his duties.
>
> *Opportunities* — not only opportunities for advancement, but opportunities to exercise his capacities and satisfy his interests.
>
> *Personality* — the sum total of a workers' reaction to his experiences and environment, personality is manifest by an individuals' reception by others. The employees' personality has great influence upon his opportunities.

Since the employee is both a social and economic entity, possessing different characteristics in various work situations; there can be a perfect adjustment of the employee in his work unit if the he possesses the exact capacities required for the work. The work similarly affords the *opportunity* for exercising these capacities, and his interests are generally satisfied in the performance of his job. However, a happy combination of the four elements are seldom achieved in actual practice; and a lack of balance forms one of the major causes of waste in production. The best or ideal personnel management, therefore, recognises the individual differences involving these elements and tries to eliminate or reduce them.

Fourth, since recruitment, selection development and utilisation of, and accommodation to people are an integral part of any organised effort, Personnel Management is inherent in all organisations. It is not confined to industry alone; it is equally useful and effective in government departments, military organisations, and non-profit institutions. It is a major part of the general management function and has roots and branches extending throughout and beyond each organisation. Therefore, it is rightly the central pervasive system of all organisations. This point has been summarized by Pigors and Myers in these words: "Personnel administration permeates all types of functional management, such as production management, financial management, sales management and research management. It applies in non-industrial organisations, government, non-profit institutions, and armed services. Unless these managers themselves expect to perform all the duties for which they are responsible, they have to secure the co-operation of other people within their part of the total organnisation. In short, every member of the management group, from top to bottom, must be an effective 'personnel administrator' because he depends on the co-operative efforts of his subordinates."

As Bakke says: "Human relations, industrial relations and personnel relations are just new names for an aspect of the general managerial function as old as management itself." It is more than the management of people by supervisors; and it is also more than the responsibilities assigned to the personnel department. As a field of discipline, personnel management is faced with many challenging problems centering around social responsibility, work design, staffing, style of leadership and supervision, compensation and appraisal, collective bargaining, organisational development and organisational climate.

Fifth, personnel management is of a continuous nature. In the words of George R. Terry: "It cannot be turned on and off like water from a faucet; it cannot be practised only one hour each day or one day a week. Personnel management requires a constant alertness and awareness of human relations and their importance in everyday operations."

Finally, personnel management attempts at getting the willing co-operation of the people for the attainment of the desired goals, for work cannot be effectively performed in isolation without the promotion and development of an *esprit de corps.*

Taking the above characteristics into consideration, it may be observed that personnel management is an approach; a point of view; a new technique of thinking and a philosophy of management, which is concerned not only with managing people, but also with solving the human problems of an organisation intelligently and equitably, and in a manner which ensures that employees' potential is properly developed, that maximum satisfaction is derived by them from their work, that the objectives of the organisation are achieved and that good human relations are maintained within the organisation.

Personnel management can be of full value to an organisation only when it is consistently thought out and applied at all levels and to all management functions; in corporate policies, in the systems, procedures and in employment practices, etc. This integrative aspect of personnel management is, therefore, of vital importance.

LINE AND STAFF ASPECT OF HUMAN RESOURCE MANAGEMENT

All managers who get work done through their subordinates are in a sense HR managers. Some of HR functions are performed by all Line Managers whose basic functions are their respective departmental responsibilities. However, there is a separate HR department which functions as staff department. We shall understand this by defining *Line* and *Staff.*

Authority — is the right to make decisions, to direct the work of others, to give orders.

Line Managers — are authorised to direct the work of their subordinates, are responsible for accomplishing organisation's goals.

Staff Managers — are authorised to assist and advise line managers in accomplishing these basic goals. HR Managers are staff managers and advise Line Managers in areas of recruiting, compensation, training etc.

What is expected of a Line Manager when he is directing or supervising his subordinate —

(1) Placing right person on the right job;

(2) Orientation and induction of new employees;

(3) Training subordinates for new jobs;

(4) Performance monitoring and improving;

(5) Interpreting company's policies and procedures;

(6) Controlling costs, wastages;

(7) Developing abilities of each employee;

(8) Protecting employees' health (safety, accident prevention);

(9) Creating and maintaing employee morale;

(10) Creating smooth working relationship.

HR Manager's Staff Functions are: serving and assisting line managers by— employing, training, evaluating, rewarding, promoting, counselling, firing employees. He administers benefit programmes also known as welfare work which includes canteen, health, accident, insurance, retirements, vacations and others like complying with legal aspects of employment, employee relations (union management relations).

CHARACTERISTICS AND QUALITIES OF A PERSONNEL MANAGER

Personnel Management is a delicate subject, and often it matters more to know 'who' says something than to know 'what' he says. Unless the personnel manager has the active support of the top management, he will be like a ship without a rudder. On the other hand, if he does not win the confidence of the employees and their union, he will not be respected by the management. Moreover, he has to earn the esteem of his colleagues especially those in the line who are more interested in immediate rather than long-term results. He walks on a tight rope. Tact and imagination are his only guides.

To be successful in his job, a Personnel Manager must be a specialist in organisation theory and as such be an effective adviser to top management in organisational matters as well as being able to organise his own Department/Division in such a manner as to minimise frictions, promote goodwill, and release the latent energies of his own people and associates to be expended on their primary assignments.

He should have real expertise in personnel administration — knowledge of relevant laws, procedures, techniques and of developments in theory and practice in comparable economies, behavioural sciences' contribution to personnel management, a bent for research in man-management, and should have an adequate knowledge of behavioural sciences which study the reactions of individuals and the groups to particular sets of conditions and environments in an organisation or a factory.

Prof. Jucius has emphasised that personnel managers should possess the following types of general knowledge, besides their specialisation in the field of personnel areas: (1) *Philosophy,* which seeks for the underlying explanations of human nature and conduct. (2) *Ethics,* which is concerned with moral and value judgements. (3) *Logic,* which is concerned with the rules and principles of reasoning. (4) *Mathematics,* which treats of exact relations between quantities, magnitudes and systems. (5) *Sociology,* which deals with the forms and functions of human groups. (6) *Anthropology,* which is concerned with physical and environmental relations to people's social and cultural patterns. (7) *Medicine,* which in all its branches is concerned with the well-being of the people. (8) *History,* which seeks to record and explain past events. (9) *Economics,* whose interests are in optimizing choices among competing uses of limited resources. (10) *Management* which is concerned with a skilful leadership of organisational groups. (11) *Political Science,* which, in the best sense, is concerned with how people are governed and how they govern themselves.

He must have a keen sense of social justice and be fully appreciative of the rights and interest of the men and women at work, as well as of the economic necessities of management. His philosophy of social justice should include two fundamental concepts: *(i)* industry is a partnership between management, men and owners whose objective is to earn profits through service: *(ii)* industry can profit greatly by developing and co-ordinating the capacities, the interests, and the opportunities of each worker and of each of management. He must be able to couple this sense of social justice with a warm personal interest in people. This is turn, must be controlled by a wealth of common sense, which will protect him from sentimentality on the one hand and from coldness on the other.

The other important qualities that a personnel manager should possess are:

(i) a mind with a capacity for creative thinking, for analysing situations and reasoning objectively;

(ii) he should know problem-solving techniques and have an ability to inspire, motivate and direct employees;

(iii) a devoted sense of vocation and faith in humanity;

(iv) capacity for leadership, a sense of social responsibility and a standard of social justice;

(v) personal integrity so that employees may repose confidence in him;

(vi) capacity for persuasion, coupled with patience and tolerance;

(vii) a friendly, approachable nature, which is tactful and sympathetic, and a pleasing personality, a well-groomed appearance, sophisticated taste and habits, and capable of working with and through other people;

(viii) initiative and decision-making ability;

(ix) mobility of facial expression (which encourages confidence, conveys interest, registers sympathy and allays distrust);

(x) an ability to generate trust among his colleagues and develop acceptability, recognition for himself and his ideas of communication with readiness and fluency;

(xi) a readiness to co-operate with the subordinates in times of difficulty and never to interfere or thrust his advice on them; and finally,

(xii) a promptitude in giving them the feedbacks in their handling of personnel matters whenever necessary in the interest of functioning of the organisation and established personnel policies of the company.

Regarding the qualities of a personnel manager, Northcott has rightly observed:"The personnel requirements are admittedly high, but a profession which deals with so large a part of industrial life will always be held in honour and calls for men and women of sterling qualities."

In sum, a personnel man must be a person who has the human relations skill, a sensitivity to behavioural issues, and a conceptual skill to see the broad picture and predict situations rather than react to problems as they occur.

THE ROLE OF PERSONNEL MANAGER

Looking back at the historical manifestation of the role of a Personnel Manager in industry, it may be said that by and large it reflected the top management's own concept of the personnel function and the methods of managerial control they believed in. The personnel manager has been playing a variety of roles at different stages in the past, like that of a police agency, a legal defender of rights and a negotiator, a catering man meeting the welfare needs of the employees. But the theme has always been set by the thinking at the top level management.

It is difficult precisely to relate the present day functions of personnel to his role as conceptualized earlier. If the personnel management is what personnel managers do, the picture that emerges is indeed confusing, for what personnel managers do can be compared to a Sunday morning jumble sale — a collection of incidental chores, fire-fighting tasks, welfare functions, and a watch-dog function.

In the modern era, the personnel manager typically performs a variety of roles, such as the roles of conscience, of a counsellor, a mediator, a company spokesman, a problem-solver and a change agent. He performs many miscellaneous roles in accordance with the needs of a situation, such as:

(i) The conscience role is that of a humanitarian who reminds the management of its moral and ethical obligations to its employees.

(ii) The personnel manager plays the role of a counsellor to whom the employees frequently go for consultation and with whom they discuss their marital, health, mental, physical and career problems.

(iii) As a mediator, he plays the role of a peace-maker, offering to settle the disputes that may arise among individuals or groups. He acts as a liaison and communicating link between an individual and a group and between labour and management.

(iv) The personnel manager has always been a frequent spokesman for or representative of the company because he has a better overall picture of his company's operations, since he deals intimately with many key organisational activities and functions.

(v) The personnel manager also acts as a problem-solver with respect to the issues that involve human resources management and overall long range organisational planning.

(vi) He works as a change agent within the organisation because he is best suited to introduce and implement major institutional changes. He takes initiative for installing organisational development programmes and convinces the top management of their need. It is he who alerts the top management regarding managerial obsolescence in his organisation.

(vii) He helps line managers learn to detect and solve their problems.

(viii) The personnel manager plays many other roles as well. Any matter which needs someone's attention and which nobody wants to deal with is often handled by the personnel department. Such activities may be peripheral but important and crucial to the efficient and effective operation of an organisation.

It has been now fully recognised that the basic role of the Personnel Manager is "the management of manpower resources." Such management is concerned with 'leadership' both in group and individual relationship, and labour-management relations. It effectively describes the process of planning, and directing development and utilization is now considered as one of the four main functions, *viz.,* finance, production, marketing and human relations.

The functions of the personnel manager are very comprehensive and varied and are determined and influenced by such factors as the size, nature and location of organisation, business or industry, its short and long-term objectives, nature of industry and product, market conditions, degree of competitiveness among rivals, economic, cultural, political and legal environment, the structure of the executive and administrative officers, the mental make-up of the personnel managers, and the over-all organisational philosophy of business.

The personnel manager undertakes all those functions which are concerned with "human elements" or "relations in organisation as well as in material elements." Whatever items are listed therein (as the functions), the main objective is to see that human resources are purposefully utilised for the optimum good of the organisation and there should be meaningful co-operation for achieving the objectives of management. Expertise is brought together in a scientific manner and attitude so created that motivate the group to achieve the organisational goals economically, effectively and speedily, and also fulfil and satisfy its physiological, psychological, economic and social needs and realise its potential abilities.

The role of personnel manager is ever expanding and is strengthened by greater interest shown in human relations problems by specialists such as behavioural scientists, industrial engineers, social psychologists, labour and legal advisers, industrial and computer technologists — all of whose researches have enriched the field of personnel management, its functions and changed their nature making them wide and humanitarian.

CHART 1.1

The Role of a Personnel Manager

Personnel Role	Welfare and Counsellor's Role	Administrative Role	Fire-fighting and Legal Role
(a) Advisory — advising management on effective use of human resources.	*(a)* Managing services — canteens, transport co-operatives, creches, etc.	*(a)* Salary & Wage administration — incentives	*(a)* Grievance handling
(b) Manpower Planning Recruitment, selection etc.	*(b)* Group Dynamics Group councelling motivation, leader ship, communication etc.	*(b)* Maintenance of records.	*(b)* Settlement of disputes
(c) Training and develop ment of employee	*(c)* Research in Personnel & Organisational Problems	*(c)* Human Engineering Man-Machine relation	*(c)* Handling disciplinary and legal matters
(d) Measurement and assessment of individual and group behaviour		*(d)* Effective utilisation of human resource	*(d)* Collective bargaining
			(e) Joint Consultation, and Participation

The ideal personnel manager is not a "decision-maker" but a counsellor not "a collector of responsibilities" but "an advisor" to help the management make more reliable personnel decisions. In any enterprise it is these "line men" who determine the "personnel climate" for the entire organisation. If the personnel man can meet the challenge of "staff role" he would make the most effective contribution to industry.

OBJECTIVES OF PERSONNEL MANAGEMENT

One of the principles of management is that all the work performed in an organisation should, in some way, directly or indirectly, contribute to the objectives of that organisation. This means that the determination of objectives, purposes or goals is of prime importance and is a prerequisite to the solution of most management problems. *Objectives are pre-determined ends or goals at which individual or group activity in an organisation is aimed.*

The formulation of the objectives of an organisation is necessary for the following reasons:

(i) Human beings are goal-directed. People must have a purpose to do some work. Announced organisational goals invest work with meaning.

(ii) Objectives serve as standards against which performance is measured.

(iii) The setting of goals and their acceptance by employees promotes voluntary co-operation and co-ordination; self-regulated behaviour is achieved.

(iv) The objectives stand out as guidelines for organisational performance. They help in setting the pace for action by participants. They also help in establishing the "character" of an organisation. Ralph C. Davis has divided the objectives of an organisation into two categories: *(a)* Primary objectives, and *(b)* Secondary objectives.

(a) Primary objectives, in the first instance, relate to the creation and distribution of some goods or services. The personnel department assists those who are engaged in production, in sales, in distribution and in finance. The goal of personnel function is the creation of a work force with the ability and motivation to accomplish the basic organisational goals. *Secondly*, they relate to the satisfaction of the personal objectives of the members of an organisation through monetary and non-monetary devices. Monetary objectives include profits for owners; salaries and other compensation for executives; wages and other compensation for employees; rent for the landowners and interest for share/stock-holders. Non-monetary objectives include prestige, recognition, security, status, *Thirdly,* they relate to the satisfaction of community and social objectives, such as serving the customers honestly, promoting a higher standard of living in the community, bringing comfort and happiness to society, protecting women and children, and providing for aged personnel.

(b) The *secondary objectives* aim at achieving the primary objectives economically, efficiently and effectively.

The fulfillment of the primary objectives is contingent upon:

(i) The economic need for, or usefulness of, the goods and services required by the community/society.

(ii) Conditions of employment for all the members of an organisation which provide for satisfaction in relation to their needs, so that they may be motivated to work for the success of the enterprise.

(iii) The effective utilization of people and materials in productive work.

(iv) The continuity of the enterprise.

The methods adopted by business organisations in fulfilling the primary purposes must be consistent with the ethical and moral values of society and with the policies and regulations established by legislative action.

On the personnel men lies the responsibility for ensuring a satisfactory accomplishment of the objectives of an organisation and of its employees, for if they are not reasonably achieved, the basic objectives of the organisation will suffer. It is for this reason that, while framing company personnel objectives care is taken to consider the interests and needs of the employees and of employee goals. This is done by integrating the employee interests and the management interests with a view to achieving the objectives of the entire organisation. The concept of integration of employee-management interests, and the relationship between objectives and programmes, have been illustrated in the following chart.

CHART 1.2

Integration of Interests of Employees and Management

Employee's Interests ↓	Management's Interests ↓
1. Recognition as an individual.	1. Lowest unit personnel cost.
2. Opportunity for expression and development.	2. Maximum productivity of employees.
3. Economic security and growth employees.	3. Availability and stability of employees
4. Interest in work.	4. Loyalty of employees.
5. Safety, healthy working conditions.	5. Co-operation and Commitment of employees.
6. Acceptable hours of work and adequate wages.	6. High organisational morale.
7. Fair and efficient leadership.	7. Intelligent initiative of employees.

Pigors and Myers observed, "Managing is organisational leadership, and one of its central tasks is effective co-ordination and utilization of available human and non-human resources to achieve the objectives of the organisation. These objectives may be, for example, to maximise profit or increase the firm's share of the market in business enterprises; to improve efficiency or expand the scope of services provided by the firm; to get more members or to bargain more effectively for members in a labour union; or to improve the quality of instruction, expand facilities for training and undertake research."

The American Management Association has very succinctly summarized the objectives of personnel administration. It says: "The purpose of a business enterprise is the profitable production of goods and services to fulfil economic needs in such a way as to provide satisfactory returns to both economic and social suppliers, owners and members of the organisation, under conditions which provide for the maximum conservation of human and material resources over a continuing period."

Following this statement, the objectives of personnel management may be laid down as follows:

(i) To achieve an effective utilization of human resources (besides other resources) in the achievement of organisational goals (which may be the production and distribution of goods and services needed by society).

(ii) To establish and maintain an adequate organisational structure and a desirable working relationship among all the members of an organisation by dividing of organisation tasks into functions, positions, jobs, and by defining clearly the responsibility, accountability, authority for each job and its relation with other jobs/personnel in the organisation.

(iii) To secure the integration of the individuals and groups with an organisation, by reconciling individual/group with those of an organisation in such a manner that the employees feel a sense of involvement, commitment and loyalty towards it. In the absence of such an integration, friction may develop in an organisation which may lead to its total failure. Friction produces inefficiency. Friction may result from political aspirations, from difficulties in communication, and from faults inherent in a particular organisational structure. The behaviour of individuals and groups in any organisation also involves frictions — personal jealousies and rivalries, prejudices and idiosyncracies, personality conflicts cliques and factions, favoritism and nepotism.

(iv) To generate maximum individual/group development within an organisation by offering opportunities for advancement to employees through training and job education, or by effecting transfers or by offering retraining facilities.

(v) To recognize and satisfy individual needs and group goals by offering an adequate and equitable remuneration, economic and social security in the form of monetary compensation, and protection against such hazards of life as illness, old age, disability, death, unemployment, etc., so that the employees may work willingly and co-operate to achieve an organisation's goals.

(vi) To maintain a high morale and better human relations inside an organisation by sustaining and improving the conditions which have been established so that employees may stick to their jobs for a longer period.

Personnel management tries to improve morale by giving adequate training to workers and by achieving for itself a knowledge of human nature which is "the totality of motives that cause human actions; it is a mosaic of reflexes and instincts, of inherited and acquired habits, of individual and group traditions."

The American Management Association observes: "These basic objectives remain the same whether or not certain groups among the members of the organisation belong to a labour union. Further, the objectives are not in opposition to those objectives of organised labour which are consistent with the private enterprise system.... The objectives are in the best interests of all those to whom management is responsible; owners of enterprises, the community, the consumers of its goods and services, and members of the organisation itself, including groups who may belong to unions."

PRE-REQUISITES FOR THE ACHIEVEMENTS OF THE OBJECTIVES

In brief, the objectives of an organisation may be: *the fullest contribution of human resources for the achievement of the organisation goal, of long and short-term plans, and of the operations of the organisation in an environment of high morale and vitality consistent with profitability and social milieu, with the ethical values of society and with the policies and regulations established by the country's legislature.*

To achieve these objectives, the following pre-requisites must be satisfied:

(a) Capable people should be picked up on the basis of the qualifications fixed.

(b) Individual and group efforts/potentialities must be effectively utilised by providing suitable work opportunities, tools and raw materials, by showing an appreciation of work well done, and by offering better chances for future advancement and training.

(c) Willing co-operation of the people to achieve the objective must be available by creating such feelings as "people work with us" rather than saying that "people work for us."

(d) The tasks of an organisation should be properly divided in accordance with a sound plan into functions and positions, each indicating clear-cut authority, responsibility and duties, as also the relationship of one position with another.

(e) The goals to be achieved should be specially made known to all concerned in the language best understood by them. *Specificity and clarity are both important in defining the objectives.* The objectives should also be comprehensive.

(f) Since objectives have to be shared by many senior persons in an organisation, a wide-scale enquiry and consultation should be undertaken before their formulation and efforts should subsequently be made to develop a common understanding of the objectives among managers at various levels.

(g) The objectives should be clearly defined, failing which a great deal of confusion may arise. Without clear-cut objectives, the management of organisational records cannot be kept in balance, and the management of one section may interfere with that of another. Moreover, without clear-cut objectives, the management of organisational records cannot be kept in balance, and the management of one section may interfere with that of another. Moreover, without clear-cut objectives, there can be no standards by which to evaluate the performance of an individual or that of the whole organisation. Again, an absence of objectives often leads to organisational disaster. On the other hand, the refining or revising of objectives is the most fundamental task of all managers at all levels.

(h) Suitable monetary and non-monetary incentives, in the form of adequate and reasonable pay-packets, service benefits and security against hazards of life and of employment and against the arbitrary actions of supervisors

should be available to employees. A properly prepared grievance handling procedure and disciplinary plan should also be available.

A determination of objectives is the responsibility of the top management, particularly of the President or Chairman and the Board of Directors.

IMPACT OF ENVIRONMENT ON ORGANISATIONAL OBJECTIVES

Various aspects of the national environment have a decesive impact upon the objectives. These are:

(i) National or commercial attitudes, such as a growing social consciousness on the part of the management to fulfil its responsibilities of providing employment to special category of people (the women, the handicapped, the scheduled tribe or scheduled class people), meeting employee needs, etc.

(ii) The needs of national defence on an emergency situation, or shortage of critical materials, may force certain organisations to change their objectives from earning high profits to a proper distribution of goods and services in the community.

(iii) Innovations in technology and service such as television, refrigerators, transistors, new vaccines have had a great impact on the objectives of an organisation, by making them more useful.

(iv) Union-management relations and the need for the payment of higher wages may force some marginal producers to go out of the market or may force organisations to instal new equipment or systems in order to compete successfully in the market. Trade union checks on management may have the effect of forcing the executive to define or revise objectives.

(v) The personal likes and dislikes of owners or directors of an organisation also have an effect on objectives. Some directors may prefer rapid growth, others may want only a moderate growth at all. Some owners or directors may not be interested in certain products or services, even though may be economically feasible to enter into competition with those particular goods or services.

(vi) The labour market also has an important effect on organisational objectives.

TOOLS, TECHNIQUES AND METHODS NEEDED TO ACHIEVE OBJECTIVES

To achieve the objectives of an organisation, *in the first place,* it is necessary to develop an appropriate organisation and an administrative system. This requires that systematic data should be collected both from within the organisation and from external sources (such as the universities and other enterprises). *In the second place,* there must be a periodic review of administrative practices in the organisation and of the changes made, whenever necessary. *In the third place*, the personnel manager should assume the responsibility of attaining the requirements of his enterprise and those imposed upon it by environmental changes.

We give an example of the objectives followed by the Tata Iron & Steel Company Ltd., Jamshedpur. (See Chart 1.3).

CHART 1.3

STATEMENT OF OBJECTIVES OF TATA IRON AND STEEL COMPANY LTD.

The fundamental objective of the TISCO is to strengthen India's base through increased productivity, effective utilisation of material and manpower resources, and applied and continued application of modern scientific and managerial methods as well as through systematic growth in keeping with national aspirations.

The Company recognises that, while honesty and integrity are the essential ingredients of a strong and stable enterprise, profitability provides the main spark for economic activity. It affirms its faith in democratic values and in the importance of the success of the individual, collective and corporate enterprise for the economic emancipation and prosperity of the Company.'

Guided in its policies and objectives by the philosophy and ideals of its founder, Jamshedji Tata, the Company believes in the effective discharge of its duties and obligations towards:

I. SHAREHOLDERS

(i) by protecting and safeguarding their investment, and

(ii) by ensuring to them a fair return.

II. EMPLOYEES

(i) by a realistic and generous understanding and acceptance of their needs and rights and an enlightened awareness of the social responsibilities of industry;

(ii) by providing adequate wages, good working conditions, job security, an effective machinery for speedy redressal of grievances, and suitable opportunities for promotion and self-development;

(iii) by promoting feelings of trust and loyalty through a humane and purposeful awareness of their needs and aspirations; and

(iv) by creating a sense of belonging and team spirit through their closer association with the management at various levels.

III. CUSTOMERS

(i) by providing products of proven quality at a fair price;

(ii) by fulfilling its commitments impartially and courteously in accordance with sound; and straightforward business principles; and

(iii) by earning their continuing confidence in its productive ability and its technical competence to keep improving the quality of its products.

IV. COMMUNITY

(i) by respecting the dignity of the individual and his activity according to the ideals of social justice;

(ii) by encouraging talent and promoting a civic sense among members of the community;

(iii) by availing of opportunities to develop the democratic qualities involved in collective work undertaken in the interest of the community; and

(iv) by assuming its proper share of social responsibilities in the communities in which the Company operates.

These policies and objectives are directed towards making the TISCO:

"The best Company to buy from;

A sound Company to invest in;

A good Company to work for;

A reliable Company to sell to;

A leading Company in the life of the community and the country."

SUMMARY

Organisations are institutions created by society to undertake tasks, aid, achieve the planned goals and objectives. There are more than one person to fulfil the organisation objectives. The relationship between these employees — known as human resources are structured, defined, monitored and developed to achieve the set goals.

Human resources management is concerned with people working in the organisation. It concerns with procuring skilled employees, developing them, motivating them for higher performance and ensuring their commitment to the organisation. HR management is very much a part of every line manager's responsibility.

HR manager and his department has basically three responsibilities: (a) to exert a line manager's authority on his unit and employees in HR department. He coordinates to ensure HR objectives and policies of the organisation. He provides various staff services to the line managers like recruiting, training, rewarding, disciplining of employees at all levels.

HR manager has to play a major role in an organisation and cope with the changes in the environment and the trends include workforce diversity, technological change, globalization and changes in the nature of work such as moving towards a service society, growing emphasis on education and human capital.

He has to work within the framework of the organisation which determines, strategic goals, improve business performance, develop organisation culture, foster innovation, flexibility and create a competitive advantage through its human resources.

❑❑❑

2

Functions of Personnel Management

INTRODUCTION

As the term implies, personnel management is the management of human resources in an organisation and is concerned with the creation of harmonious working relationship among its participants and bringing about their utmost individual development. Such management is concerned with leadership in both groups and 'individual relationship' and 'labour relations' and 'personnel management.' It effectively describes the process of planning and directing, development and utilization of human resources in employment. In fact, personnel management undertakes all those activities which are concerned with human elements or relations as well as with material elements in an organization. Whatever functions are listed therein, the main objective of these functions is to bring together expertise in a scientific way and to create attitudes that motivate a group to achieve its goals economically, effectively and speedily.

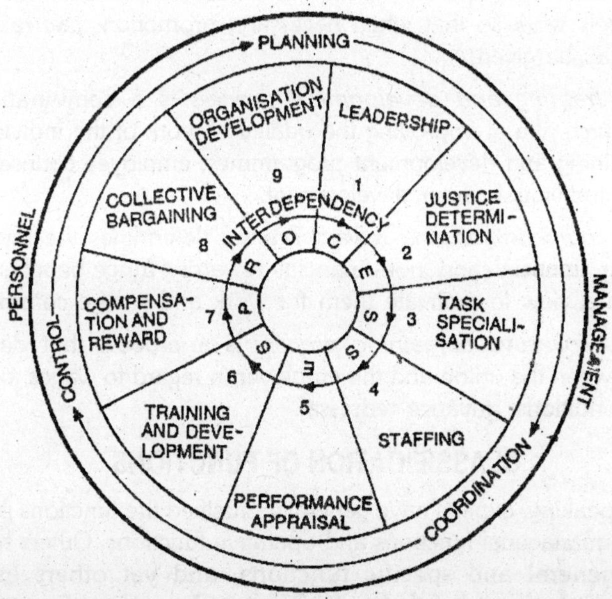

Fig. 2.1 Major Personnel Management Process in Organisation

Every function in Organisation includes a flow of *inputs* (materials, energy or information), *and transforming these into outputs* (the product or services and waste).

Functionally, "personnel management" is the planning, co-ordinating, and controlling of a network of organisation — and facilitating work pertaining to recruitment, selection, utilisation, development of human resources. The function include the most vital aspects of personnel management: leadership, justice determination, task specialisation (job and organisation design), staffing, performance appraisal, training and development, compensation and reward, collective bargaining, and organisation development. The processes involved are:

(i) The *leadership process* involves in influencing the individual and group behaviour towards achievement of organisation goals. It is concerned with traits, philosophy, and behaviour of the leader, the characteristics of subordinates, and the superiors.

(ii) The *justice determination process* is concerned with the giving of awards and penalties to the employees in proportion to their relative contribution to the output. This provides for "equal treatment to all and a fair compensation for the work."

(iii) The *task-specialisation process* consists of division of the total task into individual jobs. In other words, it consists of setting of organisational objectives; job designing; communication of the job design to employees through job descriptions and performance standards and training; job specification and the work rules.

(iv) The *staffing process* is the more complex and important process, involving manpower planning, authorisation for staffing, developing sources for recruitment; evaluation of applicants, employment decisions; offers of employment induction and orientation, transfers, promotions, demotions, and separations, etc.

(v) The *performance appraisal process* is concerned with continuous evaluation of the employee's work so that when necessary, promotion, pay raises, transfers, training etc., may be given.

(vi) The *training and development process* is a combination of many subprocesses which aim at improving the quality of work of the individual, through provision of training and development programmes, employee counselling, offering suggestions for individual career development.

(vii) The *compensation and reward process* determines the mechanism and form for giving financial and non-financial rewards, fringe-benefits, etc. to the employees with a view to motivate them for work and ensure commitment.

(viii) The *collective bargaining process* is a process that determines the relationship between the union and the employer in regard to wages, benefits, hours and working conditions, grivance redressal.

CLASSIFICATION OF FUNCTIONS

Broadly speaking, experts have generally classified the functions into two major categories, *viz.,* managerial functions and operative functions. Others have classified functions as general and specific functions, and yet others as 'Personnel Admininstration Functions' and 'Industrial Relations Functions.' Functions have also been classified on the basis of the capacities; or on the basis of authority.

This type of classification of functions has been discussed as below:

(A) THE GENERAL AND SPECIFIC FUNCTIONS

Under *'General'* type of functions, the personnel management is required: *(i)* to conduct personnel research, *(ii)* to assist in the programmes of personnel administration, *(iii)* to develop appraisal plans, *(iv)* to launch education and training programmes, *(v)* to develop a competent work force, and *(vi)* to establish and administer varied personnel services delegated to personnel department.

Under *specific functions,* the personnel management may involve itself in areas of employment, safety, wage and salary, benefit schemes, community relations and advice and counselling the employees.

(B) PERSONNEL ADMINISTRATION AND INDUSTRIAL RELATIONS FUNCTIONS

Personnel administration functions relate to the function of managing people from the lower to the upper level of the organisation and embraces policy determination as well as implementation of policies by the personnel at the lower levels. Accordingly, "personnel administration" refers to "creating, developing and utilising a 'work group' and involves all types of inter-personnel relationships between superiors and subordinates."

The *'Industrial Relations' functions,* on the other, are "not directly related to the function of 'managing people', but refer to interactions between the management and the representatives of the unions." Such functions involve all activities of employer-employee relationship, such as organisation of the union members, negotiation of contracts, collective bargaining, grievance handling, disciplinary action, arbitration, etc. — the purpose of all these being to prevent conflict between the two participants.

The above two functions are inter-related and inter-dependent and, hence, the most common term used is "Personnel Management/Administration and Industrial Relations."

(C) FUNCTIONS CLASSIFIED ON THE BASIS OF CAPACITIES

This classification has been adopted by Saltonstall. According to him, "Although personnel managements' function is the 'staff function,' it also performs three roles," *viz.:*

(i) He performs a *line function* not only because he directs the work in his own department but also in some service functions such as recruitment, administration of benefits, the plant canteen and allied activities.

(ii) He functions as a *co-ordinator* of personnel activities, in so far as he controls the functions of other departments. This he does through regular reporting on labour turnover, absenteeism, accidents and grievances to different levels of management. He also assists/advises the top management in accomplishing personnel objectives, policies and procedures.

(iii) He performs a *typical staff function* in the form of assisting and advising the line personnel to solve their problems.

Saltonstall suggests two approaches for the development of line officials, *viz., (a)* the "reductive" or "threat approach"; and *(b)* the "augmentive" or "source of help" approach. The latter approach is more close to "behavioural approach to management."

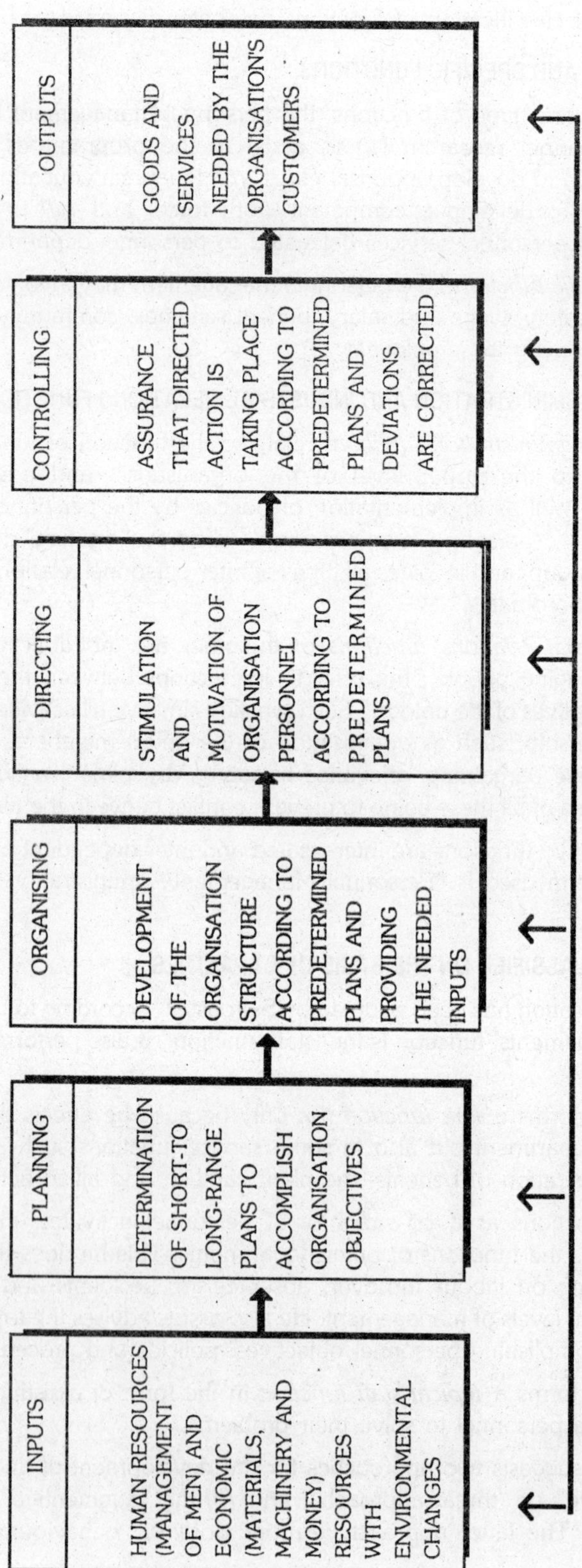

Fig. 2.2 Functions of Management

Thus, according to him:

— The *typical staff functions* are indirectly related to action and characterised by development, consultation, planning, interpretation, evaluation, diagnosis, research, investigation and recommendation; and the *typical line functions* are related to command action and characterised by direction, control, decisions, enforcement, application, performance and instruction.

(D) FUNCTIONS ACCORDING TO THE DEGREE OF AUTHORITY

Dale Henning and French made an interesting observation that "The personnel man is described in the textbooks and journals is like '*Abominable Snowman*' much talked about but seldom seen." They have classified his functions into three categories thus:

(a) Area of maximum authority, e.g., direction of payroll calculations, orientation procedure, transfer rules, etc.;

(b) Area of combined use of authority and persuasion, e.g., establishment of disciplinary procedure, inter-departmental data gathering, determining the number of participants in a training programmes, etc.; and

(c) Area of maximum persuasion, e.g., salary changes under the rules of the plant, employment of individuals recommended by the personnel department in other departments, initiating disciplinary action, etc.

We now discuss below the functions of personnel management under two broad heads, *viz.,* (1) Managerial functions, and (2) Operative functions.

MANAGERIAL FUNCTIONS

"Management is a multi-purpose organ which has three jobs, two of which are directly related to personnel managing a business: 'managing managers' and 'managing workers' and the work." Lawrence Appey says that "Management is the accomplishment of results through the efforts of other people." In the opinion of Harold Koontz, "It is the art of getting things done through people and with informally organised groups."

In our view, management may be thought of *as the process of allocating an organisation's inputs (human and economic resources) by planning, organising, directing and controlling for the purpose of producing outputs (goods and services) desired by its customers so that organisation objectives are accomplished. In the process, work is performed with and through organisation personnel in an everchanging business environment.*

Management is, thus, personnel administration.... It is the development of the people and not the direction of things.. Managing people is the heart and essence of being a manager. Thus, a Personnel Manager is a manager and as such he must perform the basic functions of management. He exercises authority and leadership over other personnel. His functions involve (what Luther Gullick calls) POSD CORB, *i.e.,* planning, organising staffing, directing, co-ordinating, reporting and budgeting the work of those who are entrusted with the performance of operative functions.[8] In other words, managers procure, process and peddle, find and employ resources, develop services, and find markets for their output.

(a) Planning: Is a pre-determined course of action. According to Allen, "it is a trap laid to capture the future." Terry is of the view that "planning is the foundation of most successful actions of any enterprise." Planning is the determination of the plans, strategies, programmes, policies, procedures, and standard needs to accomplish the desired organisation objectives. In fact, "planning today avoids crisis tomorrow." Planning is a hard job, for it involves the ability to think, to predict, to analyse, and to come to decisions, to control the actions of its personnel and to cope with a complex, dynamic fluid environment. They bridge the gap between where they are and where they want to go. For this purpose they determine personnel programmes well in advance. The two most important features of planning are research and forecasting. These two are inter-related, for forecast is possible only as a result of research. Personnel administration should be able to predict trends in wages, in labour market, in union demands, in other benefits and in personnel policies and programmes. The task of forecasting personnel needs in relation to changes in production or seasonal variations and the levelling out of differences in production is extremely important, both for employees and for management. Therefore, planning or decision-making has to be undertaken much in advance of an action so that unforeseen or anticipated problems and events may be properly handled. This is also stressed by the saying: "Good managers make things happen."

(b) Organising: After a course of action has been determined, an organisation should be established to carry it out. According to J.C. Massie, "An organisation is a structure, a framework and a process by which a cooperative group of human beings allocates its tasks among its members, identifies relationships and integrates its activities towards common objectives." This is done by designing the structure of relationships among jobs, personnel and physical factors. An organisation is the wedding of authority and responsibility because, in its essentials, it consists of the assignment of specific functions to designated person or departments with authority to have them carried out, and their accountability to management for the results obtained. It seeks to achieve the maximum return with minimum effort by decentralisation, whereby the power of decisions is brought down as near as possible to the individual concerned. How far this can be done will depend upon the top management's philosophy and appreciation of the benefits of delegation and decentralisation. In the words of Drucker: "The right organisational structure is the necessary foundation; without it, the best performance in all other areas of management will be ineffectual and frustrated."

(c) Directing (Motivating, Actuating or Commanding): Directing the subordinates at any level is a basic function of the managerial personnel. According to McGregor, "many managers would agree that the effectiveness of their organisation would be at least doubled if they could discover how to tap the unrealised potential present in their human resources." Directing is involved with getting persons together and asking them (either through command or motivation) to work willingly and effectively for the achievement of designated goals. Directing deals not only with the dissemination of orders within an organisation units and departments, but also with the acceptance and execution of these orders by the employees. The decisions are taken by the top management, but only after consultation with the personnel department. A review or checking of the safety instalments, wage-rate ranges, disciplinary action and general wage changes are all the responsibility of the personnel department. Final action is taken only when the green signal has been obtained from

it. However, securing acceptance and execution generally requires a certain amount of motivation of individuals and groups. Otherwise, the actual performance level may be well below that which is desired.

(d) Co-ordinating and Controlling: Coordinating refers to balancing timing and integrating activities in an organisation, so that a unity of action in pursuit of a common purpose is achieved. In the words of Terry, "Co-ordination deals with the task of blending efforts in order to ensure a successful attainment of an objective." Co-ordination in the management of personnel takes place at all levels, from the top management through to the supervisor and those for whom he is responsible. The personnel department has to co-ordinate the tasks of developing, interpreting and reviewing personnel policies, practices and programmes, such as safety programmes, employee benefits, job evaluation, training or development, and communication. These activities are generally put into operation by and through the line people; but it is the personnel department which follows them through, unifies them, and checks to see how they work.

Controlling is the act of checking, regulating and verifying whether everything occurs in conformity with the plan that has been adopted, the instructions issued and the principles established. It is greatly concerned with actions and remedial actions. "It is not just score-keeping. It is not just plotting the course and getting location reports; but rather it is steering the ship." It is through control that actions and operations are adjusted to pre-determined standards; and its basis is information in the hands of the managers. "By check, analysis, and review, the personnel department assists in realizing the personnel objectives. Auditing training programmes, analysing labour turn-over records, directing morale surveys, conducting separation interviews, interviewing new employees at stipulated intervals, comparing various features of the programme with other organisation programmes in the area, industry and nation — these are some of the means for controlling the management of personnel."

This monitoring process provides management with actual performance information for comparison with pre-determined performance standards. If there are unavoidable deviations from the planned performance, corrective action can be taken immediately.

This last function of control closes the system loop by providing feedback of significant deviations from the planned performance. The feedback of pertinent information can affect the inputs or any of the management functions.

Though all the above functions are performed at all levels of management, the amount of time devoted to each function varies for each management level (See Fig. 2.3). The top management performs planning functions more than does the supervisory management. On the other hand, supervisors at the third rung of the management pyramid devote more of their time to directing and controlling production.

OPERATIVE FUNCTIONS

The operative functions of personnel management are concerned with the activities specifically dealing with procuring, developing, compensating, and maintaining an efficient work force. These functions are also known as *service functions.*

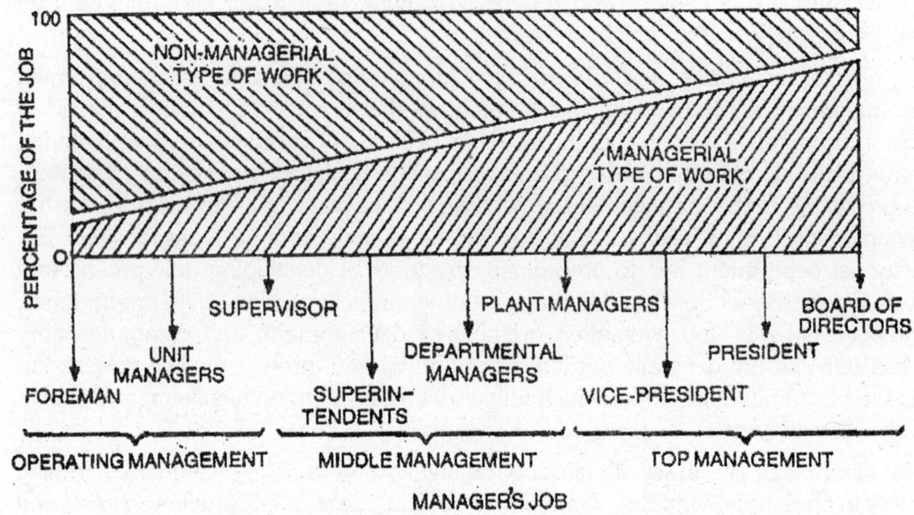

Fig. 2.3 Management Functions and Managerial Levels

(1) The *procurement function* is concerned with the obtaining of a proper kind and number of personnel necessary to accomplish an organisation's goals. It deals with specifically with such subjects as the determination of manpower requirements, their recruitment, selection and place (comprising activities to screen and hire personnel, including application forms, psychological tests, interviews, medical check-up reference calling), induction, follow-up, transfers, lay-offs, discharge and separation, etc.

(2) The *development function* is concerned with the personnel development of employees by increasing their skill through training so that job performance is properly achieved. Drafting and directing training programmes for all levels of employees, arranging for their on-the-job, office and vestibule training, holding seminars and conferences, providing for educational and vocational counselling and appraising employee potential and performance are undertaken under this function.

(3) The *compensating function* is concerned with securing adequate and equitable remuneration to personnel for their contribution to the attainment of organisational objectives. Functions related to wage surveys, establishment of job classifications, job descriptions and job analyses, merit ratings, the establishment of wage rates and wage structure, wage plans and policies, wage systems, incentives and profit-sharing plans, etc., fall under this category.

(4) The integration function: after the employee has been procured, his skill and ability developed and monetary compensation determined, the most important, yet difficult of the personnel management is to bring about an "integration" of human resources with organisation, and to cope with inevitable conflicts that ensue. "Integration" is concerned with the attempt to effect a reasonable reconciliation of individual, societal, and organisation interests. It rests upon the premise that significant overlappings of interests do exist in the organisation in such programmes as job

enlargement, job evaluation, variable compensation plans. The greater the overlap, the more productivity would coincide with employees that they would prefer to avoid, *e.g.,* assignment to narrow and repetitive tasks, meeting high output standards, acceptance of managerial decisions. For this reason, organisations have disciplinary action programmes as well as some freedom to do away with the services of particular employees. On the other hand, there are certain things that employees desire which the organisation is reluctant to provide, *e.g.,* increased wages, totally safe working conditions, time off with pay, shorter hours of work, premium pay for overtime work, etc. To get these benefits, outside pressure might be brought upon the employers.

Managerial activities that bring about a reasonable integration of human resources and the organisation objects, are termed as "human relations." The goal is to lead to productive and creative collaboration toward mutual objectives. 'Human relations' programme tend to decrease accidents, absenteeism, turnover and operating errors, while simultaneously raising morale, quality and productivity such programmes also prevent undesirable behaviour such as sabotage, insubordination, strikes, etc. All these problems are handled under grievance procedure, disciplinary action and labour union programmes.

(5) The *maintenance function* deals with sustaining and improving the conditions that have been established. Specific problems of maintaining the physical conditions of employees (health and safety measures) and employee service programmes are the responsibility of the personnel department.

Flippo rightly says: "The purpose of all of these activities is to assist in the accomplishment of the organisation's basic objectives. Consequently, the starting point of personnel management as of all management, must be a specification of those objectives and a determination of the sub-objectives of the personnel function. The expenditure of all funds in the personnel department can be justified only in so far as there is a net contribution toward company objectives."

It may be noted that the personnel management cannot afford to lay greater emphasis on one and neglect the other two major functions. In this connection the observations of John F. Mee merit mention: "It is essential to grasp the significance of this dual division of personnel functions if the mistake of becoming pre-occupied with the demand of detailed problems to the neglect of managerial duties is to be avoided. It is easy, as many executives have learned to their regret, to become so busy with such tasks as hiring, transferring, counselling, and training that they fail to foresee the shifting conditions which call for changes in operative functions; they fail to recognise the work of subordinates satisfactorily and they fail to keep a good check-up on the work of subordinates."

CLASSIFICATION OF PERSONNEL FUNCTIONS BY SOME AUTHORS

Below are given some important classifications of personnel functions made by experts in the field:

Yoder's Classification: According to Yoder, in a typical industrial relations and personnel department, the principal activities of manpower management are:

(i) Setting general and specific management policy for relationships and establishing and maintaining a suitable organisation for leadership and co-operation.

(ii) Collective bargaining, contract negotiations, contract administration and grievances.

(iii) Staffing the organisation, finding, getting and holding prescribed types and number of workers.

(iv) Aiding the self-development of employees at all levels, providing opportunities for personnel development and growth as well as for requisite skills and experience.

(v) Incentivating, developing and maintaining motivation for work.

(vi) Reviewing and auditing manpower management in an organisation.

(vii) Industrial relations research, carrying out studies designed to explain employment behaviour and thereby effecting improvements in manpower management.

Yoder and Nelson's Classification: On another occasion, on the basis of an enquiry regarding descriptions of 1984 employee-relations jobs conducted in 189 companies, Dale Yoder and Robert J. Nelson classified seven functional categories as follows.

(i) *Departmental Administration Programme:* Planning, report preparing, policy formulation and general administration.

(ii) *Employment and Placement:* Recruitment, selection, placement, orientation, personnel rating, job analysis and description.

(iii) *Training:* Induction, on-the-job training, supervisory training and management development.

(iv) *Collective Bargaining:* Contract negotiation, contract administration and grievances.

(v) *Wage and Salary Administration:* Job evaluation, wage and salary surveys.

(vi) *Benefits and Services:* Insurance, health, hospitalisation, medical care, and retirement plan administration.

(vii) *Personnel Research:* Continuing studies of all employee-relations policies, programmes and practices.

Scott, Clothier and Spriegel's Classification: Scott, Clothier and Spriegel divide the functions of the personnel management into these specific categories, namely:

(i) Employment;

(ii) Promotion, transfer, termination, demotions, and separations;

(iii) Formulation and direction of training programmes;

(iv) Job analysis and evaluation;

(v) Remuneration and incentives;

(vi) Health and Sanitation;

(vii) Safety and institutional protection;

(viii) Financial aids to employees;

(ix) Employee service activities;

(x) Research, record keeping, reports and follow-up;

(xi) Employee-employer and community cooperation; and

(xii) Labour union contracts and cooperation.

Straus's and Sayles' Classification:

(i) *Recruitment, Selection and Placement: (a)* Contact with and evaluation of advertising media, employment agencies, including State employment services, college and school recruiting; *(b)* Screening and testing techniques, including physical examination; *(c)* Assistance for in-company transfer, career development; *(d)* Assistance for lay-offs and plant closing through job searches for redundant personnel; *(e)* Labour market surveys and projection of potential shortages; and *(f)* Manpower planning, projecting future company needs.

(ii) *Job Analysis, Job Description and Job Evaluation: (a)* Development of methods that will facilitate personnel placement and assignment of money values to skill and experience; *(b)* Development of promotional ladders by means of job analysis; and *(c)* Position guides for organisational planning and information for new placements.

(iii) *Compensation and Appraisal Plans: (a)* Design and implementation of personnel appraisal plans; *(b)* Wage administration; *(c)* Control of merit increases: *(d)* Design and installation of incentive and bonus plans; and *(e)* Administration of deferred compensation plans such as profit-sharing and bonus plans.

(iv) *Employment Records: (a)* Maintenance of job histories, skill inventories and aptitude and education information; and *(b)* Maintenance of wage and hour records, output records, overtime, vacation payments, incentive earning.

(v) *Employee Benefit Programme: (a)* Administration of life insurance, pension and health and welfare benefits; *(b)* Approval of action, disability and compensation payments; *(c)* Suggestion and saving plans, credit union administration; *(d)* Recreation and athletic programmes; *(e)* Cafeteria, employee clubs; *(f)* Company medical services, first aid, preventive medicine; *(g)* Community referrals (psychiatric, alcoholic), and *(h)* Counselling service.

(vi) *Special Services: (a)* Safety inspection, safety plans and controls; *(b)* Company guards and protection services, including fire-fighting; *(c)* Staff reception areas; and *(d)* Communication services, printing house organs, policy manuals, and instructional manuals.

NATIONAL INSTITUTE OF PERSONNEL MANAGEMENT'S CLASSIFICATION

The National Institute of Personnel Management, India, classifies the functions of personnel management into the following categories.

(i) Improvement of industrial relations;

(ii) Promotion of joint consultation;

(iii) Helping management to formulate a labour policy and improving communication between management and employees;

(iv) Advising the management on the fulfilment of statutory obligations relating to safety, health and welfare of the employees;

(v) Improving factory amenities and welfare provisions; and

(vi) Advising the management on the training and further education of employees.

In sum, the N.I.P.M. is of the view that "all those functions which are concerned with the human element in industry, as distinct from the mechanical elements, may be categorised into three classes — welfare activities; labour or personnel aspects; and industrial relations aspects."

(1) Functions associated with the labour or personnel aspect comprising activities concerned with manpower planning, recruitment, selection placement, induction, promotion, transfer, demotion, separation, lay-off, retrenchment, training, and development; incentives and motivations; wage and salary administration.

(2) Functions associated with the welfare aspect of labour are concerned with the conditions of work, and amenities such as the provision of canteens, creches, housing, transport, medical, education, recreational and cultural facilities, and health and safety provisions.

(3) Functions associated with industrial aspect: that is, activities concerned with trade union negotiations, settlement of disputes, grievance handling, disciplinary action, collective bargaining, joint consultation, benefits and services such as insurance, unemployment security, sickness, leave, loan funds, etc.

In practice, all these functions are bound to merge into one another for all are concerned with the human element in industry as distinct from the mechanical or material resources.

FUNCTIONAL AREAS OF PERSONNEL MANAGEMENT

On the basis of the various functions which the personnel management generally undertakes, the functional areas of personnel management may be set forth as below:

(i) Organisational Planning, Development and Task Specialisation;

(ii) Staffing and Employment;

(iii) Training and Development;

(iv) Compensation, Wage and Salary Administration;

(v) Motivation and Incentives;

(vi) Employee Services and Benefits;

(vii) Employee Records;

(viii) Labour or Industrial Relations; and

(ix) Personnel Research and Personnel Audit.

I. ORGANISATIONAL PLANNING AND DEVELOPMENT

"Organisational planning" is concerned with the division of all the tasks to be performed into manageable and efficient units (departments, divisions or positions) and with providing for their integration. Both differentiation and integration are vital for the achievement of pre-determined goals.

(1) A determination of the needs of an organisation in terms of a company's short and long-term objectives, utilization of technology (industrial engineering, industrial psychology, and mechanical engineering) of production, deciding about the nature of product to be manufactured, keeping in view the external environment and public policy.

(2) The planning, development and designing of an organizational structure through the fixing of the responsibility and authority of the employees, so that organisational goals may be effectively achieved.

(3) Developing inter-personal relationship through a division of positions, jobs and tasks; the creation of a healthy and fruitful interpersonal relationship; and the formation of a homogeneous, cohesive and effectively interacting informal group.

II. STAFFING AND EMPLOYMENT

The staffing process is a flow of events which results in a continuous manning of organizational positions at all levels — from the top management to the operative level. This process includes manpower planning, authorization for planning, developing sources of applicants, evaluation of applicants, employment decisions (selection), offers (placement), induction and orientation, transfers, demotions, promotions and separations (retirement, lay-off, discharge, resignation, disability, and death).

(1) Manpower planning is a process of analysing the present and future vacancies that may occur as a result of retirements, discharges, transfers, promotions, sick leave, leave of absence, or other reasons, and an analysis of present and future expansion or curtailment in the various departments. Plans are then formulated for internal shifts or cut-backs in manpower, for the training and development of present employees, for advertising openings, or for recruiting and hiring new personnel with appropriate qualifications.

(2) Recruitment is concerned with the process of attracting qualified and competent personnel for different jobs. This includes the identification of existing sources of the iabour market, the development of new sources, and the need for attracting large number of potential applicants so that a good selection may be possible.

(3) Selection Process is concerned with the development of selection policies and procedures and the evaluation of potential employees in terms of job specifications. This process includes the development of application blanks, valid and reliable tests, interview techniques, employee referral systems, evaluation and selection of personnel in terms of job specifications, the making up of final recommendations to the line management and the sending of offers and rejection letters.

(4) Placement is concerned with the task of placing an employee in a job for which he is best fitted, keeping in view the job requirements, his qualifications and personality needs.

(5) By induction and orientation is meant the introduction of an employee to the organisation and the job by giving him all the possible information about the organisation's history, objectives, philosophy, policies, future development opportunities, products, goodwill in the market and in the community, and by introducing him to other employees with whom and under whom he has to work.

(6) Transfer process is concerned with the placement of an employee in a position in which his ability can be best utilised. This is done by developing transfer policies and procedures, counselling employees and line management on transfers and evaluating transfer policies and procedures.

(7) Promotion is concerned with rewarding capable employees by putting them in higher positions with more responsibility and higher pay. For this purpose, a fair, just and equitable promotion policy and procedure have to be developed; line managers and employees have to be advised on these policies, which have to be evaluated to find out whether they have been successful.

(8) Separation process is concerned with the severing of relationship with an employee on grounds of resignation, lay-off, death, disability, discharge or retirement. Exit interviews of employees are arranged, causes of labour turnover are to be analysed and advice is given to the line management on the causes of, and reduction in, labour turnover.

A number of devices and sub-systems are used in the systems designs to manage the staffing process. These are: *(a)* Planning tables and charts; *(b)* Application blanks; *(c)* Interviews; *(d)* Psychological tests; *(e)* Reference checks; *(f)* Physical examination; *(g)* Performance reviews; and *(h)* Exit interviews.

III. TRAINING AND DEVELOPMENT

It is complex process and is concerned with increasing the capabilities of individuals and groups so that they may contribute effectively to the attainment of organisational goals. This process includes:

(1) The determination of training needs of personnel at all levels, skill training, employee counselling, and programmes for managerial, professional and employee development; and

(2) Self-initiated developmental activities (formal education), during off-hours (including attendance at school/college/professional institutes); reading and participation in the activities of the community.

Under this area, the training needs of the company are identified, suitable training programmes are developed, operatives and executives are identified for training, motivation is provided for joining training programmes, the line management is advised in matters of conducting training programmes, and the services of specialists are enlisted. The effectiveness of training programmes has to be evaluated by arranging follow-up studies.

IV. COMPENSATION, WAGE AND SALARY ADMINISTRATION

It is concerned with the process of compensation directed towards remunerating employees for services rendered and motivating them to attain the desired levels of performance. The components of this process are:

(1) Job evaluation through which the relative worth of a job is determined. This is done by selecting suitable job evaluation techniques, classifying jobs into various categories, and then determining their relative value in various categories.

(2) Wage and salary programme consists of developing and operating a suitable wage and salary programme, taking into consideration certain facts such as the ability of the organisation to pay, the cost of living, the supply and demand conditions

in labour market, and the wage and salary levels in other firms. For developing a wage and salary programme, wage and salary surveys have to be conducted, wage and salary rates have to be determined and implemented, and their effectiveness evaluated.

(3) The incentive compensation plan includes non-monetary incentives which have to be developed, administered and reviewed from time to time with a view to encouraging the efficiency of the employee.

(4) The performance appraisal is concerned with evaluating employee performance at work in terms of pre-determined norms/standards with a view to developing a sound system of rewards and punishment and identifying employees eligible for promotions. For this purpose, performance appraisal plans, techniques and programmes are chalked out, their implementation evaluated, and reports submitted to the concerned authorities.

(5) Motivation is concerned with motivating employees by creating conditions in which they may get social and psychological satisfaction. For this purpose, a plan for non-financial incentives (such as recognition, privileges, symbols of status) is formulated; a communication system is developed, morale and attitude surveys are undertaken, the health of human organisation diagnosed and efforts are made to improve human relations in the organisation. The line management has to be advised on the implementation of the plan and on the need, areas and ways and means of improving the morale of employees.

V. EMPLOYEE SERVICES AND BENEFITS

These are concerned with the process of sustaining and maintaining the work force in an organisation. They include:

(1) Safety provision inside the workshop. For this purpose, policies, techniques, and procedures for the safety and health of the employees are developed; the line management is advised on the implementation and operation of safety programmes; training has to be given to first line supervisors and workers in safety practices; the causes of accidents have to be investigated and data collected on accidents; and the effectiveness of the safety programmes evaluated periodically.

(2) Employee counselling is the process through which employees are given counsel in solving their work problems and their personal problems. The line management has to be advised on the general nature of the problems which the employees may face from time to time.

(3) The medical services include the provision of curative and preventive medical and health improvement facilities for employees, free or otherwise. A periodical medical check-up of employees, training in hygienic and preventive measures are undertaken.

(4) The r*ecreational and other welfare facilities* include entertainment services like filmshows, sports and games; and housing, educational, transport and canteen facilities, free or at subsidised rates. Suitable policies and programmes are framed and efforts are made to administer these services satisfactorily. The effectiveness of such programmes has also to be evaluated.

(5) Fringe benefits and supplementary items are made available to employees in the form of: *(a)* Old age survivor's and disability benefits, unemployment and

workmen's compensation; *(b)* Pensions, gratuities and such other payments as are agreed upon — death benefits, sickness, accident and medical care, insurance, expenses of hospitalisation, voluntary retirement benefits; *(c)* Paid rest periods, lunch periods, wash-up time, travel time, get-ready time; *(d)* Payments for the time during which no work is done — paid vacation or bonus in lieu of vacation, payment for holidays, paid sick and maternity leave; and *(e)* Profit-sharing benefits, stock options contribution to employees' provident fund, employees educational expenditure and special wage payments ordered by the courts.

These benefits are usually given to employees in order to tempt them to remain in the organisation, to provide them social security, and to reduce absenteeism and labour turnover. Policies and programmes for implementing these have to be properly developed.

VI. EMPLOYEE RECORDS

In employee records complete and up-to-date information is maintained about employees, so that these (that is the records) may be utilized, if need be, at the time of making transfers/promotions, giving merit pay, or sanctioning leave and at the time of termination of service.

Such records include information relating to personal qualifications, special interests, aptitudes, results of tests and interviews, job performance, leave promotions, rewards and punishments.

VII. LABOUR RELATIONS

By labour relations is meant the maintenance of healthy and peaceful labour-management relations so that production/work may go on undisturbed.

Under this area:

(1) Grievance handling policy and procedures are developed, after finding out the nature and causes of grievances, and locating the most delicate areas of dissatisfaction.

(2) Rules and regulations are framed for the maintenance of discipline in the organisation, and a proper system of reward and punishment is developed.

(3) Efforts are made to acquire a knowledge of, and to observe and comply with, the labour laws of the country and acquaint the line management with the provisions which are directly concerned with organisation. Collective bargaining has to be developed so that all the disputes may be settled by mutual discussions without recourse to the law court. Such bargaining, negotiating and administering agreements relating to wages, leave, working conditions and employee-employer relationship falls in this area.

VIII. PERSONNEL RESEARCH AND PERSONNEL AUDIT

This area is concerned with:

(1) A systematic inquiry into any aspect of the broad question of how to make more effective an organisation's personnel programmes — recruitment, selection, development, utilization of, and accommodation to human resources:

(2) Procedures and policies and findings submitted to the top executive;

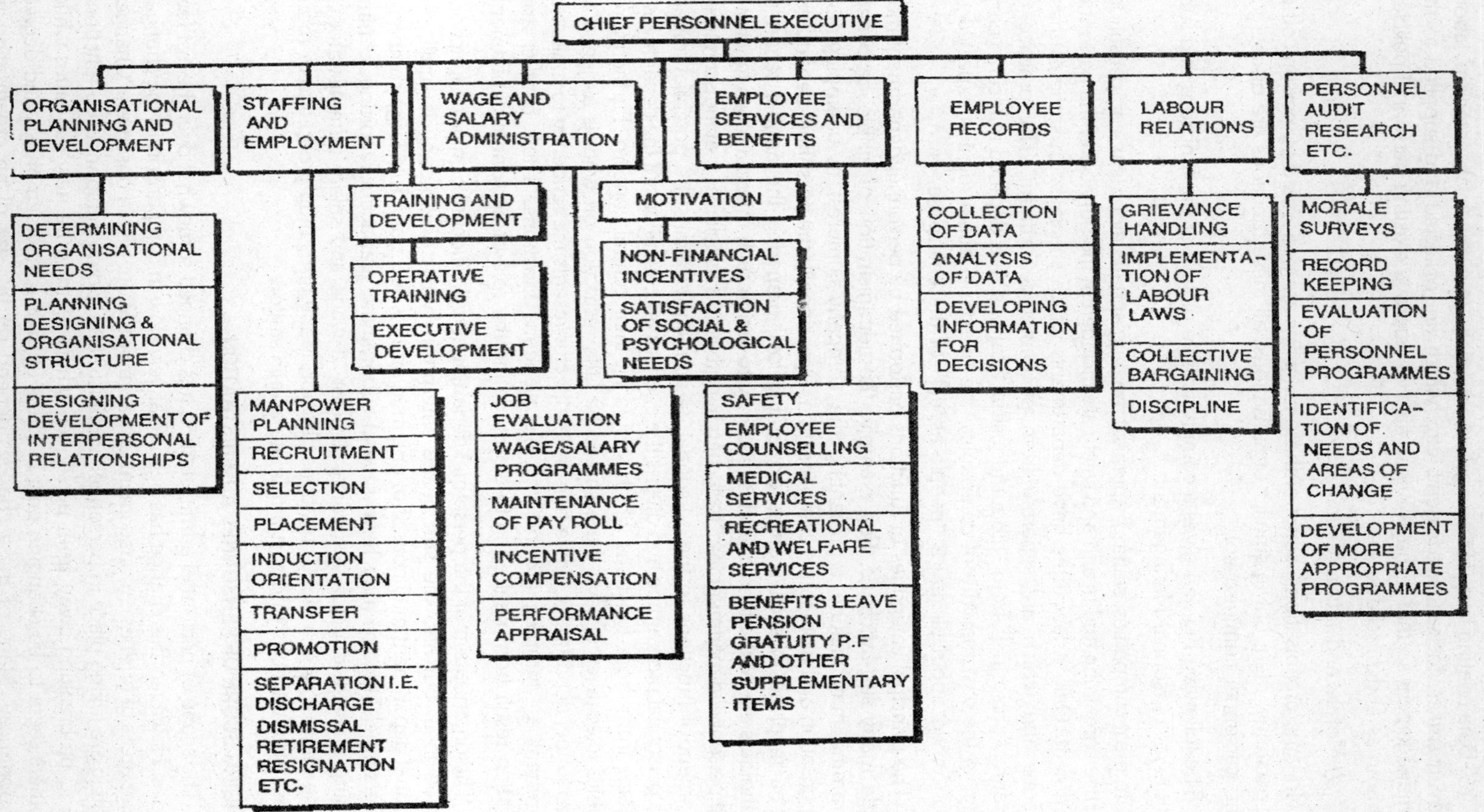

Fig. 2.4 Major Functions and Sub-functions of Personnel Management

(3) Data relating to quality, wages, productivity, grievances, absenteeism, labour turnover, strikes, lock-outs, accidents etc., which are collected and supplied to the top management so that it may review, alter or improve existing personnel policies, programmes and procedures;

(4) Morale and attitude surveys.

In large organisations, some of these functions are performed by persons other than personnel men; but in smaller organisations, all these functions are discharged by the personnel administrator.

The following Fig. 2.4 gives a comprehensive picture of the functions and sub-functions of Personnel Management.

In most companies, staffing, appraisal, training and development, compensation, collective bargaining and health and safety are included in the purview of the personnel department. Only a few firms have departments which specialise in some of these functions and which are separate from personnel department. The practice of separating "personnel" from "labour/industrial relations" has declined in recent years. Today, in the vast majority of companies, the personnel department is expected to be concerned about all major "people aspect" of the enterprise.

The principal categories of functions performed by personnel department may include many sub-functions. For example, the administration of employee benefit programme may include representing the company's interest in unemployment compensation and workmen's compensation. Occasionally the personnel department may be involved in such matters as parking lots, preparing the annual report to shareholders etc. McFarland calls this tendency to assign such miscellaneous functions to the personnel department the "trashchen hypothesis." He believes that indiscriminate assignment of functions to the personnel department weakens the potential impact of the personnel programme and diverts the energies and attentions of the department's members from those functions which should be their central concern. Furthermore, the chief executives believe there should be little restriction on what is assigned to the personnel department, while personnel director resents the tendency to make the department a 'dumping ground" of miscellaneous functions. Thus, conflict and frustration result from neglecting to clearly define the role of personnel department.

The organisation of the personnel department will reflect not only the functions assigned to it, but also the size of the enterprise. When a company is small, the personnel department may consist of one man and his secretary. In a large company, the Personnel Director may have several subordinate managers reporting to him, including a safety director, a medical director, a wage and salary administrator, a training director, and a labour relations director. Many firms may group two or more of these sub-functions under subordinate administrators.

CHANGING SCOPE OF PERSONNEL ADMINISTRATION

The scope of personnel administration has changed somewhat over the last few decades. However, this change has been relatively slow in comparison to the changes in other areas of business, management and administration. Sikula observes: "Changes definitely are taking place in personnel administration. Some personnel sub-functions seem to be breaking away from personnel, others seem to be new sub-areas while still others seem to be changing only in terms of their relative emphasis and degree of importance." Many of these changes depend on the size of an organisation in which the personnel function occurs, the managerial personnel philosophies, the growing importance of the functions, the changing organisational demands, employee needs and societal concerns. Managerial and organisational development, manpower planning, organisational planning, human resource development are incoming areas, *i.e.,* they are now going to receive substantially more attention; they did not have any prominence in the past. Training and managerial development and personnel research have become increasingly important today; while the importance of personnel appraisal, wage and salary administration, has somewhat declined in terms of relative emphasis. Employee benefit and services, and workers' health and safety have always been important personnel concerns. Labour relations, public relations and plant security are "outgoing" personnel sub-areas which have been taken away from the personnel department because of their increased organisational importance.

TRENDS IN THE NATURE OF WORK

(i) Technological changes — have already taken over the age old management in manufacturing, communications, designing raw material — supply, storage movements, by accepting near to method techniques, products, machines, raw materials supply chain, logistics, thus helping increasing productivity and reduce number of employees. Labour intensive blue collar and clericals jobs have started declining with arrival of the new techniques. Technology will also force companies to be competitive, job redesigning, change in organisation structures are being accepted.

Information technology has also speeded up what experts call the "call of hierarchy", in other words managers depend less and less on yesterday's stick-to-the chain of command approach to organising.

(ii) Another trend refers to Globalization — This refers to the tendencies of companies to extend their sales or manufacturing to the new markets abroad for business, internationally, production is becoming globalised too, as manufacturing facilities are put around the world by manufacturers, at places which give them better advantages.

This globalization of markets and manufacturing has vastly increased international competition, changes are taking place in the nature of work, jobs due to the trends in tehcnological change and globalization. Information technolgoy including fax machines, personal computers and after e-business applications have allowed companies to relocate operations to locations with lower wages.

There is trend to use temporary and part time workers, employees on contract basis and as consultants. There is trend to get work done through service industry, to get knowledge through Information Technology. An enormous shift from manufacturing jobs to service jobs is taking place in America and Western Europe.

Other trends affecting Human Resource Management relate to legal protection to employees in the matter of employment, health of employees, safety provisions, union-management relations.

These changes require a new approach to management of human resources.

EMERGING ROLE OF PERSONNEL MANAGEMENT

It has been rightly apprehended that there are dangers of the personnel manager giving way to the new specialists who are coming up — the experts in information technology, in the management of research and development, and in manpower and planning, unless the personnel manager tries and acquires advance knowledge of and prepares for the change. He should, therefore, concern himself with the following major areas of change which are emerging:

(a) Changing composition of work force, with the white-collar gradually becoming a dominant group;

(b) growing unionisation among the work force is greatly increasing their strength to demand increasing participation in the decision-making activities influencing their interests;

(c) increasing role of government in enacting protective legislation to bring about a balance in the interests and rights of the participants in the organisation;

(d) revolution in information technology and other technological innovations, which might adversely affect the interests of the work force and their occupational mobility;

(e) rapidly changing jobs and skills requiring long-range man-power planning; and

(f) increasing concern of many firms for accepting greater social responsibility.

In all these areas of change; personnel management people would be needing larger amount of training, re-training, mid-career re-training. Furthermore, they must also be familiar with the findings of the Behavioural Sciences so that they could rely more on management by intergration of professional goals with the goals of the organisation and by self-control rather than on management by centralised direction and control. They also cannot afford to neglect the "bread and butter" problems of day-to-day personnel administration.

People at work and their interpersonal relations are in a state of transition. Although personnel management and personnel departments have witnessed an almost universal recognition and acceptance by top executives of the important role that personnel management can perform in planning and administering systems of human resources, the coming decade presents major new challenges in various fields, as described below.

The individual is and will be the basic unit of activity. Individual human beings supply the knowledge, skills, and much of energy utilised in organisations. It would not be incorrect to presume that each individual human being will continue to have needs, drives, and expectations; but no two people would be identical in their goals, ambitions, strengths and weaknesses. Such people may expect even more from their employment relationship. For example, Bennis has suggested that the increased level of education and mobility will change the values people have towards work. "People will be more intellectually committed to their jobs and will probably require more involvement, participation and autonomy in their work."

The educational level of the work force is expected to continue to rise. The work force will become more diverse in backgrounds, age concentrations, and ideological philosophies. Groups previously considered to be minorities of the work force (such as the women, the handicapped persons, the members of the scheduled castes, etc.) will increase in number and percentages, and their demands will become more vocal. Many workers might be having more leisure time because of change in work patterns. Managers will be required to face a wide variety of demands from employees.

Changes in the institutions of the society — the family unity, religion, education, organised labour — are likely to occur. The effect of these changes will be significant upon people at work.

The over-supply of unskilled labour, the under-supply of skilled labour in some areas, and over education of some workers for jobs available will result in organisational stress.

Social applications, both formal and informal, will have a large influence on the attitudes and behaviour of people at work. Because people are normally socially oriented, the attitudes and values of organisational peer groups, family members, off-the-job friends, and others to whom they may socially relate will influence heavily their perceptions and actions. The job of managing may therefore, become more challenging and more variable than it has hitherto been.

The organisations of the future would be larger, more complex and with more inter-related structurings of the people. Accordingly, such organisations will become more impersonal and more dehumanising. Such organisations might be required to decentralise decision-making and other activities. They might also expect that the employees should recognise a common set of objectives, plans, and goals so that they can contribute collectively toward mutually beneficial goals. High level managers will need to devote more of their time to integrative decision-making to unite the efforts of all organisational members.

Technology, discoveries and innovations will result in new pressures on organisations and individuals and call for changes in objectives of organisations and methods and procedures to achieve their objectives. Skill requirements will be altered as a result of technology. In some instances, technology might cause workers and their tasks to become more interrelated, while in others there might be tendencies toward separation and even social isolation. Computer technology may result in the reshaping of a number of organisational roles and goals and will have a particularly significant impact on decision-making. These changes indicate the challenge that lies ahead for future managers.

Being human being managers are and will be subject to their own mental and physical limitations, to their own philosophical commitments, to their own biases and prejudices, and to outside pressures from many directions. However, future managers should be able to profit from the increasing body of knowledge and experiences of the present and past managers so that they are in a position to serve more effectively and more constructively the various sectors of people.

ROLE OF THE PERSONNEL MANAGERS OF TOMORROW

The future manager will be more knowledgeable about people, organisations and the total environment, as observed by Bergey and Slover. They state:

"The future manager will be better grounded in social sciences, world affairs, and the humanities in general. He will effectively integrate the techniques of information technology with the human resources available to him."

To meet future challenges, professionalism among the managers will be on the increase. They will be receiving more formalised educational training in managerial techniques and responsibilities. These managers will also need different types of skills, *e.g., top managers* will need more conceptual, analytical, and decision-making abilities; *first line supervision* may need technical skills and interpersonal leadership abilities, and *middle-level managers* may need a blend of the above skills in addition to coordinative abilities. However, all managers will be benefitted from the development and utilisation of skills and abilities in interpersonal relations.

Future managers should develop the ability to be perceptive toward themselves, their superiors, colleagues and subordinates; their organisation, its goals, resources, etc., and many additional elements. They should be sensitive and empathetic to the people, events, and objects around them. They must be perceptive in discerning changes in knowledge, attitudes, behaviour, value systems, need levels, technical requirements, etc. They must have the ability to get to the real heart of the situation.

Because the managers will have to constantly encounter changes, they must be open-minded, and receptive to new ideas and new operational techniques and innovations. They must also possess patience and tolerance so that they may not only perceive the problems, but also diagnose cause, work with other individuals, bear their views, and find out suitable solutions.

The strength of future manager would be in helping others make decisions for themselves. This means that he should know how to lead group efforts, how to counsel with individuals and how to be a good listener. The personnel manager should put more emphasis on "positive motivation" — on helping people achieve personal goals while striving toward organisational objectives. This type of environment induces employees to be more productive because they are forced to perform. At the same time, the manager should not avoid the use of "negative motivational techniques" when they may be useful.

Besides, he and his staff should be deeply involved in encouraging "participative management" or "job enrichment", either of which may have a major impact on job design. The corporate personnel staff should be increasingly concerned with organisational planning, preparation of organisation manuals, and advice to the chief executive on over-all organisational structure, and implementing plans of reorganisation.

The future personnel staff must seek opportunities to be heavily involved in manpower planning, initial selection, orientation, promotional decisions, and career planning. It should also fulfil several other functions, such as "training for change," "systems counselling", "developing new incentives", and "building collaborative problem-solving teams."

SUMMARY

In conclusion, it may be said that future has many challenges for the managers of tomorrow. The most important challenge is how personnel executive and his staff can help in improving organisational effectiveness; and how best he can utilise the results of behavioural scientists for the benefit of the people at work. One part of the challenge lies in "how to create and manage the various personnel sub-systems in a way compatible with the thrust toward more participative, results-oriented, adaptive, and humanistic organisation." Systems of job design, staffing, appraisal, compensation, collective bargaining, organisational justice, and training and development must all be examined and improved toward these ends. The technological and information technology innovations have changed methods of getting work done. The trend is to reduce direct employees and depend more on external sources of getting work, tasks, results, through service industry.

In the words of French, "This challenge is made all the more real and urgent by two sometimes seemingly contradictory imperatives which are rapidly overtaking us — the imperative toward more efficient production of quality goods and services, and the imperative toward a higher quality of life in organisations. *Personnel management must — and will — play a major role in furthering a creative synthesis of these two imperatives.*"

❑❑❑

3

Personnel Management in India

GENESIS AND GROWTH

The *Personnel Function* in India has been a product of various factors, labour legislation being one of them. The importance of labour officers in Indian industry was realised as early as 1929, when the Royal Commission on Labour was set up. In 1931, the Commission recommended the appointment of a labour officer in order to "protect the workers from the evils of jobbery and indebtedness, to act as a spokesman of labour and to promote an amicable settlement between the workers and management." The Commission observed that:

(i) The jobber should be excluded from the engagement and dismissal of labour and that, instead, a labour officer be appointed for this purpose;

(ii) The qualities required of a labour officer should be integrity, personality, energy, and the gift of understanding individuals and he should have a linguistic facility. If he is of the right type, the workers will rapidly learn to place confidence in him and regard him as a friend;

(iii) All labour should be engaged by him, and none should be dismissed without consulting him; and

(iv) The labour officer should fulfil many duties, and should particularly initiate and administer welfare measures.

In 1931, the Bombay Millowers' Association appointed labour officers on their own, who were required to attempt to settle grievances and disputes. Similar officers were appointed in the jute industry in Bengal under the directions of the Jute Mills' Association. These officers were entrusted with the responsibility of setting up food shops, promoting sports and welfare activities. Personnel officers in the textile industry came up from the department concerned with recruitment and the settlement of grievances rather than from one administering welfare activities, as in other countries (the USA and the UK). Their functions as Industrial Relations Officers to handle grievances and prevent disputes were stressed from the beginning.

During the Second World War, these officers were generally entrusted with the handling of welfare and labour administration. Their functions were subsequently enlarged and were influenced by the social reform movement in the country, public concern for improving labour administration and the growth of the modern management movement. Their functions thus included activities relating to welfare, personnel and industrial relations.

The Factories Act of 1948 provides for the statutory appointment of a welfare officer in a factory. Section 49 (1) and (2) of the Factories Act lays down that: (1) in every factory wherein 500 or more workers are ordinarily employed the occupier shall employ in the factory such number of welfare officers as may be prescribed; (2) the state government may prescribe the duties, qualifications and conditions of service of officers employed under sub-section (i). According to the Plantations Labour Act, 1951 every plantation wherein 300 or more workers are ordinarily employed the employer shall employ such number of welfare officers as may be prescribed. The state government may prescribe their duties, qualifications, and conditions of service. The Mines Act, 1952 also provides that every mine wherein 500 or more persons are ordinarily employed, the owner, agent or manager has to appoint a suitably qualified person as welfare officer. These Acts also prescribed the manner of their recruitment, their salaries and conditions of service; and also laid down an elaborate list of duties to be performed by them, including those concerned with welfare, with day-to-day personnel administration and with industrial relations.

In the beginning, personnel management was neither given any particular attention nor place in the organisation system, nor did professionals find themselves involved in the process. Its existence without any apparent assignment or responsibility was the usual picture and the so called champions and protectors of labour welfare used to remain only on the fringe of industrial activities as an appendage to the system. Subsequently, it was entrusted with the *policing function* within the organisation, *i.e.,* to report on and assist the organisation in dealing with mostly discipline and getting rid of trouble-makers. At this stage, it was mostly engaged in "fire fighting tasks", *i.e.,* going to the forefront at the moments of crisis, without having carried out any preventive or organising action. Incidentally, it was at this stage that, at times, the use of welfare officers for aiding and abetting the exploitation of the working class by certain organisations brought them on the periphery of notoriety. However, by and large, their appointment in industries remained only symbolic, satisfying the statutory requirements, without any specific, constructive role to play. The "personnel man," who was initially known as "welfare officer," has moved on to be known as "labour welfare officer," "personnel officer," "industrial relations officer" and is now identified as "human resource manager."

QUALIFICATIONS OF LABOUR WELFARE OFFICER

A welfare officer to be appointed should possess: *(i)* a university degree; *(ii)* degree or diploma in social sciences, social work or social welfare from any recognised institution; and *(iii)* adequate knowledge of the language spoken by the majority of the workers in the area where the factories, mines and plantations are situated.

The National Commission on Labour has stated that "laws were made to ensure that the managements appointed a person exclusively to look after the welfare of their workers and help them in discharging their statutory obligations in respect of welfare measures. Welfare Officers should form part of the administration in order to discharge their responsibilities effectively. Therefore, the eligibility of a Welfare

Officer must be ensured before his appointment. The Welfare Officer should not be called upon to handle labour dispute on behalf of the management."

The *Committee on Labour Welfare,* after going through the views expressed by the State Governments, public sector undertakings, private employers' organisations, workers' organisations and eminent persons in the field of relations and on the role and status of welfare officer, recommended that:

"The management should designate one of the existing officers to their personnel department as welfare officer to fulfil the purpose of the law. The management should ensure that only such officers of the personnel department are designated to look after the welfare activities as are properly qualified to hold these posts and have aptitude for welfare work."

FUNCTIONS OF LABOUR WELFARE OFFICERS

In actual practice, the welfare officer has been entrusted with the following functions:

(a) Supervision of:

(i) Safety, health and welfare programmes; housing, recreation, and sanitation services;

(ii) looking after the working of the joint committee;

(iii) grant of leave with wages; and

(iv) redressal of workers' grievances.

(b) Counselling Workers on:

(i) Personal and family problems;

(ii) adjusting to work environment; and

(iii) understanding rights and privileges.

(c) Advising the Management on Matters of:

(i) Formulating welfare policies;

(ii) apprenticeship training programmes;

(iii) meeting statutory obligations to workers;

(iv) developing fringe benefits; and

(v) workers' education and use of communication media.

(d) Establishing Liaison with Workers to:

(i) Understand the various limitations under which they work;

(ii) appreciate the need of harmonious industrial relations in the plant;

(iii) interpret company policies to workers; and

(iv) persuade workers to come to a settlement in the event of a dispute.

(e) Establishing Liaison with the Management to:

(i) Appreciate the workers' viewpoint on various matters;

(ii) intervene on behalf of the workers in matters under the consideration of the management;

(iii) help different department heads to meet their obligations;

(iv) maintain harmonious industrial relations in the plant; and

(v) suggest measures for the promotion of the general well-being of workers.

(f) Working with the Management and Workers to:

(i) Maintain harmonious industrial relations in the plant;

(ii) arrange a prompt redressal of grievances and speedy settlement; and

(iii) improve the productivity and productive efficiency of the enterprise.

(g) Working with the Public to:

(i) Secure a proper enforcement of the various provisions of the Acts as applicable to the plant by establishing contact with factory inspectors, medical officers and other inspectors;

(ii) to help workers to make use of community services.

It is obvious that the duties and functions entrusted to a Welfare Officer range from assisting the management in policy formulation and implementation to supervising welfare programme, establishing contacts with workers and the public, solving workers' problems and grievances.

The National Commission on Labour has stated, "the care of workers in all matters affecting their well-being, both at the place of work and outside, puts a special responsibility on the welfare officer. He should be a 'maintenance engineer on human side.' In many cases, he also handles grievances and complaints of workers relating to terms and conditions of service and domestic and other matters which lie in the domain of personnel management. There is, thus, virtually, no demarcation between personnel management functions and welfare functions." The Commission recommended that "in order to reduce the hierarchical hiatus in the status of these two officers, there should be an interchange to encourage professional functional mobility and to eliminate the functional monopoly as well the hierarchical status problems."

In the Chart 3.1 below are shown the functions of a labour welfare officer.

From the chart it will be seen that a Welfare Officer in India is a "multi-purpose personnel officer." He is a mainly concerned with welfare of the staff with a role of staff adviser or specialist. He is expected to act as an adviser counsellor, mediator and a liaison-man between the management and labour, *i.e.*, to act as a "maintenance engineer on the human side."

CHART 3.1

Labour Welfare Officer

Labour Welfare Functions

↓

Advice and Assistance in Implementing Legislative Provisions Relating to:

1. Health and Safety
2. Working Conditions
3. Sanitation and Grievances
4. Recreation
5. Welfare Amenities
7. Services like Co-ops., Credit Society.
8. Formation of Welfare Committees
9. Housing
10. Implementation of Welfare Acts.

Labour Administration Functions

↓

These may cover:

1. Organisational Discipline and Non-legislative
2. Safety and Medical Cleanliness
3. Wage and Salary Administration
4. Administration of Legislation Covering Industrial Relations.

Labour Relations Functions

↓

These may Consist of:

1. Administration of Standing Orders
2. Settlement of Administration
3. Settlement of Disputes through Statutory Procedures
4. Trade Unions and Union Management
5. Steps to Increase Productive Efficiency.

The Central Model Rules, 1957, define the duties of welfare officers so widely (Rule 7) as to comprise:

(1) helping maintain harmonious relation between factory management and workers.

(2) redressal of workers' grievances.

(3) providing feedback to management regarding labours' point of view "to shape and formulate labour policies and to interpret these policies to the workers."

(4) to watch industrial relations and settle disputes by "persuasive efforts."

(5) to advise management on the implementation of health and safety programmes.

(6) to promote productive efficiency.

(7) amelioration of the working conditions and helping workers to adjust and adapt themselves to the working environment, and

(8) personnel counselling — advising workers on individual personal problems, etc.

It will, thus, be observed that practically the whole gamut of personnel management, except disciplinary action, recruitment, and promotion seem to be comprised in this formulation.

Based on these Central Model Rules we give below the duties authority and responsibilities of Labour Welfare Officer in India.

In the United Kingdom, these duties are performed by personnel officers. It may, therefore, be said that the government has unconsciously attempted to develop the institution of personnel management through the appointment of welfare

CHART 3.2

Responsibilities and Authority of Labour Welfare Officer in India

Nature of Authority	*Area of Responsibility*
(1) Advisory: To advise To suggest To encourage To promote To secure	In the formulation of company labour policies *(a)* Should promote training and apprenticeship programmes; *(b)* Induction programmes and improved working conditions; *(c)* Welfare programmes, housing, recreational and educational facilities for workers and their families; *(d)* Joint consultation and methods of communicating with the workers.
(2) Service: To help To explain	*(i)* To workers: *(a)* In personal and family problems; *(b)* In adjusting to work environment; *(c)* In understanding their rights and principles; *(d)* In making applications for leave etc. *(ii)* To Management: By helping workers to understand the various limitations under which they have to work.
(3) Supervisory: To inspect To supervise To regulate	*(a)* Welfare and benefit programmes; *(b)* Health and safety programmes; *(c)* Paid vacations; *(d)* Joint committees.
(4) Functional: To ensure To deal with	*(a)* Implementation of labour laws; *(b)* Wages and Employment.
(5) Policies: To bring To notice of To watch To restrain	*(a)* The factory\management the grievances of the workers, individual as well as collective. *(b)* To watch industrial relations with a view to using his influence in the event of a dispute between the factory management and workers. *(c)* To exercise a restraining influence over workers going on an illegal strike and over the management declaring illegal lockouts and to help prevent anti-social activities.
(6) Mediation:	*(a)* To establish contacts and hold consul-tations with a view to maintaining harmonious relations between the factory management and workers. *(b)* To secure an expeditious redressal of the workers grievances and to to act as a negotiating officer with trade unions. *(c)* To help bring about a settlement of an industrial dispute by persuasive efforts: and *(d)* To maintain a neutral attitude during a legal strike or lockout and to help in bringing about a peaceful settlement.

officers in industries. However, in the USA and the UK, the personnel manager is an integral part of the top level management and is on a par with the manufacturing and marketing managers. He is clearly defined "staff" and not "line" function. He is in touch with all personnel, enjoys the trust, confidence and respect of all ranks, a position which enables him to advise both management and labour. In that sense the personnel manager is the most powerful bridge connecting the management with labour. He is the central figure in any productivity programme. Contrary to this, the personnel function in India has not made rapid advances. This may be attributed to the impediments in its way.

IMPEDIMENTS TO THE PROGRESS OF PERSONNEL MANAGEMENT IN INDIA

There are various factors which have hindered the growth and development of personnel management in India. Some of the important reasons are:

1. The legal status of a Personnel Officer requires him to work in the field of welfare and day-to-day personnel administration and industrial relations. But since the personnel function is a line responsibility and a staff function, it cannot be properly performed by a personnel officer.

2. The attitude of the employees towards personnel officers has not been favourable. Management in India is still traditional and does not take the personnel officer into its confidence. "The line executives are often regarded as those who get the material, cut it up, put it together and ship it out, while staff executives are those who attempt to prevent the line boys from doing their jobs." Such ideas about the role of the personnel managers, generate frustration among them. In the words of Peter Drucker, "the personnel manager tends to conceive his job partly as a file clerk's job, partly as a house-keeping job, partly as a social worker's job and partly as a fire-fighter to head off union trouble or settle it."

3. Personnel officers are even now required to spend a major portion of their time in attending to disputes and the grievances of workers. The plethora of labour laws has encouraged trade unions to keep some matters always under litigation for the advancement of their selfish interests. This factor keeps a personnel officer preoccupied in litigation and away from his more important duties. As a result, he has neither the time nor inclination for long-range planning.

4. Lack of professional training facilities, a sense of insecurity and lack of job satisfaction among a large number of personnel executives drive them away from the profession.

5. The profession has not so far attracted the most meritorious among young persons. Mostly those of ordinary calibre have found place in this profession. One of the reasons being that this profession is still considered by many to be somewhat like a *pinjrapole,* an abode of useless cows.

6. The educational institutions which supply the 'material', have still the age-old curriculum which falls far short of equipping the incumbents with the desired type of fast changing knowledge and skill — which could enable them to deal with human problems effectively at the first instance.

7. The urge for updating the personnel people themselves is also mostly absent, which keeps them from being developed. The lack of initiative renders them obsolete and incompetent for the challenging jobs.

8. Their pre-occupation with their own personal aspirations make them overlook and, at times, ignore the expectations of all others, including the organisations.

9. By and large such professionals have not been tested in any trying situation and, when actually put in it, have generally emerged as failures succeeding rarely. In their behaviour, tendencies like making false promises for cheap popularity and taking credit for the performance of others make it difficult for them to be acceptable to others.

10. The inability to take decisions and the lack of courage to take responsibility for decisions based on their advice have been their greatest handicaps. The professional courage to disagree is a rare virtue. Absence of such professional courage of conviction and lack of confidence in their own competence often compel them to take the line of least resistance.

11. Many a time, the personnel mean — whether due to professional zeal or personal ambition — have tried to impose their will on other professions. This tendency has been responsible for their alienation. They should shed this trait and make an effort to integrate the expectations of all other professionals in industry without creating the feeling of an imposition.

12. Finally, personnel management has not yet been accorded the totality of acceptance by all concerned. It is because unlike professions such as engineering and medicine, where the result of any faulty action or decision becomes almost immediately obvious, the loss felt and the person responsible identified, the result of faulty decision on the management of human resources is not, by and large felt immediately and the responsibility for it can safely be shifted to someone else. Further, unlike other professions, the acceptance of "man-management" as a profession has to come from employers, trade unions as well as the government. This fact makes the profession an easy prey to politicization by government machinery, trade unions and even by those within the organisation.

PROFESSIONALISATION OF PERSONAL MANAGEMENT

The following are some suggestions to improve personnel management profession in India.

1. The employers and the organisation having professional men should give the same status as extended to other professions, and give the personnel man's advice the same weightage as given to others. The areas in man-management should be left to be handled by personnel managers and they must be allowed to contribute their utmost in the formulation of sound personnel policies.... It is high time that management of human beings is not made to like anybody's business. The idea, that by virtue of being a man, everybody is capable of handling other human beings, must go. The practice of encroachment by all and sundry in the area of management must stop.

2. The trade unions must recognise this profession as a speciality in the area of man-management and deal with accordingly .... *Firmness with fairness must replace the practice of appeasement of the trade unions without creating any misunderstanding.*

3. The Government must also professionalize personnel management in the public sector, which is supposed to be the model for others to follow.... The Government should reduce its involvement in the day-to-day relationship of workers and managers, and should encourage bipartism to play its role in its fullness. *It should remain the watch dog to restrain, direct and guide the parties as and when required.*

4. On the side of the management themselves, it is expected that *personnel management should read the writings on the wall.* It must be able to identify the goals of the organisation with those of theirs, by appreciating the needs and aspirations of all others.

FUTURE ROLE OF PERSONNEL MANAGER IN INDIA

About the future role of personnel manager in India, Shri Pandey observes:[7]

"Just as the business of finance men is to manage the finances of the organisation to get the optimum return on investment, just as it is the business of production men to utilise the various resources at their disposal in such manner that optimum output is obtained, so is the business of 'personnel men' to manage human resource ensuring harmony, motivation, satisfaction and commitment.

"The line managers and other functionaries should continue to directly deal with the 'men' under them and, therefore, this relationship must continue. The personnel men's role should be to aid and assist the line managers and others in such a way that the human resource is put to its optimum use. Areas of expertise like wage negotiations, implementation of compensation plans, collective bargaining, recruitment, training in organisational development, management development, manpower planning, manpower audit, employees' service, community development and social welfare and the like are the areas which need professional strategy and skills of personnel men. *In these areas they must be given a decisive role to play.* By virtue of education and training as well as the time at their disposal, personnel men will be most suited persons to handle these matters.

"The concept of 'line' and 'staff' functions must undergo a change and the word 'adviser' (staff) and 'line' need be redefined. Because in a highly competitive and interdependent process of production, where group dynamics plays significant role, drawing an 'iron-curtain' between these two functions cannot work. It is the teamwork that matters and will matter most in dealing with people. An organisation is an organic system, and management a composite team. The various disciplines in management must be cohesive and given equal importance. From this angle, *personnel function should be given appropriate place at all levels of management.*

"Status is earned and not asked for. Each personnel man will have to undergo a serious introspection about his role and himself. The power always lies in one's effectiveness and usefulness. It also lies in its capacity to influence other organisational disciplines as well as workers. In a nutshell, personnel man's power and status will depend to a large extent on how pragmatic is his approach.

"In a fast changing society as our own, self-development in professional field is a continuing feature which must be kept up at all levels lest obsolescence would eat our vitalities."

"At present, the personnel officer in India presents a kaleidoscopic picture of his multi-role structure, namely, that of the *buffer zone* between labour and management; that of the *third force* in industry; that of the *non-aligned* professional, of the *social worker* in an industrial setting, and, above all, of a *staff advisor* in the organisation and an *executive* in the personnel and welfare spheres. A clearer perception of the view depends upon four crucial focus-factors, *viz., (i)* the external conditions generally circumscribing the scope of the role, *(ii)* the internal environment of the undertaking characterizing the motivational analysis and the organisational relations concerning him; *(iii)* the person's ability to deliver the goods as reflected in the kind of training (in knowledge, acquisition of skills and development of attitudes) received by him for the efficient discharge of his duties; and above all; and *(iv)* the personality traits and leadership qualities of the individual concerned." The effective discharge of his duties depends upon his capacity and his resilience to meet the challenges of the circumstances as they arise.

The independence of the country and the beginning of a planned economic society, the rapidly developing management movement, rapid technological improvements and the increasing impact of mechanisation, which have brought in their wake changes in organisational structures and group relations; the growing complexity and size of business, the development of employees' associations, the new findings in behavioural science and the changes in political, economic and social climate of the country, together with the changing patterns of industrial relations; the Government's increasing role in promoting this specialised function — all these pose a new challenge to Indian management, which may broadly be described as "a challenge of survival and expansion" — *survival* because, on account of the increasing costs of production and the creation of increasing competitive conditions, it has become difficult for any business to survive; and *expansion* because, with a national economic policy geared to rapid economic growth, every business has to make a contribution towards increasing production in its own sphere of activity. To meet this challenge of survival and expansion is an up-hill task for personnel executives. Therefore, the future need of organisations is better management and managerial skills so that they may ably cope with the changing social, economic and industrial environment.

One of the primary responsibilities of the personnel manager is to participate in the process of change and make the acceptance of this change smooth and orderly. This would involve the matching of manpower with the new tasks and new methods of work which, in its turn, calls for a lot of uprooting and re-adjustment in the present functions of the Personnel Department. This may create problems of replacing, not obsolescent plant and machinery, but also men. Their retraining and better mobility would lead to stresses, strains and resistance, for which new approaches will have to be adopted. The personnel manager, therefore, will have to be *'more of a development man'* than a *'mere administrator of personnel services.'* He would, moreover, need to be equipped with up-to-date knowledge in the fields of industrial engineering, social psychology, behavioural services, law and accountancy etc.

The future personnel officer should be invested with the necessary authority to implement his decisions; and he should be consulted in the framing of labour and industrial relations policies. He should perform the role of an advisory staff in employer-employee relations, industrial relations and management training; and he should have executive authority in the area of employment, health and safety, employee services and benefits, wage and salary administration, productivity, joint consultation, grievance handling, organisation discipline, and maintenance of personnel records and research.

In the selection of unskilled, semi-skilled and skilled employees, the personnel officer should have a more decisive role, while in the highly skilled supervisory and professional categories, his recommendations should be given due weight.

Induction, workers' education, apprenticeship training and executive development programme should be his responsibilities and his views taken into consideration while making decisions about training programmes.

The creation of an environment of paper work should be conducive to effective work performance and it must relate to the maintenance of suitable working conditions, the provision of employee services, health, safety, welfare and other benefits, and their administration and supervision. All these should be the sole responsibility of the personnel officer.

The development of a just and reasonable promotion and transfer policy; the placement of employees according to their qualifications, and plans which aim at increasing efficiency, promoting job satisfaction, motivating employees; and finally, the administration and adoption of wage and other incentive plans — all these should be looked after by the Personnel Department.

The maintenance of discipline, the handling of grievances and complaints, consultation in matters of disputes, arrangements for negotiations between the parties at dispute with a view to bringing about an amicable settlement of issues, should be some of the other functions of personnel officers.

Engaging in planning and meaningful personnel research on problems relating to personnel; keeping pace with the changing social, political and economic conditions; stimulating managers to anticipate the employee problems which may arise as a result of the introduction of changes in personnel policies, manufacturing processes and procedures and labour-management agreements; conducting attitude surveys to check on current management agreements; conducting attitude surveys to check on current management practices with a view to assisting line managers to improve upon them; examining and assessing the functions of his own department, pruning obsolete functions, becoming cost-conscious in regard to any personnel proposals he submits to the top management; and bringing home to managers the importance of individual dignity, job satisfaction and social approval with a view to wining the co-operation and building up the morale of workers — these, too, are some of the functions of a personnel officer. He should, moreover, be a person who will move, mix and work with all the employees in an organisation, develop an insight into the workings of the human mind, its attitudes and aspirations, improve interdepartmental relations and promote team-work through effective communication.

The future personnel men should keep pace with changes, get very much involved in basic organisational planning, and help the management to gear up human resources to new tasks. In fact, the personnel officer is certainly no less responsible and important in the success of any organisation than one who procures finance, or who produces or who markets the manufactured products. That is why in countries like the USA, the UK and the USSR, his importance has been increasingly recognised. This is equally true of India.

The future role of personnel managers will depend upon:

(i) The responsibilities delegated to personnel managers and their relationship with their bosses, and subordinates;

(ii) Having authority delegated to them for co-operative or service functions;

(iii) Their being able to function unfettered in giving objective advice;

(iv) Their guarding themselves constantly against obsolescence;

(v) Their placing adequate emphasis on personnel research, without which they will turn into corporate refugees;

(vi) Their preparing an adequate training base for the new members of the profession;

(vii) Their ability to slash through procedural brambles in order to achieve results; and

(viii) Their being prepared to accept the full responsibility of their position as senior executives of an enterprise.

SUMMARY

In conclusion, it may be said that the future personnel managers should strive hard towards excellence — individually as well as collectively, so that as a body they may occupy a rightful place in the management along with other co-professionals. If they could do it, they would prove worthy of the motto "To Learn to Serve." Due to rapid changes in the Government policies towards Commerce, Industry and Economic Development there will be change in the process, like manufacturing, distribution, sales, which will necessitate change in employer-employee relationship and the import of Information Technology will bring about new concept of completing tasks, getting work done. Globalisation too, will have enormous impact on product and services being provided.

The HR manager will have to participate in the strategic planning and implementation of new management techniques and keep pace with the changes. He will have to reorient himself and be a part of the learning organisation.

❑ ❑ ❑

4

Human Resource Planning

IMPORTANCE OF HUMAN RESOURCE

"Manpower" or "human resource" may be thought of as "the total knowledge, skills, creative abilities, talents and aptitudes of an organisation's work force, as well as the values, attitudes and benefits of an individual involved.... It is the sum total of inherent abilities, acquired knowledge and skills represented by the talents and aptitudes of the employed persons." Of all the "Ms" in management (*i.e.,* the management of materials, machines, methods, money, motive power), the most important is "M" for men or human resources. It is the most valuable asset of an organisation, and not the money or physical equipment. It is in fact an important economic resource, covering all human resources — organised or unorganised, employed or capable of employment, working at all levels — supervisors, executives, Government employees, "blue" and "white" collar workers, managerial, scientific, engineering, technical, skilled or unskilled persons, who are employed in creating, designing, developing, managing and operating productive and service enterprises, and other economic activities. Human resources are utilized to the maximum possible extent in order to achieve individual and organisational goals. An organisation's performance and resulting productivity are directly proportional to the quantity and quality of its human resources. Hence, the importance of human resource.

MANPOWER PLANNING DEFINED

"Manpower Planning" and "human resource" planning are synonymous. In the past, the phrase manpower planning was widely used; but now the emphasis is on human resource planning which is more broad based. Human resource or manpower planning is "the process by which a management determines how an organisation should move from its current manpower position to its desired manpower position. Through planning, a management strives to have the right number and the right kind of people at the right places, at the right time, to do things which result in both the organisation and the individual receiving the maximum long-range benefit.

Coleman has defined h uman resource or manpower planning as "the process of determining manpower requirements and the means for meeting those requirements in order to carry out the integrated plan of the organisation."

Stainer defines manpower planning as "Strategy for the acquisition, utilisation, improvement, and preservation of an enterprise's human resources. It relates to establishing job specifications or the quantitative requirements of jobs determining the number of personnel required and developing sources of manpower."

According to Wickstrom, human resource planning consists of a series of activities, *viz.,*

(a) *Forecasting* future manpower requirements, either in terms of mathematical projections of trends in the economic evironment and development in industry, or in terms of judgemental estimates based upon the specific future plans of a company;

(b) *Making an inventory of* present manpower resources and assessing the extent to which these resources are employed optimally;

(c) *Anticipating* manpower problems by projecting present resources into the future and comparing them with the forecast of requirements to determine their adequacy, both quantitatively and qualitatively; and

(d) *Planning* the necessary programmes of requirement, selection, training, development, utilization, transfer, promotion, motivation and compensation to ensure that future manpower requirements are properly met.

Thus, it will be noted that *manpower planning consists in projecting future manpower requirements and development manpower plans for the implementation of the projections.* This planning cannot be rigid or static; it is amenable to modification, review and adjustments in accordance with the needs of an organisation or the changing circumstances.

Human resource planning is a double-edged weapon. If used properly, it leads to the maximum utilisation of human resources, reduces excessive labour turnover and high absenteeism; improves productivity and aids in achieving the objectives of an organisation. Faultily used, it leads to disruption in the flow of work, lower production, less job satisfaction, high cost of prodction and constant headaches for the management personnel. Therefore, for the success of an enterprise, human resources planning is a very important function, which can be neglected only at its own peril. It is as necessary as planning for production, marketing, or capital investment.

For an individual, it is important because it helps him to improve his skills and utilize his capabilities and potential to the utmost. For an organisation, it is important because it improves its efficiency and productivity. It is only through initial human manpower planning that capable hands are available for promotion in the future.

NEED FOR HUMAN RESOURCE PLANNING

Human resource planning is deemed necessary for all organisations for one or the other of the following reasons:

(i) To carry on its work, each organisation needs personnel with the necessary qualifications, skills, knowledge, work experience and aptitude for work. These are provided through effective manpower planning.

(ii) Since a large number of persons have to be replaced who have grown old, or who retire, die or become incapacitated because of physical or mental

ailments, there is a constant need for replacing such personnel. Otherwise, the work would suffer.

(iii) Human resource planning is essential because of frequent labour turnover which is unavoidable and even beneficial because it arises from factors which are socially and economically sound such as voluntary quits, discharges, marriage, promotions; or factors such as seasonal and cyclical fluctuations in business which cause a constant ebb and flow in the workforce in many organisations.

(iv) In order to meet the needs of expansion programmes human resource planning is unavoidable (It becomes necessary due to increase in the demand for goods and services with growing population, a rising standard of living — larger quantities of the same goods and services are required.

(v) The nature of the present workforce in relation to its changing needs also necessitates the recruitment of new labour. To meet the challenge of a new and changing technology and new techniques of production, existing employees need to be trained or new blood injected in an organisation.

(vi) Manpower planning is also needed in order to identify areas of surplus personnel or areas in which there is a shortage of personnel. If there is a surplus, it can be redeployed; and if there is shortage, it may be made good.

The objective of human resource planning is to maintain and improve the organisation's ability to achieve its goal by developing strategies that will result in optimum contribution of human resources. For this purpose, Stainer recommended the following nine strategies for the manpower planners:

(a) they should collect, maintain and interpret relevant information regarding human resources; *(b)* they should report periodically manpower objectives, requirements and existing employment and allied features of manpower; *(c)* they should develop procedures and techniques to determine the requirements of different types of manpower over a period of time from the standpoint of organisation's goals: *(d)* they should develop measures of manpower utilisation as component of forecasts of manpower requirements along with independent validation; *(e)* they should employ suitable techniques leading to effective allocation of work with a view to improving manpower utilisation; *(f)* they should conduct research to determine factors hampering the contribution of the individuals and groups to the organisation with a view to modifying or removing these handicaps; *(g)* they should develop and employ methods of economic assessment of human resources reflecting its features as income-generator and cost and accordingly improving the quality of decisions affecting the manpower; *(h)* they should evaluate the procurement, promotion and retention of the effective human resources; and *(i)* they should analyse the dynamic process of recruitment, promotion and loss to the organisation and control these processes with a view to maximising individual and group performance without involving high cost.

Human resource planning is the responsibility of both the line and the staff manager. The line manager is responsible for estimating manpower requirements. For this purpose, he provides the necessary information on the basis of the estimates of the operating levels. The staff manager provides the supplementary information in the form of records and estimates. The staff manager is expected to: *(i)* report about manpower utilisation in the present and the past: *(ii)* provide help and advise managers on the assessment of manpower utilisation and to develop sources of information and techniques for purposes of comparison; *(iii)* administer the procedure of forecasting or objective setting; *(iv)* present the overall forecasts of departmental managers; and *(v)* to advise line managers on forecasting techniques.

BENEFITS OF HUMAN RESOURCE PLANNING

(i) Upper management has a better view of the human resources dimensions of business decisions;

(ii) Personnel costs may be less because management can anticipate imbalances, before they become unmanageable and expensive;

(iii) More time is provided to locate source talent;

(iv) Better opportunities exist to include women and minority groups in future growth plans;

(v) Better planning of assignments to develop managers can be done;

(vi) Major and successful demands on local labour markets can be made.

Human resource planning is practically useful at different levels, as stated by Narayanrao. According to him:

(i) *At the national level,* it is generally done by the Government and covers items like population projections, programme of economic development, educational facilities, occupational distribution, and growth, industrial and geographical mobility of personnel.

(ii) *At the sector level,* it may be done by the Government — Central or State — and may cover manpower needs of agricultural, industrial and service sector.

(iii) *At the industry level,* it may cover manpower forecast for specific industries, such as engineering, heavy industries, consumer goods industries, public utility industries, etc.

(iv) *At the level of the individual unit,* it may relate to its manpower needs for various departments and for various types of personnel.

PROCESS OF HUMAN RESOURCE PLANNING

The process of human resource planning is one of the most crucial, complex and continuing managerial functions which, according to the Tata Electrical Locomotive Company, "embraces organisation development, management development, career planning and succession planning." The process has gained importance in India with the increase in the size of business enterprises, complex production technology, and the adoption of professional management technique. It may be rightly regarded as a multi-step process, including various issues, such as:

(A) Deciding goals or objectives;

(B) Estimating future organisational structure and manpower requirements,

(C) Auditing human resources;

(D) Planning job requirements and job descriptions; and

(E) Developing a human resource plan.

(A) Objectives of Human Resource Planning: Human resource planning fulfils indivi dual, organisational and national goals; but, according to Sikula, "the ultimate mission or purpose is to relate future human resources to future enterprise needs so as to maximise the future return on investment in human resources." In effect, the main purpose is one of matching or fitting employee abilities to enterprise requirements, with an emphasis on future instead of present arrangements." The objectives may be laid down for a short-term *(i.e.,* for one year). For example, the short-term objective may be to hire 25 persons from Scheduled Tribes or Backward Class for purposes of training. The long-term objective may be to start a new industry, to expand the market, to produce a new product, to develop its own sales force rather than depend on distributors, or to have minority group members eventually in position of middle and upper management cadres.

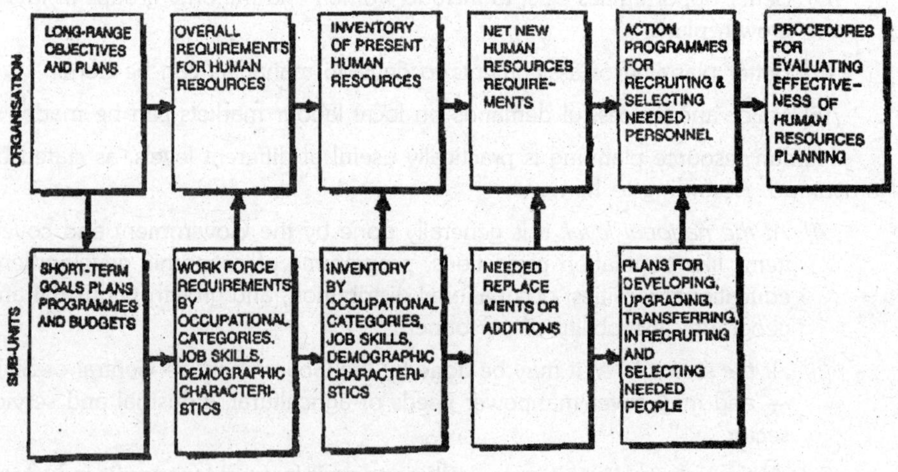

Fig. 4.1 Human Resource Planning System

(B) Estimating the Future Organisational Structure OR Forecasting the Manpower Requirements: The management must estimate the structure of the organisation at a given point in time. For this estimate, the number and type of employees needed have to be determined. Many environmental factors affect this determination. They include business forecasts, expansion and growth, design and structural changes, management philosophy, government policy, product and human skills mix, and competition.

Forecasting provides the basic premises on which the manpower planning is built. Forecasting is necessary for various reasons, such as:

(a) The eventualities and contingencies of general economic business cycles (such as inflation, wages, prices, costs and raw material supplies) have an influence on the short-range and long-run plans of all organisations. *(b)* An expansion following enlargement and growth in business involves the use of additional machinery and personnel, and a re-allocation of facilities, all of which call for advance planning of human resources. *(c)* Changes in management philosophies and leadership styles. *(d)* The use of mechanical technology (such as the introduction of automatic controls,

or the mechanisation of materials handling functions) necessitate changes in the skills of workers, as well as a change in the number of employees needed. *(e)* Very often, changes in the quantity or quality of products or services require a change in the organisation structure. Plans have to be made for this purpose as well.

After estimating what the future organisation structure should be, the next step is to draw up the requirements of human resources, both for the existing departments and for new vacancies. For this purpose, a forecast of labour force is needed, and requisitions should be obtained from different departments, *i.e.,* forecast has to be made in returns of functional category; the members needed; and the levels at which they are required. Vacancies, occurring in any department, should be notified in writing by different department heads to the personnel department, stating clearly the number of vacancies to be filled, job or category-wise types of personnel needed, their technical qualifications and experience, and the reasons for acquisition *(i.e.,* whether for replacement or addition); a statement of duties, types of jobs, pay scales, age, and previous experience should also be made. Requisitions should be based on accurate job specifications by first line supervisors. They should, as far as possible, be clear-cut about the exact demands of a job.

In determining the requirements of human resources, the expected losses which are likely to occur through labour turnover — quits, retirement, death, transfers, promotions, demotions, dismissals, disability, resignations, lay-offs, and other separations — should be taken into account. Changes in the human quality resulting from the experience gained in the jobs during the period and the training achieved also need to be considered. The addition of new lines of production and new projects also influence the demand estimates of human resources. The basic fact to remember is that the human resource in an organisation constantly changes in terms of its present and future size. Additional human resources are gained through new employment of personnel, promotions, through transfers and demotions; but personnel is lost through voluntary quits, death, dismissals, terminations and retirements.

After making adjustments for wastage, anticipated and expected losses and separations, the real shortage or surplus may be found out. If a shortage is there, efforts are made to meet it either by new recruitment or promotion from within, or by developing the existing staff. If there is a surplus, it is to be decided how it will be dealt with, *i.e.,* whether there should be transfers, lay-offs, retrenchment or reduction in the hours of work of all.

Underestimation of the quality and number of the employees required would lead to shortfalls in performance, while overestimation would result in avoidable costs to the organisation. According to Dr. Ram Tarneja, "management can ensure control of labour costs by avoiding both shortages and surpluses of manpower through proper manpower planning."

It may be noted that for purposes of manpower planning, the main dimensions to be taken into consideration are:

(i) The total number of personnel available, this could be obtained from the pay-rolls and other personnel records, such as the applications for employment. The total number has to be classified on some basis, such as manual workers *(i.e.,* daily-rated, weekly-rated or monthly-rated); clerical employees, ministrial staff, managers and other executives; specialists and skilled and unskilled workers; sex-wise distribution, etc.

(ii) *The job-family, i.e.,* a detailed job-description for each position such as stenographers who may belong to various departments, *e.g.,* finance, marketing, personnel, public relations, general administration, etc.

(iii) *Age distribution of the employees,* available in the present departments, say in the age-groups 20-29 years; 30-45 years; 46 years and above.

(iv) *Qualification and experience desired,* such as a person with 5 years or 10 years experience in a particular branch/job; and whether under-graduate, post-graduate, or MBAs or graduates in Science, Commerce, Arts, Engineering or professional diploma holders, etc.; or with specialised knowledge in the field of marketing, finance, computer programming or engineering work.

(v) *The salary range,* etc.

(C) Auditing Human Resources: Once the future human resource needs are estimated, the next step is to determine the present supply of manpower resources. This is done through what is called "Skills Inventory." A skills inventory contains data about each employee's skills, abilities, work preference and other items of information which indicate his overall value to the company.

CHART 4.1

Skills Inventory Proforma

Personal Factors

Name .... Birth place ....

Age ....Occupation of parents ....

Sex ....Present address ....

Dependants ....Permanent address ....

Marital status...................................Telephone number (if any) ....

EDUCATION AND TRAINING

School attended with years ....

Degrees/Diplomas obtained...

Training achieved...

EXPERIENCE AND SKILLS

Job areas..	Special skills (such as ability to speak/write foreign languages)
Job titles..	Reasons for leaving supervisory
Job dates..	responsibilities ....

ADDITIONAL INFORMATION

Salary	Test results ....
Grade..	Performance ratings.....................
Absenteeism record..........................	Location of relatives....................
Disciplinary record...........................	Appraisal data............................
Career plans....................................	Any other information.................

The above facts are usually recorded by an employee in some forms from which the information is fed into a computer. Other data pertaining to his performance ratings and his superiors' evaluation of his potential for promotion may also be fed into the computer. The result may either be kept in a file (on tape or otherwise stored) containing information as to the number of employees in the organisation, and other data about each employee, and an indication of his fitness for promotion. A specimen employee information card is given in Chart 4.2.

CHART 4.2

Employee Information Card

Employee No.. Address ....Town ....

Deptt. .... Code. ....

Position.......................

Exp. Date...

Employee status	Regular/Part-time/Co-operative
Shift	1/2/3
Marital status	Married/Single/Widowed/Separated/Divorced
No. of dependent children	1/2/3/4/5
Relatives in company	Yes/No............................ Who?
Union membership (which one)	
Experience of skills	Clerical/Mechanical/Sales/Supervisory/Others.
Special training	Departmental/On-the-job/Vestibule
Accidents	Loss time (mits)............Hospitalisation (Yes/No)
Member of the Credit Union	Yes/No
Abseenteeism	Days ....

Date ....

Operator..

Some organisations do not compile a Skills Inventory but prepare *Organisation Charts* to determine "how many people, at what level, in what position and what kind of experience and training would be required to meet the objectives." These charts show a person's age, the number of years he has been in a particular position, and his fitness for promotion. These Charts or Skills Inventories help in determining and evaluating the quantity and quality of the present human resources of an organisation. They tell us 'what exists in stock' and 'what is needed to be added to that stock', taking into account the capability, qualifications, experience, skill, knowledge and promotional potential of employees. Some companies maintain a *Manning Table,* which lists all the jobs in the unit and the number of workers holding each job. Other Companies also use *Manpower Replacement Charts*, which show the present performance of each position holder and the promotional potential of possible replacements.

Once the present manpower resources are determined, the personnel department can estimate what changes will occur in the present labour force in the next few years, say, 5 years.

(D) Job Analysis: After having decided how many persons would be needed, it is necessary to prepare a job analysis, which records details of training, skills, qualification, abilities, experience and responsibilities, etc., which are needed for a job. Job analysis includes the preparation of job descriptions and job specifications. This has been discussed in the later section of this chapter.

(E) Developing a Human Resource Plan: This step refers to the development and implementation of the human resource plan, which consists in finding out the sources of labour supply with a view to making an effective use of these sources. The first thing, therefore, is to decide on the policy — should the personnel be hired from within through promotional channels or should it be obtained from an outside source. *The best policy* which is followed by most organisations is *to fill up higher vacancies by promotion and lower level positions by recruitment from the labour market.*

The labour market is a geographical area from which employers recruit their work force and labour seeks employment. Here, the forces of demand and supply interact. A labour market generally has the following characteristics:

(a) It is highly unstructured and unorganised, for a majority of workers are illiterate and ignorant and do not have any information about available job opportunities.

(b) The procedures by which companies recruit workers and the methods by which workers go about getting jobs are highly variable.

(c) A great range of wage rates for the same occupation exists in the labour market, depending upon the attitude of the management towards wage levels, the employer's ability to pay and the productivity of labour.

(d) Labour is mostly not mobile either because it has incomplete or inaccurate knowledge of job opportunities and available wages or because of lack of job security.

(e) The supply of labour fluctuates and is influenced by the population in the labour market, the attractiveness of a job (benefits, services, wage rates, the reputation of a company), the extent of unemployment, and the particular skills that are in demand.

(f) Manual labour for unskilled jobs has been replaced by activities that require skills, scientific knowledge, technical acumen and professional training.

Various external factors influence the outflow and inflow of manpower resources. *At the local level* such factors are:[12] *(i)* population density at various distances from the factory or work place; *(ii)* local unemployment level, particularly of the categories which are relevant for the operation of the organisations; *(iii)* availability of part-time labour, *(iv)* current competition for similar categories of manpower from other organisations; *(v)* output from the educational system (general as well as technical; *(vi)* pattern of in-migration and out-migration within the area and between it and *(vii)* transport facilities and communication pattern.

At the corporate level other factors operate, *viz., (i)* trends in the growth of the working population; *(ii)* Government training schemes and systems of technical, vocational, professional, and general education, and their out-turn; *(iii)* impact of social security measures on manpower supply; *(iv)* mobility of the products of the technical, professional and vocational institutions; *(v)* cultural factors and customs, social norms, affecting school leaving age, labour force participation of women, children and young persons.

The personnel manager should have a thorough knowledge of the labour market. Which particular source in the labour market will be tapped will depend upon the policy of a firm, the position of labour supply, the arrangements with labour unions, and Government regulations. However, it is always safe for the personnel manager to be in close liaison with these different sources and use them as and when the need arises.

RESPONSIBILITY FOR HUMAN RESOURCES PLANNING

Human resource planning is the responsibility of the personnel department. In this task, it is aided by the industrial engineering department, the top management and the team of directors of different departments. It is mostly a staffing or personnel function. The over-all responsibility lies with the Board of Directors because, as the manpower planning scheme of Hindustan Lever indicates, "these members are in a position to direct the future course of business, set appropriate goals for the management concerned in the formulation of personnel policies." The personnel department's responsibility is "to recommend relevant personnel policies in respect of manpower planning, devise methods of procedure, and determine the quantitative aspects of manpower planning."

The responsibilities of the personnel department in regard to manpower planning have been stated by Geisler in the following words:

(i) To assist, counsel and pressurise the operating management to plan and establish objectives;

(ii) To collect and summarise data in total organisation terms and to ensure consistency with long-range objectives and other elements of the total business-plan;

(iii) To monitor and measure performance against the plan and keep the top management informed about it; and

(iv) to provide the research necessary for effective manpower and organisational planning.

POINTS TO CONSIDER

The Personnel Department/Director must first decide on a plan period, *i.e.,* the time span for which the plan is to be made. A plan period of less than three years or more than five years would be unrealistic. The process of recruitment, training and placement often takes three or more years.

Having decided on the time span (say five years), it should be seen that it runs span of five years and in blocks. Only then the plan can be kept realistic and functioning.

The plan should be worked out in sufficient detail. Its implementation should be evaluated and controlled properly. *This requires a great deal of tenacity, persistence and vigilance on the part of personnel managers.*

Every component of the plan has to be compatible with policies regarding recruitment, promotion, termination, inter-departmental transfers, retirement and training. *Policy formulation is an essential pre-requisite for manpower planning.*

Whatever plan is made, it has to be realistic. A plan has to be put into operation and, therefore, *whatever is not feasible should be excluded.*

For every part of the plan, allowances should be made for lead time, otherwise the result will be adversely affected. A balance between conflicting requirements of standards and time available has to be achieved. In other words, *practicability has to be given precedence over perfection.*

Finally, the paramount consideration should be to make the plan an integral part of the corporate plan. *It has to mesh with plans in other functional areas.*

MANPOWER PLAN COMPONENT

The manpower plan can be broken down into three components: *(i) Forecasting* — estimating future needs and stock taking of available resources in the organisation; *(ii) Recruitment plan,* to meet the gap between the internal resource and estimated need by external recruitment; *(iii) Training and Development plan* to utilise fully the human resources of the organisation and to develop the potential resources.

In practice it has been found that short-term (under 2 years) and medium-range plans (2 to 5 years) are easier to formulate with greater degree of certainity.

Chart 4.3 summarises factors related to two major forms of human resource planning.

CHART 4.3

Three Ranges of Manpower Forecasting

	Short-Range (0-2 years)	*Intermediate Range (2 to 5 years)*	*Long-Range (beyond 5 years)*
Demand for Labour	Authorised expansion technological changes; new legislation; Employee turnover; lay-offs, and contractual restrictions.	Operating needs from budgets or plans. Expansion or Contraction or adjustments	Geographical capacity; size of the organisation and system; product lines; services offered; load anticipated. Changes in environment and techn-ology essentially judgemental. Labour saving equipment, efficiencies, productivity, etc.
Supply of Labour: Internal	Departmental, divisional rosters; promotions. expected losses; quits, death.	Merger or acquisition plans; managerial and supervisory development programmes.	Management expectations of changing characteristics of employees and future available manpower.
Supply of Labour: External	Area employment levels; Number of employees needed.	Labour Market projections, business development plans, general institutional plans to hire.	Management expectations of future conditions affecting immediate decisions.

SHORT-RANGE ANALYSIS

It usually grows out of normal budgetary processes. Fig. 4.2 illustrates the key steps in the short-term forecasting/planning process.

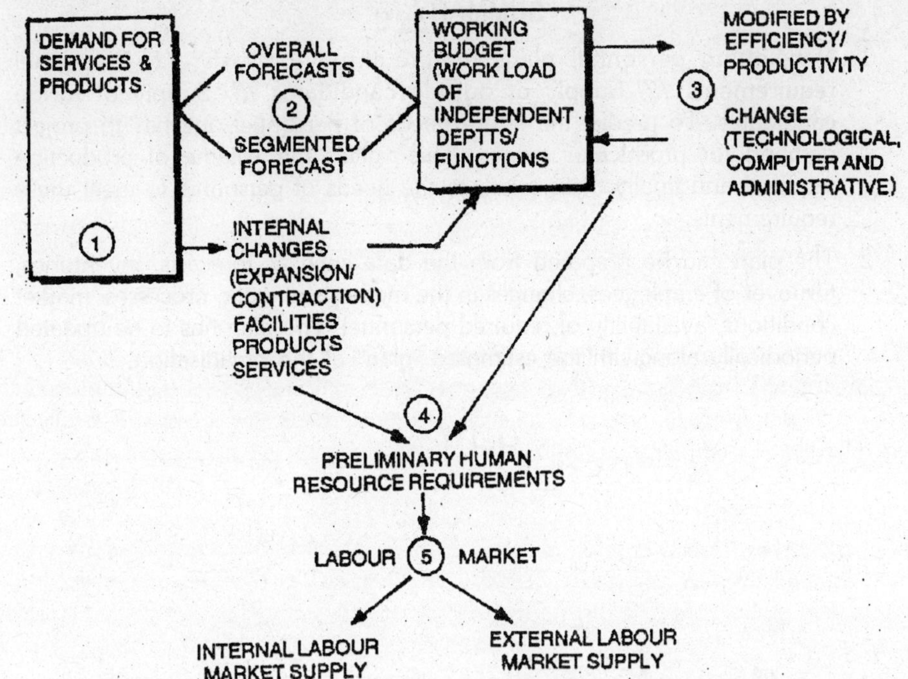

Fig. 4.2 Short-Range Human-Resource Forecasting Organisational Perspective

LONG-RANGE ANALYSIS

The parameters of short-range forecasting usually are fairly well-defined. They are handled in the normal course of budget preparation and require simple arithmetic calculations. Long-range planning is more complex and is dependent upon mathematical and statistical models, as knowledge of demand variables and appropriate measurement techniques.

Two general kinds of forecasting techniques are used: indirect and direct methods. *Indirect methods* involve the forecasting of general rules — production figures, for example — that must be translated into specific requirements or measures. *Direct techniques* involve the use of methods of estimate (directly) labour hours, number of supervisors or particular occupational needs.

Aggregate models are based on several key variables that are known to directly affect the organisation's overall human resource needs. Every organisation has special characteristics or problems, and a planner can use an aggregate model to get the big picture. These models may apply to a geographic region or to the overall system.

Estimates techniques models are used for situations where circumstances make it difficult to use mathematical or statistical approaches. Here expert opinion and experience are used. The volume of future activity of business conditions, including legislation, change, innovation, or competition — situations that are almost impossible to qualify — can provide workable answers to problems.

At the end, it may be noted that all organisations — those that have a high labour turnover — must systematically plan their short-term, medium-term and long-term manpower needs. These requirements need periodical reviews and adjustments to meet changing conditions.

SUMMARY

1. Developing personnel plans require three forecasts: *(1)* Personnel requirements *(2)* Supply of outside candidates *(3)* Supply of inside candidates. To predict the future needs of personnel one has to project demand for product or service. This gives the volume of production required and finally these relate to the needs of personnel to meet these requirements.
2. The plan can be prepared from the data such as forecasts, inventories, turnover of employees, changes in the methods of work, processes, market conditions, availability of required personnel. The plan has to be updated periodically alongwith the estimated "plan" of the organisation.

❑ ❑ ❑

5

Job Analysis, Job Design — Job Evaluation

Developing an orgnisation structure results in jobs which have to be staffed. "Work" is an organisation's primary function. The 'basic work activities' may relate to three categories — Data, People and Things. Under *Data* are included synthesizing, co-ordinating, analysing, compiling, computing, copying and comparing activities. *People* relate to monitoring, negotiating, instructing, supervising, diverting, persuading, speaking, signalling, serving and taking instructions. *Things* are concerned with setting up, precision working, operating-controlling, driving-operating, manipulating, feeding-off bearing and handling.

While manpower inventory is concerned with telling 'what employees *can do*,' job analysis assesses 'what employees *are doing*.' From job analysis, specific details of what is being done and the skills utilised in the job, is obtained. Job analysis enables managers to understand jobs and job structures to improve to work flow or develop techniques to improve productivity. It also involves job design or redesign, co-ordinating demands on available time, individual psychological needs, technical procedures, and desired performances.

Before we proceed to discuss job analysis in detail, certain terms relating to job need be understood. These terms are:

Job: A job may be defined as a "collection or aggregation of tasks, duties and responsibilities which as a whole, are regarded as a regular assignment to individual employees," and which is different from other assignments. In other words, when the total work to be done is divided and grouped into packages, we call it a "job." Each job has a definite title based upon standardised trade specifications within a job; two or more grades may be identified, where the work assignments may be graded according to skill, the difficulty of doing them, or the quality of workmanship. Further, a job may include many positions, for a position is a job performed by, related to, a particular employee.

Thus, it may be noted that a position is a "collection of tasks and responsibilities regularly assigned to one person;" while a job is a "group of positions, which involve essentially the same duties, responsibilities, skill and knowledge." A position consists of a particular set of duties assigned to an individual. There may be, say five persons, all of whom are classified under the same job; and yet each may perform a slightly different work. Therefore, each may perform a slightly different work. Therefore, each person would have a different position — position of a secretary, for example. It may be noted that while a *"job is impersonal the position is personal."*

Job Analysis: It is a procedure by which pertinent information is obtained about a job, *i.e.*, it is a detailed and systematic study of information relating to the operations and responsibilities of a specific job. An authority has defined job analysis as "the process of determining, by observation and study, and reporting pertinent information relating to the nature of a specific job....It is the determination of the tasks which comprise the job and of the skills, knowledge, abilities and responsibilities required of the worker for a successful performance and which differentiate one job from all other."

The information that is collected for job analysis is:

(a) Work activities — such as cleaning, setting, selling, teaching or painting. This may why, when and how the worker perform each activity.

(b) Human behaviour — such as communicating, decision-making, writing include plus what the job demands like, lifting weights, walking etc.

(c) Machine Tools, equipment and other work aids — includes also products made materials, processed etc.

(d) Performance standards — required such as quantity, quality, speed of each job.

(e) Job context — includes physical working conditions, work schedules, incentives for doing the job.

It is a procedure and a tool for determining the specified tasks, operations and requirements of each job. "It is the process of getting information about jobs: specially, what the worker does; how he gets it done; why he does it; skill, education and training required; relationship to other jobs; physical demands; environmental conditions." In other words, *it refers to the anatomy of the job.* It is a complete study of job, embodying every known and determinable factor, including the duties and responsibilities involved in its performance, the conditions under which the performance is carried on, the nature of the task, the qualities required in the worker, and such conditions of employment as pay, hour, opportunities and privileges. It also emphasises the relation of one job to others in the organisation.

Job Description: It is a written record of the duties, responsibilities and requirements of a particular job. It "is concerned with the job itself and not with the work." It is a statement describing the job in such terms as its title, location, duties, working conditions and hazards. In other words, it tells us 'what is to be done' and 'how it is to be done' and 'why.' It is a standard of function, in that it defines the appropriate and authorised contents of a job.

Job Specification: It is a standard of personnel and designates the qualities required for an acceptable performance. It is written record of the requirements sought in an individual worker for a given job. In other words, it refers to a summary of the personal characteristics required for a job. It is a statement of the minimum acceptable human qualities necessary for the proper performance of a job.

Job Design: It is the division of the total task to be performed into the manageable and efficient units — positions, departments and divisions — and to provide for their proper integration. The sub-division of work is both on a horizontal scale — with different tasks across the organisation being performed by different people and on the vertical scale, in which higher levels of the organisation are responsible for the supervision of more people, the co-ordination of sub-groups, more complex planning, etc.

PURPOSE AND USES OF JOB ANALYSIS

A comprehensive JA programme is an essential ingredient of sound personnel management. It is the major input to forecasting future human resource requirements, job modifications, job evaluation, determination of proper compensation, and the writing of job evaluation, determination of proper compensation, and the writing of job descriptions. It is of fundamental importance to manpower management programmes because of the wider applicability of its results. The information provided by JA is useful, if not essential, in almost every phase of employee relations.

1. Organisation and Manpower Planning: It is helpful in organisation planning, for it defines labour needs in concrete terms and co-ordinates the activities of the work force, and clearly divides duties and responsibilities.

2. Recruitment, Selection: By indicating the specific requirements of each job *(i.e.,* the skills and knowledge), it provides a realistic basis for the hiring, training, placement, transfer and promotion of personnel. "Basically, the goal is to match the job requirements with a worker's aptitude, abilities and interests. It also helps in charting the channels of promotion and in showing lateral lines of transfer."

3. Wage and Salary Administration: By indicating the qualifications required for doing a specified job and the risks and hazards involved in its performance, it helps in salary and wage administration. Job analysis is used as a foundation for job evaluation.

4. Job Re-engineering: Job analysis provides information which enables us to change jobs in order to permit their being manned by personnel with specific characteristics and qualifications. This takes two forms: *(a) Industrial engineering activitity,* which is concerned with operational analysis, motion study, work simplification methods and improvement in the place of work and its measurement, and aims at improving efficiency, reducing unit labour costs, and establishing the production standard which the employee is expected to meet; and *(b) Human engineering activity,* which takes into consideration human capabilities, both physical and psychological, and prepares the ground for complex operations of industrial administration, increased efficiency and better productivity.

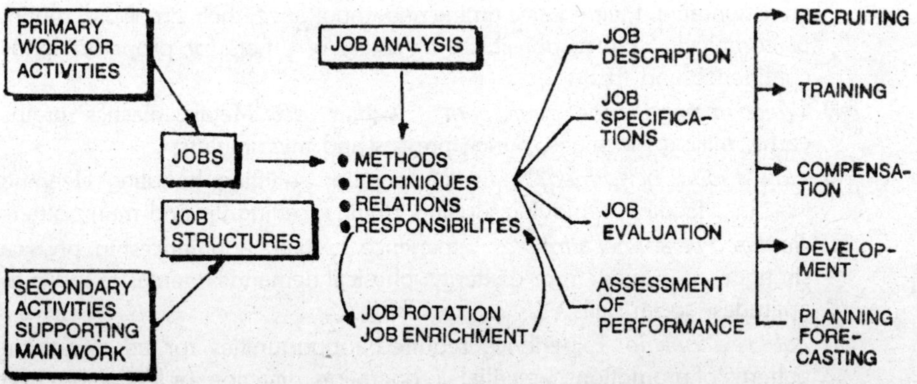

Fig. 5.1 Job Analysis: Area of Application

5. Employee Training and Management Development: Job analysis provides the necessary information to the management of training and development programmes. It helps it to determine the content and subject matter of in-training courses. It also helps in checking application information, interviewing, weighing test results, and in checking references.

6. Performance Appraisal: It helps in establishing clearcut standards which may be compared with the actual contribution of each individual.

7. Health and Safety: It provides an opportunity for identifying hazardous conditions and unhealthy environmental factors so that corrective measures may be taken to minimize and avoid the possibility of accidents.

In sum, it may be noted that job analysis is a systematic procedure for securing and reporting the information which defines a specific job. It has many uses in the management of personnel. It determines the qualifications required for a job; provides guidance in recruitment and selection; evaluates current employees for transfer or promotion; and establishes the requirements for training programmes. It is used as a foundation for job evaluation and helps in employee development by means of appraisal and counselling; for establishing improved methods of analysing problems of health, safety and fatigue; it functions as a guide in connection with discipline and grievances and as a basis for transfers, lay-offs and as a basis of comparison of the pay rates obtaining in other organisations; and it establishes workloads and job assignments. It also helps in redesigning the jobs to improve operational performance or to enrich job content and employee improvement. Managers may develop ways of giving their employees an increased sense of personnel accomplishment and control over themselves and their work.

JA produces four kinds of documentation and procedures that are crucial to personnel activities: *(i)* Job descriptions; *(ii)* Job specifications; *(iii)* Job evaluation, and *(iv)* Personnel assessment. In turn, the procedures and documentation are basic inputs for diverse personnel functions.

CONTENTS OF JOB ANALYSIS

A job analysis provides the following information:

(i) Job identification: Its title, including its code number;

(ii) Significant characteristics of a job: Its location, physical setting, supervision, union jurisdiction, hazards and discomforts;

(iii) What the typical worker does: Specific operation and tasks that make up an assignment, their relative timing and importance, their simplicity, routine or complexity, the responsibility or safety of others for property, funds, confidence and trust;

(iv) Which materials and equipment a worker uses: Metals, plastics, grains, yarns, milling machines, punch presses and micrometers;

(v) How a job is performed: Nature of operation — lifting, handling, cleaning, washing, feeding, removing, drilling, driving, setting up and many others;

(vi) Required personnel attributes: Experience, training, apprenticeship, physical strength, co-ordination or dexterity, physical demands, mental capabilities, aptitudes, social skills;

(vii) Job relationship: Experience required, opportunities for advancement, patterns of promotions, essential co-operation, direction, or leadership from and for a job.

It is obvious from the foregoing that a job analysis is usually a clear indication of a *job description and job specification.* The diagrammatic representation given in Chart 5.1 may be found useful.

CHART 5.1
JOB ANALYSIS
(A Process for Obtaining All Pertinent Job Facts)

Job Description

Statement containing items such as:

(a) Job Identification (job title, location, occupational code, alternative name in use, name of division, department and unit where it exists.

(b) Job Summary (gives a quick capsule explanation of the contents of a job, its hazards and discomforts).

(c) Duties performed (says the what, how and why of a job; also describes a worker's responsibilities in regard to custody of money, supervision of other workers, training of subordinates, etc.)

(d) Relation to other jobs (gives how many persons may be supervised).

(e) Supervision given/taken (helps in locating a job in the job hierarchy).

(f) Machines, tools, equipment (what type of tools/equipment material is used).

(g) Materials and forms used.

(h) Conditions of work *Location* — factory/office/inside/outside/overhead/underground/solitary gang; *Time* — day; night, overtime, peak loads, uniformity of work; *Posture* — standing, sitting, stopping, clinging, walking, reaching, lifting; *Speed* — quick, moderate, slow; *Accuracy* — coarse, fine, exacting, *Health hazards* — ventilation, illumination, nerve strain, eye-strain, physical strain, moisture, heat, dust, humidity, fumes, acids, exposure to such disagreeable features as dirt, noise, etc.

(i) Hazards (accident hazards).

Job Specification

A statement of the human requirements for doing a job:

(a) Physical make-up or characteristics.

(b) Psychological characteristics.

(c) Personal characteristics.

(d) Responsibilities.

(e) Other factors of a demographic nature (sex, age, education, language, ability to read, write and speak).

THE STEPS IN JOB ANALYSIS

There are five basic steps required for doing a job analysis, *viz.,*

Step 1: Collection of Background Information : According to Terry, "the make-up of a job, its relation to other jobs, and its requirements for competent performance are essential information needed for a job evaluation. This information can be had by reviewing available background information such as *organisation charts* (which show how the job in question relates to other jobs and where they fit into the overall organisation); *class specifications* (which describe the general requirements of the class of job to which the job under analysis belongs); and the existing *job descriptions* which provide a starting point from which to build the revised job description.

Step 2: Selection of Representative Job to be Analysed: Since the analysis of all jobs would be time-consuming, few representative positions should be analysed.

Step 3: Collection of Job Analysis Data: Job data on features of the job, required employee qualifications and requirements, should be collected either from the employees who actually perform a job; or from other employees (such as foremen or supervisors) who watch the workers doing a job and thereby acquire knowledge about it; or from the outside persons, known as the *trade job analysts* who are appointed to watch employees performing a job.

The duties of such a trade job analyst are: *(i)* to outline the complete scope of a job and to consider all the physical and mental activities involved in determining what the worker does. For this purpose, he studies the physical methods used by a worker to accomplish his task (including the use of machinery, tools and his own movements and necessary mental facilities); *(ii)* find out why a worker does a job; and for this purpose he studies why each task is essential for the overall result; and *(iii)* the skill factor which may be needed in the worker to differentiate between jobs and establish the extent of the difficulty of any job.

Step 4: A Job Description: The information collected is to be developed in the form of a job description. This is a written statement that describes the main features of the job, as well the qualifications/activities which the job incumbents must possess.

Step 5: Developing Job Specification: The last step is to convert the Job Description statements into Job Specifications, *i.e.,* to specifically mention what personal qualities, traits, skills and background is necessary for getting the job done.

TECHNIQUES OF JOB ANALYSIS DATA

The determination of job tasks, the concomitant skills and abilities necessary for successful performance, and the responsibilities inherent in the job can be obtained through such *methods* or *approaches* as the following:

(i) Personal observation;

(ii) Sending out questionnaires;

(iii) Maintenance of log records; and

(iv) Conducting personal interviews.

(i) Personal Observation: The materials and equipment used, the working conditions and probable hazards, and an understanding of what the work involves are the facts which should be known by an analyst. Direct observation is especially useful in jobs that consist primarily of observable physical ability, like the jobs of draftsman, mechanic, spinner or weaver.

(ii) Sending Out Questionnaires: The method is usually employed by engineering consultants. Properly drafted questionnaires are sent out to job-holders for completion and are returned to supervisors. However, the information received is often unorganised and incoherent. The idea in issuing questionnaire is to elicit the necessary information from job-holders so that any error may first be discussed with the employee and, after due corrections, may be submitted to the job analyst.

(iii) Maintenance of Log Records: The employee maintains a daily diary record of duties he performs, making the time at which each task is started and finished. But this system is incomplete, for it does not give us any desirable data on supervisor relationship, the equipment used, and working conditions. Moreover, it is time-consuming.

(iv) Personnel Interviews: may be held by the analyst with the employees, and answers to relevant questions may be recorded. But the method is time-consuming and costly.

However, it may be noted that the personal observation and interview approach are more or less complete and accurate. If a particular job is simple and repetitive, observation may be the only technique required. Otherwise, in most cases, interviews coupled with observation constitute the desirable approach.

Caroll L. Shartle, Otis and Lenhert have provided the following suggestions for making the job analyst's task simple:

(i) Introduce yourself so that the worker knows who you are and why you are there;

(ii) Show a sincere interest in the worker and the job that is analysed;

(iii) Do not try to tell the employee how to do his job;

(iv) Try to talk to the employees and supervisors in their own language;

(v) Do not confuse the work with the workers;

(vi) Do a complete job study within the objectives of the programmes; and

(viii) Verify the job information obtained.

An example of Job Analysis and Job Description used in a large sized Company is given in Chart 5.2.

CHART 5.2

Job Analysis Record Form

	Name of Company	Job Analysis Form		
For a	Present Job Title	Staff Division		Date
Division's Use:	Proposed Job Title	Organisation Components	Employee Report	Supervisor Report to
For Central Staff Use	Position Title	Position Code		Date

DESCRIPTION OF DUTIES

(i) General Summary Statement: Indicate the extent of supervision received or exercised; summarise the basic and distinguishing characteristics of the nature of work, and show the general level of responsibility.

(ii) Typical Duties: When describing duties, be as detailed as possible in outlining the main duties of a position, considering what is done and how it is done, and list them in order of their importance. Indicate whether work is performed as a regular routine or intermittently.

FACTORS

(i) Previous Experience Required: Indicate the period of time required in lower or related jobs, measured from the time when the qualification level of education, cited in factor (ii) is acquired, that are essential for starting on, and a proper performance of a work.

(ii) Specialised or Technical Education Required: Indicate in definite terms the minimum level of academic education essential for a proper performance of a job, citing specific qualifications and/or recognised levels of attainment.

(iii) Manual or Physical Skill Required: What kind of manual or physical skills is required in the performance of the duties?

(Examples: Typing, Shorthand, Comptometer, Book-keeping machine.)

(iv) Physical Effort Required: What kind of physical effort is required and what is the duration of such exertion? *(Examples:* Continuous, walking, standing, lifting of heavy object, etc.)

(v) Complexity and Difficulty of Work:

(a) The extent to which decisions made and action taken are controlled by precents, prescribed work practices, regulations or other guidelines;

(b) The degree of originality, judgement and development work involved;

(c) The variety and the scope allowed by timing schedules.

Assessment	
Divisional	*Central Staff*

(vi) Seriousness of Errors: What type of errors are possible in a job; and what would be the consequences of such errors in terms of additional expense to the company, rework or loss of goodwill?

(vii) Hazards: What type of hazards and risks to health are involved in the performance of duties? State frequency.

(viii) Adverse Working Conditions: Are there any physical conditions surrounding the work that are definitely disagreeable or uncomfortable? (Such as dirt, noise, weather, etc.)

(ix) Contacts with Customers, the General Public or other Companies: Indicate the organisational level of persons in other companies dealt with; the type, difficulty and importance of transactions handled; and the potential effects of such contacts on company goodwill. How contact is made — by telephone, personal contact or correspondence?

(x) Contacts with Other Departments: Indicate type, volume, importance and difficulty of transactions with other departments of the company. How contact is made — by telephone, personal contact or correspondence?

(xi) For the Safety of Others: Show the extent of responsibility of protecting, safeguarding or eliminating hazard to fellow employees or the general public.

(xii) For Company Funds or Property: Does a job involve actual custody of, or personal accountability for, any company funds or portable tools and equipments? If so, state the amount of money or type of tools and equipment involved.

(xiii) For Confidential Information: Does the work involve contact with any confidential data? Does a job involve discretion to reveal the data? If so, explain the nature of data and extent of discretion.

(xiv) For Performance of Work Without Immediate Supervision: Who assigns the work to an incumbent? How is the progress of work assignments checked by the supervisor? How frequently? What is the average duration of an assignment?

(xv) For the Supervision of Others: Does the work involve supervision or direction by other? If so:

(a) Describe the type of work and indicate the number of employees;

(b) The percentage of time spent on work similar to that to the subordinates involved.

Analyst

Approved by

Notes:

JOB DESCRIPTION (JD)

"Job description" is an important document which is basically descriptive in nature and contains a statement of job analysis. It provides both *organisational information* (location in structure, authority, etc.) and *functional information* (what the work is). It defines the scope of job activities, major responsibilities, and positioning of the job in the organisation. It provides the worker, analyst, and supervisor with a clear idea of what the worker must do to meet the demands of the job.

"Job description" is different from "performance assessment." The former concerns such functions as planning, co-ordinating, and assigning responsibility; while the latter concerns the quality of performance itself. Though job description is not assessment, it provides an important basis for establishing assessment standards and objectives.

Job Description describe 'jobs,' not 'job holders.' The movement of employees due to promotion, quits, etc. would create instability to job descriptions if people rather than jobs are described.

USES OF JOB DESCRIPTION

Job description has several uses, such as:

(i) Preliminary drafts can be used as a basis for productive group discussion, particularly if the process starts at the executive level.

(ii) It aids in the development of job specifications, which are useful in planning recruitment, 'in training and in hiring people with required skills.

(iii) It can be used to orient new employees toward basic responsibilities and duties.

(iv) It is a basic document used in developing performance standards.

(v) It can be used for job evaluation, a wage and salary administration technique.

A job description enables the manager to frame suitable questions to be asked during an interview. It is particularly helpful when the application form is used as a tool for eliminating the unfit personnel. According to Zerga, who analysed 401 articles on job description about 30 years ago, a job description helps us in:

(i) Job grading and classification;

(ii) Transfers and promotions;

(iii) Adjustments of grievances;

(iv) Defining and outlining promotional steps;

(v) Establishing a common understanding of a job between employers and employees;

(vi) Investigating accidents;

(vii) Indicating faulty work procedures or duplication of papers;

(viii) Maintaining, operating and adjusting machinery;

(ix) Time and motion studies;

(x) Defining the limits of authority;

(xi) Indicating case of personal merit;

(xii) Studies of health and fatigue;

(xiii) Scientific guidance;

(xv) Determining jobs suitable for occupational therapy;

(xvi) Providing *hiring* specifications; and

(xvii) Providing performance indicators.

Job description helps top executives, especially when they jointly discuss one another's responsibilities. Overlapping or confusion can then be pointed out; questions can be raised about the major thrust of each position, and problems of structure can be identified. *A job description becomes a vehicle for organisational change and improvement.*

Some companies have more than one job description for each job. A detailed version may be used in training and in evaluating a job, while a shorter version may be used in planning and hiring of management.

Components or Content of Job Description: A job description contains the following data.

1. *Job identification, or Organisational Position* which includes the job title, alterative title, department, division, plant and code number of the job. The job title identifies and designates the job properly. The department, division, etc., indicate the name of the department where it is situated — whether it is the maintenance department, mechanical shop, etc. The location gives the name of the place. The portion of job description gives answer to two important questions: to what higher level job is this job accountable; and who is supervised directly?

2. *Job Summary* serves two important purposes. *First* it provides a short definition which is useful as an additional identification information when a job title is not adequate. *Second,* it serves as a summary to orient the reader towards an understanding of detailed information which follows. It gives the reader a "quick capsule explanation" of the content of a job usually in one or two sentences.

3. *Job duties and responsibilities* give a comprehensive listing of the duties together with some indication of the frequency of occurrence or percentage of time devoted to each major duty. *It is regarded as the heart of a job.* It tells us what needs to be done? how it should be done? and why it should be done? It also describes the responsibilities related to the custody of money, the supervision of workers and the training of subordinates.

4. *Relation to other jobs:* This helps to locate the job in the organisation by indicating the job immediately below or above it in the job hierarchy. It also gives an idea of the vertical relationships of work flow and procedures.

5. *Supervision:* Under it is given the number of persons to be supervised along with their job titles, and the extent of supervision involved — general, intermediate or close supervision.

6. *Machine, tools and equipment* define each major type or trade name of the machines and tools and the raw materials used.

7. *Working conditions* usually give us information about the environment in which a job holder must work. These include cold, heat, dust, wetness, moisture, fumes, odour, oily conditions, etc. obtaining inside the organisation.

8. *Hazards* give us the nature of risks to life and limb, their possibilities of occurrence, etc.

DEVELOPING JOB DESCRIPTIONS OR GUIDELINES FOR WRITING 'A JOB DESCRIPTION'

Opinions differ on how to write job descriptions. Some experts are of the view that these should be written in detail and in terms of work flow. Others feel that these should be written in terms of goals or results to be achieved, in other words as performance standards (or what is popularly known as "management by objectives"). The prevalent thinking is that job descriptions should be written in terms of duties and responsibilities, *i.e.,* in terms of functions performed.

Job descriptions are written by Personnel Department or its representatives.

Although there is no set way of writing a job description, the following pattern is fairly typical, and used by many companies:

(i) A paragraph is allocated to each major task or responsibility.

(ii) Paragraphs are numbered and arranged in a logical order, task sequence or importance.

(iii) Sentences are begun with an active verb, *e.g.*, "types letters," "interviews the candidates," "collects, sorts out, routes and distributes mail."

(iv) Accuracy and simplicity are emphasised rather than an elegant style.

(v) Brevity is usually considered to be important but is largely conditioned by the type of job being analysed and the need for accuracy.

(vi) Examples of work performed are often quoted and are useful in making the job description explicit.

(vii) Job descriptions, particularly when they are used as bases for training, often incorporate details of the faults which may be encountered in operator tasks and safety check-points.

(viii) Statements of opinion, such as "dangerous situations are encountered," should be avoided.

(ix) When job description are written for supervisory jobs, the main factors (such as manning, cost control, etc.) are identified and listed. Each factor is then broken down into a series of elements with a note on the supervisor's responsibility.

The British Institute of Management Publication adds four more guidelines:

(i) Give a clear, concise and readily understandable picture of the whole job;

(ii) Describe in sufficient detail each of the main duties and responsibilities;

(iii) Indicate the extent of direction received and supervision given;

(iv) Ensure that a new employee understands the job if he reads the job description.

LIMITATIONS OF JOB DESCRIPTION

In any use of job descriptions, it should be remembered that these descriptions are not perfect reflections of the job. "The object of a job description is to differentiate it from other jobs and set its outer limits." Further, executives tend to carry work patterns with them into new jobs, thus modifying the job drastically.

To avoid such problems, care must be exercised in writing a job description to make it as accurate as possible, and at the managerial or professional level, it should be reviewed and discussed after the job. *Jobs tend to be dynamic, not static and a job description can quickly go out of date. Therefore, jobs should be constantly revised and kept up-to-date,* and the personnel and the other departmental heads should be apprised of changes.

Both supervisors and subordinates should understand the uses to which a job description would be put so that appropriate information is recorded by them. The relevant parties should agree that a job description fairly reflects the job; otherwise job evaluation and job performance review would seem to be unfair.

CHART 5.3
A Specimen of a Job Description for a Supervisor

Job Title .... Supervisor.................................

JOB

Factor	*Elements*	*Supervisor's Actions*
(i) Manning	*(a)* Requisition for instructors	Act
	(b) Preparation advertisements	Recommended
	(c) Interviewing candidates for instructor jobs — Accept/Reject	Act
	(d) Assessment of instructor's performance/merit for pay purposes	Recommended
	(e) Discharging for mis-conduct	Recommended
	(f) Supervision of training centre instruction and ensuring that established performance standards are met	Act
	(g) Supervision of clerical and secretarial duties of training centre secretary	Act
(ii) Equipment	*(a)* Developing a system for safeguarding and distributing tools	Act
	(b) Operating a system for safeguarding and distributing tools	Delegate
	(c) Authorising within the budget limitations the purchase of small items of capital equipment, i.e., tools	Act
	(d) Purchase of major items, *i.e.,* machines	Recommended
(iii) Safety	*(a)* Ensuring compliance with training centre safety regulations	Act
	(b) Preparation of accident reports	Act and Delegate
	(c) Requisition and issue of protective clothing	Act
	(d) Ensuring the use of protective clothing	Act and Delegate
(iv) Cost Control	*(a)* Preparation of annual cost budget for Training Centre	Prepare and Recommend
	(b) Submission of reports on reasons for monthly budget variances to superiors	Act
(v) Inspection	Receipt of inspection reports onbelow standard work	Advise instructors
(vi) Apprentice Trainees	*(a)* Instruction of aprrentices in training school	Delegate
	(b) Placement of apprentices in appropriate course	Act
	(c) Examination of reports on apprentices and allocation of apprentices today; Release for subsequent sessions	Act

(d) Assessment from apprentice feedback of the value of specific courses	Act
(e) Selection of alternative courses if the existing ones are inadequate	Recommended
(f) Preparation of documentation for rates for age rewards	Act
(g) Authorisation of rate for age rewards	Act
(h) Assessement from the reports of instructor and foreman for additional annual merit awards	Recommended
(i) Placement of apprentices on completion of training	Act with appropriate line supervisor
(j) Raising and processing documentation for those apprentices who resign	Act
(k) Discharge of apprentices failing to meet 80% performance level	Recommended
(l) Maintenance of apprentice records	Delegate
(m) Preparation of work rotation for apprentices.	Act

CHART 5.4

An Example of a job description for certain positions, as used by the National Machinery Manufacturers, Ltd.

Categories	*Requirements*
(i) Unskilled Jobs Mazdoors, sweepers, officeboys and helpers.	Literate, robust in health, and preferably local candidates.
(ii) Semi-skilled Jobs Mechanists, khalasis, painters, coolies, mukadams, furnacemen, case makers, dressers, chippers, grinders in-dressing department, moulding machine operators, fitters, learners, moulders, wiremen.	Prefereably ITI trained candidates; where such candidates are not available literate candidtates with 3 to 4 years experience in the line.
(iii) Skilled Jobs Crane drivers, setters, khalasis, mukadams, fitters, electricians, turners, welders, moulders.	SSC's possessing ITI trade certificate, with a minimum of 5 years experience in the line.
(iv) Highly Skilled and Special Jobs Pattern-makers, turners, millers, jig borers, electricians, horizontal borers.	SSC's possessing ITI trade certificate, with a minimum experience of 5 years in the line. Local candidates preferred.
(v) Clerical Jobs	Graduates with English and Mathematics and a sound general knowledge and smart disposition.
(vi) Typists	Graduates with proficiency in typing; smart, well-behaved, and at least 2 years experience as typist.

JOB SPECIFICATION

The job specification takes the job description and answers the question. "What human traits and experience are needed to do the job well?" *It tells what kind of person to recruit and for what qualities that person should be tested.*

Job specifications translate the job description into terms of the human qualifications which are required for a successful performance of a job. They are intended to serve as a guide in hiring and job evaluation. As a guide in hiring, they deal with such characteristics as are available in an application bank, with testing, interviews, and checking of references.

Job specification are developed with the co-operation of the personnel department and various supervisors in the whole organisation. The personnel department co-ordinates the writing of job descriptions and job specifications and secures agreement on the qualifications required.

These specifications relate to:

(a) *Physical characteristics,* which include health, strength, endurance, age-range, body size, height, weight, vision, voice, poise, eye, hand and foot co-ordination, motor co-ordination, and colour discrimination.

(b) *Psychological characteristics* or special aptitudes which include such qualities as manual dexterity, mechanical aptitude, ingenuity, judgement, resourcefulness, analytical ability, mental concentration and alertness.

(c) *Personal characteristics or traits of temperament,* such as personal appearance, good and pleasing manners, emotional stability, aggressiveness or submissiveness, extroversion or introversion, leadership, co-operativeness, initiative and drive, skill in dealing with others, unusual sensory qualities of sight, smell, hearing, adaptability, conversational ability, etc.

(d) *Responsibilities,* which include supervision of others, responsibility for production, process and equipment; responsibility for the safety of others; responsibility for generating confidence and trust; responsibility for preventing monetary loss.

(e) *Other features of a demographic nature,* which are age, sex, education, experience and language ability.

The items to be included in job specifications vary according to the nature of an organisation and the uses to which they are put. However, items like age, sex, experience, skill, education, dexterity and personality are invariably included in job specifications: for example, 5 years experience; ability to lift 30 kgs; versatility in languages and fluency in speech; ability to type 100 words per minute and take shorthand dictation at 120 words per minute.

Job specifications are mostly based on the educated guesses of supervisors and personnel managers. They give their opinion as to who do they think should be considered for a job in terms of education, intelligence, training etc. One of the most extensive "judgemental" approaches to developing job specifications is contained in a Dictionary of Occupational Titles, published by the U.S. Training and Employment service. Its description for a Personnel Manager's job is as follows:

"Personnel Manager: Director personnel; manager, employee relations; Personnel supervisor.

"Plans and carries out policies relating to all phases of personnel activities:

"Organisations, recruitment, selection and training procedures, and directs activities of subordinates directly concerned. Confers with company and union official to establish pension and insurance plans, workmen's compensation policies, recreational, and educational activities. Studies personnel records for information, such as educational background, work record and supervisor's reports, to determine personnel suitable for promotions and transfers. May represent — company in negotiating wage agreements with labour representatives. May act as liaison between management and labour within organisation."

Job specifications may also be based on statistical analysis. This is done to determine the relationship between: (1) some *predictor* or *human trait* (as height, intelligence, finger dexterity, etc.) and (2) some *indicator* or *criterion* of job effectiveness (such as performance as rated by the supervisor.)

The statistical analysis comprises five steps: *(i)* analysing the job and determining criteria of success; *(ii)* selecting personnel traits which should predict successful performance; *(iii)* testing candidates for these traits; *(iv)* measuring these candidates' subsequent job performance; and *(v)* statistically analysing the relationship between the 'human trait' and job performance.

CHART 5.5

Specimen of Personnel Specifications of Works Manager

Personnel Specifications

(Interpretation of job description in terms of the kind of person suitable for the job)

(i) Physical Characteristics

Essential	Good health.
	No significant disabilities in voice, hearing and eyesight.
Dress	Neat conventional dress.
	Well groomed and takes trouble with details of personal appearance.

(ii) Attainments

Essential	At least a Bachelor of Science or engineering, evidence of occupational success in previous employment; production management experience — minimum of 5 years. Age, not above 30 years. Knowledge of work study, work programming, quality control and stock control techniques and experience of negotiating with trade unions at plant level.
Desirable	A degree in business management.

(iii)

Essential	Top 10 per cent.
	An intellifent approach to the solution of business problems

(iv) Special Aptitudes

Essential	Fluency in speaking and writing; analytical skills; ability to prepare and understand basic statistical information;

	competence in arithmetic; ability to read B/S and P&L A/c. and understand their significance; high degree of listening skill; evidence of ability to plan ahead and organise the work of others.
(v) Interests	
Essential	Evidence of some interest outside work but nothing specific.
(vi) Disposition	
Essential	Acceptability to other people and previous occupational evidence of influencing others: ability to accept responsibility without undue strain; cooperative in relations with others.
(vii) Motivation	
Essential	Ambitious — evidence of fairly rapid promotion and the achievement of high but realistic goals; must be willing to control output to meet vigorous Performance Standards targets.
(viii) Circumstances	
Essentail	Ability to work long hours if required.

JOB EVALUATION

Job evaluation is the output provided by job analysis. As seen earlier, *Job analysis* describes the duties of a job, authority relationships, skills required, conditions of work, and additional relevant information. *Job evaluation* on the other hand, uses the information in job analysis to evaluate each job — valuing its components and ascertaining relative job worth. It involves, in other words, a formal and systematic comparison of jobs in order to determine the worth of one job relative to another, so that a wage or salary hierarchy results. So *it is a process by which jobs in an organisation are evaluated.*

When jobs are evaluated, the relative worth of a given collection of duties and responsibilities to the organisation is assessed. This process is adopted to help a management to maintain high levels of employee productivity and employee satisfaction. If job values are not properly studied, it is very likely that jobs would not be properly priced, i.e., high valued jobs may receive less pay than low-valued jobs. When employees realise that this is happening, they become dissatisfied. They may leave the organisation, reduce their efforts or perhaps adopt other modes of behaviour detrimental to the organisation. Therefore, in modern society, a great deal of attention is paid to the value of a job. What a particular job should be paid is greatly influenced by the value of judgement about the worth of a job. In other words, a person is paid for what he brings to a job — his education, training and experience provided that these are related to the requirements of the job which he is assigned.

DEFINITION OF JOB EVALUATION

Below are given some important definitions of job evaluation:

The I.L.O. defines job evaluation as "an attempt to determine and compare demands which the normal performance of a particular job makes on normal workers without taking into account the individual abilities or performance of the workers concerned."

The Bureau of Labour Statistics, U.S.A., says that "job evaluation is the evaluation or rating of jobs to determine their position in the job hierarchy. The evaluation may be achieved through the assignment of points or the use of some other systematic method for essential job requirements, such as skills, experience and responsibility."

In the words of the Netherlands Committee of Experts on Job Evaluation, "job evaluation is a method which helps to establish a justified rank order of jobs as a whole being a foundation for the setting of wages. Job evaluation is the only one of the starting points for establishing the relative differentiation of base wage rates."

Kimball and Kimball define job evaluation as "an effort to determine the relative value of every job in a plant to determine what the fair basic wage for such a job should be."

According to Wendell French, "job evaluation is a process of determining the relative worth of the various jobs within the organisation, so that differential wages may be paid to jobs of different worth." The relative worth of a job means value produced by such factors as *responsibilities skill, effort and working conditions.*

We may define job evaluation as *a process of analysing and describing positions, grouping them and determining their relative value by comparing the duties of different positions in terms of their different responsibilities and other requirements.*

It is the quantitative measurement of relative job worth for the purpose of establishing consistent wage rate differentials by objective means. It measures the differences between jobs differences between job requirements, the objective being the setting of pay for wage administration purposes.

It does not set the price of a job; it merely fixes its relative worth. It presents an effort to determine the relative value of every job in a plant, and to determine what the fair basic wage for such a job should be. It is not evaluating the merit of the worker who is doing the work. It rates the job and not the qualities of the individual worker on the job, which is the task of employee rating.

OBJECTIVE OF JOB EVALUATION

Says an I.L.O. Report, "the aim of the majority of systems of job evaluation is to establish, on agreed logical basis, the relative values of different jobs in a given plant or machinery, i.e., *it aims at determining the relative worth of a job.* The principle upon which all job evaluation schemes are based is that of describing and assessing the value of all jobs in the firms in terms of a number of factors, the relative importance of which varies from job to job."

(i) To secure and maintain complete, accurate and impersonal descriptions of each distinct job or occupation in the entire plant;

(ii) To provide a standard procedure for determining the relative worth of each job in a plant;

(iii) To determine the rate of pay for each job which is fair and equitable with relation to other jobs in the plant, community or industry;

(iv) To ensure that like wages are paid to all qualified employees for like work;

(v) To promote a fair and accurate consideration of all employees for advancement and transfer;

(vi) To provide a factual basis for the consideration of wage rates for similar jobs in a community and in an industry; and

(vii) To provide information for 'work organisation, employees' selection, placement, training and numerous other similar problems.

In fact, *the primary purpose of job evaluation is to set wages and salary on the basis of the relative work or jobs in the organisation.* It does this by providing a ground for the following matters:

(a) Equity and objective of salary administration, i.e., paying the people whose work is alike the same wages, and establishing appropriate wage differentials between jobs calling for different skills and responsibilities;

(b) Effective wage and salary control;

(c) Union-management negotiations on wages; and

(d) Comparison of wage and salary rates with those of other employees.

Besides setting wages, job evaluation also helps in:

(a) Providing standardisation of, and improvement in, working conditions;

(b) Clarifying the functions, authority and responsibility of employees;

(c) Establishing references for the settlement of grievances arising out of individual rates and for negotiations with a trade union on internal wage structure and differentials;

(d) Developing machinery for a systematic reviewing of job rates as job contents change; and

(e) Developing personnel statistics.

Knowles and Thomson state that job evaluation is useful in eliminating many of the evils to which nearly all systems of wage and salary payments are subject. These are:

(i) Payment of high wages and salaries of persons who hold jobs and positions not requiring great skill, effort and responsibilities;

(ii) Paying beginners less than they are entitled to receive in terms of what is required of them;

(iii) Giving a raise to persons whose performance does not justify the raise;

(iv) Deciding rates of pay on the basis of seniority rather than ability;

(v) Payment of widely varied wages and salary for the same or closely related jobs and positions; and

(vi) Payment of unequal wages and salaries on the basis of race, sex, religion or political differences.

It may, however, be noted that a job evaluation system does not accomplish all the purpose; rather it facilitates them. Basically, it provides a systematic catalogue of the jobs in an organisation, which is indispensable for management purposes.

PRINCIPLES OF JOB EVALUATION PROGRAMME

There are certain broad principles, which should be kept in mind before putting the job evaluation programme into practice. According to Kress, these principles are:

(i) Rate the job and not the man. Each element should be rated on the basis of what the job itself requires.

(ii) The elements selected for rating purposes should be easily explainable in terms and as few in number as will cover the necessary requisites for every job without any overlapping.

(iii) The elements should be clearly defined and properly selected.

(iv) Any job rating plan must be sold to foremen and employees. The success in selling it will depend on a clear-cut explanation and illustration of the plan.

(v) Foremen should participate in the rating of jobs in their own departments.

(vi) Maximum co-operation can be obtained from employees when they themselves have an opportunity to discuss job ratings.

(vii) In talking to foremen and employees, any discussion of money value should be avoided. Only point values and degrees of each element should be discussed.

(viii) Too many occupational wages should not be established. It would be unwise to adopt an occupational wage for each total of point values.

BASIC PROCEDURE OF JOB EVALUATION

The basic procedure of job evaluation is to compare the *content* of jobs in relation to one another, in terms of their skills or responsibility or some other requirement. The *job contents* may be decided upon in two ways, i.e., *either* by making an intuitive "overview" i.e., by deciding that one job is "more important" than another, and not going any deeper in why — in terms of specific job-related factors; *Or* by comparing one job to another by focussing on certain 'basic factors', which may be common in each job. Such factors are called *compensable factors* — which determine the definition of job content; that determine how the jobs compare to each other; and they also help determine the compensation paid for each job. The organisation might develop its own compensable factors or use those factors adopted by others. For example, the "Equal Pay for Equal Work Act" (in USA) focuses on four factors: *skills, efforts, responsibility and working conditions.* While some other system (say Hay system in the States) focuses on know-how, problem-solving and accountability. Often several basic factors are chosen initially and then subdivided into sub-factors. For example, refer to the following table.

Table 5.1
Compensable Factors

Universal Factors	*Sub-factors*	*No. of Degrees*
Knowledge	Education	8
	Experience	8
	Skill	8
Problem-Solving	Interpretation	8
	Compliance	8
	Communication	8
Decision-Making	Interpersonal	8
	Managerial	8
	Asset	8

When compensable factors are available, jobs can be evaluated more systematically. Each job is compared with all the others using the same factors, sub-factors, and number of degrees. Sometimes job specifications are based on these factors, stating the "human requirements" of the job in terms of compensable factors like education, skills, problem-solving, and decision-making.

In India, the National Institute of Personnel Management, has laid down the following steps which should be taken to install a job evaluation programme:

(i) *Analyse and Prepare Job Description:* This requires the preparation of a job description and also an analysis of job requirements for successful performance.

(ii) *Select and Prepare a Job Evaluation Plan:* This means that a job must be broken down into its component parts, i.e., it should involve the selection of factors, elements needed for the performance of all jobs for which money is paid, determining their value and preparing written instructions for evaluation.

(iii) *Classify Jobs:* This requires grouping for arranging jobs in a correct sequence in terms of value to the firm, and relating them to the money terms in order to ascertain their relative value.

(iv) *Install the Programme:* This involves explaining it to employees and putting it into operation.

(v) *Maintain the Programme:* Jobs cannot continue without updating new jobs and job changes in obedience to changing conditions and situations.

ADVANTAGES OF JOB EVALUATION

An I.L.O., publication claims following advantages for job evaluation:

(i) Job evaluation is a logical and, to some extent, an objective method of ranking jobs relative to one another. It may help in removing inequalities in existing wage structures and in maintaining sound and consistent wage differentials in a plant or industry.

(ii) In the case of new jobs, the method often facilitates fitting them into the existing wage structure.

(iii) The method helps in removing grievances arising out of relative wages; and it improves labour-management relations and workers' morale. In providing a yardstick, by which workers' complaints or claims can be judged, the method simplifies discussion of wages to be explained and justified.

(iv) The method replaces the many accidental factors, occurring in less systematic procedures, of wage bargaining by more impersonal and objective standards, thus establishing a clear basis for negotiations.

(v) The method may lead to greater uniformity in wage rates, thus simplifying wage administration.

(vi) The information collected in the process of job description and analysis may also be used for the improvement of selection, transfer and promotion procedures on the basis of comparative job requirements.

(vii) Such information also reveals that workers are engaged in jobs requiring less skill and other qualities than they possess, thereby pointing to the possibility of making more efficient use of the plant's labour.

LIMITATIONS OF JOB EVALUATION

These are:

(i) Though many ways of applying the job evaluation techniques are available, rapid changes in technology and in the supply and demand of particular skills have given rise to problems of adjustment. These need to be probed.

(ii) Substantial differences exist between job factors and the factors emphasised in the market. These differences are wider in cases in which the average pay offered by a company is lower than that prevalent in other companies in the same industry or in the same geographical area.

(iii) A job evaluation frequently favours groups different from those which are favoured by the market. This is evident from the observations of Kerr and Fisher. They observe, "the jobs which tend to rate high as compared with the market are those of janitor, nurse and typist, while craft rates are relatively low. Weaker groups are better served by an evaluation plan than by the market; the former places the emphasis not on force but on equity."

(iv) Job factors fluctuate because of changes in production technology, information system, and division of labour and such other factors. Therefore, the evaluation of a job today is made on the basis of job factors, and does not reflect the time job value in future. In other words, continuing attention and frequent evaluation of a job are essential.

(v) Higher rates of pay for some jobs at the earlier stages than other jobs or the evaluation of a higher job higher in the organisational hierarchy at a lower rate than another job relatively lower in the organisational hierarchy often give rise to human relations problems and lead to grievances among those holding these jobs.

(vi) When job evaluation is applied for the first time in any organisation, it creates doubts and often fear in the minds of those whose jobs are being evaluated. It may also disrupt the existing social and psychological relationships.

(vii) A large number of jobs are called *red circle jobs.* Some of these may be getting more and others less than the rate determined by job evaluation.

(viii) Job evaluation takes a long time to install, requires specialised technical personnel, and may be costly.

(ix) When job evaluation results in substantial changes in the existing wage structure, the possibility of implementing these changes in a relatively short period may be restricted by the financial limits within which the firm has to operate.

BASIC JOB EVALUATION METHODS / SYSTEMS

There are four basic, traditional systems of job evaluation: (1) the ranking system; (2) the grading or job classification system; (3) the point system; and (4) the factor comparison system. The first two systems are popularly known as the *non-analytical* or *non-quantitative* or *summary systems,* because they utilise non-quantitative methods of listing jobs in order of difficulty and are, therefore, simple. The last two systems are called the *analytical* or *quantitative systems,* because they use quantitative techniques in listing the jobs. They are more complex and are time consuming.

The principal differences between these methods reflect:

(1) Consideration of the 'job as a whole,' versus consideration of 'compensable factors'; and

(2) judging and comparing jobs with each other rather than assigning numerical scores on a rating scale. Plans commonly used today represent variations of these basic methods.

1. THE RANKING SYSTEM

Mechanism: Under this system, all jobs are arranged or ranked in the order of their importance from the simplest to the hardest, or in the reverse order, each successive job being higher or lower than the previous one in the sequence. It is not necessary to have job descriptions, although they may be useful. Sometimes, a series of grades or zones are established, and all the jobs in the organisation are arranged into these. A more common practice is to arrange all the jobs according to their requirements by rating them and then to establish the group or classification. The usually adopted technique is to rank jobs according to "the whole job" rather than a number of compensable factors.

According to this method, the ranking for a university may be like thus.

Table 5.2
Ranking of University Personnel

Ranking Order	*Pay Scale Range*
Professor	Rs. 5000-8000
Associate Professors	Rs. 4000-7000
Assistant Professors	Rs. 3500-6000
Registrar	Rs. 4000-7000
Dy. Registrar	Rs. 3500-5000
Assistant Registrar	Rs. 3000-4500
Clerk Grade I	Rs. 1000-2500
Clerk Grade II	Rs. 900-1800
Class Four Servants	Rs. 500-800

After ranking, additional jobs between those already ranked may be assigned an appropriate place/wage rate.

Generally speaking, the following *five steps* are involved in system:

Step 1: *Preparation of job description,* particularly when the ranking of jobs is done by different individuals and there is a disagreement among them.

Step 2: *Selection of Raters,* jobs may be usually ranked by department or in "Clusters" (i.e., factory workers, clerical workers, menials, etc). This eliminates need for directly comparing factory jobs and clerical jobs. Most organisations use a *committee of raters.*

Step 3: *Selection of rates and key jobs,* usually a series of *key jobs* or *bench-mark jobs* (10 to 20 jobs, which include all major departments and functions) are first rated; then the other jobs are roughly compared with these key jobs to establish a rough rating.

Step 4: *Ranking of all jobs.* Each job is then compared in detail with other similar jobs to establish its exact rank in the scale. For this each rater may be given a set of 'index card,' each of which contains a brief description of a job. These jobs are then ranked from 'lowest to highest' or from 'highest to the lowest' are ranked first and then the next highest and next lowest and so forth until all the cards have been ranked.

Step 5: *Preparation of job classification from the rating:* The total ranking is divided into an appropriate number of groups or classifications, usually 8 to 12. All the jobs within a single group or classification receive the same wage or range of rates.

The ranking system of job evaluation usually measures each job in comparison with other jobs in terms of the relative importance of the following five factors:

(i) Supervision and leadership of subordinates;

(ii) Co-operation with associates outside the line of authority;

(iii) Probability and consequences of errors (in terms of waste, damage to equipment, delays, complaints, confusion, spoilage of product, discrepancies, etc.);

(iv) Minimum experience requirement; and

(v) Minimum education required;

Merits: (i) The system is simple, easily understood, and easy to explain to employees (or a union). Therefore, it is suitable for small organisations with clearly defined jobs.

(ii) It is far less expensive to put into effect than other systems, and requires little effort for maintenance.

(iii) It requires less time, fewer forms and less work, unless it is carried to a detailed point used by company.

Demerits: (i) As there is no standard for an analysis of the whole job position, different bases of comparison between rates occur. The process is initially based on judgement and, therefore, tends to be influenced by a variety of personal biases.

(ii) Specific job requirements (such as skill, effort and responsibility) are not normally analysed separately. Often a rater's judgement is strongly influenced by present wage rates.

(iii) The system merely produces a job order and does not indicate to what extent it is more important than the one below it. It only gives us its rank or tells us that it is higher or more difficult than another; but it does not indicate how much higher or more difficult.

2. JOB CLASSIFICATION OR GRADING METHOD

Under this system, a number of pre-determined grades or classifications are first established by a committee and then the various jobs are assigned within each grade or class. Grade descriptions are the result of the basic job information which is usually derived from a job analysis. After formulating and studying job descriptions and job specifications, jobs are grouped into classes or grades which represent different pay levels ranging from low to high. Common tasks, responsibilities, knowledge and experience can be identified by the process of job analysis. Certain jobs may then be grouped together into a common grade or classification. General grade descriptions are written for each job classification, and finally these are used as a standard for assigning all the other jobs to a particular pay scale.

Mechanism: The following five steps are generally involved:

(i) The preparation of job descriptions, which gives us basic job information, usually derived from a job analysis.

(ii) The preparation of grade descriptions, so that different levels or grades of jobs may be identified. Each grade level must be distinct from the grade level adjacent to it; at the same time, it should represent a typical step in a continuous way and not a big jump or gap. After establishing the grade level, each job is assigned to an appropriate grade level on the basis of the complexity of duties, non-supervisory responsibilities and supervisory responsibilities.

(iii) Selection of grades and key jobs. About 10 to 20 jobs are selected, which include all the major departments and functions and cover all the grades.

(iv) Grading the key jobs. Key jobs are assigned to an appropriate grade level and their relationship to each other studied.

(v) Classification of all jobs. Jobs are classified by grade definitions. All the jobs in the same grade receive the same wage or range of rates. For example, menials may be put into one class; clerks in another; junior officers in a higher class; and the top executive in the top class.

Table 5.3 gives us the gradations of five classes designed by a title lable and increasing in value.

Merits: (i) This method is simple to operate and understand, for it does not take much time or require technical help.

(ii) The use of fully described job classes meets the need for employing systematic criteria in ordering jobs to their importance. Since many workers think of jobs in, or related to, clusters or groups, this method makes it easier for them to understand rankings.

Table 5.3
Description of Job Classification

Grades	*Description of Job Classification*
Clerk Grade III	Pure routine concentration, speed and accuracy, works under supervision; may or may not be held responsible for supervision.
Clerk Grade II	No supervision by others, specially skilled for the job by having an exhaustive knowledge of the details.
Clerk Grade I	Must have the characteristics of a second class clerk and assume more responsibility.
Senior clerk	Technically varied work, occassionally independent thinking and action due to difficult work which require exceptional clerical ability and extensive knowledge of principles and fundamentals of the business of his department. Not charged with the supervision of others to any extent; works subject to a limited check; dependable, resourceful and able to take decisions.
Head clerk	Those handling or capable of taking a major decision on the work they do; complicated work requiring much independent thinking; able to consider details outside the control.

(iii) If an organisation consists of 500 people holding to different jobs, the jobs might be broken up into perhaps 5 classes, arranged in order of importance from high to low, and described class by class. This class description broadly reflects level of education, mental skill, profit impact or some combination of these.

(iv) The grouping of jobs into classifications makes pay determination problems administratively easier to handle. Pay grades are determined for, and assigned to, all the job classification.

(v) It is used in important government services and operates efficiently; but it is rarely used in an industry.

Demerits: This system suffers from the following defects:

(i) Although it represents an advance in accuracy over the ranking method, it still leaves much to be desired because personal evaluations by executives (unskilled in such work) establish the major classes, and determine into which classes each job should be placed.

(ii) Since no detailed analysis of a job is done, the judgement in respect of a whole range of jobs may produce an incorrect classification.

(iii) It is relatively difficult to write a grade description. The system becomes difficult to operate as the number of jobs increases.

(iv) It is difficult to know how much of a job's rank is influenced by the man on the job.

(v) The system is rather rigid and unsuitable for a large organisation or for very varied work.

3. THE POINTS SYSTEM

This method is the most widely used type of job evaluation plan. It requires identifying a number of compensable factors (i.e., various characteristics of jobs) and then determining degree to which each of these factors is present in the job. A different number of points is usually assigned for each degree of each factors. Once the degree to each factor is determined, the corresponding number of points of each factor are added and an overall point value is obtained. The point system is based on the assumption that it is possible to assign points to respective factors which are essential for evaluating an individual's job. The sum of these points gives us an index of the relative significance of the jobs that are rated.

Mechanism: This system requires a detailed examination of the jobs. The steps in this method followed are:

Step 1: The jobs have to be determined first which are to be evaluated. They are usually clustered. The jobs which require *(i)* similar activities, *(ii)* the same workers characteristics or traits (corresponding machines, tools, materials and instruments) and work on the same kind of material (say wood or metal are placed in the same cluster or family. Gonyea and Lunneborg have clustered 22 occupations in five groups, based on common factors in five groups.

Table 5.4
Clustering of 22 Occupations on the basis of Common Factors in Five Groups (after Gonyea and Lunneborg)

Group	*Occupation*
A — Business Group	Includes buyer, office manager, personnel manager, interior decorator, Insurance salesman, accountant , and secretary.
B — Masculine Group	Includes aviator, automobile mechanics, surveyor, radio operator, policeman and engineer.
C — Aesthetic Group	Artist, writer, interior decorator.
D — Service Group	Policeman, social worker, lawyer, physician, personnel counseller.
E — Scientific Group	Medical lab technician, chemist, physician, engineer, auto mechanic and wire less operator.

Step 2: For the purpose, *a pre-determined number of factors are arbitrarily selected by raters.* The number of factors used varies a great deal from company to company, ranging from as few as 3 to as many as 50, although most companies use less than 15. Sometimes, only three factors (job conditions, physical ability and mental requirements) may be used. Another company may use 4 factors (skill, effort, responsibility and job conditions). As far as possible, the factors selected are such as are common to all the jobs.

The common factors are: Education and training; experience; physical skills and effort; planning for the supervision of others; external contacts, internal contacts; confidential information and working conditions. Moreover, the factors which overlap in their meaning are avoided and factors which are unique and relative to each other described in terms of varying degrees. They should also be so defined and described that everyone associated with the plan gets the same meaning of the words that are used.

Step 3: The next step is to break down each factor into degrees or levels, and to assign a point value to each level or degree. For example, experience, which is one of the most commonly used job factors, may be sub-divided into 5 degrees. The first degree, three months or less may be assigned 5 points; the second degree, 3 to 6 months, given 10 points, the third degree, 6 to 12 months, assigned 15 points; the fourth degree 1 to 3 years, assigned 20 points; and the fifth degree is over 3 years, and is assigned 25 points. This same procedure is followed for each factor at each level or degree represented by an appropriate number of points. The point to note is that the major factors are assigned total points and that each of these factors is broken up into sub-groups (with written definitions for each), and these sub-groups are assigned points within the total established for the major group.

Le Tourneau has given an example of job work point rating scale.

CHART 5.6

Some Items from the rating system developed by Le Tourneau with the scale values assigned to different factor (indicated by numbers)

Rated by .... Job .... Department .... Date

Factor	Check the Correct Item for Each Factor				
I. Education School	College 5	High 4	Elem. Maths 3	Addl. Subjects 2	Read & Write 1
II. Experience	Over 12 Months 12	9 to 12 Months 12	6 to 9 Months 9	3 to 6 Months 6	1 to 3 Months 3
III. Learning Period	Over 3 yrs. 10	1 to 3 yrs. 8	6 months to 1 yr. 6	3 months to 6 months 4	1 to 3 months 2
IV. Mental Effort	Very High 5	High 4	Average 3	Below Average 2	Low/Slight 1
V. Mechanical Ability	Very High 5	High 4	Average 3	Below Average 2	Slight 1
VI. Physical Effort	A,B,C,D 10	E,F,G 8	H,I,J 6	K,L 4	M 2
VII. Job Conditions	A 10	B,C 8	D,E 6	F,G 4	H,I 2
VIII. Hazards	Very High 5	High 4	Average 3	Below 2	Slight 1

IX.	Responsibility Equipment	Over $ 50 M	$ 25 M to $ 50 M	$ 10 M to $ 25 M	$1 M to $ 10 M	Less $ 1M
		5	4	3	2	1
X.	Responsibility (persons)	Over 16	11 to 15	6 to 10	2 to 5	1
		5	4	3	2	2
XI.	Responsibility	Over $ 60M	$25M to $ to M	$10M to 25M	$1M to $ 10M	Less $ 1 M
		5	4	3	2	1
XII.	Complexity	Very High	High	Average	Below	Slight
		5	4	3	Average 2	1
XIII.	Effect on	Very High	High	Average	Below Average	Slight
		5	4	3	2	1
XIV.	Attention to Operations	Very High	High	Average	Below Average	Slight
		5	4	3	2	1
XV.	Know other Operation	Very High	High	Average	Below Average	Slight
		5	4	3	2	1
XVI.	Coordination	Very High	High	Average	Below Average	Slight
	5	4	3	2	1	

Generally speaking, the four job factors common to the point method of job rating are skill, effort, responsibility and job conditions. The relative values of these are skill, 50 per cent; effort, 15 per cent; responsibility, 20 per cent; and job conditions, 15 per cent.

Step 4: *Determination of relative values or weights* to assign to each factor. For each job or cluster of jobs some factors are more important than others. For example, for executives, the "mental requirements" factor would carry more weight than "physical requirements." The opposite might be true of "factory jobs."

Step 5: The next step is to *assign money values to points.* For this purpose, points are added to give the total value of a job; its value of a job; its value is then translated into terms of money with a pre-determined formula.

Table 5.5 shows the job points translated into job rupees.

Table 5.5
Job Points Translated into Job Rupees

Point Range	Hourly Basic Rate Range	Job Grade
101-150	Rs. 6 to 10	1
165-200	Rs. 8 to 12	2
201-250	Rs. 10 to 15	3
251-300	Rs. 15 to 20	4
301-350	Rs. 20 to 25	5
351-400	Rs. 25 to 30	6
401-450	Rs. 30 to 35	7
451-500	Rs. 35 to 45	8

SAMPLE DEFINITION OF FACTORS USED IN POINTS SYSTEM

(I) SKILL

A. (acquired) Facility in muscular co-ordination, as in operating machines; repetitive movements, careful co-ordination, dexterity, assembling, sorting etc.

B. (acquired) Specific job knowledge necessary for the muscular co-ordination acquired by the performance of a job and not to be confused with general education or specialised knowledge. It is very largely training in the interpretation of sensory impressions.

EXAMPLES

(i) In operating an adding machine, the knowledge of which key to depress for a sub-total would be a skill.

(ii) In automobile repairs, the ability to determine the significance of a certain knock in the motor would be a skill.

(iii) In a hand firing boiler, the ability to determine from the appearance of the firebed how coal should be shovelled over the surface would be a skill.

Education relates to the schooling requirements which are essential for a satisfactory performance of the job.

The *experience factor* pertains to the extent of job training which is necessary for a person before he gains a satisfactory proficiency.

Initiative and ingenuity appraise the independent action, exercise of judgement, the making of decisions or the amount of planning that a job requires.

(ii) EFFORT

In some jobs, particularly factory and other manual work more physical efforts are needed; while in higher jobs, more of mental requirements is a must.

A. Physical Requirements

(1) Physical efforts; sitting, standing, walking, climbing, pulling, lifting; both the amount exercised and degree of continuity should be taken into account.

(2) Physical status, including age, height, weight, sex, strength and eye-sight.

B. Mental Requirements

Either the possession of and/or the active application of the following:

(1) (inherent) Mental traits, such as intelligence, memory, reasoning, facility for verbal expression, ability to get along with people and imagination.

(2) (acquired) General education, such as knowledge of grammar and arithmetic; general information as to sports, world events, etc.

(3) (acquired) Specialised knowledge such as chemistry, engineering, accounting, advertising, etc.

(iii) RESPONSIBILITY

The *responsibility factor,* for different items, measures responsibility for preventing damage to machinery or equipment which may result from error or negligence, and also measures the probability of damage to materials, parts in process or finished goods.

(1) For raw materials, processed materials, tools, equipment and property.
(2) For money or negotiable securities.
(3) For profit or loss, savings or methods improved.
(4) For public contacts.
(5) For records.
(6) For supervision.

(i) Primarily, it means the complexity of supervision given to subordinates; the number of subordinates is a secondary feature. Planning, direction, co-ordination, instruction, control and approval characterise this kind of supervision.

(ii) The degree of supervision received. If jobs A & B gave no supervision to subordinates, but job A receives a much closer immediate supervision than B, then B would be entitled to a higher rating than A in the supervision factor.

To summaries the four degrees of supervision:

Highest degree	—	Gives much, gets less.
High degree	—	Gives more, gets much.
Low degree	—	Gives none, gets little.
Lowest degree	—	Gives none, get much.

(iv) WORKING CONDITIONS

The *working conditions factor* appraises the surroundings or physical conditions under which a job must be done and the extent to which such conditions make the job disagreeable. Consideration will have to be given to the presence, relative amount and continuity of exposures to dust, dirt, heat, fumes, cold, noise, vibrations, wetness or other unpleasant conditions.

(1) Environmental influences, such as atmosphere, ventilation, illumination, noise, congestion, fellow-workers, etc.

(2) Hazards from the work or its surroundings.

(3) Hours.

Merits: The system enjoys the following merits:

(i) It gives us a numerical basis for wage differentials; by analysis a job by factors it is usually possible to obtain a high measure of agreements on job value.

(ii) Once the scales are developed, they can be used for a long time.

(iii) Jobs can be easily placed in distinct categories.

(iv) Definitions are written in terms applicable to the type of jobs being evaluated, and these can be understood by all.

(v) Factors are rated by points which make it possible for one to be consistent in assigning money values to the total job points.

(vi) The workers' acceptance of the system is favourable because it is more systematic and objective than other job evaluation methods.

(vii) Prejudice and human judgement are minimised, i.e., the system cannot be easily manipulated.

(viii) It has the ability of handling a large number of jobs and enjoys stability as long as the factors remain relevant.

The availability of a number of ready-made plans probably accounts for the wide use of points plans in job evaluation.

Demerits: The drawbacks of the system are:

(i) The development and installing of the system calls of heavy expenditure.

(ii) The task of defining job factors and factor degrees is a time-consuming and difficult task.

(iii) If many rates are used, considerable clerical work is entailed in recording and summarising the rating scales.

(iv) It is difficult to determine the factor levels within factors and assign values to them. It is difficult to explain to supervisors and employees. Workers find it difficult to fully comprehend the meaning of concepts and terms, such as factors, degrees and points.

In spite of these drawbacks, this system is used by most organisations because its greater accuracy possibly justifies the large expenditure of time and money.

4. THE FACTOR COMPARISON METHOD

Under this system, jobs are evaluated by means of standard yardstick of value. It entails deciding which jobs have more of certain compensable factors than others. Here the analyst or the Evaluation Committee selects some 'key' or 'benchmark' jobs for which there are clearly understood job descriptions and counterparts in other organisations, and for which the pay rates are such as are agreed upon and are acceptable to both management and labour. Under this method, *each job is ranked several times — once for each compensable factor selected.* For example, jobs may be ranked first in terms of the factor 'skill.' Then, they are ranked according to their mental requirements. Next they are ranked according to their 'responsibility,' and so forth. Then these ratings are combined for each job in an over-all numerical rating for the job.

Mechanism: The major steps in this system consist of the following:

Step 1: Clear-cut job descriptions are written and job specifications then developed: Preferably in terms of compensable factors. The people writing job specifications are generally provided with a set of definitions which have been used in each of the compensable factor selected. Usually five factors are used: *(i)* mental requirements, *(ii)* physical requirements; *(iii)* skill requirements; *(iv)* responsibility and *(v)* working conditions. These factors are universally considered to be components of all the jobs.

Step 2: Selecting of Key-Jobs: Such jobs are those jobs which represent the range of jobs under study; and for which pay is determined to be *'standard' or 'reference points'* and for which there is no controversy between the management and the employees. These 'key' jobs serve as standards against which all other jobs are measured. They are selected in such a way that they cover the range from the 'low' to the 'high' paid jobs. Besides, such jobs must be those on the pay of which analysts and executives do not disagree. Again, they should be definable in accurate and clear terms. Usually 10 to 30 jobs are picked up as 'key' jobs.

Step 3: Ranking of 'Key' Jobs: Several different members of the job Evaluation Committee rank the key jobs on each of the five factors (mental requirements, physical requirements, skill, responsibility, and working conditions). Ranking is made individually and then a meeting held to develop a consensus (among raters) on each job.

Mental Requirements involve inherent mental trait (such as memory, intelligence, reasoning, ability to get acquired education, and acquired specialisation of education or knowledge).

Physical Requirements consist of physical effort (climbing, pulling, walking and lifting); and physical conditions (age, height, weight, sex, eye-sight and strength); *skill requirements* are concerned with acquired facility in muscular co-ordination, assembling, sorting, and dexterity of fingers; and acquired job knowledge for an effective performance of the job.

Responsibility involves responsibility for raw and processed materials, tools, equipment and property; money securities; profit and loss; supervision; and maintenance of records.

Working Conditions include atmospheric conditions (illumination, ventilation, noise, congestion); hazards of work and its surroundings; and hours of work.

Step 4: Valuing the Factors: The basic pay for each 'key' job is allocated to each factor. Pay for such jobs should range from about the lowest to, at or near the highest, and there must be complete agreement on job selected. Usually, 15 to 20 jobs are chosen against which to evaluate all the other jobs.

Step 5: Comparing all Jobs with Key Jobs: All the other jobs are then compared with the key jobs, factor by factor, to determine their relative importance and position in the scale of jobs, to determine also their money value.

This identical process is repeated for all the other factors. The pay rate assigned to a job is obtained by adding the determined amounts as indicated by the money values shown in the five scales that individually set a job money value in relative comparison to fixed key jobs.

Step 6: Establishing the Monetary Unit Value for all Jobs: Monetary values are assigned to each factor of every key job. This should reflect a range from the lowest to the highest.

Table 5.6
Factors used in a Typical System

Cents per Hour	*Mental Requirement*	*Skill Requirements*	*Physical Requirements*	*Responsibility*	*Working Conditions*
200	Toolmaker*	Labourer			
180	Toolmaker		Electrician*		
160			Toolmaker*	Inspector*	
140	Electrician*	Machinist		Toolmaker*	Toolmaker*
120	Machinist†	Electrician†	Machinist*		Inspector*
100	Assembler†	Assembler†	Inspector	Machinist*	Electrician
60	Inspector*	Inspector*	Assembler†	Electrician	Machinist†
50	Labourer†			Assembler†	Assembler†
25		Labourer†		Labourer†	Labourer†

*Indicates key job.

†Indicates non-key or unanalysed job.

The following example will clearly show how the system works:

Suppose job E and job A are similar in skill (Rs. 3.00); job B in responsibility (Rs. 0.85); job C in effort (Rs. 1.40); and job D in working condition (Rs. 1.20); then its correct rate of pay will be Rs. 6.45, i.e., the sum total of all.

Table 5.7
Key Jobs, Job Factors and Correct Rates of Jobs

Job Factor	*Job A Correct Rate: Rs. 20*	*Job B Correct Rate: Rs. 16*	*Job C Correct Rate: Rs. 14*	*Job D Correct Rate: Rs. 12*	*Job E Correct Rate: Rs. 24*
1. Skill	10	8	7.50	5	11
2. Effort	5	3	4	4	6
3. Responsibility	3	1	1	1	4
4. Working Conditions	2	4	1.50	2	3

This system is usually used to evaluate white collar, professional and managerial positions.

Merits: This system enjoys the following benefits:

(i) It is a systematic, quantifiable method for which detailed step by step instructions are available.

(ii) Jobs are compared to other jobs to determine a relative value.

(iii) It is a fairly easy system to explain to employees.

(iv) There are no limits to the value which may be assigned to each factor.

(v) The plan does not require a translation from points to money. It involves a comparative process wherein jobs are priced against other jobs rather than against some established numerical scale.

(vi) The reliability and validity of the system are greater than the same statistical measures obtained from group standardized job analysis plans.

(vii) The limited number of factors (usually 5) tends to reduce the possibility of overlapping and over-weighting of factors.

Demerits: The system suffers from the following shortcomings:

(i) It is costly to install, and somewhat difficult to operate for anyone who is not acquainted with the general nature of job evaluation techniques.

(ii) Wage levels change from time to time, and their minor inconsistencies may be adjusted to bring all the jobs into alignment. Jobs in which discrepancies are too wide are discarded as key jobs.

(iii) Money rates, when used as a basis of rating, tend to influence the actual rate more than the abstract point.

(iv) The system is complex and cannot be easily explained to, and understood by, every day non-supervisory organisational employee.

(v) The use of five factors is a growth of the technique developed by its originations. Yet using the same five factors for all organisations and for all jobs in an organisation may not always be appropriate.

IMPLEMENTATION OF THE EVALUATED JOB STRUCTURE

The evaluated job structure has to be translated into a structure of wage rates. This depends upon:

(i) The range of wages to be paid, i.e., what should be the maximum and minimum wages for the grade.

(ii) Should there be any overlapping between pay ranges for adjacent pay grades? If so, by how much?

(iii) How many grades should be used?

(iv) On what basis will an individual employee be advanced in wages through the established pay range for the grade?

These issues are inter-related, and a change in any of these calls for a change in at least one or the other issue.

As far as the first issue is concerned, it may be noted that the difference between the maximum and the minimum is referred to as the 'wage range' or 'wage differential.' While evaluating a wage structure, it should be seen that the range is not too high and that the job evaluated wage curve does not have too many deviations from the existing industry wage line. This should be done to prevent the turnover of workers and avoid dissatisfaction amongst them.

A wage range can be made with or without an overlap. Theoretically, there should be no overlap because, in that case, an employee near the top of a lower grade gets higher wages than the employee in the higher grade. Too great an overlap may cause dissatisfaction amongst employees and minimise the rewards for superior performance. However, though a too great overlap should be avoided, there should be some overlapping between the grades so that employees in the lower grades may, following an excellent performance, get higher wages than an employee working in a higher grade but showing a poor performance.

As regards the number of grades to be adopted in many wage structures, the accuracy may be secured upto *six* grades; 12 or more grades result in a higher accuracy. Generally, the number of grades considered are between 6 to 11. If more grades are adopted, the overlapping between them would be greater.

ESSENTIALS OF SUCCESS OF JOB EVALUATION PROGRAMMES

When it is finally decided to install a formal system of job evaluation irrespective of which system is decided upon, the utmost care must be exercised to ensure that human as well as technical aspects are taken into account.

In order that a job evaluation system works efficiently, it is necessary that all those who are concerned with job evaluation should be fully conversant with the techniques and implications of the different available systems. Otherwise, the chances of success are doubtful. The following measures may be adopted:

(i) Supervisors should have full knowledge of the system. They should understand it, and be able to explain to their workers the purpose of the plan and how it works. They must accept the desirability of the plan, for if they are not convinced that it is useful, they will certainly not be able to convince the employees.

(ii) Supervisors as a group should receive a thorough training in advance of the actual introduction of the plan to enable them to explain the policies, principles and procedures to anyone who wants to understand them.

(iii) The management must give the widest publicity to every phase of the programme, utilising employee publications, notice boards, departmental meetings and letters to employees' homes.

(iv) Separate pay structures should be maintained for major groups of employees. For example, it would be difficult to work out a plan equally applicable to factory workers, office workers, salesmen, and departmental heads. The wages that are offered must be at or about the prevailing rate in order that there may be a successful competition for capable people.

(v) Whatever plan or system is selected for each group will arouse some fears or apprehensions. To overcome these, the details of the administration of the plan should be as simple as possible, and the management should endeavour to involve a broad range of employees from a number of departments.

According to the findings of the International Relations Sections of the Princeton University, the following conditions are necessary for the successful operation of a job evaluation programme:

(a) It must be carefully established by ensuring that: *(i)* the management's aims are clear to all concerned and that not only the manual workers but also all levels of supervision and management employees fully understand its implications; and *(ii)* all the relevant internal and external factors have been taken into account in arriving at the final form of the scheme.

(b) It must have the full approval and continued support and backing of the top management.

(c) It must have obtained the acceptance of trade unions.

(d) Adequate administrative control must be set up to ensure: *(i)* a centralised co-ordination of the scheme; *(ii)* the evaluation of new and changed jobs; *(iii)* a proper control of individual rate ranges; and *(iv)* the conduct of wage surveys to provide the necessary information about the intra-plant ranges.

(e) The importance of factors, other than job content, in wage rate determination (employment market conditions, sex, wage differentials, geographical wage differentials, and the relative bargaining power of the management and the trade union) must be recognised and taken into consideration while launching a job evaluation programme.

(f) Before launching a job evaluation programme, certain issues should be decided beforehand. There are: *(i)* which category of employees are to be covered (i.e., whether hourly paid job or salaried job employees) and up to what range? *(ii)* who will evaluate a job — outside consultants or trade analysts or the personnel of the personnel department? *(iii)* how will the employees be consulted in regard to the method of putting the programme through? and *(iv)* does a proper atmosphere exist for launching of the programme?

APPENDIX 5.1

DEFINITION OF FACTORS USED IN RATING JOBS

The factors usually considered in any rating procedure are education, training, experience, mental effort, physical effort, visual attention, initiative, responsibility, working conditions, and physical hazards. These factors are sub-divided into degrees — usually six; and points are allocated to these.

1. EDUCATION

This factor appraises the educational background of an individual to determine whether he will do the job satisfactorily.

First Degree: Ability to read, write and follow simple written or oral instructions.

Second Degree; Basic school education or its equivalent to do small arithmetical calculations involving addition, subtraction, division and multiplication of decimals and fractions.

Third Degree: High school education to determine knowledge of elementary accounting or general shop practice and manufacturing methods.

Fourth Degree; Intermediate education to determine the ability to understand and perform work calling for a knowledge of general engineering principles, commercial theory, principles of advanced drafting, knowledge of general accounting fundamentals and of complicated shop procedures and processes, etc.

Fifth Degree: Graduation to determine the ability to understand and perform work of a specialised or technical nature, knowledge of finance, business administration, chemistry, physics, journalism or any other technical or specialised field.

Sixth Degree: Post-graduate research experience in any technical or specialised field.

2. TRAINING

This factor appraises the period of training needed by an average individual to perform his job efficiently.

First Degree: Upto 6 months;

Second Degree: 6 to 12 months;

Third Degree: 12 to 15 months;

Fourth Degree: 15 to 18 months;

Fifth Degree; 18 to 21 months;

Sixth Degree: Over 21 months.

3. EXPERIENCE

This factor appraises the length of period needed by an average employee with a previously specified educational standard to be able to perform the job satisfactorily.

First Degree: Upto 3 months;

Second Degree: 3 to 6 months;

Third Degree: 6 months to 2 years;

Fourth Degree: 2 to 4 years;

Fifth Degree: 4 to 6 years;

Sixth Degree: Over 6 years.

4. MENTAL EFFORTS

This factor appraises the mental effort required of an individual to perform his job satisfactorily.

First Degree: Minimum mental effort required to do a simple rating job.

Second Degree: Some mental effort required.

Third Degree: Considerable mental effort needed.

Fourth Degree: Considerable organising ability required.

Fifth Degree: Sustained and diversified mental effort required.

Sixth Degree: Sustained and diversified mental effort required, as also clarity of concepts and ideas.

5. PHYSICAL EFFORTS

This factor appraises the physical effort needed from an employee for a satisfactory performance of a job.

First Degree: Very light physical effort required.

Second Degree: Light physical effort required, as in an office job.

Third Degree: Continuous physical activity required.

Fourth Degree: Moderately heavy physical activity required.

Fifth Degree: Great physical effort to lift or push heavy objects.

Sixth Degree: Extremely arduous physical effort required.

6. VISUAL ATTENTION

This factor appraises the extent and continuity of the visual attention needed on a job.

First Degree: Minimum visual attention required.

Second Degree: Ordinary visual attention required.

Third Degree: Fairly close attention required.

Fourth Degree: Close visual attention required to check the quality of products.

Sixth Degree: Extremely close work with intense and constant visual attention.

7. INITIATIVE

This factor appraises the capacity for independent decision or action required of an individual.

First Degree: Elementary type of job. The employee receives detailed instructions and is expected to perform the job exactly, as indicated, without deviations.

Second Degree: Repetitive type of job. Requires a close following of instructions and procedures.

Third Degree: Requires more frequent simple decisions on the part of the employee, but only when definite clear-cut precedents are available.

Fourth Degree: In addition to frequent simple decisions, the job calls for occasional decisions or actions following only general procedures in the absence of clear-cut procedures.

Fifth Degree: Difficult and complex type of job. Requires independent and original action to achieve the desired results.

Sixth Degree: Extremely difficult and complex type of job requiring independent and original action to achieve the desired results.

8. RESPONSIBILITY

This factor appraises the responsibility which goes with the job for preventing damage to tools, equipment or materials used in the performance of a job.

First Degree: Probable damage to tools upto Rs. 100 for an average mishap.

Second Degree: Probable damage to tools between Rs. 100 and Rs. 200.

Third Degree: Probable damage to tools between Rs. 200 to Rs. 500.

Fourth Degree: Probable damage to tools upto Rs. 5,000 per mishap.

Fifth Degree: Probable damage to tools, equipment and materials not to exceed Rs. 10,000 per mishap.

Sixth Degree: Probable damage exceeding Rs. 10,000 per mishap.

9. WORKING CONDITIONS

This factor appraises the physical environment under which a job is performed. Physical environment includes heat, cold, dampness, darkness, glare, dust, fumes, noise, etc.

First Degree: Excellent working conditions.

Second Degree: Occasional exposure to dust or fumes.

Third Degree: Constant exposure to one or more unpleasant conditions.

Fourth Degree: More disagreeable conditions.

Fifth Degree: Continuous exposure to disagreeable conditions.

Sixth Degree: Continuous exposure to various intensely disagreeable conditions.

10. PHYSICAL HAZARDS

This factor appraises the accident or health hazards which exist even though safety devices have been installed.

First Degree: No hazard exists.

Second Degree: Minor injuries may be sustained if an accident takes place.

Third Degree: If an accident takes place, an employee would receive severe cuts or burns.

Fourth Degree: The job is quite risky and the employee may catch some industrial disease.

Fifth Degree: There may be loss of some part of the body in the accident.

Sixth Degree: If an accident takes place, the employee is more likely to be killed or permanently disabled by injuries.

WAGE STUDY

After establishing the job hierarchy with the help of evaluation method(s), wage and salary differentials have to be fixed. Before fixing such differentials, wage rate must be ascertained. It is in this context that the wage study assumes importance.

The first step in a wage study is to select key jobs, the duties of which are clearly defined, reasonably stable, and representative of all levels of job worth. Thus, a sample of jobs is created. Secondly, a sample of firms in the labour market area must be chosen. The labour market for different job categories may vary from local to regional to national in scope. With both samples being selected, the final task is to obtain appropriate wage information, taking care to ensure that the job comparisons being made are sound. Job content, the varying qualities of personnel on these jobs, and the total compensation programme must be carefully analysed, compared, and equated. The data obtained from the study are analysed and averaged.

SUMMARY

1. *Developing an organisation structure:* results in fixing jobs that have to filled by suitable job holders. Job analysis is a procedure that entails — what kind of people should be recruited with what skills, knowledge and abilities.
2. *Job description should indicate:* duties to be performed by the job holder and the manner he should complete the tasks.
3. *Job specification:* answer the question "what human traits and experience are necessary to do the job. It portrays what kind of person to recruit and for what qualities that person should be tested.
4. *Job evaluation:* is a systematic comparison done in order to determine worth of one job relative to another and eventually results in wage or salary fixation for the job based on efforts, responsibility and skills. Different methods are used for evaluating jobs.
5. *Job classification:* is a method used for categorising jobs into groups. The groups are called classes if they contain similar jobs.
6. *Pay rates:* Establishing pay rates involve these steps: (i) conducting salary survey in comparative organisations, (ii) evaluating jobs in your own organisation, (iii) developing pay grades.

❑ ❑ ❑

6

Recruitment and Selection Process

RECRUITMENT

Recruitment forms the first stage in the process which continues with selection and ceases with the placement of the candidate. It is the next step in the procurement function, the first being the manpower planning. Recruiting makes it possible to acquire the number and types of people necessary to ensure the continued operation of the organisation. *Recruiting is the discovering of potential applicants for actual or anticipated organisational vacancies.* In other words, it is a 'linking activity' bringing together those with jobs and those seeking jobs.

As Yoder and others point out: "Recruitment is a process to discover the sources of manpower to meet the requirements of the staffing schedule and to employ effective measures for attracting that manpower in adequate numbers to facilitate effective selection of an efficient working force." Accordingly, the purpose of recruitment is to locate sources of manpower to meet job requirements and job specifications.

Recruitment has been regarded as the most important function of personnel administration, because unless the right type of people are hired, even the best plans, organisation charts and control systems would not do much good. Flippo views recruitment both as 'positive' and 'negative' activity. He says: "It is a process of searching for prospective employees and stimulating and encouraging them to apply for jobs in an organisation. It is often termed *positive* in that it stimulates people to apply for jobs to increase the 'hiring ratio,' *i.e.*, the number of applicants for a job. Selection, on the other hand tends to be *negative* because it rejects a good member of those who apply, leaving only the best to be hired."

FACTORS AFFECTING RECRUITMENT

All organisations, whether large or small, do engage in recruiting activity, though not to the same extent. This differs with: *(i)* the size of the organisation; *(ii)* the employment conditions in the community where the organisation is located; *(iii)* the effects of past recruiting efforts which show the organisation's ability to locate and keep good performing people; *(iv)* working conditions and salary and benefit packages offered by the organisation — which may influence turnover and necessitate future recruiting; *(v)* the rate of growth of organisation; *(vi)* the level of seasonality of operations and future expansion and production programmes; and *(vii)* cultural, economic and legal factors, etc.

Factors governing recruitment may broadly be divided as internal and external factors.

The internal factors are:

(i) Recruiting policy of the organisation;

(ii) Human resource planning strategy of the company;

(iii) Size of the organisation and the number of employees employed;

(iv) Cost involved in recruiting employees, and finally;

(v) Growth and expansion plans of the organisation.

The external factors are:

(i) Supply and demand of specific skills in the labour market;

(ii) Political and legal considerations such as reservation of jobs for SCs, STs, and so on.

(iii) Company's image-perception of the job seekers about the company.

THEORIES REGARDING RECRUITMENT

Recruitment is a two-way street: it takes a recruiter and a recruitee. Just as the recruiter has a choice whom to recruit and whom not, so also the prospective employee has to make the decision if he should apply for that organisation's job. The individual makes this decision usually on three different basis, the objective factor, critical contact, and subjective factor.

"The *objective factor theory* views the process of organisational choice as being one of weighing and evaluating a set of measurable characteristics of employment offers, such as pay, benefits, location, opportunity for advancement, the nature of the work to be performed, and educational opportunities."

"The *critical contact theory* suggests that the typical candidate is unable to make a meaningful differentiation of organisation's offers in terms of objective or subjective factors, because of his limited or very short contact with the organisation. Choice can be made only when the applicant can readily perceive the factors such as the behaviour of the recruiter, the nature of the physical facilities, and the efficiency in processing paper work associated with the application."

"The *subjective factor theory* emphasises the congruence between personality patterns and the 'image' of the organisation, *i.e.,* choices are made on a highly personal and emotional basis."

CONSTRAINTS LIMIT THE FREEDOM OF MANAGER TO RECRUIT

No employer could ever freely choose the "best" candidate because various forces impinge upon such selection. Such constraints are:

1. The Image of the Organisation: The prospective candidate may not be interested in getting job in the particular organisation either because its reputation or goodwill is not good in the community, or because the conditions of work are unsafe or it is indifferent to the need of the community. All such factors reduce its ability to attract the best personnel available.

2. The Unattractive Job: If the job is regarded as boring, hazardous, anxiety creating or lacking in promotion potential, people would not be attracted to such an organisation.

3. Internal Organisational Policies: If the policy aims at providing promotion to its employee from within, people would be attracted to it, because such a policy enjoys several advantages such as that of creating good public relations, building high morale, encouraging good people who are ambitious and improving the probability of a good selection.

4. Union Requirements can also Restrict Recruiting Sources: Some unions emphasise on recruitment to members of the unions only. Where such situation occurs, management has to recruit from a restricted supply.

5. Governments Influence: An employer cannot distinguish any individual, on the basis of physical appearance, sex or religious background, for purposes of recruitment.

STEPS ON RECRUITMENT PROCESS

As was mentioned earlier, recruitment refers to the process of identifying and attracting job seekers so as to build a pool of qualified job applicants. The process comprises five inter-related stages, viz., (i) planning, (ii) strategy development, (iii) searching, (iv) screening, and (v) evaluation and control.

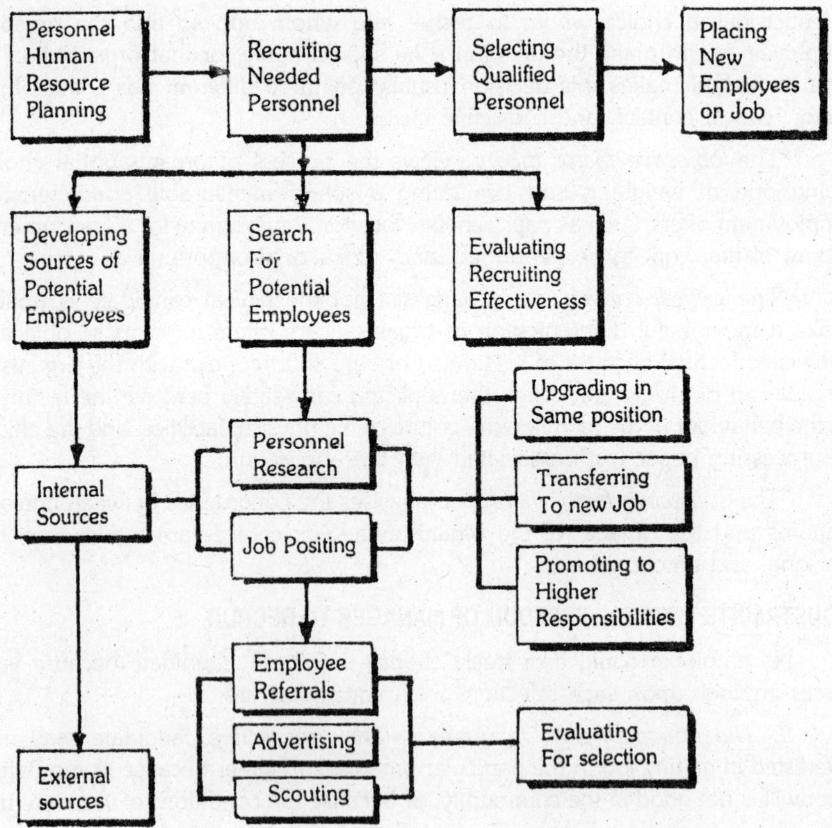

Fig. 6.1 Place of Recruitment in Selection System

According to Famularo, personnel recruitment process involves five elements, *viz.,* a recruitment policy, a recruitment organisation, a forecast of manpower, the development of sources of recruitment, and different techniques used for utilising these sources, and a method of assessing the recruitment programme.

Figure 6.1 shows the place of recruitment in the entire selection process.

RECRUITMENT POLICY

Such a policy asserts the objectives of the recruitment and provides a framework of implementation of the recruitment programme in the form of procedures. As Yoder and other observe:

"Such a policy may involve a commitment to broad principles such as filling vacancies with the best qualified individuals. It may embrace several issues such as extent of promotion from within, attitudes of enterprise in recruiting its old employees, handicaps, minority groups, women employees, part-time employees, friends and relatives of present employees. It may also involve the organisation system to be developed for implementing recruitment programme and procedures to the employed."

Therefore, a well considered and pre-planned recruitment policy, based on corporate goals, study of environment and the corporate needs, may avoid hasty or ill-considered decisions and may go a long way to man the organisation with the right type of personnel.

A good recruitment policy must contain these elements:

(a) Organisation's objectives — both in the short-term and long-term — must be taken into consideration as a basic parameter for recruitment decisions and needs of the personnel — area-wise, job-family-wise.

(b) Identification of the recruitment needs to take decisions regarding the balance of the qualitative dimensions of the would be recruits, *i.e.,* the recruiters should prepare profiles for each category of workers and accordingly work out the main specifications, decide the sections, departments or branches where they should be placed and identify the particular responsibilities which may be immediately assigned to them.

(c) Preferred sources of recruitment, which would be tapped by the organisation, e.g., for skilled or semi-skilled manual workers, internal sources and employment exchanges may be preferred; for highly specialised categories and managerial personnel, other sources besides the former, may be utilised.

(d) Criteria of selection and preferences: These should be based on conscious thought and serious deliberations which include merit and suitability.

(e) The cost of recruitment and financial implications of the same.

A "recruitment policy," in its broadest sense, "involves a commitment by the employer to such general principles as:

(i) To find and employ the best qualified persons for each job;

(ii) To retain the best and most promising of those hired;

(iii) To offer promising opportunities for life-time working careers; and

(iv) To provide programmes and facilities for personal growth on the job."

According to Yoder, "the recruitment policy is concerned with quantity and qualifications (*viz.,* and Q1 and Q2) of manpower." It establishes broad guidelines for the staffing process. Generally, the following factors are involved in a recruitment policy:

(i) To carefully observe the letter and spirit of the relevant public policy on hiring and, on the whole, employment relationship;

(ii) To provide individual employees with the maximum of employment security, avoiding, frequent lay-off or lost time;

(iii) To provide each employee with an open road and encouragement in the continuing development of his talents and skills;

(iv) To assure each employee of the organisation interest in his personal goals and employment objectives;

(v) To assure employees of fairness in all employment relationships, including promotions and transfers;

(vi) To avoid cliques which may develop when several members of the same household or community are employed in the organisation;

(vii) To provide employment in jobs which are engineered to meet the qualifications of handicapped workers and minority sections; and

(viii) To encourage one or more strong, effective, responsible trade unions among the employees.

PREREQUISITES OF A GOOD RECRUITMENT POLICY

The recruitment policy of an organisation must satisfy the following conditions:

(i) It should be in conformity with its general personnel policies;

(ii) It should be flexible enough to meet the changing needs of an organisation;

(iii) It should be so designed as to ensure employment opportunities for its employees on a long-term basis so that the goals of the organisation should be achievable; and it should develop the potentialities of employees;

(iv) It should match the qualities of employees with the requirements of the work for which they are employed; and

(v) It should highlight the necessity of establishing job analysis.

The nature and extent of the recruitment programme depends on a number of factors, including the skills required, the state of the labour market, general economic conditions, and the image of the employer. A company which has a reputation of paying fair wages, providing good employee benefits and taking interest in employee welfare activities would attract a larger number of applicants than it needs without making any extra recruiting effort. Small companies which hire only a few persons each year may not need to do more than spread the word around the plant or office that a vacancy exists. However, as a result of regulations and pressures from society and the government, the recruitment programme now requires the employers to go out and actively seek job applicants from groups of those who may not otherwise apply for employment.

RECRUITMENT ORGANISATION

There is no general procedure for hiring new personnel which is applicable to all business enterprises. Each enterprise has its "tailor-made" procedure which brings it the desired quantity and quality of manpower at the minimum possible cost. The most commonly adopted practice is to centralise the recruitment and selection function in a single office. All employment activity should be centralised if the policies of the top management are to be implemented consistently and efficiently. Only when personnel requisitions go through one central source and all employment records are kept up-to-date is there a possibility of maximum efficiency and success in hiring.

The advantages of centralising of recruitment and selection are:

(i) It reduces the administrative cost associated with selection by consolidating all activities in a single office;

(ii) It relieves line officers of the details involved in hiring workers, which is common under a decentralised plan;

(iii) It tends to make the selection of workers scientific;

(iv) It makes possible the development of a centralised manpower pool in a company;

(v) It provides a wider opportunity for placing an applicant in several departments of the company;

(vi) It tends to reduce favouritism as a basis for selection.

This centralised department is generally known as the *Employee Office*, or the *Recruitment Section*. The staff personnel is attached to it. This enables specialists to concentrate upon the recruitment function; and soon they become very efficient in the use of various recruitment techniques.

This office should be properly equipped with furniture. Its waiting room should be roomy, clean and well ventilated; it should have lighting facilities and drinking water, and it should be comfortable. This room should also have a table or a counter so that candidates may fill in their application blanks conveniently. It is desirable that personnel records be filed in a room accessible to the interviewer.

This office is concerned with the following functions:

(i) Establishing employment standards;

(ii) Making initial contact with prospective employees;

(iii) Testing before selection;

(iv) Conducting physical examinations;

(v) Conducting final interviews;

(vi) Filling out necessary forms and record keeping;

(vii) Introducing the employee to his superior; and

(viii) Following up the employee.

It may be noted that in a small organisation, recruiting procedure is merely informal and generally the "line official" may be responsible to handle this function. But in larger organisations, it is entrusted to a staff unit with Personnel or Industrial Relations Department. However, *recruitment remains the line responsibility as far as the personnel requisition forms are originated by the line personnel.*

FORECAST OF MANPOWER REQUIREMENTS

This aspect has already been discussed in the previous chapter.

It is only to be stated here that a 'requisition' or an 'indent' for recruitment has to be submitted by the line official. Such 'indents' usually specify: *(i)* the jobs or operations or positions for which the persons should be available; *(ii)* duration of their employment; *(iii)* salary to be offered and any other conditions and terms of employment which the indenting officer feels necessary (iv) Necessary qualifications and experience.

The indents are then checked against the posts allotted to the department/branch and also against authorisation for expansion, if already granted. Financial implications of the proposed appointments and additional expenditure are worked out — of course, these would be within the budgetary sanctions of the department concerned. If the indents are found correct, the proposed recruitments are authorised and the initial pay, the scale and other admissible allowances are determined.

Finally, job-specifications and man-specifications are determined, in consultation with the line managers.

SOURCES OF RECRUITMENT

Before an organisation activity begins recruiting applicants, it should consider the most likely source of the type of employee it needs. Some companies try to develop new sources, while most only try to tackle the existing sources they have. These sources, accordingly, may be termed as internal and external.

INTERNAL SOURCES

Internal sources are the most obvious sources. These include personnel already on the pay-roll of an organisation, *i.e.,* its present working force. Whenever any vacancy occurs, somebody from within the organisation is upgraded, transferred, promoted or sometimes demoted. This source also includes personnel who were once on the pay-roll of the company but who plan to return or whom the company would like to rehire, such as those on leave of absence, those who quit voluntarily, or those on production lay-offs.

Merit: The use of an internal source has some merits:

(i) It improves the morale of employees, for they are assured of the fact that they would be preferred over outsiders when vacancies occur.

(ii) The employer is in a better position to evaluate those presently employed than outside candidates. This is because the company maintains a record of the progress, experience and service of its employees.

(iii) It promotes loyalty among the employees, for it gives them a sense of job security and opportunities for advancement.

(iv) As the persons in the employment of the company are fully aware of, and well acquainted with, its policies and know its operating procedures, they require little training, and the chances are that they would stay longer in the employment of the organisation than a new outsider would.

(v) They are tried people and can, therefore, be relied upon.

(vi) It is less costly than going outside to recruit.

Demerits: However, this system suffers from certain defects as well.

(i) It often leads to inbreeding, and discourages new blood from entering an organisation.

(ii) There are possibilities that internal sources may "dry up", and it may be difficult to find the requisite personnel from within an organisation.

(iii) Since the learner does not know more than the lecturer, no innovations worth the name can be made. Therefore, on jobs which require original thinking (such as advertising, style, designing and basic research), this practice is not followed.

(iv) As promotion is based on seniority, the danger is that really capable hands may not be chosen. The likes and dislikes of the management may also play an important role in the selection of personnel.

This source is used by many organisations; but a surprisingly large number ignore this source, especially for middle management jobs. In other words, *this source is the lode that is rarely mined.* It is not only reasonable but wise to use this source, if the vacancies to be filled are within the capacity of the present employees; if adequate employee records have been maintained, and if opportunities are provided in advance for them to prepare themselves for promotion from "blue-collar" to "white-collar" jobs.

EXTERNAL SOURCES

These sources lie outside the organisation. They usually include:

(i) New entrants to the labour force, *i.e.,* young, mostly inexperienced potential employees — the college students; technical school students;

(ii) The unemployed — with a wide range of skills and abilities;

(iii) Retired experienced persons such as mechanics, machinists, welders, accountants, salesman;

(iv) Others not in the labour force, such as married women and persons from minority groups.

Merits: (i) External sources provide the requisite type of personnel for an organisation, having skill, training and education up to the required standard. *(ii)* Since persons are recruited from a large market, the best selection can be made without any distinctions of caste, sex or colour. *(iii)* In the long run, this source proves economical because potential employees do not need extra training for their jobs.

Demerits: However, this system suffers from what is called "braindrain," especially when experienced persons are *raided* or *hunted* by sister concerns.

METHODS OR TECHNIQUES OF RECRUITMENT

Dunn and Stephens summarise the possible recruiting methods into three categories: direct, indirect and third party.

DIRECT METHODS

These include sending *travelling recruiters* to educational and professional institutions, employees' contacts with public, and manned exhibits. One of the widely used direct methods is that of sending of recruiters to colleges and technical schools. Most college recruiting is done in co-operation with the placement office of a college. The placement office usually provides help in attracting students, arranging interviews, furnishing space, and providing student resumes. For managerial, professional and sales personnel, campus recruiting is an extensive operation. Persons reading for MBA or other technical diplomas are picked up in this manner. For this purpose, carefully prepared brochures, describing the organisation and the jobs it offers, are distributed among students, before the interviewer arrives. The DCM, TATAs, and other enlightened firms maintain continuing contacts with institutions' placement officials with a view to recruiting staff regularly for different responsible positions.

Sometimes, firms directly solicit information from the concerned professors about students with an outstanding record.

Many companies have found employees' contact with the public a very effective method.

Other direct methods include sending recruiters to conventions and seminars, setting up exhibits at fairs, and using mobile offices to go to the desired centres.

INDIRECT METHODS

Indirect methods involve mostly advertising in newspaper, on the radio, in trade and professional journals, technical magazines and brochures.

Advertising in newspapers and/or trade journals and magazines is the most frequently used method, when qualified or experienced personnel are not available from other sources. Senior posts are largely filled by such methods when they cannot be filled by promotion from within.

Advertising is very useful for recruiting blue-collar and hourly workers, as well as scientific, professional, and technical employees. Local newspaper can be a good source of blue-collar workers, clerical employees, and lower-level administrative employees.

The main point is that the higher the position is in the organisation, or the more specialised the skills sought, the more widely dispersed advertisement is likely to be. The search for top executive might include advertisements in a national periodical; while the advertisement of blue-collar jobs is usually confined to the daily newspaper or regional trade journals.

The classified advertisement section of a daily newspaper or the Sunday weekly edition of The Hindustan Times, The Times of India, The Tribune, The National Herald, The Free Press Journal, The Pioneer, Amrit Bazar Patrika, The Economic Times, The Hindu, The Indian Express etc., carry advertisements for all types of positions. Such advertisements enable prospective candidates to screen themselves in order to find out whether they are fit for the job for which the advertisement has been issued.

In order to be successful, an advertisement should be carefully written. If it is not properly written, it may not draw the right type of applicants or it may attract too many applicants who are not qualified for the job. It should be so framed as to attract attention — for example, by the use of different sizes and types of print. The first line should limit the audience somewhat and the next few lines should further screen out the readers who do not possess the necessary qualifications. It should provide specific information on job requirements and opportunities for advancement, the benefits to be enjoyed by working in the company; and it should emphasise facts related to the dignity of the job and to its professional aspects. "Frilly advertisements, containing exaggerated claims and gimmicky appeals, are to be avoided." Advertising can be very effective if its media are properly chosen.

According to Advertisement Tactics and Strategy in Personnel Recruitment, three points need to be borne in mind before an advertisement is inserted. *First,* to visualise the type of applicant one is trying to recruit. *Second,* to write out a list of the advantages a company offers; in other words, why the reader should work for the company. *Third,* to decide where to run the advertisement, not only in which area but in which newspaper having a local, state or nation-wide circulation.

Many organisations often place what is referred to as a *blind advertisement,* one in which there is no identification of the organisation. Respondents are asked to reply to a 'Post Office Box Number' or to a consulting firm that is acting as an intermediary between the applicant and the organisation. The large organisations with regional or national reputation do not usually use blind advertisements.

Other methods include advertising in publications, such as trade and professional journals, and radio or television announcements, as is done by many Indian manufacturers. Professional journals are read by people with specialised backgrounds and interests. Therefore, advertisements in these are generally selective.

THIRD PARTY METHODS

These include the use of commercial or private employment agencies, state agencies, placement offices of schools, colleges and professional associations, recruiting firms, management consulting firms, indoctrination seminars for college professors, and friends and relatives.

Private employment agencies are widely used. They charge a small fee from an applicant. They specialise in specific occupations: general office help, salesmen, technical workers, accountants, computer staff, engineers and executives. These private agencies are brokers who bring employers and employees together. The specialisation of these agencies enhances their capacity to interpret the needs of their clients, to seek out particular types of persons and to develop proficiency in recognising the talent of specialised personnel.

State or public employment agencies also known as *Employment or Labour Exchanges,* are the main agencies of public employment. They provide a clearing house for jobs and job information. Employers inform them of their personnel requirements, while job-seekers get information for them about the types of jobs that are referred to by employers. These agencies provide a wide range of services — counselling, assistance in getting jobs, information about the labour market, labour and wage rates.

Schools, Colleges and Professional Institutions offer opportunities for recruiting their students. They operate placement services where complete biodata and other particulars of the students are available. The companies that need employees maintain contact with the Guidance Counsellors of Employment Bureaus and teachers of business and vocational subjects. The prospective employers can review credentials and interview candidates for management trainees or probationers. Whether the education sought involves a higher secondary certificate, specific vocational training, or a college background with a bachelor's, master's, or doctoral degree, educational institutions provide an excellent source of potential employees for entry-level positions in organisations. These general and technical/professional institutions provide blue-collar applicants, white-collar and managerial personnel.

Sometimes, the organisations provide Work Study Programme to the students or summer jobs for undertaking a project in the establishment so as to get them interested in the organisation in question, and after completion of this, they may be absorbed by the companies concerned.

Professional organisations or recruiting firms or executive recruiters maintain complete information records about employed executives. These firms are looked upon as 'head hunters', 'raiders' and 'pirates' by organisations which lose personnel through their efforts. However, these same organisations may employ "executive search firms" to help them find executive talent. These consulting firms recommend persons of high calibre for managerial, marketing, and production engineers' posts.

Indoctrination seminars for colleges professors are arranged to discuss the problem of companies and employees. Professors are invited to take part in these seminars. Visits to plants and banquets are arranged so that the participant professors may be favourably impressed. They may later speak well of a company and help it getting the required personnel.

Employee Referrals: Friends and relatives of present employees are also a good source from which employees may be drawn. When the labour market is very tight, large employers frequently offer their employees bonuses or prizes for any referrals who are hired and stay with the company for a specific length of time. Some companies maintain a register of former employees whose record was good to contact them when there are new job openings for which they are qualified. This method of recruitment, however, suffers from a serious defect that it encourages nepotism, *i.e.,* persons of one's community or caste are employed, who may or may not be fit for the job.

Casual Labour or Applicant at the Gate : Most industrial units rely to some extent on the casual labour which presents itself daily at the factory gate or employment office. However, this source is uncertain, and the candidates cover a wide range of abilities. Even then, many of our industries make use of this source to fill up casual vacancies.

Unconsolidated Applications : For positions in which large number of candidates are not available from other sources, the companies may gain in keeping files of applications received from candidates who make direct enquiries about possible vacancies on their own, or may send unconsolidated applications. The information may be indexed and filed for future use when there are openings in these jobs. If necessary, the candidates may be requested to keep the organisation posted with any change in their qualifications, experience or achievements made.

Voluntary Organisations, such as private clubs, social organisations, might also provide employees — handicapped, widowed or married women, old persons, retired hands, etc. in response to advertisements.

Computer Data Banks: When a company desires a particular type of employee, job specifications and requirements are fed into a computer, where they are matched against the resume data stored therein. The output is a set of resumes for individuals who meet the requirements. This method is very useful for identifying candidates for hard-to-fill positions which call for an unusual combination of skills.

Which particular source is to be tapped will depend on the policy of a firm, the position of labour supply, Government regulations and agreements with labour organisations. However, the personnel manager must be in close touch with these different sources and use them in accordance with his needs. *The best management policy regarding recruitment is to look first within the organisation. If that source fails, external recruitment must be tackled.*

According to Flippo, the present tendency among most business firms is to "home grow" their executive leaders. Koontz and O' Donnel rightly observe that the policy should be to "raise" talent rather than "raid" for it.

TABLE 6.1

Recruiting Practices and a Firm's Position in the Labour Market

Degree of Tightness in the Labour Market	*Sources Used for Recruitment*	*Area Covered for Recruitment*
1. Most loose	Direct hiring	Immediate vicinity
2. Intermediate	Friends and relatives, private and public agencies	Part of an urban industrial area
3. Tight	Advertising, nearby special sources (colleges, private agencies)	The whole urban industrial area
4. Most tight	Labour scouting	Regional and national

RECRUITMENT PRACTICES IN INDIA

The different sources for recruitment in India have been classified thus: *(i)* Within the organisation; *(ii) Badli* or temporary workers; *(iii)* Employment agencies; *(iv)* Casual callers; *(v)* Applicants introduced by friends and relatives in the organisation; *(vi)* Advertisements; and *(vii)* Labour contractors *(viii)* Educational Training Institutes.

According to a survey of public and private sector employers by Prof. Basavaraj, the following methods were used to recruit employees:

(a) In the public sector (steel units), the major sources of recruitment in order of preference are: *(i)* Casual callers or employment seekers; *(ii)* Newspaper advertisements; *(iii)* Employment exchanges; *(iv)* Other public undertakings; *(v)* Internal advertisement; *(vi)* Displaced persons; *(vii)* Relative and friends; *(viii)* Employee recommendations; and *(ix)* Institutions.

In the public sector (heavy engineering), the sources for non-supervisory staff are: *(i)* Employment exchanges; *(ii)* External advertisement; *(iii)* Internal advertisement; *(iv)* Central training institute; *(v)* Introduction by the liaison officer of a corporation; *(vi)* Deputation personnel; and *(vii)* Transfers from other public undertakings.

(b) In the private sector, the survey disclosed that the procedures, though formulated, were not institutionalised in character. In some organisations, preference was given to sons and relatives of employees and to local people. In order of

preference, the major sources are: *(i)* Advertisements; *(ii)* Educational Institutions; *(iii)* Relatives and friends; *(iv)* Database in the company; *(v)* Employee recommendations; *(vi)* Company recruitment; *(vii)* Recruting agencies.

THE PROBLEM OF THE "SONS OF THE SOIL"

A controversy has arisen in recent years over giving preference in recruitment to "Sons of the Soil." In this connection the National Commission on Labour has observed: "The solution has to be sought in terms of the primacy of common citizenship, geographical mobility and economic feasibility of locating industrial units, on the one hand, and local aspiration on the other." It has suggested that:

(a) Young persons from families whose lands are acquired for industrial use should be provided training opportunities for employment in jobs which are likely to be created in new units set up on these lands;

(b) To remove unjustified apprehensions among local candidates, the following steps should be taken to supervise the implementation of the directives of the Government of India on recruitment for public sector projects;

(i) While recruiting unskilled employees, first preference should be given to persons displaced from the areas required for the projects. The next to be preferred should be those who have been living in the same vicinity.

(ii) The selection of persons to posts in lower scales should not be left entirely to the head of the unit. It should be made through a recruitment committee.

(iii) In the case of middle level technicians whose recruitment has to be on an all-India basis, a member of the State Public Service Commission should be associated in making selections in addition to the State Government official on the Board of Directors for public sector undertakings.

(iv) Apart from the report sent to the concerned Ministry at the Centre, the undertaking should send a statement to the State Government at regular intervals, preferably every quarter, about the latest employment and recruitment position.

Although the Commission has suggested these steps for employment in the public sector, it is of the opinion that they should apply equally to recruitment in the private sector, though the mechanism to regulate this recruitment would necessarily differ from that in the public sector. In India, for recruitment of industrial labour, traditional methods (casual or *badli* workers on lists maintained by the factory; the use of jobbers, *sardars, mukadams,* etc., employees' relatives and dependants and undertaking's own labour force, etc., and contract labour) are still used for getting labour in textile industry, for building and construction industry, digging of canals, building of roads and dams, etc.

Besides these, large industrial complexes have developed a more 'committed' labour force. For supplying skilled operators there are a number of Crafts Training Schools (Industrial Training Institutes; Advanced Vocational Training Institutes at Mumbai, Kolkata, Hyderabad, Kanpur, Ludhiana and Chennai; Seven Craft Instructors Training Schools; and an Institute for Training of Foremen at Bangalore).

RECRUITMENT PRACTICES IN INDIA AND ELSEWHERE

All public sector enterprises are required to consider candidates sponsored by the Employment Exchanges (over 535) and, in most cases, confine the selection to these candidates. However, the private sector is not under any such formal obligation.

Under the Apprentices Act, 1961, young craftsmen having received pre-employment training in Industrial Institutes have to be employed by 'specialised' industries during their training period as a percentage of the total number of regular employees. Reservation of 25% of vacancies for Scheduled Castes and Scheduled Tribes candidates and preferential treatment of displaced persons is a part of statutory requirement of Government and public sector employment in India.

The recruitment of supervisory personnel in all organised industries is generally by promotion from within the organisation. Some industries first recruit a number of young persons as management trainees and after 2 or 3 years absorb them completely. Executives too are mostly promoted from within. Sometimes good persons are also recruited from Indian Institutes of Technology, All-India Institutes of Management at Calcutta, Institutes of Technology, All-India Institutes of Management at Calcutta, Ahmedabad and Bangalore; from universities offering MBA courses, etc.

Retired military and police personnel also provide an important source of recruitment, particularly for security jobs, and for personnel jobs.

In the U.S.A. four sources of applicants are most used in obtaining hourly workers — direct applications at the company office, public employment sources, recommendations by employees, and newspaper advertising. In the case of blue-collar workers, the sources most successfully used are newspaper advertising, direct application, public employment offices, employee's recommendations, and private employment agencies. In the case of scientific, professional and technical employees, the most productive sources are advertising, on-campus recruiting and employment agencies.

Thus, it may be observed that there is virtually no definite work that develops employer's reasons for selecting various methods of recruitment. No single method is predominant and that recruitment practices are adapted to fill vacancies, employment rates, and other circumstances faced by the employer.

ASSESSMENT OF THE RECRUITMENT PROGRAMME

Sources for recruiting should be periodically evaluated. For this purpose, the criteria may be the cost per applicant, the applicant/hiring ratio, tenure, performance appraisals, etc. The organisation should first identify how an applicant was attracted to the firm. A simple way of securing this information is to include in the application blank a question: "How did you learn of the job vacancy for which you have applied?" The next step is to determine whether any one method consistently attracts better applicants. The last step is to use this information to improve the recruiting process. Recruiting should take into consideration ethical practices, such as use of "truth in hiring," *i.e.,* telling an applicant all about the firm and its position, both good and bad, to enable him to decide whether or not to join the firm, if selected.

A successful and effective recruitment programme necessitates a well-defined recruitment policy, a proper organisational structure, procedures for locating sources of manpower resources, suitable methods and techniques for utilising these and a constant assessment and consequent improvement.

SELECTION

SELECTION PROCEDURE

The selection procedure is concerned with securing relevant information about an applicant. This information is secured in a number of steps or stages. The objective of selection process is to determine whether an applicant meets the qualifications for a specific job and to choose the applicant who is most likely to perform well in that job.

Selection is a long process, commencing from the preliminary interview of the applicants and ending with the contract of employment.

The hiring procedure is not a single act but it is essentially a series of methods or steps or stages by which additional information is secured about the applicant. At each stage, facts may come to light which may lead to the rejection to the applicant. A procedure may be compared to a series of successive hurdles or barriers which an applicant must cross. These are intended as screens, and they are designed to eliminate an unqualified applicant at any point in the process. This technique is known as the *successive hurdles technique.* Not all selection processes include all these hurdles. The complexity of a process usually increases with the level and responsibility of the position to be filled.

According to Yoder, "the hiring process is of one or many 'go, no-go' gauges. Candidates are screened by the application of these tools. Qualified applicants go on to the next hurdle, while the unqualified are eliminated." Thus, an effective selection programme is a non-random process because those selected have been chosen on the basis of the assumption that they are more likely to be "better" employees than those who have been rejected. Table 6.2 gives the hiring requirements as outlined by Yoder.

TABLE 6.2

Hiring Requirements

Types of Qualifications or Specifications	*Types of Gauges*
1. Arbitrary, Security, Age, Sex	1. Application blank
	2. Security check
	3. Police records
	4. Personnel records
2. Physical health and adequacy	Physical Examination
3. Skills (including specialised knowledge)	1. Application blank
	2. Education, training, apprenticeship
	3. Grades
	4. Employment records
	5. References
	6. Biography
	7. Trade tests
4. Experience	1. Application blank
	2. Biography

	3. Employment records
	4. References
	5. Interviews
5. Aptitude (including intelligence)	1. Employment records
	2. Personnel appraisals
	3. References
6. Interests	1. Application blank
	2. Reference
	3. Biography
7. Emotional maturity, moods, motivations	1. Biography
	2. Employment records
	3. Tests
8. Attitudes	1. Interviews
	2. References
	3. Personnel appraisals
	4. Attitude-morale scales.

Selection processes or activities typically follow a standard pattern, beginning with an initial screening interview and concluding with the final employment decision. The traditional selection process includes: preliminary screening interview; completion of application form; employment tests; comprehensive interview; background investigations, physical examination and final employment decision to hire.

SELECTION POLICY

While formulating a selection policy, due consideration should be given to organisational requirements as well as technical and professional dimensions of selection procedures. Yoder and others have suggested goals, technological issues, cost factors, extent of formality, etc. In other words, an effective policy must assert the "why" and "what" aspects of the organisational objectives.

ESSENTIALS OF SELECTION PROCEDURE

The selection procedure adopted by an organisation is mostly tailor made to meet its particular needs. The thoroughness of the procedure depends upon three factors:

First, the nature of selection, whether faulty or safe, because faulty selection affects not only the training period that may be needed, but also results in heavy expenditure on the new employee and the loss that may be incurred by the organisation in case the job-occupant fails on his job.

Second, the policy of the company and the attitude of the management. As a practice some companies usually hire more than the actual number needed with a view to removing the unfit persons from the jobs.

Third, the length of the probationary or the trial period. The longer the period, the greater the uncertainty in the minds of the selected candidate about his future.

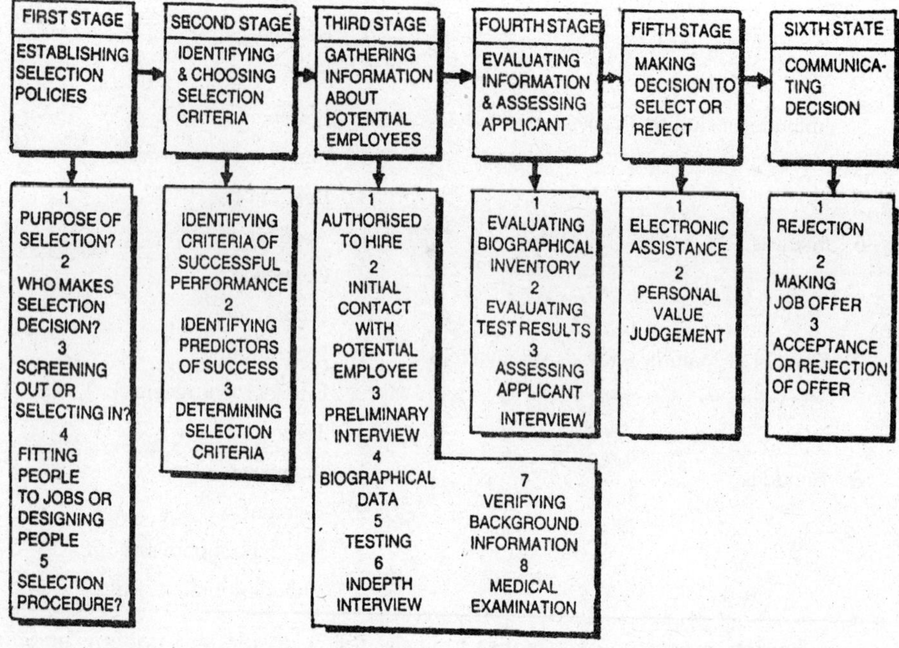

Fig. 6.2 Model Procedure for Effective Personnel Selection

The hiring process can be successful, if the following preliminary requirements are satisfied:

(i) Some one should have the authority to hire. This authority comes from the employment requisition, as developed by an analysis of the work-load and work force.

(ii) There must be some standard or personnel with which a prospective employee may be compared, *i.e.,* there should be available, beforehand, a comprehensive job description and job specifications as developed by a Job Analysis.

(iii) There must be a sufficient number of applicants from whom the required number of employees may be selected.

STEPS IN SELECTION PROCEDURE

There is no shortcut to an accurate evaluation of a candidate. The hiring procedures are, therefore, generally long and complicated. Many employers make use of such techniques and pseudo-sciences as phrenology, physiognomy, astrology, graphology etc., while coming to hiring decisions. However, in modern times, these are considered to be unreliable measures.

The following is a popular procedure though it may be modified to suit individual situation:

1. Reception or preliminary interview or screening;
2. Application blank — a fact-finder which helps one in learning about an applicant's background and life history;

3. A well conducted interview to explore the facts and get at the attitudes of the applicant and his family to the job;
4. A physical examination — health and stamina are vital factors in success;
5. Physiological testing to explore the surface area and get an objective look at a candidate's suitability for a job; conducting other tests if any.
6. A reference check;
7. Final selection approval by manager; and communication of the decision to the candidate.

In the paragraphs that follow, we shall be discussing items 1, 2, 4, 5 and 6. The remaining items have been treated in the two subsequent chapters.

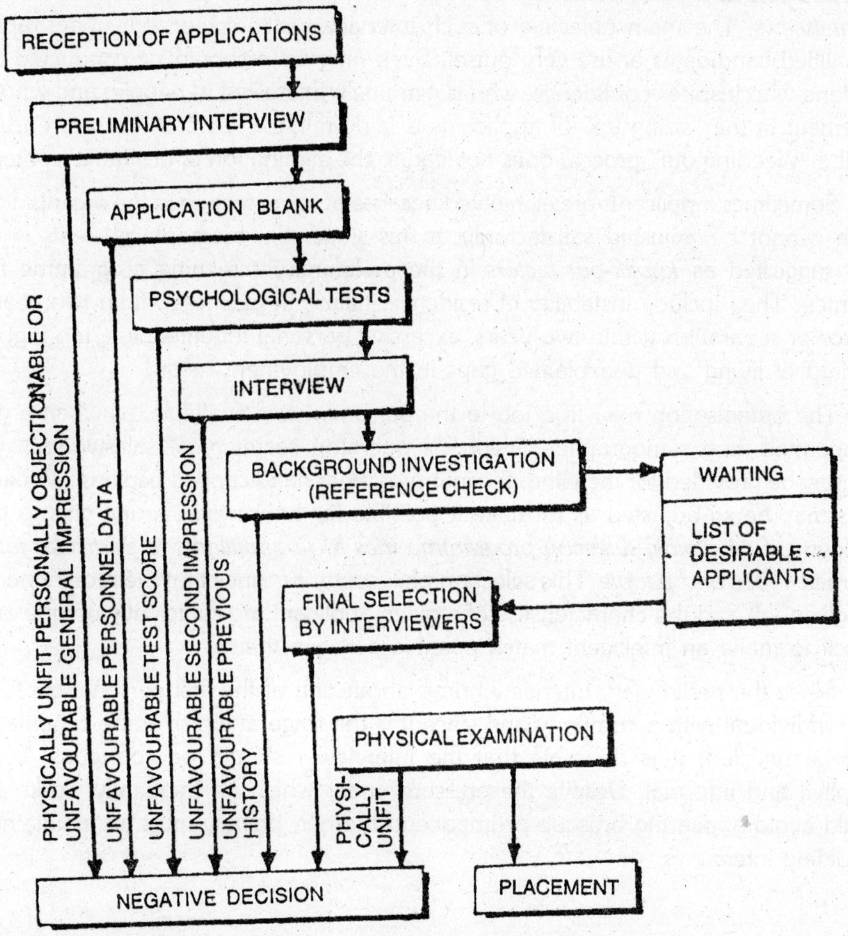

Fig. 6.3: Selection Process Flow Chart

RECEPTION, INITIAL OR PRELIMINARY INTERVIEW OR SCREENING

The initial screening is usually conducted by a special interviewer or a high calibre receptionist in the employment office. When a large number of applicants are available, the preliminary interview is desirable both from the company's point of view and that of the applicant seeking employment. This interview is essentially a sorting process in which perspective applicants are given the necessary information about the nature of the jobs in the organisation. The necessary information, then, is elicited from the candidates relating to their education, experience, skill, salary demanded, the reasons for leaving their present jobs, their job interests and whether they are available for the job, their physical appearance, age, "drive" and facility in speech. If a candidate meets with the requirements of the organisation, he may be selected for further action. If he does not fit into the organisational structure (because of lack of requisite qualifications, physical disability, weak sight, or poor physique), he is eliminated at the preliminary stage. Such interviews are usually short and may be conducted at a desk, across a counter or railing and they are known as *stand-up interviews.* The main objective of such interviews is to screen out undesirable/unqualified candidates at the very outset. Such interviews should be conducted by someone who inspires confidence, who is genuinely interested in people, and whose judgement in the "sizing up" of applicants is fairly reliable. Care is taken to ensure that the "Weeding out" process does not lead to the elimination of desirable workers.

Sometimes, applicants are eliminated because of some feature in the organisation which cannot be adjusted satisfactorily at this stage. Six biographical items have been suggested as *knock-out factors* in the preliminary screening programme for salesmen. They include instability of residence, failure in business within two years, divorce or separation within two years, excessive personal indebtedness, too high a standard of living and unexplained gaps in the employment record.

The organisation may fit a job to the person who is available, as when a girl is appointed as a stenographer, telephone operator, secretary or saleswoman. Or jobs may be provided for the blind, the infirm or other handicapped persons. Working hours may be so adjusted as to make it possible for housewives/young girls to get employment. *A typical selection programme tries to fit applicants to particular jobs, i.e., match jobs and people.* This selection philosophy assumes that the requirements of a given job and the characteristics of a given applicant are sufficiently unique and explicit to make an intelligent match possible between them.

Since the preliminary interview brings about one of the first personal contacts of an individual with a company and since it is the stage at which some candidates must be rejected, it is desirable that the interviewer should be courteous, kind, receptive and informal. Despite the pressure under which he frequently works, he should avoid appearing brusque or impatient. Further, privacy must be maintained in holding interviews.

CHART 6.1

Guidelines for Preliminary Screening

Name of the Candidate: ....

(a)	Personality: Grade	A	B	C	D ....
(b)	Expression (in English)	A	B	C	D ....
	(in Hindi)	A	B	C	D ....
(c)	Technical Knowledge				
	Theory:	A	B	C	D..............
	Application:	A	B	C	D ....
(d)	General Knowledge	A	B	C	D ....
(e)	Any other remarks	A	B	C	D ....

Selected for Employment Test .... Yes .... No.........................

Date of Interview .... Signature of the Interviewer........ ....

* Grade A — Outstanding: B — Good; C — Average; D — Poor.

APPLICATION BLANK OR APPLICATION FORM

An application blank is a traditional, widely accepted device for getting information from a prospective applicant which will enable a management to make a proper selection.

The blank provides preliminary information as well as aid in the interview by indicating areas of interest and discussion. It is a good means of quickly collecting verifiable (and therefore fairly accurate) basic historical data from the candidate. It also serves as a convenient device for circulating information about the applicant to appropriate members of management and as a useful device for storing information for, later reference.

The information required to be given in the applicant's own hand-writing is needed to identify him properly and to draw tentative inferences about his suitability for employment. Many types of application forms — sometimes very long and comprehensive and sometimes brief — are used. Information is generally called on the following items:

(a) Biographical Data: Name, father's name, date and place of birth, age, sex, nationality, height, weight, identification marks, physical disability, if any, marital status, and number of dependants.

(b) Educational Attainment: Education (subjects offered and grades secured), training acquired in special fields and knowledge gained from professional/technical institutes or evening classes or through correspondence courses.

(c) Work Experience: Previous experience, the number of jobs held with the same or other employers, including the nature of duties, and responsibilities and the duration of various assignments, salary received, grades, and reasons for leaving the present employer.

(d) Salary and Benefits: Present and expected.

CHART 6.2

A Specimen of a Short Application Form for Unskilled Manual Employees

KHANDELWAL BROTHERS PVT. LTD.

FORT, MUMBAI - 400 001.

Date..........................

Name: ....

Address: ....

Date of Birth: .... Single/Married/Widowed/Divorced

Position Applied for: ....

Details of the last two jobs, including present one if still employed.

Name and address of the Employer	Type of work done	To	From	Reason for leaving
1.				
2.				

Physical disabilities:

Have you ever worked for this concern before? Yes/No

Engaged/Not Engaged.................................. Department: ....

Due to start... Interviewer: ....

(e) Personal Items: Association memberships, of NCC or NSS, extra-curricular activities, sports, hobbies, and any other pertinent information supporting a candidate's suitability for a post.

(f) Other Items: Names and addresses of previous employers, references, etc.

An application blank is a brief history sheet of an employee's background and can be used for future reference, in case or need.

The data submitted in an application form should help predict the candidate's chances for making a success of his job. The information sought in it should be relevant to the objective of selection. To ensure that the information given by the applicant is true, the application blank usually carries a threat of discharge at any time after employment if the information furnished in it proves to be false.

The questions included in an application blank should be such as are valid and necessary. Superfluous questions should be avoided. They should not by their wording or nature, encourage dishonest answers. In brief, an application form should be complete enough to relieve the interviewer of the burden of recording considerable factual data.

CHART 6.3

Long Application Blank

THE ARAVALI PUBLISHING COMPANY PVT. LTD.

(for staff)

Registered office: Aravali Buildings

Udaipur (Rajasthan)

FORM FOR APPLICATION

NOTE: (a) All entries must be made in candidate's handwriting.

(b) All subsequent change in the particulars given in the application must be intimated to the Personnel Department within a week of such change.

(c) If space against any query is not adequate a separate sheet should be attached.

(d) Canvassing in any form will disqualify a candidate.

(e) The candidate will render himself liable to summary dismissal if it is found that any information given by him is incorrect or any relevant information has been supressed.

1. Full Name (with surname) in Block Letters:..
2. Nationality: .... Caste: .... Religion: .... Sex: ....
3. Father's Name and Occupation: ....
4. Present Address: ....
5. Permanent Address: .... Village .... Mohalla ....

   H. No: .... P.O. .... Dist. .... State ....
6. Age: .... Date of Birth ....Place of Birth ....
7. Academic/Technical Qualifications stating examinations passed from High School SLC/Hr. Secondary onwards:

	Name of University	Examinations Passed	Subjects Offered	Year of Passing	Division Class (Marks obtained if there is no division of class)
(a)					
(b)					
(c)					

8. Apprenticeship/Practical Training:

Nature of Apprenticeship/Training	Organisation in which served	Duration From (Date)	To (Date)	Result

9. Languages: (a) Can Speak: Hindi English/Gujarati, Marathi any other

   (b) Can Speak read and write:
10. Physique: Games played: ....

    (a) Height: (in cms).................... Hobbies: ....

    (b) Weight: (in kgs) ....

    (c) Strength of glasses (if worn): ....

    (d) Any disability: (current): ....

(e) Any major disability or ailment suffered in the past: ....

(f) Identification Marks: ....

11. Past Experience:

	Name of employer with complete address	Total number of staff and workers	Post held and exact nature of duties	Period Date of joining leaving	Salary: basic and allowances at start and leaving and other benefits	Reasons for Leaving
1.						
2.						
3.						
4.						
5.						

Information regarding specialization in a particular subject and other matters of interest

....

12. (a) Have you ever been removed from your job. If so, state where and why

....

(b) Have you been convicted by a court of law? If so, give particulars

....

13. (a) Have you ever applied to been interviewed by this Company before?

....

(If yes, please state the name of the post and the date of interview)

14. References (other than relations) (Name and full address to be given)

(i) ....

(ii) ....

15. Minimum salary acceptable (including all allowances):

....

16. Time required for joining (if selected):

17. Number of dependants:.......................... Male .... Female ....

18. Marital status: Married/Bachelor Divorced/Widowed/Separated

19. (a) Children ....

(b) Ages of children .... Sons ....

Daughters .... Name of relative ....

Department .... Relationship ....

20. Any acquaintance in our Company? If so, give name and full particulars of each acquaintance:

....

....

21. Copies of Testimonials enclosed.
    1.
    2.
    3.
    4.
    5.

Place ....

Date .... Signature of Applicant

(TO BE FILLED IN BY THE PERSONNEL DEPARTMENT)

Interviewed 1. .... (on date)

2. ....

3. ....

Remarks:

....

....

....

....

Appointed by: ....

Date of Appointment: ....

Salary Fixed: ....

Post to which appointed: ....

Nature of vacancy: Temporary/Peramanent: ....

Period of Probation: ....

For THE ARAVALI PUBLISHING COMPANY PVT.LTD.

Manager

To be filled in by the selected candidates only.

I have read and understood the Company's Service Rules and agree to abide by them including any changes made therein by the Management from time to time.

Specimen Signature: ....

Specimen Initials: ....

From the analysis of the above Application Blank, four types of information can be gathered:

First, one can make judgements on *substantative matters,* such as "does the applicant have the education and experience to do the job?"

Second, one can draw conclusions about the applicants previous *progress and growth* (especially in the case of management candidates).

Third, one can also draw tentative conclusion concerning the applicant's *stability* based on his previous work record.

Fourth, one may be able to use the data in the application to *predict* which candidates will succeed on the job and which would not.

In practice, most organisations use different application forms. For technical and managerial personnel, for example, the form may require detailed answers to questions regarding the candidate's education, etc. For blue-collar jobs, the form might stress on tools and equipment the applicant has used.

WEIGHTED APPLICATION BLANK

Some companies analyse the information on an application blank and determine statistically its relation to later success in the job. The answers are weighted according to the extent of job success. Such application blanks are known as weighted application blanks. Such forms may speed up both recruitment and selection.

A weighted application form should be established and used with a caution. Its objectives should be clearly determined. For example, there may be a selection of more stable employees to decrease labour turnover or increase job efficiency. The factors that bring about success may also be taken into account. For this purpose, the varying conditions in an organisation should be noted. The blank should be continually up-dated. Finally, no firm should try to select an employee solely on the basis of one or two important facts.

CHART 6.4
Weighted Application Blank for the Post of Secretary

Item	*Percentage*		*Weight*
	Short-term	*Long-term*	
Age			
20 or under	10	0	0
21-25	50	12	4
26-30	20	12	0
31-35	20	23	0
Over 35	10	53	5
Marital Status			
Married	20	47	2
Single	63	41	1
Widowed	0	0	0
Divorced	10	6	0
Separated	7	6	0
Education			
Attended Grade School	0	0	0
Grade School Graduate	0	0	0

Attended High School	0	12	0
High School Graduate	33	41	0
Attended College	40	41	0
College Graduate	27	6	1
Business School	10	29	0
Years on Last Job			
Less than 1	50	0	– 5
1 to 1½	7	35	2
1½ to 2½	37	12	– 1
2½ to 3	0	6	0
More than 3	10	35	2
Years of Experience			
0	3	18	0
Less than 1	20	0	– 1
1 to 2	20	0	– 1
2½ to 3	30	0	– 3
Over 3	27	71	5

BIO-DATA

Sometimes, when a management wants to appoint an existing employee to a higher position, it may ask him to submit his necessary bio-data for consideration at the time of selection or interview. In such circumstances, an employee need not fill in an application blank. Such bio-data may also be got from different organisations having good employees for whom chances of advancement in their own organisation are very bleak.

CHART 6.5
Bio-Data of Mr. X

Name: ....Sex: ....

Date of Birth:.................................Age: ....

Father's Name:............................ Address: ....

Educational Qualifications:...

Exams Passed	Institution	From	To	University	Marks Obtained	Subjects Offered	Division Obtained
1	2	3	4	5	6	7	8

Previous Experience:	Employed in what Capacity	During Period	Reason for Leaving	Salary Grade
9	10	11	12	13

Extra curricular activities/hobbies: ....

Salary expected: ....

References (Three): 1 ....

2. ....

3. ....

Any other fact ....

....

....

Place: ....

Date: .... Signature of the applicant

---

BIOGRAPHICAL INVENTORIES

These inventories are specially constructed for the purpose of predicting success in a given type of work. The items included are those which a person, who conducts an analysis, believes to have some potential as predictors. A typical inventory contains a large number of items, utilizes a multiple-choice format exclusively, and deals with those matters that are normally not covered in an application blank. Such items deal with experiences in early life, hobbies, social relations, values and opinions, etc.

CHART 6.6
Typical Biographical Inventory Questions

Classification Data:

What is your present marital status?

1. Single
2. Married, no children
3. Married, with one or more children
4. Widowed
5. Separated or divorced

Health:

Have you every suffered from?

1. Allergy
2. Asthama
3. High blood pressure
4. Tuberculosis
5. Ulcers
6. None of these

Human Relations:

What are your relations with your neighbours?

1. Not interested in them
2. Like them but seldom see them
3. Visit each-other's homes occassionally
4. Spend a lot of time together

Parental Home Childhood. Teens:

With whom did you live for most of the time before you were 18?

1. Parents
2. Relatives
3. Hostel

Personal Attributes:

How creative do you think you are?

1. Highly creative
2. Somewhat more creative than most in your field
3. Moderately creative
4. Somewhat less creative than most in your field

Present Home, Spouse and Children:

Regarding moving from location to location, my wife

1. Would go willingly wherever I do
2. Would not move under any circumstances
3. Would move only if it were absolutely necessary
4. Has not told me how she feels about moving
5. Not married

Self-Impressions:

Do your generally do your best?

1. At whatever job you are doing
2. Only in what you are interested
3. Only when it is demanded of you

Recreation, Hobbies, Interest:

How do you pass your leisure time?

1. Going to a movie
2. Visiting friends
3. Playing games
4. Reading light material
5. Gardening
6. Stamp collecting
7. Others

Values, Opinions and Preferences:

Which one of the following seems most important to you?

1. Having a pleasant home and family life
2. Getting a challenging and exacting job
3. Forging ahead in the world
4. Making the most of your particular ability

Work:

How do you feel about travelling on business?

1. Would you enjoy it tremendously?
2. Would you like to do some travelling?
3. Would travelling be troublesome if it were necessary?
4. Do you definitely dislike travelling?

PHYSICAL EXAMINATION

Certain jobs require unusual stamina, strength or tolerance of hard working conditions. A physical examination reveals whether or not a candidate possesses these qualities. It brings out deficiencies, not as a basis of rejection but as a positive aid to selective placement and as indicating restrictions on his transfer to other positions.

Purpose: A physical examination serves the following purposes:

(i) It gives us an indication whether a candidate is physically able to perform the job. Those who are physically unfit are rejected.

(ii) It discovers existing disabilities and obtains a record of the employee's health at the time of hiring so that the question of the company's responsibilities (both legal and ethical) may be settled in the event a workman's compensation claim for an injury is preferred.

(iii) It prevents the employment of those who suffer from some type of contagious diseases.

(iv) It places properly those people who are otherwise employable but whose physical handicaps may necessitate assignment only to specific jobs.

The basic purpose of a physical examination is to place persons in jobs which they can handle without injury or damage to their health.

Candidates are medically examined either by the company's physician or by a medical officer approved by the company for the purpose.

Contents: Usually a medical check-up involves a quick examination of the eyes, ears and throat. Bronchial weakness is looked for as an indication of nervousness, tuberculosis and hernia. Heart and lungs may also be thoroughly examined.

It is worth noting that those to whom heavy manual work is to be assigned are tested for physical strength as well as physical health; while those who are to be placed in the office should be particularly tested for eyesight, the condition of the pulmonary system and for signs of tubercular tendencies.

Stone and Kendall have outlined the following contents of physical examination:[29]

(a) The applicant's *medical history* is obtained by interviews between the applicant and the medical officer.

(b) *Physical measurements* such as height, weight, chest and the abdominal circumferences.

(c) *General examination,* including an examination of the skin, musculature and joints.

(d) *Examination of special senses* of the applicant — visual and auditory activity to be checked closely.

(e) *Clinical examination* of eyes, ears, nose, throat and teeth.

(f) *Examination of chest and lungs.*

(g) *Check-up of blood pressure and heart.*

(h) *Laboratory tests to urine, blood, etc.*

(i) *X-Ray examination of chest, and other parts of the body.*

(j) Specialist's test, such as basal metabolic rate or consultation by a specialist.

(k) A *neuro-psychiatric examination* particularly when medical history or a physician's observations indicate an adjustment problem.

CHART 6.7
Specimen of a Medical Report

Name: .... Age ....Sex ....
Address: ....
General Appearance: ....Height :.............Weight ....
Eyes (R):...................................Ears(R): ....
(L):...................................(Hears with) (L):...
Nose: ....Throat ....
Neck: ....Teeth: ....
Pulse: ....Blood Pressure: ....
Chest Contour ....Lungs ....
Abdomen: ....Urine:..
Spine ....Stool ....
Blood Group ....Skin ....
Identification Mark ....
Past Medical History ....
Notes:...
Place: .... Date:...

(Signature of the Doctor)

In some organisations, the procedure for the physical examination and selection is a farce. A candidate is often approved within a few minutes and without having really been examined by a qualified physician. In other organisations, particularly when the appointment of a top executive is being considered, the medical examination is very comprehensive and thorough, and determines whether the candidate should or should not be offered the job.

REFERENCE CHECKS

The use of references is common in most selection procedures, for it involves only a little time and money, and minimum of effort.[3]

The procedure places reliance on the evaluation of former employers, friends and professional personnel. Checks on references are made by mail or by telephone, and occasionally in person, or by using a reference form, which require specific answers.

CHART 6.8

A Sample Reference Form

Mr.. has applied to us for the post of ....

He claims to have been in your employ from..................to ....Having had an opportunity to observe the above candidate as an employee your frank answers to the questions on the reverse side of this card will be valuable to us, and would be greatly appreciated. We assure you that your replies will be kept strictly confidential.

REVERSE

1. When was the applicant in your employ? From..............................To..............................
2. Positions held...
3. Attendance Regular? Yes.........................No.................If not, what was the cause of absence?
4. Liked by his co-workers (well-liked, acceptable, sometimes criticised)?...............................
5. Evaluation of his performance..
6. Asked to resign or resigned voluntarily?...
7. Would you re-employ him in a similar position? Yes.....................No.................. If not why?
8. What is your knowledge of the applicant's character, ability and dependability, how? .... what? ....

The opinions of previous employers and others, who have known the applicant, are generally useful in getting a picture of his potential performance in a particular job when background checks are used. It is important to get more than two viewpoints. It is vitally important that references should indicate how long and in what capacity the referees had the contact with the applicant.

However, some employers are of the opinion that references are useless because a referee rarely gives an unfavourable opinion about the application. But other employers consider reference-checking to be an integral part of the total overall selection and assessment programme.

EMPLOYMENT INTERVIEW

INTERVIEWING CANDIDATE IS AN IMPORTANT STEP IN THE SELECTION PROCESS

An interview is a procedure designed to get information from a person and to assess his potential for the job he is being considered, on the basis of oral responses by the applicant to oral inquiries by the Interviewer. Interviewer is a formal in-depth conversation with the applicant, to evaluate his suitability. It is one of the most important tool in the selection process. This tool is used when interviewing skilled, technical, professional and even managerial employees. It involves two-way exchange of information. The interviewer learns about the applicant and the candidate learns about the employer. Although an indispensable management tool interviews do have shortcomings.

Objectives of Interviews: Interview helps: *(i)* to obtain additional information from the candidate; *(ii)* facilitates giving to the candidate information about the job, company, its policies, products etc.; *(iii)* to asses the basic suitability of the candidate.

The selection interview can be

(i) One to one between the candidate and the interviewer;

(ii) Two or more interviewers by employers representatives — sequential;

(iii) By a panel of selections, i.e., by more than representative of the employer.

The sequential interview involves a series of interviews; each interviewer meeting the candidate separately.

The panel interview consists of two or more interviews meeting the candidate together.

Types of interviews: Interviews can be classified in four ways according to:

(a) degree of structure

(b) purpose

(c) content

(d) the way in which it is conducted.

Interviews are of the following types:

(1) *unstructured or non directive:* in which you ask questions as they come to mind. There is no set format to follow;

(2) *structured or directive:* in which the questions and acceptable responses are specified in advance. The responses are rated for appropriateness of content.

Structured and non-structured interviews have their pros and cons. In structured interviews all applicants are generally asked all required questions by all interviewers. Structured interviews are generally more valid. However structured interviews do not allow the flexibility to pursue points of interests as they develope.

The purpose of interview: A selection interview is a type of interview designed to predict future job performance, on the basis of applicant's responses to the oral questions asked to him.

A stress interview is a special type of selection interview in which the applicant is made uncomfortable by series of awkward and rude questions. The aim of stress interview is supposedly to identify applicant's low or high stress tolerance. In such a interview the applicant is made uncomfortable by throwing him on the defensive by series of frank and often discourteous questions by the interviewer.

The content of interview can be of a type in which individual's ability to project a situation is tested. This is a situation type interview. In Job-related interview, interviewer attempts to assess the applicant's past behaviours for job related information, but most questions are not considered situational.

In a behaviour interview a situation in described and candidates are asked how they behaved in the past in such a situation.

While in situational interviews candidates are asked to describe how they would react to situation today or tomorrow. In the behavioural interview they are asked to describe how they did react to the situation in the past.

Are interviews useful? While interviews are used by all employers, statistical analysis indicates their validity is actually mixed. Recent studies indicate that the key to the usefulness of an interview depends upon the manner in which it is administered.

The following conclusions based on a recent study of interview, is worthnoting, "with respect to predicting job performance, situational interviews yield a higher mean validity than do job related (behavioural) interviews. Behaviour interviews yield a higher mean validity than the psychological interviews."

Structural interviews, regardless of contents are more valid than unstructured interviews for predicting job performance.

Both in structured or unstructured interviews, individual interviews (by competent interviewer) are more valid than are panel interviews, in which more than one interviewer provide ratings in one sitting.

Structured situational interviews, conducted on one to one basis appear to be most useful for predicting job performance.

Unstructured interviews in general and panel interviews are somewhat less useful for predicting job performance.

HOW TO CONDUCT THE STRUCTURED INTERVIEW

In an effective structured interview, a series of hypothetical job oriented questions with predetermined answers that are consistently asked of applicants for a particular job.

It should be conducted by a committee of persons familiar with job and based on actual job duties.

The interviewer should follow the following steps:

1. Job analysis in the form of job duties required knowledge, skills, abilities and other qualifications should be proposed.
2. Rating the important duties on its importance to job success should be written down.
3. Develop interview questions based on list of job duties.
4. Develop model answers to these questions and make rating scale for each question with specific answers to these questions.

These types of interviews are generally conducted by a panel consisting of three or more persons. Before the interview starts the job duties, questions and model answers are distributed to the panel members.

SOME GUIDELINES FOR CONDUCTING AN INTERVIEW

1. Plan the interview: A quiet place, structured questions, rating scales should be prepared.

2. Establish rapport: with the candidate by putting the candidate at ease and start the interview by asking non-controversial questions and making him feel comfortable, not tense, relaxed.

3. Ask questions: which are prepared before — it is suggested to actually write down the questions on a sheet of paper (to be used by the panel members) and record the answers by the candidate.

4. Close the interview: by asking the candidate if he has any questions to ask. Try to end the interview on a positive note — the candidate should be told what steps you intend to take.

(5) Review the interview after the candidate leaves: You should be able to summarise the candidate's general strength and limitations and be able to draw conclusion about the person's intellectual capacity, knowledge/experience, motivation and personality.

This will help you to match the candidate to the job.

PLACEMENT

After an employee has been recruited he is provided with basic background information about the employer, working conditions and the information necessary to perform his job satisfactorily. The new employee's initial orientation helps him perform better by providing him information of the company rules, and practices.

Orientation is one component of the new employee socialization process. Socialization is the ongoing process of instilling in all new employees prevailing attitudes, standards, values, patterns of behaviour that are expected by the organisation and its departments.

Placement is a process in which the new employee is allocated the job he is hired for and it is an assignment of a new employee to the job. The job he is assigned to may be (i) independent (ii) sequential (he may be one of the team who has to perform in sequential order the work he is expected to do) (iii) or may be in the pool where he works with others to complete the assigned work whether independent, sequential or team work, he has to adjust himself to the new environment which includes other employees in the department.

Placement is the responsibility of the superior or colleague with whom the employee has to work. The human resources department should monitor the right placement so that the new entrant settles down satisfactorily in the work place.

SUMMARY

In the selection and placement process the human resources department plays a crucial role of selecting the right man for the right job and inducting him into the organisation or department successfully. The process includes interviewing the candidate to decide his suitability for the job. The process of interview, rendering tests, assessing the applicant for the job and important components of selection task. The fine tuning in the selection process is obtained by knowing the job itself, through job analysis and matching the person by an objective interviews. Induction, placement are equally important components of the selection process. A written documented paper on placement process will assist the personnel man to help the new employee settle down on his job.

❑ ❑ ❑

SECTION - II

7. Promotions, Transfers, and Career Planning
8. Employee Training and Development
9. Performance Appraisal
10. Wage Salary Administration, Incentives, Fringe Benefits and Services
11. Human Resources Development (HRD)
12. Participation in Management
13. Personnel Manual

7

Promotions, Transfers and Career Planning

INTRODUCTION

Promotion, transfer and separation are activities through which an adjustment in the size of workforce of an enterprise can be made to cope with the changing situations. Such adjustments in work force may be needed to meet special situations, such as changes in organisational structure involving regrouping of jobs, changes in the jurisdictions of the departments and relocation of individuals, jobs and departments; fluctuations in volume of production and employment due to introduction of new or complete stoppage of old products, services, processes, methods, etc. The three functions — promotion, transfer and separation — provide work force flexibility and mobility to suit the requirements of the organisation. These functions can be accomplished informally or formally. Usually formal systems are adopted to secure operative consistency and efficiency.

PROMOTIONS

"Promotion" is a term which covers a change and calls for greater responsibilities, and usually involves higher pay and better terms and conditions of service and, therefore, a higher status or rank.

According to Scott and Clothier: "A promotion is the transfer of an employee to a job which pays more money or one that carries some preferred status."

A promotion may be defined as an upward advancement of an employee in an organisation to another job, which commands better pay/wages, better status/ prestige, and higher opportunities/challenges, responsibility, and authority, better working environment, hours of work and facilities, and a higher rank.

Promotion is a bit different from *upgrading,* which is concerned with minor promotions, promotions within grade or horizontal promotions.

PURPOSE OF PROMOTIONS

A promotion is a vertical move in rank and responsibility. Involved in a promotion may be some measure of skill; and responsibility, e.g., it may be from a machinist B grade to a machinist A grade, or it may involve an entirely different type of work, for example, from salesman to a sales manager or from a fitter Grade III to a fitter Grade II, or from a clerk to the post of a section in-charge. Promotions are usually given:

(i) To put the worker in a position where he will be of greater value to the company and where he may derive increased personal satisfaction and income from his work;

(ii) To remove a worker from his job as an alternative to avoid the embarrassment of firing or demoting him;

(iii) To recognise an individual's performance and reward him for his work so that he may have an incentive to forge ahead. Employees will have little motivation if better jobs are reserved for outsiders;

(iv) To increase an employee's organistional effectiveness; and employee loyalty.

(v) To build up morale, loyalty, and a sense of belonging on the part of the employees when it is brought home to them that they would be promoted if they deserve it;

(vi) To promote job satisfaction among the employees and give them an opportunity motivation, for unbroken, continuous service;

(vii) To provide a process of "selective socialization." Employees whose personalities and skills enable them to fit into an organisation's human relations programme tend to stay on; while those whose personalities with those of the organisation clash tend to leave;

(viii) To attract suitable and competent workers for the organisation;

(ix) To create among employees a feeling of contentment with their present conditions and encourage them to succeed in the company.

Watkins, Dodd and others mention that purposes of promotion are:

(a) To furnish an effective incentive for initiative, enterprise and ambition;

(b) To conserve proved skill, training and ability;

(c) To reduce discontent and unrest;

(d) To attract suitable and competent employees; and

(e) To suggest logical training for advancement of an individual.

As Yoder and others observe, "promotion provides incentive to initiative, enterprise, and ambition; minimises discontent and unrest; attracts capable individuals; necessitates logical training of advancement and forms an effective reward for loyalty and co-operation, long service, etc."

Promotions have a salutary effect on the satisfaction of the promoted person's needs for esteem, belonging and security. They also afford an opportunity for greater self-actualization through more varied and challenging assignments. It helps in retaining competent, talented, useful employees.

TYPES OF PROMOTIONS

Promotions may be *multiple chain promotions* which provide for a systematic linking of each position to several others. Such promotions identify multi-promotional opportunities through clearly defined avenues of approach to and exit from each position in the organisation.

In a *up or out promotion,* a person must either earn a promotion or seek employment elsewhere. Many universities and other organisations follow this practice. Such promotions often lead to termination of services.

Dry promotions are those which are given in lieu of increases in compensation, i.e., when all compensation is adjusted upward to keep pace with the cost of living we have dry promotions.

Promotion becomes a delicate problem not in the matter of selection of the right incumbent for the right job, but it poses a constant challenge to executives at all levels and impels them to chalk our a well-thought-out programme by which the best and the most capable individuals may find an opportunity to go up to the top. The procedure for promotion, therefore, starts right at the bottom from the shop floor and ends with the managing director of a company.

All promotions should be carefully arranged so that the promoted person proves himself useful and successful in the new assignment.

PROMOTION PROGRAMME AND PROCEDURE

A promotion programme consists of the following basic elements:

Deciding the Policy: The management must provide realistic opportunities which will encourage promising employees to take the risks involved in moving upward. It must not discourage valuable employees from seeking advancement by making service in an unpopular job a prerequisite for promotion. It must provide for employees who do outstanding work but who are unwilling to take on new and additional responsibilities. It must provide alternatives for professionals who are reluctant to assume supervisory responsibilities.

"Organisation that have failed to reward excellence in service, or that have relied too heavily on personal relationships or length of service, suffer in terms of both efficiency and morale."

Each organisation needs to strike a balance between the internal sources of personnel promotion and external source (through recruitment) on the one hand and between merit and ability as against length of service on the other. "The organisation that fails to develop a satisfactory procedure is bound to pay a severe penalty in terms of administrative costs, misallocation of personnel, low morale, and ineffectual performance, among both non-managerial employees and their supervisors."

Since promotions mean advancement for some, the promotional process itself must ensure that successful candidates are sufficiently acceptable to their subordinates and others so that leadership in, and effective administrative of organisational progress is unhindered and unhampered. A management should frame the policy on the basis of which promotions may be made.

A sound promotion policy must satisfy the following criteria:

(a) *It should enjoy consistency,* i.e., it will be applied irrespective of the persons concerned. Consistency demands that the policy should be so correlated to career planning that there should not be a sudden spurt of promotion in the organisation conferring premature benefits on a number of persons, followed by a long period of absence of promotion.

(b) *It should be fair and impartial,* i.e., the management should be able to remove all suspicion of arbitrariness, adhocism, improvisation to suit particular individuals, nepotism, etc.

(c) *Promotion should be a planned activity,* i.e., the management should make a correct assessment of the requirements or opportunities of promotion within the organisation so that there is no phenomenon of 'bunching' or no period of 'promotional drought', i.e., no over-estimation or under-estimation.

The promotion policy should involve *six elements* as follows:

1. *Promotion Policy Statement,* which should consider whether vacancies are primarily to be filled up from within an organisation or by recruitment from outside. Is any preferential treatment to be given to direct recruits? Would it be sound to deny promotion to otherwise qualified personnel? Whether an increase in pay is to be given? if so, when and how much? Usually, internal promotions are preferred over external recruitment and increase is given at the time of promotion, otherwise promotion is meaningless.

2. *Establish as Plan of Jobs,* i.e., decide on what basis promotions are to be given. Whether on performance appraisal, or on the basis of confidential records, or job and post-bid system. Which positions are to be filled up? Usually promotions are decided on the basis of performance appraisals. "Job-post and bid system", i.e., positing of job vacancies indicating job titles, duties, pay and qualifications on company notice boards, is also utilised.

3. *Trace Transfer Routes,* i.e., having some type of formal and systematic promotion channels. Ladders giving paths of advancement, *promotional charts, opportunity charts or fortune sheets* clearly distinguish each job and by lines and arrows, connect various jobs; and show the lines/routes of advancement up to and away from them. *Stepping jobs* should be clearly identified and recorded on paper. *Dead-end jobs* should be labelled and the path upward well marked.

4. *Prepare Employees for Advancement, through the Provision of some Training,* either on the job in professional/technical institutions, or through job rotation, multiple management, under-study and conferences.

5. *Communicate the Policy,* the organisation should communicate its promotion policy either in the form of a manual or in the agreement signed with the union or in the form of a set of Standing Orders. To have a policy and not to communicate it to the employees will only create suspicions and misgivings. However, for higher level personnel a precise formulation of such a policy may not be effective.

6. *Detailed Personnel and Service Records are Kept Ready* on the basis of which promotions may be made.

The following indices are available for judging whether candidates are suitable for promotion:

The *margin of performance* on his present job, i.e., does he run it with ease and with margin to spare or is he barely able to manage his job?

Flexibility or versatility, i.e., has been successful on different types of jobs requiring different skills and different abilities, or does he seem to be only interested in a restricted field?

Intelligence, i.e., how does he think? How has he learnt on work he has carried out?

Equipment, i.e., how compatible are his education, literacy, expression and personality with the critical needs of the job?

Motivation, i.e., what are his wants? What is important for him? What are his goals, his objectives in work and life?

Team-member— how successful he has been working in a group and whether he has qualities of leadership.

PROMOTION SYSTEM

Thus, a promotion system involves clear-cut definitions of line of future advancement, detailed personnel records, specific promotion plans, definite allocation of responsibility for identifying promotable individuals and a centralised coordination of promotion function.

Beach has very aptly described promotion systems for different categories of personnel in the organisation. He observes: "For unskilled and semi-skilled workers, entry is made into 'labour pool' and thereafter upgrading takes place on the basis of seniority or a combination of both seniority and ability. The skilled craftsmen are recruited as helpers or apprentices and thereafter upward mobility occurs up to position of foremen, inspectors or production co-ordinators. Entry in clerical jobs is through appointment as clerks, typists or stenographers and subsequently promotions are made to higher positions such as that of secretaries or administrative assistants. In professional jobs, entry is made as assistant engineers, engineers, senior engineers, project engineers or even managers. Jobs in managerial positions are filled up by individuals who enter as management trainees or assistant supervisors, finally they are promoted to middle level management positions and ultimately to top management positions."

Promotions may be based on either the "rank-in-the-job" or "rank-in-the-man." In former system, the content of the job including level of skill, efforts and responsibility form the basis. In this system emphasis is laid on job analysis, job evaluation, organisational planning, etc. These determine the pay and status in the organisation. In the latter system, emphasis is put on proficiency of the individuals. It determines the position level in the hierarchy of career pattern.

PROMOTION POLICY

The usual policy is to take merit into consideration. Sometimes length of service, education, training courses completed, previous work history, etc., are factors which are given weight while deciding on a promotion. Although promotions are made on the basis of ability, hard work, co-operation, merit, honesty, many informal influences are powerful determinants of a promotional policy.

For higher posts, persons are picked by the top executives:

(i) Who think and feel just as he does;

(ii) Who value loyalty to him and to the organisation; and

(iii) Who have social, political, economic and religious interests similar to his own.

Top executives lend to choose those who are carbon copies of themselves.

Seniority versus Merit: "Seniority" refers to length of service in the company or in its various plants, or in its departments, or in a particular position. Under *straight plant-wise seniority* in all jobs, promotions go to the oldest employees, provided that he is fit for the job. *Occupational seniority* may be within a department, within a division or in the entire plant.

Seniority offers certain rights and benefits. These are:

(a) Some rights are based on competitive seniority among employees. Rights to promotion, transfer, lay-off and recall are such examples.

(b) Other benefits have nothing to do with one man relative to another, e.g., a man may be entitled to have 15 days' casual leave in a year, a pension after 30 years and a certain amount of sick leave after 6 months' service.

There is a great controversy on the question of whether promotions should be given on the basis of seniority or ability. Trade unions are of the view the promotions should be given on the basis of seniority, while managements favour promotions on the basis of merit and ability.

If a promotion is given to a qualified man in recognition of his performance or with a view to creating an incentive for him, then it should be based on his ability.

If, on the other hand, promotion is given to recognise and reward senior employees, then it should be on the basis of seniority.

The most widely used basis for promotion combines both ability and seniority. The best policy would be to ensure that whenever there are two employees of equal seniority, ability or merit should be the deciding factor in a promotion. Where, however, there are two employees of almost equal competence, seniority should be the decisive factor. Such a policy would satisfy the management which prefers ability, and trade unions which prefer seniority.

ARGUMENTS FOR AND AGAINST PROMOTION BY SENIORITY SYSTEMS

Promotion by seniority is preferred by trade unions and most employees because:

(a) The system is simple to understand and operate. All employees are assured that promotion will come automatically when it is due.

(b) It satisfies the personal aspirations of the employees for growth, builds morale and is conducive to better labour-management relations.

(c) It leads to an optimum utilisation of the existing work force by training and development.

(d) This system is much more economical than open market recruitment or recruitment by negotiation with other candidate belonging to another organisation.

(e) The management will have a known man of good performance in a higher position than take a risk in bringing an unknown outsider.

But this system suffers from certain drawbacks too such as:

(a) The internal sources may be quite inadequate, and possibilities are that people who do not quite come up to the requirements of higher jobs, may be promoted.

(b) Since the working system and technology change very fast, it is necessary that new blood should be infused with new and up-to-date knowledge and ideas, which the older persons in the organisation may be lacking.

(c) The worth of an individual is not appreciated and given due recognition. This generates frustration and may constrain a good employee to leave the organisation.

(d) When there are wholesale promotions, promotion from within might cause disorganisation and upset the working of the organisation.

On the other hand, the system of *promotion by merit* enjoys these benefits:

(a) It brings rewards for meritorious work, extra competence, achievement and initiative;

(b) It encourages an employee to work hard so that he may get an opportunity for advancement in the organisation;

(c) It leads to increased productivity, for individuals are satisfied that their merit and competence will be properly appreciated and rewarded.

PRACTICE IN INDIA

In India, in some companies, promotions are made on the basis of merit, potential and seniority. Internal Promotions are also granted on the basis of performance, commitment and loyalty.

In public sector organisations, elaborate rules exist for regulating the seniority of employees in different service cadres. Promotions are made from this list. But often, due to political pressures, the rules are violated and a person standing much lower in the list is given priority over the senior-most men.

In the private sector enterprises, the promotions are generally not based upon any clear-cut rule. Efficiency is the main consideration, unless it is a family enterprise where relationship with the proprietors or patronage might play a part. But even there only a limited number of posts would be filled upon the basis of relationship or by way of patronage. Even in such firms where employees are concerned there is generally a well-defined promotion policy and nepotism is avoided, as far as possible, where the employees are well organised. The rule followed is: "*Promote the best man available.*"

While making promotions, the management must ensure that:

(a) Proper talents are first made available by a correct programme of recruitment;

(b) Employees are enabled to satisfy their own aspirations within the framework of the company's own objectives and projects and

(c) A programme of training, development and career planning, coupled with periodic assessment is followed in accordance with established practice.

It is worth noting that in a developing economy like India, with rapid technological advances and need for training and education it is not always possible to promote the older workers who can neither be adequately trained nor are willing to be exposed to new concepts, ideas and methods of work. As for the higher level promotions, only in large organisation can a policy of promotions from within be practicable; but even there such promotions cannot be confined entirely to the existing personnel of the organisation, unless management development and career planning are an essential part of the company's promotion policy.

DEMOTION

'Demotion' has been defined as "the assignment of an individual to a job of lower rank and pay usually involving lower level of work and responsibility."

In other words, *demotion refers to the lowering down of the status, salary and responsibilities of an employee.* It is used as a punitive measure when there are serious breaches of duty on the part of an employee when it is often a preliminary to a dismissal. When an employee is demoted, his pride suffers a more severe jolt than it does when he is superseded by his junior.

CAUSES OF DEMOTION

Demotions may be caused by factors beyond an employee's control:

(i) When departments are combined and jobs eliminated, employees are often required to accept lower-level position until normalcy is restored. Such demotions are not a black mark against an employee.

(ii) Inadequacy on the part of the employees in terms of job performance, attitude and capability — as happens when an individual finds it difficult to meet job requirement standards, following his promotion; and

(iii) When, because of a change in technology, methods and practices, old hands are unable to adjust, or when employees, because of ill health or personal reasons, cannot do their job properly.

(iv) Demotion is also used as a disciplinary measure.

Demotion Policy: Yoder, Heneman, Turnbull and Stone have suggested a five-fold policy in regard to demotion practice:

(i) A clear and reasonable list of rules should be framed, violations of which would subject an employee to demotion;

(ii) This information should be clearly communicated to employees;

(iii) There should be a competent investigation of any alleged violation;

(iv) If violations are discovered, there should be a consistent and equitable application of the penalty, preferably by the immediate supervisor;

(v) There should be a provision for review. (In a unionised case, this will be automatic via the grievance procedure; in a non-unionised case, the employer will need to make other provisions for review).

Demotions serve a useful purpose in the sense that they keep the employees alert and alive to their responsibilities and duties.

For persons with a long and meritorious service, there should be no demotion. However, some of their duties and responsibilities may be taken from them and assigned to others. The other alternative is to create a job for the person at the same pay and status but with lower job demands.

A demotion should never be made as a penalty for a violation of the rules of conduct, poor attendance record, or insubordination because such action will not improve the performance of the individual. Only discipline and training can set the things right.

Demotions have a serious impact on the morale and need fulfilment of the employee. Needs for esteem and belonging are frustrated, leading to a defensive behaviour on the part of the person demoted; there is complaining, emotional turmoil, inefficiency or resignation. Hence, demotions are made quite infrequently. Many managers prefer to discharge employees rather than face the problems arising from demotion.

TRANSFER

Yoder and associates have defined transfer as "a lateral shift causing movement of individuals from one position to another usually without involving any marked change in duties, responsibilities, skills needed or compensation."

A transfer is a horizontal or lateral movement of an employee from one job, section, department, shift, plant or position to another at the same or another place where his salary, status and responsibility are the same. It generally does not involve a promotion, demotion or a change in job status other than movement from one job or place to another. Transfers can be regular and frequent to suit work situations.

PURPOSES OF TRANSFERS

Transfers are generally effected to build up a more satisfactory work team and to achieve the following purposes:

(a) To satisfy such needs of an organisation as may arise out of a change in the quantity of production, fluctuations in work requirements, and changes in the organisational structure; the introduction of new lines of production, the dropping of existing product lines, the reallocation of, or reduction in the work force due to a shortage or a surplus in the same section so that lay-offs may be avoided; filling in of the vacancies which may occur because of separations or because of the need for suitable adjustments in business operations. Such transfers are known as *production transfers, flexibility transfers,* or *organisational transfers.* The purpose of such transfers is to stabilise employment in an organisation. They are generally controlled centrally through and by the personnel department.

(b) To meet an employee's own request, when he feels uncomfortable on the job because of his dislike of his fellow workers, or because better opportunities for his future advancement do not exist there, or because of family circumstances which may compel him to change the place of his residence. Such transfers generally have their root in faulty selection and erroneous placement, and are known as *personal transfers.* They enable employees to feel at home in the work of their choice.

(c) To utilise properly the services of an employee when he is not performing satisfactorily and adequately and when the management feels that he may be more useful or suitable elsewhere, where his capacities would be better utilised. Such transfers are called *remedial transfers.* They act as a follow-up measure of the selection-and-placement procedure and help employees to adjust themselves to suitable jobs.

(d) To *increase the versatility of the employee,* by shifting him from one job to another so that he may have ample opportunities for gaining a varied and broader experience of work. Such transfers are known as *versatility transfers.* They

make it possible for an employee to enjoy the facility of job enrichment, which in turn gives to the management a more effective and experienced employee for a higher job.

(e) To adjust the work force of one plant with that of another particularly when one is closed down for reasons beyond the control of the employer. Such transfers are known as *plant transfers* and are generally effected on humanitarian grounds to ensure that persons who have been long in service of an organisation are not thrown out of employment.

(f) To replace a new employee by an employee who has been in the organisation for a sufficiently long time. Such transfers are known as replacement transferred from night shift to morning shift or from the first to the second shift (as in the case of women workers who may like to look after their children and do the necessary domestic work in the morning hours). Such transfers are known as *shift transfers.*

(g) To help employees work according to their convenience so far as timings are concerned; for example, an employee is transferred from night shift to morning shift or from the first to the second shift (as in the case of women workers who may like to look after their children and do the necessary domestic work in the morning hours). Such transfers are known as *shift transfer.*

(h) To penalise the employee transfers are also done, under which either a difficult trade union activist or intriguer or sealawyer may be transferred to a remote branch or office where he cannot continue his activities. In Government organisations, this practice is widespread, and is also preferred by the employee to the grim alternative of disciplinary action.

(i) Transfer for the maintenance of a tenure system. In senior administrative services of the Government and also in industries, or where there is a system of annual intake of management trainees such transfers are common. Here the employee holds a certain job for a fixed tenure but he is made to move from job to job with a view to enabling him to acquire a variety of experience and skills and also to ensure that he does not get involved in politicking informal groups.

Scott and others have classified transfers according to:

(i) The convenience of the company:

- *(a) Temporary* transfers arising from temporary absenteeism; shifts in the work load; vacation;
- *(b) Permanent* transfers arising out of shifts in the work load; vacancies which need the special skill or ability of the transferred employee.

(ii) The convenience of the employee:

- *(a) Temporary* transfers arising from the ill health of, or an accident to an employee; for family reasons or for taking care of some private affair;
- *(b) Permanent* transfers arising out of ill health or accident; out of outside interest — for example, for the purpose of attending a professional school or similar activities; out of family consideration; out of a desire to learn a particular skill.

TRANSFER POLICY

Every organisation should have a just and impartial transfer policy which should be known to each employee. The responsibility for effecting transfers is usually entrusted to an executive with power to prescribe the conditions under which requests for transfers are to be approved.

For successful transfer policies, it is necessary to have a proper organisation structure, job description and job analysis indicating levels of responsibilities. Care should be taken to ensure that frequent or large-scale transfers are avoided by laying down adequate selection and placement procedures for the purpose.

(i) Specifically clarify the types of transfers and the conditions under which these will be made;

(ii) Locate the authority in some officer who may initiate and implement transfers;

(iii) Indicate whether transfers can be made only within a sub-unit or also between departments, divisions/plants and at different locations;

(iv) Indicate the basis for transfer, i.e., whether it will be based on seniority or on skill and competence or any other factor;

(v) Decide the terms to be offered to the transferee (e.g., same, better);

(vi) Intimate the fact of transfer to the person concerned well in advance and counsel him to accept it;

(vii) Transfer should be in writing and duly communicated to all concerned;

(viii) Not be made frequently.

In making transfers, the usual practice that is followed is to pay to the employee the actual cost of moving the household to the place of transfer and bear other expenses involved.

PROCEDURE FOR TRANSFER

Intra-departmental transfers or transfers within the same section of the same department are decided by the foreman or plant manager, and these are effected without the issue of any transfer order to the employee. He may be given oral instructions. The personnel manager, however, must be informed of such transfers.

Inter-departmental transfers or transfers from one department to another are decided by mutual consultations among the departmental heads/plant managers when such transfers are of a permanent nature or of long duration. Written orders, signed by the personnel manager are issued to the employee.

Transfers from one place or unit to another place or unit, involving a considerable change in working conditions and cost to the company, have to be made in writing, after giving due notice to the employees. But, as far as possible, such transfers are generally discouraged.

CAREER PLANNING

INTRODUCTION

Individual's Career Planning assumed greater significance with the growth and speed of knowledge, phenomenal increase in educational and training facilities and widespread increase in job opportunities. Similarly, organisational career planning also gained importance with the change in technology, human needs, values and aspirations, increase in organisational size, complexity and number of openings at different levels. Reasons for interest in career management are presented in Chart 7.1.

CHART 7.1

Reasons for Interest in Career Planning

Several factors account for the growing interest in career Planning

1. Technological change and obsolescence have resulted in layoffs and underemployment, causing both individuals and organizations to recognize the need for planning a career and for developing multiple skills.
2. Increased education has created rising expectations about what constitutes a happy and fulfilling life. Employees of all ages, especially younger ones, are demanding greater personal and career autonomy and are less concerned with the demands of the organization.
3. Continuing pressure from policies demands of the ensures not only that firms hire more females and members of protected groups, but also that they plan for the development and steady movement of these individuals through the organization development and growth.
4. Organizations typically lose as many as 30 to 50 per cent of their "younger" employees during the first two years on the job. Similarly, there is a growing trend toward job changes in midcareer as members seek greater career satisfaction and a higher quality of life. Also, organizations are seeking ways to reduce the expensive turn-over as more workers ask, "Am I in the right job?" "Would I be happier doing something else?" This type of question is being asked by all kinds of employees, at all levels.
5. Shortage of capable managers and certain skilled, professional, and technical workers has resulted in organizations looking for ways to develop such personnel from within through career planning and development.

(I) WHAT IS CAREER PLANNING?

A career is all the jobs that are held progressively during one's working life.[1] Edwin B. Flippo defined a career as a sequence of separate but related work activities that provides continuity, order and meaning in a person's life. Douglas T. Hall defined a career as "an individually perceived sequence of attitudes and behaviours associated with work related experiences and activities over the span of the person's life." Career goals are the future positions one strives as part of a career. Career Planning is the deliberate process by which one selects career goals and the path to these goals. Career development is those personal improvements one undertakes to achieve a personal career plan. Career management is the process of designing and implementing goals, plans and strategies to enable the organisation to satisfy employee needs while allowing individuals to achieve their career goals through growth process.

CAREER STAGES

Careers can be analysed based on the career stages. There are five career stages through which most of us have gone through or will go through. These stages include: exploration, establishment, mid-career, late career and decline.

Exploration: Exploration is a career stage that usually ends in one's mid twenties as one makes the transition from college to work. This stage has the least relevance from the organisational point of view as it happens prior to employment.

Establishment: It is a career stage in which one begins to search for work. It includes getting one's first job. It takes many years to search for a right job. The problems of this stage include making mistakes, learning from those mistakes and assuming increased responsibilities.

Mid-career Stage: This stage is marked by a continuous improvement in performance, leveling off in performance or the start of deterioration in performance. Remaining productive at work is a major challenge of career at this stage. Some employees reach their goals at the early stage and go on to even higher heights. These employees are "climbers." Maintenance is another possible outcome. These employees are plateaued, not failed. These employees are technically competent and no longer as ambitious as the climbers.

Late Career: A career stage, in which one is no longer learning about his or her job. He is also not expected to try to outdo his/her levels of performance from previous years. This stage is usually a pleasant stage. The employee enjoys playing a part of the elder statesperson. The employee can rest on his laurels and gain the respect of younger employees.

NEED FOR CAREER PLANNING

Career planning is necessary due to the following reasons:

- To attract competent persons and to retain them in the organisation.
- To provide suitable promotional opportunities.
- To enable the employees to develop and make them ready to meet the future challenges.
- To increase the utilisation of managerial talents within an organisation.
- To correct employee placement.
- To reduce employee dissatisfaction and turnover.
- To improve motivation and morale.

PROCESS OF CAREER PLANNING AND DEVELOPMENT

Steps in Career Planning and Development includes:

(a) Analysis of individual skills, knowledge, abilities, aptitudes etc.

(b) Analysis of career opportunities both within and outside the organisation.

(c) Analysis of career demands on the incumbent in terms of skills, knowledge, abilities, aptitude etc., and in terms of qualifications, experience and training received etc.

(d) Relating specific jobs to different career opportunities.

(e) Establishing realistic goals both short-term and long-term.

(f) Formulating career strategy covering areas of change and adjustment.

(g) Preparing and implementing action plan including acquiring resources for achieving goals.

Various stages of career planning and development are shown in Chart 7.2.

CHART 7.2

Organisational and Individual Career Planning

Organisational Career Planning	*Individual Career Planning*
Human resource needs development	Identifying your interests, skills, and potential
Upgrading of human resources for increased productivity	Identifying your life-goals and career goals
Career paths definition	Developing a written plan (including schedule) to achieve your goals
Assessment of individual potential job	Seeking and obtaining the best first
Matching of organisational needs and career needs	Communicating to management your career plan
Career counseling for quality of work life	Seeking counsel from your manager and from the HR department on career plans and progress
Audit and control of the career planning and development system	Evaluating internal and external (other company) opportunities
	Seeking aid from sponsors
	Making known (publicizing) yourself and your accomplishments

(II) SUCCESSION PLANNING

Survival, growth and efficient continuous existence of an organisation requires a succession of people to fill various important jobs. The purpose of succession planning is to identify, develop and make the people ready to occupy higher level jobs as and when they fall vacant. Higher level jobs fall vacant due to various reasons like retirement, resignation, promotion, death, creation of new position and new assignments.

Succession may be from internal employees or external people. Succession from internal employees is advantageous to the organisation as well as to the internal employees. Organisation can buy the employees loyalty and commitment, belongingness, shared feeling of development along with the organisation by promoting the internal employees. Employees get the benefits of growth in the organisation. The organisation mostly prefer to encourage the growth and development of its employees and as such tend to prefer succession from within.

Organisations, appraise employees potentialities, identify training gaps for future vacancies, develop them for higher and varied jobs. The scope of succession plan would be more when the organisation grows steadily and employees have potentialities to take up higher responsibilities.

Professionally run organisations ask their managers to identify the internal employees having potentialities and develop them in order to occupy their positions as and when they fell vacant.

However, it is necessary to allow the inflow of new blood also. Hence, organisations should also search for outside talent in certain cases like when competent internal people are not available, when major expansion, diversification and growth plans are in offing, complete dependence on either internal source or external source is not advisable to any organisation. Hence, a judicial balance between these two sources should be maintained.

(III) CAREER DEVELOPMENT

STEPS INVOLVED IN ESTABLISHING A CAREER DEVELOPMENT SYSTEM

Career development programmes are not of recent idea.

There are four steps in establishing a career development system. They are: *(i) needs* — defining the present system, *(ii) vision* — determining new directions and possibilities, *(iii) action plan* — deciding on practical first steps, and *(iv) results* — maintaining the change.

Step 1: Needs: This step involves in the conducting a needs assessment as a training programme.

Step 2: Vision: The needs of the career system must be linked with the interventions. An ideal career development system known as the vision links the needs with the interventions.

Step 3: Action Plan: An action plan should be formulated in order to achieve the vision. The support of the top management should be obtained in this process.

Step 4: Results: Career development programme should be integrated with the organisation's on-going employee training and management development programmes. The programme should be evaluated from time to time in order to revise the programme.

Chart 7.3 shows the steps and tasks in establishing a career development system.

CHART 7.3

STEPS AND TASKS IN ESTABLISHING A CAREER DEVELOPMENT SYSTEM

Step 1: Needs: Defining the Present System

Establish roles and responsibilities of employees, managers, and the organization.

Identify needs; establish target groups.

Establish cultural parameters; determine organizational receptivity, support, and commitment to career development.

Assess existing HR programs or structures; consider possible links to a career development program.

Determine prior attempts at solving the problem or need.

Establish the mission or philosophy of the program.

Design and implement needs assessment to confirm the data or collect more data.

Establish indicators or criteria of success.

Step 2: Vision: Determining New Directions and Possibilities

Create a long-term philosophy.

Establish the vision or objetives of the program.

Design interventions for employees, managers, and the organization.

Organize and make available career information needed to support the program.

Step 3: Action Plan: Deciding on Practical First Steps

Assess the plan and obtain support from top management.

Create a pilot program.

Assess resources and competencies.

Establish an advisory group.

Involve advisory group in data gathering, program design, implementation, evaluation, and monitoring.

Step 4: Results: Maintaining the Change

Create long-term formalized approaches.

Publicize the program.

Evaluate and redesign the program and its components.

Consider future trends and directions for the program.

Source: Z.B. Leibowitze, C. Farren, and B.L. Kaye, *Designing Career Development Systems,* San Francisco, CA: Jossey-Bass, 1986, p. 273.

Career development is essential to implement career plan. Career development consists of personal improvements undertaken by the individual employee, training, development and educational programmes provided by the organisation and various institutes. The most important aspect of career development is that every employee must accept his/her responsibility for development. Various career development actions prove useful if an employee is committed to career development. The Career development actions are:

CAREER DEVELOPMENT ACTIONS

(a) Job Performance: Employee must prove that his performance on the job is to the level of standards established, if he wants career progress.

(b) Exposure: Employee's desire for career progress should expose their skills, knowledge, qualifications, achievements, performance etc., to those who take the decision about career progress.

(c) Resignations: Employees may resign the present job in the organisation, if they find that career opportunities elsewhere are better than those of the present organisation.

(d) Change the Job: Employees who put organisational loyalty above career loyalty may change the job in the same organisation if they find that career opportunities in other jobs in the same organisation are better than those in the present job.

(e) Career Guidance: And counselling provides information, advice and encouragement to switch over to other career or organisation, where career opportunities are better.

Career development actions are presented in Chart 7.4

CHART 7.4
Career Development Actions

- Self-assessment tools
  - Career planning workshops
  - Career workbooks
- Individual counselling
- Information services
  - Job posting systems
  - Skills inventories
  - Career ladders and paths
  - Career resource centers
- Organizational assessment programs
  - Assessment centers
  - Psychological testing
  - Promotability forecasts
  - Succession planning
- Developmental programs
  - Assessment centers
  - Job rotation programs
  - Tuition fees paid by the company
  - Internal training programs
  - Mentoring programs
- Programs to address issues confronting employees at various career stages
  - Early-career issues
  - Anticipatory socialization programs
  - Realistic recruitment
  - Employee orientation programs
- Mid-career issues
  - Job rotation
  - Downward moves
  - Developmental programs
- Late-career issues
  - Workshops on older worker issues
  - Preretirement programs
  - Incentives for early retirement
  - Flexible work patterns
- Career programs for special target groups
  - Fast-track or high-potential employees
  - Terminated employees (outplacement programs)
  - Supervisors
- Women, minorities, and employees with disabilities
- Programs to assist employed spouses and parents
  - Policies on hiring couples
  - Work-family programs
  - Job-sharing programs
  - Relaxed policies on transfers and travel
  - Flexible work arrangements
  - Paid and unpaid leave (maternity, paternity)
  - Child-care services

Source: J.E.A. Russell, Career Development Interventions in Organizations, *Journal of Vocational Behaviour,* 38, 1991, p. 244.

PRE-REQUISITES FOR THE SUCCESS OF CAREER PLANNING

- Strong commitment of the top management in career planning, succession planning and development.
- Organisation should develop, expand and diversify its activities at a phased manner.
- Organisation should frame clear corporate goals.
- Organisation should have self-motivated, committed and hard working employees.
- Organisation's goal in selection should be selecting the most suitable man and place him in the right job.
- Organisation should take care of the proper age composition in manpower planning and in selection.
- Organisation should take steps to minimise career stress.
- Organisation should have fair promotion policy.
- Organisation should publicise widely the career planning and development programmes.

KEY ISSUES IN CAREER DEVELOPMENT

It is clear from the above discussion that there are two key issues in career development, viz., external career and internal career. External career is the objective categories used by society and organisation to describe progress of steps through a given occupation. Internal career is the set of steps or stages which make up the individual's own concept of career progression within an occupation.

There is every possibility of mismatching of internal career and external career. Hence, both the organisation and the individual have to gain more insight into the characteristics of the external career and internal career, nature of work, identifying mismatches and adjusting the mismatches through introducing changes in external career structure and internal career structure. There are different roles in career development which are mentioned below:

The Individual:

(1) Should be motivated.

(2) Should accept responsibility for his own growth.

(3) Seek information and resources for his own development.

(4) Should establish career goals and plans.

(5) Utilise opportunities for growth.

(6) Talk to his boss.

The Manager or the Boss:

(1) Provide timely performance feedback.

(2) Provide developmental assignment and support.

(3) Participate in career development discussions.

The organisation:

(1) Communicate Policies, Procedures.

(2) Provide training and development opportunities and information.

(3) Offer if possible variety of career options and provide monitoring.

ADVANTAGES OF CAREER PLANNING AND DEVELOPMENT

For Individuals:

(1) The process of career planning helps the individual to have the knowledge of various career opportunities, his priorities etc.

(2) This knowledge helps him select the career which is suitable to his life styles, preferences, family environment, scope for self-development etc.

(3) It helps the organisation identify internal employees who can be promoted.

(4) Internal promotions, upgradation and transfers motivate the employees, boost up their morale and also result in increased job satisfaction.

(5) Increased job satisfaction enhances employee commitment and creates a sense of belongingness and loyalty to the organisation.

(6) Employee will await his turn of promotion rather than changing to another organisation. This lowers employee turnover.

(7) It improves employees' performance on the job by taping their potential abilities and further employee growth.

(8) It satisfies employee esteem needs.

FOR ORGANISATIONS

A long-term focus of career planning and development will increase the effectiveness of human resource management. More specifically, the advantages of career planning and development for an organisation include:

(i) Efficient career planning and development ensures the availability of human resources with required skill, knowledge and talent.

(ii) The efficient policies and practices improve the organisation's ability to attract and retain highly skilled and talented employees.

(iii) The proper career planning ensures that the women and people belonging to backward communities get opportunities for growth and development.

(iv) The career plan continuously tries to satisfy the employee expectations and as such minimises employee frustration.

(v) By attracting and retaining the people from different cultures, enhances cultural diversity.

(vi) Protecting employees' interest results in promoting organisational good will.

Chart 7.5 Shows benefits of a career development system.

CHART 7.5

Benefits of a Career Development System

Managers/Supervisors	*Employees*	*Organisation*
Increased skill in managing own careers	Helpful assistance with career decisions	Better use of employee skills.
Greater retention of valued employees	Enrichment of present job and increased job satisfaction	Dissemination of information at all organization levels
Better communication between manager and employee	Better communication between employee and manager	Better communication within the organization as a whole
More realistic staff and development planning	More realistic goals and expectations	Greater retention of valued employees
Productive performance appraisal discussions	Better feedback on performance	Expanded public image as a people developer
Greater understanding of the organization	Current information on the firm and the future	Increased effectiveness of personnel systems
Enhanced reputation as a people developer	Greater personal responsibility for career.	Greater clarification of goals of the organization.

Source: Z.B. Leibowitz, C. Ferren, and B. L. Kaye, *Designing Career Development Systems,* San Francisco, CA: Josse-Bass, 1986, p. 7.

LIMITATIONS OF CAREER PLANNING/CAREER PROBLEMS

Despite planning the career, employees face certain career problems. They are:

(1) Dual Career Families: With the increase in career orientation among women, number of female employees is on increase. With this the dual career families have also been on increase. Consequently, one of those family members might face the problem of transfer. This has become a complicated problem to organisations. Consequently other employees may be at disadvantage.

(2) Low Ceiling Careers: Some careers do not have scope for much advancement. Employees cannot get promotions despite their career plans and development in such jobs.

(3) Declining Career Opportunities: Career opportunities for certain categories reach the declining stage due to the influence of the technological or economic factors. Solution for such problem is career shift. For example career opportunities for 'Statisticians' declined due to computerisation. The existing statisticians can overcome this problem by acquiring skills in computer operation.

(4) Career and Life Issues: Further, interaction of career issues with the issues of life stages of the employee and his family, changing needs of employee throughout his life cycle complicate the career issues.

(5) Downsizing/Delayering and Careers: Business process reengineering, technological changes and business environmental factors force the business firms to

restructure the organisations by delayering and downsizing. Downsizing activities result in fixing some employees, and degrading some other employees. These activities necessitate the organisation to provide training and to provide climate for job sharing.

SUGGESTIONS FOR EFFECTIVE CAREER DEVELOPMENT

(i) Challenging Initial Job Assignments: There is an evidence indicating that employees who take up initial challenging jobs perform better at later stages.

(ii) Dissemination of Career Option Information: Mostly employees lack information about career choices/options. The managers identify career paths and succession paths. This information should be made available to all employees concerned.

(iii) Job Positioning: Management should provide job information to employees through job positioning. For posting the jobs organisations can use bulletin board displays, company publications, electronic billboards and similar means.

(iv) Assessment Centres: The assessment centres evaluate the people regarding their ability to certain jobs. This technique helps to identify the available skills, abilities and knowledge.

(v) Career Counselling: Career counselling helps employees in setting directions, reviewing performance, identifying areas for of professional growth. The content of career counselling include:

(i) Employee's goals, aspirations and expectations with regard to future career,

(ii) The manager's views about the future opportunities,

(iii) Identification of employee's attempts for self-development.

(vi) Career Development Workshops: Managements should conduct career development workshops. There workshops help for resolving misperceptions. Entry workshops help for orientation and socialization activities. Mid career workshops help the employees with the same background and length of service. Late-career workshops are helpful for the employees preparing for retirement, employees who are frustrated over unfulfilled career goals.

(vii) Continuing Education and Training: Continuous education and training help the employees to reduce the possibilities of obsolete skills. In fact, continuous education and development are highly essential for career planning and development. Competency-based training approaches are best for career development.

(viii) Periodic Job Changes: In the modern business, the Proverb, "rolling stone gathers no mass" has a little relevance. In fact, the rolling stone gathers mass. The technique of job rotation helps the employees to acquire the organisational knowledge, and knowledge about different jobs and departments. Ultimately, the employee gains confidence of working efficiently under any environment. The periodic job changes offers diverse and expanded range of experiences that the future job will demand. Thus, this technique prepares the employee for the future careers.

Leave of Absence: Long leave of absence or sabbaticals allow the employee to work under new environment or attend an executive development programmes. Thus, leave allows the employees to learn under different environments.

Management Simulation: Under this technique, employees are taken through a number of exercises and given extensive career development feedback regarding the areas of development necessary.

Professional Associations: Professional associations enable the managers to interact among themselves and learn from each other. Further, associations arrange guest speakers on current topics. Thus, these associations help the employees to keep abreast of current career demands and expectations.

Mentor — Protege Relationships: Organisations encourage these relationships through networking, building mentor expectations into managerial job descriptions and recognising and rewarding successful mentoring efforts.[9]

SOLUTION TO THE CAREER PROBLEMS

Employees can minimise the problems by *(a)* improving the dissemination of career information in order to help the early process of career choice, *(b)* improving mechanisms for people to discover their own talents, needs and motives, *(c)* improving mechanism for career switching, and *(d)* introducing necessary educational facilities.

The organisation can also minimise the problems by *(a)* improving human resources planning and forecasting systems, *(b)* improving dissemination of career option information, *(c)* initiated career counselling, *(d)* developing effective internal and external assessment centres, *(e)* supporting educational and training programmes, *(f)* introducing more flexible reward and promotional systems and conducting career development sessions.

CHART 7.6

Career Development Sessions

The purpose of career development discussions is to allow both the supervisor and the individual to explore future areas of growth to satisfy their respective needs.

The content of the session should be as employee-centered as possible, with the supervisor providing structure and feedback. The range of areas that can be covered is practically limitless, but here are some suggested topics:

- Discover what the individual truly wants. Is this different from your own original estimate of the goal that he should strive for? If so, why are these two objectives different?
- Examine the 'individual's "self-selling" technique and offer suggestions for improving it.
- Is the individual being relatively objective in the assessment of his strengths and weaknesses?
- Is the individual limited in his scope? Is he aware of the wide range of alternatives available to him?
- Is the individual neglecting consideration of some positions because of the personalities of the person currently in those positions? Is he overrating other positions for similar reasons?
- Can the employee verbalize both the pros and cons of a position, or does he focus solely on the positive?
- Is the individual motivated more by the salary and/or status of a job than by the duties themselves?

- Is the individual sincere, or is he just saying what he thinks you, the supervisor, want to hear?
- Is the employee sufficiently motivated to undergo the training required for a new position?
- Has the individual incorporated previous supervisory feedback into his thinking?
- Is the individual focusing only on long-range goals, or has he developed smaller, more immediate steps?
- To pursue the individual's overall goal, can he expect to achieve it within the organization, or should he be looking elsewhere for satisfaction?

Source: Lee R. Ginsburg, "Career Planning: Help Your Organization Grow," *Supervisory Management,* June 1977, pp. 14-15.

SUMMARY

It will be seen that career development is a dual responsibility of the individual who wants to grow and the organisation — which should provide, opportunities, training, development support. Regular appraisals by the company should be able to highlight the individuals who are interested in growth and are ready for undertaking developmental activities by the management — training, job rotation and job enrichment, monitoring promotions are the channels through which the individual is offered career development.

❑ ❑ ❑

8

Employee Training and Development

INTRODUCTION

Every organisation needs to have well trained and experienced people to perform the activities that have to be done. If the current or potential job occupant can meet this requirement, training is not important. But when this is not the case, it is necessary to raise the skill levels and increase the versatility and adaptability of employees. Inadequate job performance or a decline in productivity or changes resulting out of job redesigning or a technological breakthrough require some type of training and development efforts. As the jobs become more complex, the importance of employee development also increases. In a rapidly changing society, *employee training and development are not only an activity that is desirable but also an activity that an organisation must commit resources to if it is to maintain a viable and knowledgeable work force.*

'Training,' 'education' and 'development' are three terms frequently used. On the face of it, there might not appear any difference between them, but when a deep thought is given, there appears some differences between them. In all 'training' there is some 'education' and in all 'education 'there is some' training. And the two processes cannot be separated from 'development.' Precise definitions are not possible and can be misleading; but different persons have used these activities in different ways.

THREE TERMS: TRAINING, DEVELOPMENT AND EDUCATION

Training is a process of learning a sequence of programmed behaviour. It is application of knowledge. It gives people an awareness of the rules and procedures to guide their behaviour. It attempts to improve their performance on the current job or prepare them for an intended job. *Development* is a related process. It covers not only those activities which improve job performance but also those which bring about growth of the personality; help individuals in the progress towards maturity and actualisation of their potential capacities so that they become not only good employees but better men and women. In organisational terms, it is intended to equip persons to earn promotion and hold greater responsibility. Training a person for a bigger and higher job is development. And this may well include not only imparting specific skills and knowledge but also inculcating certain personality and mental attitudes. In this sense, development is not much different from *education. Education* is the understanding and intervention of knowledge. It does not provide definitive answers, but rather it develops a logical and rational mind that can determine relationships among pertinent variables and thereby character, and understanding of basic principles and develop the capacities of analysis, synthesis and objectivity. Usually, education is outside the scope of an organisation's functions. It involves a range of skills and expertise which can be provided only by educational institutions. An organisation can and does make use of such institutions in order to support and supplement its internal training and development efforts.

DISTINCTION BETWEEN TRAINING AND DEVELOPMENT

" *Training* is short-term process utilising a systematic and organised procedure by which non-managerial personnel learn technical knowledge and skills for a definite purpose.... *Development* is a long-term educational process utilising a systematic and organised procedure by which managerial personnel learn conceptual and theoretical knowledge for general purpose."

"Training" refers only to instruction in technical and mechanical operations, while "development" refers to philosophical and theoretical educational concepts. Training is designed for non-managers, while development involves managerial personnel. In the words of Campbell, "training courses are typically designed for a short-term, stated set purpose, such as the operation of some piece(s) of machinery, while development involves a broader education for long-term purposes."

Training and development differ in four ways:

(a) "What" is learned;

(b) "Who" is learning;

(c) "Why" such learning takes place; and

(d) "When" learning occurs.

The difference may be stated thus:

Learning Dimensions	*Training*	*Development*
Who?	Non-managerial personnel	Managerial personnel
What?	Technical and mechanical operations	Theoretical, conceptual ideas
Why?	Specific job-related purpose	General Knowledge
When?	Short-term	Long-term

NEED FOR BASIC PURPOSES OF TRAINING

The need for the training of employees would be clear from the observations made by the different authorities.

(i) To Improve Productivity: "Purposeful instruction can help employees increase their level of performance on their present assignment. Increased human performance often directly leads to increased operational productivity and increased company profit."[3] Again, "increased performance and productivity, because of training, are most evident on the part of new employees who are not yet fully aware of the most efficient and effective ways of performing their jobs."

(ii) To Improve Quality: "Better informed workers are less likely to make operational mistakes. Quality increases may be in relationship to a company product or service, or in reference to the intangible organisational employment atmosphere."

(iii) To Help a Company Fulfil its Future Personnel Needs: "Organisations that have a good internal educational programme will have to make less drastic manpower changes and adjustments in the event of sudden personnel alternations. When the need arises, organisational vacancies can more easily be staffed from internal sources if a company initiates and maintains an adequate instructional programme for both its non-supervisory and managerial employees."

(iv) To Improve Organisational Climate: "An endless chain of positive reactions results from a well-planned training programme. Production and product quality may improve; financial incentives may then be increased, internal promotions become stressed, less supervisory pressure ensure and base pay rate increases result. Increased morale may be due to many factors, but one of the most important of these is the current state of an organisation's educational endeavour."

(v) To Improve Health and Safety: "Proper training can help prevent industrial accidents. A safer work environment leads to more stable mental attitudes on the part of employees. Managerial mental state would also improve if supervisors know that they can better themselves through company-designed development programmes."

(vi) Obsolescence Prevention: "Training and development programmes foster the initiative and creativity of employees and help to prevent manpower obsolescence, which may be due to age, temperament or motivation, or the inability of a person to adapt himself to technological changes."

(vii) Personal Growth: "Employees on a personal basis gain individually from their exposure to educational experiences." Again, "Management development programmes seem to give participants a wider awareness, an enlarged skill, and enlightened altruistic philosophy, and make enhanced personal growth possible."

It may be observed that the need for training arises from more than one reason.

(i) An increased use of technology in production;

(ii) Labour turnover arising from normal separations due to death or physical incapacity, for accidents, disease, superannuation, voluntary retirement, promotion within the organisation and change of occupation or job.

(iii) Need for additional hands to cope with an increased production of goods and services;

(iv) Employment of inexperienced, new or *badli* labour requires detailed instruction for an effective performance of a job.

(v) Old employees need refresher training to enable them to keep abreast of the changing methods, techniques and use of sophisticated tools and equipment;

(vi) Need for enabling employees to do the work in a more effective way, to reduce learning time, reduce supervision time, reduce waste and spoilage of raw material and produce quality goods and develop their potential.

(vii) Need for reducing grievances and minimising accident rates;

(viii) Need for maintaining the validity of an organisation as a whole and raising the morale of its employees.

A programme of training becomes essential for the purpose of meeting the specific problems of a particular organisation arising out of the introduction of new lines of production, changes in design, the demands of competition and economy, the quality of materials processed, individual adjustments, promotions, career development, job and personnel changes and changes in the volume of business. Collectively, these purposes directly relate to and comprise the ultimate purpose of organisational training programmes to enhance overall organisational effectiveness.

O. Jeff Harris, Jr. observes:

"Training of any kind should have as its objective the redirection or improvement of behaviour so that the performance of the trainee becomes more useful and productive for himself and for the organisation of which he is a part. Training normally concentrates on the improvement of either *operative skills* (the basic skills related to the successful completion of a task), *interpersonal skills* (how to relate satisfactorily to others), *decision-making skills* (how to arrive at the most satisfactory causes of action), or a combination of these."

The objectives of training as adopted by the Indian Oil Company will serve as an illustrative example:

(i) To impart to new entrants the basic knowledge and skill they need for an intelligent performance of definite tasks;

(ii) To assist employees to function more effectively in their present positions by exposing them to the latest concepts, information and techniques and developing the skills they will need in their particular fields;

(iii) To build up a second line of competent officers and prepare them to occupy more responsible positions;

(iv) To broaden the minds of senior managers by providing them with opportunities for an inter-change of experiences within and outside with a view to correcting the narrowness of the outlook that may arise from over-specialisation;

(v) To impart customer education for the purpose of meeting the training needs of Corporations which deal mainly with the public, e.g., Hindustan Steel Limited, Gujarat State Road Transport Corporation, B.E.S. & T, Mumbai, Heavy Electrical, Bhopal, Gujarat State Fertilizer Corporation, Vadodra, Western Railway, Bombay, and the All-India State Road Transport Corporation.

IMPORTANCE OF TRAINING

Training is the corner-stone of sound management, for it makes employees more effective and productive. It is actively and intimately connected with all the personnel or managerial activities. It is an integral part of the whole management programme, with all its many activities functionally inter-related.

There is an ever present need for training men so that new and changed techniques may be taken advantage of and improvements affected in the old methods, which are woefully inefficient.

Training is a practical and vital necessity because, apart from the other advantages mentioned above, it enables employees to develop and rise within the organisation, and increase their "market value," earning power and job security. It enables management to resolve sources of friction arising from parochialism, to bring home to the employees the fact that the management is not divisible. It moulds the employees' attitudes and helps them to achieve a better co-operation with the company and a greater loyalty to it. The management is benefited in the sense that higher standards of quality are achieved; a satisfactory organisational structure is built up; authority can be delegated and stimulus for progress applied to employees. Training, moreover, heightens the morale of the employees, for it helps in reducing dissatisfaction, complaints, grievances and absenteeism, reduces the rate of turnover. Further, trained employees make a better and economical use of materials and equipment; therefore, wastage and spoilage are lessened, and the need for constant supervision is reduced.

The importance of training has been expressed in these words: "Training is a widely accepted problem-solving device. Indeed, our national superiority in manpower productivity can be attributed in no small measure to the success of our educational and industrial training programmes. This success has been achieved by a tendency in many quarters to regard training as a panacea. It is almost traditional in America to believe that if something is good, more of the thing is even better. Hence, we take more vitamin pills to solve personal health problems and more training to solve our manpower problems. Over and under-emphasis on training stems largely from inadequate recognition and determination of training needs and objectives. They stem also from lack of recognition of the professional techniques of modern industrial training."

RESPONSIBILITY FOR TRAINING

Training is the responsibility of four main groups;

(a) The top management, which frames the training policy;

(b) The personnel department, which plans, establishes and evaluates instructional programmes;

(c) Supervisors, who implement and apply developmental procedure; and

(d) Employees, who provide feedback, revision and suggestions for corporate educational endeavours.

According to Prof. John Mee, the work of training should be done at two levels, *viz.*,

(i) The training department should assume the primary responsibility for the instruction of trainers in methods of teaching; for normal orientation; for the training of supervisors in human relations; for the development of executives, for co-operative education in schools and colleges; and for the general education of employees.

(ii) Line supervisors and employees should carry the bulk of the teaching load in the following areas: On-the-job instruction of employees; instruction in the technical and professional aspects of a business; daily development of superiors and executives through counselling; departmental communication and staff meetings as part of an over-all training programme. It is needless to say that the top line executive has the responsibility for:

(a) Authorising basic training policies;

(b) Reviewing and approving the broad outlines of training plans and programmes; and

(c) Approving training budgets.

CREATION OF A DESIRE FOR TRAINING

The employees can be persuaded to be interested in training programmes in one of the following three ways:

1. They will respond to programmes involving changed behaviour if they believe that the resulting modification in the behaviour is in their own interest, that they will receive benefits as a result of their new behaviour.
2. Trainees will change their behaviour if they *became aware* of better ways of performing (more productive or otherwise more satisfactory ways) and *gain experience* in the new pattern of behaviour so that it becomes their normal manner of operation.
3. A trainee may change his behaviour in compliance with the forced demands of his superiors or others with more power than the trainee possesses.

PRINCIPLES OR CONCEPTS OF TRAINING

Since training is a continuous process and not a one shot affair, and since it consumes time and entails much expenditure, it is necessary that a training programme or policy should be prepared with great thought and care, for it should serve the purposes of the establishment as well as the needs of employees. Moreover, it must guard against over-training, use of poor instructions, too much training in skills which are unnecessary for a particular job, initiation of other company training programmes, misuse of testing techniques, inadequate tools and equipment, and over reliance on one single technique — e.g., on slides, pictures or lectures — and not enough on practice.

A successful training programme presumes that sufficient care has been taken to discover areas in which it is needed most and to create the necessary environment for its conduct. The selected trainer should be one who clearly understands his job and has professional expertise, has an aptitude and ability for teaching, possesses a pleasing personality and a capacity for leadership, is well-versed in the principles and methods of training, and is able to appreciate the value of training in relation to an enterprise.

Certain general principles need be considered while organising a training programme. For example:

1. Trainees in work organisations tend to be most responsive to training programmes when they feel the need to learn, i.e., *the trainee will be more eager to undergo training if training promises answers to problem or needs he has as an employee.* The individual who perceives training as the solution to problems will be more willing to enter into a training programme than will the individual who is satisfied with his present performance abilities.
2. Learning is more effective where there is reinforcement in the form of rewards and punishments, i.e., *individuals do things that give pleasure and*

avoid things that give pain. In other words, after an action, if satisfaction is received, the action will be repeated. If no satisfaction is received, the action will not be repeated.

3. In the long run, awards tend to be more effective for changing behaviour and increasing one's learning than punishments.
4. Rewards for the application of learned behaviour are most useful when they quickly follow the desired performance.
5. The larger the reward for good performance following the implementation of learned behaviour, the greater will be the reinforcement of the new behaviour.
6. Negative reinforcement, through application of penalties and heavy criticism following inadequate performance, may have a disruptive effect upon the learning experience of the trainee than positive reinforcement.
7. Training that requests the trainee to make changes in his values, attitudes, and social beliefs, usually achieves better results if the trainee is encouraged to participate, discuss and discover new, desirable behaviour norms.
8. The trainee should be provided with 'feedback' on the progress he is making in utilising the training he has received. As Miller has stated, "If a person with the required abilities is to improve his performance, he must *(i)* know what aspect of his performance is not up to par; *(ii)* know precisely what corrective actions he must take to improve his performance." *The feedback should be fast and frequent,* especially for the lower level jobs which are often routine and quickly completed.
9. The development of new behaviour norms and skills is facilitated through practice and repetition. *Skills that are practised often are better learned and less easily forgotten.*
10. The training material should be made as meaningful as possible, because if the trainee understands the general principles underlying what is being taught, he will probably understand it better than if he were just asked to memorize a series of isolated steps.

The National Industries Conference Board, U.S.A., states some other principles like the following:

(i) The purpose of the training is to help meet company objectives by providing opportunities for employees at all organisational levels to acquire the requisite knowledge, skills and attitudes;

(ii) The first step in training is to determine needs and objectives;

(iii) The objectives and scope of a training plan should be defined before its development is begun in order to provide a basis for common agreement and co-operative action;

(iv) The techniques and processes of a training programme should be related directly to the needs and objectives of an organisation;

(v) Training is properly the responsibility of any one in the management who wants to attain a particular objective;

(vi) The purpose behind the training of personnel is to assist line management in the determination of training needs and in the development, administration, conduct and follow-up of training plans;

(vii) To be effective, training must use the tested principles of learning;

(viii) Training should be conducted in the actual job environment to the maximum possible extent.

LEARNING

Training is an organised procedure by which people learn knowledge and acquire the skills they need for a definite purpose. *Training is what is done to the trainee.* This training is rooted in the learning process; and "learning is that human process by which skills, knowledge, habits and attitudes are acquired and utilised in such a way that behaviour is modified." In other words, *training causes learning, a process that takes place within the trainee,* in which behavioural changes occur as a result of experience. Learning cannot be measured directly but the changes in behaviour that occur as a result of learning can only be measured.

PRINCIPLES OF LEARNING

Learning concepts and theories are based on firmly rooted and well-grounded educational and psychological principles. These are:

1. Every human being is capable of learning. Each has an intellectual capacity and the ability to learn from training.
2. It is easier for the trainee to understand/remember material that is *meaningful.* Training materials may be made more meaningful at least in six ways: *(i)* At the start of training, the trainee should be provided with the *bird's eye view* of the material to be presented. Knowing the overall picture and understanding how each part of the programme fits into it helps make the entire programme meaningful. *(ii)* When presenting material to the trainees, a variety of similar examples should be used. *(iii)* The training material is organised in a logical manner and has meaningful units. *(iv)* The materials should be split up into meaningful chunks rather than presenting it all at once. *(v)* The terms and concepts that are already familiar to the trainees should be used. *(vi)* As many visual aids should be used as possible to argument "theoretical" material.
3. The training programme should be planned in a logical manner so that each succeeding step builds upon the previous one — the probability of success increases because the trainee encounters the steps in sequence. The best course for changing behaviour is to bring about the transition through a progression of small, orderly steps.
4. A new employee may learn in order to please his boss, to get confirmed in his job, to acquire the requisite knowledge and skill to perform it in a much better and more effective manner. Supervisors may go in for training to learn how to delegate responsibility more effectively, how to save their own limited time, how to read reports quickly, how to understand their subordinates better, how to eliminate potential labour troubles, and how to administer the agreements reached between the management and the employees.

5. Different levels of learning exist. Learning may involve awareness, changed attitudes and changed behaviour. It may involve mental processes or physical strength. Different time and method requirements are needed to bring about different levels of learning.
6. The basic principles of training design consist of: *(a)* identifying the components of tasks of final desired performance; *(b)* assuring that each component is fully achieved; and *(c)* arranging the total learning situation in a sequence.
7. Learning objectives should be established for every training programme. These objectives guide the instructor in planning the training, guide the trainee, and provide criteria for evaluating how much learning has been achieved. A complete statement of learning objectives clearly specifies the behaviour expected of the trainee after the instruction has taken place, the conditions under which the trainee will be required to demonstrate the prescribed behaviour, and the standards of acceptable performance. A knowledge of standards of performance makes learning effective and the goals and bench marks enable the learner to judge his educational achievements and progress.
8. An adequate interest in, and motive for, learning are essential because people are goal-oriented. They work to satisfy their needs for self-expression, self-accomplishment, self-actualisation, and financial incentives. However, most learning is self-motivated and related to the attainment of personal goals. The trainer must explain to the trainee how his training can be instrumental in his success. He should first *clarify the goals of the training; then explain how job performance is related to rewards; and explain how the training will improve his performance and thereby boost* his rewards.
9. Learning is active and not passive. Effective education calls for action and active involvement on the part of all participants. Researchers have revealed (in America) that people remember 10% of what they read, 20% of what they hear, 30% of what they see, 50% of what they see and hear, 70% of what they say, and 90% of what they say as they perform the task. In other words, *people learn best and more by doing than by 'hearing."* The larger number of human senses involved, the more complete is the training.

   Different training methods are used for different types of learning. For example, *cognitive learning* stresses visual and audio experience to gain understanding. It may involve reading, lectures, audio-visual presentations, case problems, examinations, etc. *Affective learning* (i.e., attitude, value, and interest acquisitions) may best be learned through field-trips, role playing, open ended discussion, counselling or reflection. *Psychomotor learning* (doing skills) can be acquired best through practice, drill, behaviour modification, simulation games, demonstration, internships, etc. Therefore, *the value of multi-sensory learning exercises should be emphasised.*
10. Previous experience of the individual trainee affects his learning experiences. New material is related to his previous knowledge. New behaviour is formulated using existing foundations as a basis.

11. People learn more and even faster when they are told of their achievements, i.e., they should have *Knowledge of Results* (KR) or *feedback.* Such feedback should be specific rather than general. It should be precise and diagnostic rather than evaluative. It should be directed at the behaviour that the learner can do something right than at values or individual personality traits.

    It should be the automatic, immediate and meaningfully related to work that is done. In on-the-job-training, an employee should be informed of his success or failure so that he may adjust his efforts, if necessary or correct his mistakes. The trainer should not wait until the end of the day to tell a trainee that "he has done well." Instead, reinforcement should be frequent, whenever he does something right.

12. Training in one activity can be transferred to another if, there are similar components and principles. Once a general principle has been learned, all problems of similar nature can be solved as they arise. For example, a manager trained in the techniques of contingency leadership theory may be capable of anlysing a wide variety of motivational problems and developing solutions to them on the basis of his knowledge of a few basic principles.

    Transfer of training can be accomplished by: *(i)* maximising the similarity between the training situation and the work situation; *(ii)* providing adequate experience with tasks during training; *(iii)* providing for a variety of examples when teaching concepts or skills; *(iv)* identifying important features of the task; and *(v)* making sure that the trainee understands general principles.

13. The training that involves understanding complex problems and discovering new alternative solutions can be achieved best when the environment is relaxed and free of anxiety and the trainees are not under any immediate pressure to produce.

14. The differences in abilities, backgrounds, experiences, readiness to learn and other factors cause individual trainees to acquire new knowledge, skills, and attitudes at differing rates of speed. Training programmes necessarily must be adapted to the training speeds of the separate trainees.

15. Time must be provided to practice that which has been learned. The learning process requires a great deal of time for assimilation, testing, acceptance, and the development of confidence. Repetition, accompanied by constant efforts towards improvement, makes for an effective development of skills. Practice makes man perfect. Moreover, skills that are practised often are better learned and easily not forgotten.

16. Learning is closely related to attention and concentration. The learning process is more effective if distractions are avoided.

17. Learning is more effective when one sheds one's half-knowledge, prejudices, bias, likes and dislikes, i.e., when one abandons the "I know attitude" and adopts the "I want to know" approach.

18. Early success increases an individual's chances for effective learning, for "nothing succeeds like success."

19. Trainers are important ingredient in the learning environment.

    They should know the material, be able to communicate, and be aware of the learner's needs. The old saying, "if the student failed to learn, the teacher failed to teach," contains a great deal of truth.

STEPS IN TRAINING PROGRAMMES

Training programmes are a costly affair, and a time consuming process. Therefore, they need to be drafted very carefully. Usually in the organisation of training programmes, the following steps are considered necessary:

1. Discovering or Identifying the training needs.
2. Getting ready for the job.
3. Preparation of the learner.
4. Presentation of operation and knowledge.
5. Performance try-out.
6. Follow-up and Evaluation of the programme.

1. DISCOVERING OR IDENTIFYING TRAINING NEEDS

A training programme should be established only when it is felt that it would assist in the solution of specific operational problems and improve performance of the trainee. The most important step, in the first place, is to make a thorough analysis of the entire organisation, its operations and manpower resources available in order to find out "The trouble spots" where training may be needed. It should, however, be noted that training is not a cure-all. For example, if the efficiency of an employee is low, or he cannot get the job done, it may be due to faulty raw materials and equipment or not getting their timely supplies, or a defective engineering design, or uncongenial work environment, or low wages, or tax supervision. If that is the case, these problems should be rectified.

Identification of training needs must contain three types of analyses — organisational analysis, operations analysis, and man analysis. *Organisational analysis* centres primarily upon the determination of the organisation's goals, its resources, and the allocation of the resources as they relate to the organisational goals. The analysis of the organisational goals establishes the framework in which, training needs can be defined more clearly. *Operations analysis* focuses on the task or job regardless of the employee doing the job. This analysis includes the determination of the employee must do — the specific employee behaviour required — if the job is to be performed effectively. *Man analysis* reviews the knowledge, attitudes and skills of the incumbent in each position and determines what knowledge, attitudes or skills he must acquire and what alterations in his behaviour he must make if he is to contribute satisfactorily to the attainment of organisational objectives.

William Berliner and William McLarney say that discovering training needs involves five tasks:

(A) TASK DESCRIPTION ANALYSIS

1. List the duties and responsibilities or tasks of the job under consideration, using the Job Description as a guide.
2. List the standards of work performance on the job.

(B) DETERMINING TRAINING NEEDS

3. Compare actual performance against the standards.
4. Determine what parts of the job are giving the employee trouble — where is he falling down in his performance?
5. Determine what kind of training is needed to overcome the specific difficulty or difficulties.

Numbers 1 and 2 comprise basic *task description step* in identifying training needs. Here job requirements — the jobs the person does — and expected standards of performance are taken note of. Numbers 3, 4 and 5 involve determining job related training needs. Problems and performance discrepancies are noted and training goals set.

(a) Task Description Analysis : The job or task analysis aims at determining what constitutes the job, the methods that are used on the job, and the human skills required to perform the job adequately. The job or task description that results, lays out the requirements of task in terms of actual duties to be performed. The job specification lists the human skills and knowledge required.

(a) Task Description Analysis

(b) How often the tasks are: *Performed* is the frequency with which the tasks and sub-tasks are performed.

(c) Quantity, quality standards: For each task these are to be recorded. These should be expressed in measurable terms.

(d) Performance conditions: Here indicate the working conditions under which the tasks and sub tasks are to be performed. This is important as conditions are crucial to the training.

(e) Skills required: Here you have to list the skills or the knowledge required for each of the task, specifying what knowledge you must teach the trainee.

(b) Determining Training Needs: Training needs may be discovered/identified for the new as well as the present employees and for solving the specific problem in the following ways:

(i) Identifying Specific Problems: Such problems are: productivity, high costs, poor material and control, poor quality, excessive scrap and waste, excessive labour-management troubles, excessive grievances, excessive violation of rules of conduct, poor discipline, high employee turnover and transfers, excessive absenteeism, accidents, excessive fatigue, fumbling, discouragement, struggling with the job; standards of work performance not being met, bottlenecks in production, deadlines not being met, and delayed production. Problems like these suggest that training may be necessary. For this the task and the workers should be closely observed and the difficulties found out.

(ii) Anticipating Impending and Future Problems: Bearing on the expansion of business, the introduction of new product, new services, new designs, new plant, new technology and of organisational changes concerned with manpower inventory for present and future needs.

(iii) *Management Requests:* The supervisors and managers may make specific request for setting training programmes. Though this method is simple and a correct evaluation of the employees performance deficiencies can be made, but often such recommendations may be built on faulty assumptions; and requests may not coincide with each other or organisational goals.

(iv) *Interviewing and Observing the Personnel on the Job:* Interviewing personnel and direct questioning and observation of the employee by his superiors may also reveal training needs.

(v) *Performance Appraisal:* An Analysis of the past performance records of the perspective trainee and comparing his actual performance with the target performance may provide clues to specific interpersonal skills that may need development.

(vi) *Questionnaires:* Questionnaires may be used for eliciting opinions of the employees on topics like communication, satisfaction, job characteristics, their attitude towards working conditions, pay, promotion policies etc. These will reveal much information about where an employee's skills and knowledge are deficient.

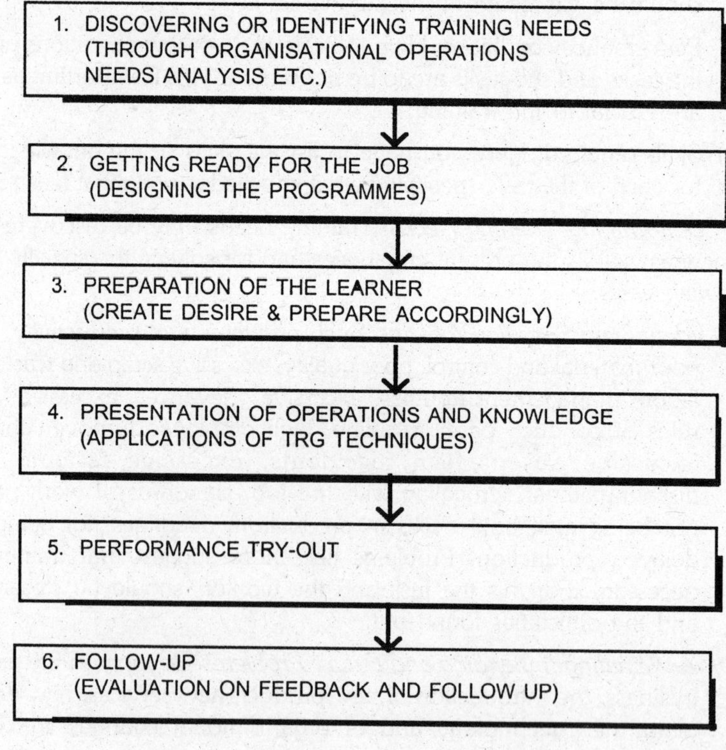

Fig. 8.1 Sequence of Training Programme

(vii) *Checklist:* The use of checklist is a useful supplement to interviews and observations. Through it, more reliable information can be obtained and the data got are quantifiable. This facilitates evaluating the training programme's effectiveness.

(viii) *Morale and Attitude Surveys:* An occasional personnel audit may be conducted to forecast future promotions, skill requirements, and merit rating, to initiate informal discussions and an examination of records and statistics regarding personnel, production, cost, rejects and wastages. All these generally reveal the potential problems to be tackled through training programmes.

(ix) In addition, tests of the interpersonal skills through handling of posed cases and incidents, may also reveal training needs.

It is interesting to note that "the determination of training needs in American industry ranges from subjective beliefs about the value of training and education to a systematic identification of problems requiring solutions. The latter seems to be the wisest course in order to ensure that training contributes to the goals of an enterprise." In a survey of 150 firms, it was found that the training needs of an organisation were determined generally by requests from the top management. Presumably, perception, judgement, intuition, the expressed needs of the first level and middle managers, or a desire to follow the practices of other firms were the determining factors in these requests. The other methods which were often used were informal observations, talks with supervisors, and group discussions and conferences; used less often were analysis of various reports (such as cost, turnover, grievances, suggestions, etc.), formal training advisory committees, employee questionnaires and merit or performance rating. In another enquiry, it was found that the development of training needs was based on supervisory commendations in 73 per cent of the firms, on the analysis of job requirements in 58 per cent and on the analysis of job performance in 32 per cent. Suggestions by employees were a factor in 66 per cent of the firms. Organisations have several sources of information which assist them in determining their training needs; and in this determination of needs, supervisors play a major role.

In India, it was found in a survey that in all the 13 private sector companies where the survey was undertaken, the training needs were determined on the basis of supervisory recommendations, analyses of job performance and job requirements, and on the basis of employee suggestions. In the case of steel and tobacco industries, the employees themselves suggested the type of training that was needed.

Based upon William Tracy, the following chart gives a checklist for identifying training needs.

CHART 8.1

Check List for Identifying Training and Development Requirements

---

I. Determine Immediate Needs.

A. Evaluate current training and development programmes to determine whether training produces the desired behavioural changes.

(i) Evaluate ongoing training programmes:

(a) Review training documents for adequacy.

(b) Observe trainers and trainees in the learning environment of a classroom, a shop or a laboratory.

(c) Analyse in-course and end-of-course test results.

(d) Interview trainers and trainees.

(ii) List and analyse shortfalls in the process of products. Determine whether they are due to:

(a) Poor organisation;

(b) Inadequate supervision;

(c) Poor communication;

(d) Improper personnel selection or policies or procedures;

(e) Unclear policies;

(f) Poor job design;

(g) Equipment or materials problems;

(h) Work methods;

(i) Inappropriate work standards;

(j) Inadequate operator or supervisor training.

B. Survey all the aspects of the operations of an enterprise to determine the areas where additional training is required.

(a) Compare job descriptions and applicant specifications with personnel records.

(b) Analyse performance ratings.

(c) Analyse all the records of an enterprise to identify areas of possible deficiency.

(d) Identify and analyse operating problems.

(e) Use interview, questionnaires, group conferences, tests, and work samples to determine training problems.

(f) Subject each problem to a careful analysis to determine whether it is due to:

(1) Poor organisation;
(2) Inadequate supervision;
(3) Unclear or ambiguous policies;
(4) Poor communication;
(5) Improper personnel selection policies;
(6) Poor job designs;
(7) Equipment or material deficiencies;
(8) Improper work methods;
(9) Inappropriate work standards;
(10) Training deficits.

II. Determine Long-range Training Needs

(a) Analyse an enterprise's plans, policies, and forecasts to determine their potential impact on staffing needs.

(b) Identify and analyse future systems, equipment, techniques, and procedures to determine their impact on personnel requirements.

(c) Determine whether current training systems will support future personal requirements in terms of:

(i) Operative personal (workers);

(ii) Supervisory personnel;

(iii) Managerial personnel;

(d) Identify training system shortfalls.

III. For each training requirement, *determine whether training be provided on or off the premises,* and whether it should be normal or on-the-job. Consider:

(a) Comparative costs; and

(b) The availability of in-house personnel, equipment and facilities.

IV. *Summarise training needs.*

V. *For off-the-premises programmes,* develop objectives, prepare contract specifications, solicit and evaluate proposals, and select contractors.

VI. *For in-house programmes,* develop objectives and guidelines following the procedures laid down for the purpose.

Armed with the knowledge of each trainee's specific training needs, programmes of improvement can be developed that are tailored to these needs. This training — programme then follows a general sequence aimed at supplying the trainee with the opportunity to develop his skills and abilities.

2. GETTING READY FOR THE JOB

Under this step, it is to be decided who is to be trained — the newcomer or the older employee, or the supervisory staff, or all of them selected from different departments. The trainer has to be prepared for the job, for he is the key figure in the entire programme. This calls for a decision on:

These have been discussed, in detail, elsewhere in this chapter under the headings; Support material for training; Training period; Training for different employees; and Training methods.

3. PREPARATION OF THE LEARNER

This step consists: *(i)* in putting the learner at ease (so that he does not feel nervous because of the fact he is on a new job); *(ii)* in stating the importance and ingredients of the job, and its relationship to work flow; *(iii)* in explaining why he is being taught; *(iv)* in creating interest and encouraging questions, finding out what the learner already knows about his job or other jobs; *(v)* in explaining the 'why' of the whole job and relating it to some job the worker already knows; *(vi)* in placing the learner as close to his normal working position as possible; and *(vii)* in familiarising him with the equipment, materials, tools and trade terms.

4. PRESENTATION OF OPERATION AND KNOWLEDGE

This is the most important step in a training programme. The trainer should clearly *tell show, illustrate* and *question* in order to put over the new knowledge and operations. The learner should be told of the sequence of the entire job, and why each step in its performance is necessary. Instructions should be given clearly, completely and patiently; there should be an emphasis on key points, and one point should be explained at a time. For this purpose, the trainer should demonstrate or make use of audio-visual aids and should ask the trainee to repeat the operations. He should also be encouraged to ask questions in order to indicate that he really knows and understands the job.

5. PERFORMANCE TRY OUT

Under this, the trainee is asked to go through the job several times slowly, explaining him each step. Mistakes are corrected, and if necessary, some complicated steps are done for the trainee the first time. The trainee is asked to do the job, gradually building up skill and speed. As soon as the trainee demonstrates that he can do the job in a right way, he is put on his own, but not abandoned.

The trainee is then tested and the effectiveness of a training programme evaluated. This is usually done by:

(a) Giving written or oral tests to trainees to ascertain how far they have learnt the techniques and principles taught to them and the scores obtained by them;

(b) Observing trainees on the job itself and administering performance tests to them;

(c) Finding out individual's or a group's reaction to the training programme while it is in progress and getting them to fill up evaluation sheets;

(d) Arranging structured interviews with the participants or sending them questionnaires by mail;

(e) Eliciting the opinion or judgement of the top management about the trainees' performance;

(f) Comparing the results obtained after the training with those secured before the training programme in order to find out whether any material change has taken place in attitude, opinion, in the quality of output, in the reduction in scrap, breakage and the supplies used and in overhead costs.

(g) Study of profiles and charts of career development of the participants and related assignment techniques.

Through one or a combination of these devices, the validity of training programmes may be ascertained. If there are any errors or weaknesses, they should be corrected and instruction repeated, if necessary, till the *trainer knows that the trainee has learnt whatever has been imparted to him.*

6. FOLLOW-UP

This step is undertaken with a view to testing the effectiveness of training efforts. This consists in:

(a) Putting a trainee "on his own."

(b) Checking frequently to be sure that he has followed instructions; and

(c) Tapering off extra supervision and close follow-up until he is qualified to work with normal supervision.

It is worth remembering that if the learner hasn't learnt, the teacher hasn't taught.

TRAINING POLICY

Every company or organisation should have well-established training policy. Such a policy represents the top management's commitment to the training of its employees, and comprises rules and procedures governing the standard of scope of training. A training policy is considered necessary for the following reasons:

(a) To indicate a company's intention to develop its personnel; to provide guidance in the framing and implementation of programmes and to provide information concerning them to all concerned;

(*b*) To discover critical areas where training is to be given on a priority basis; and

(*c*) To provide suitable opportunities to the employee for his own betterment.

TRAINING COURSES

Training may range from highly specified instruction in the procedures to be adopted while performing a particular job to every general instruction concerning the economy and society.

Training courses in general areas usually aim at making an employee a rounded individual, a happier worker and a good citizen, and at training him for "larger responsibilities" and future advancement. Such training exerts a remarkable influence on production and labour. From the producer's point of view, output would increase with decrease in scrap, spoilage, waste and the cost of production. From the point of view of labour, the employee's morale would improve; so would the rate of turnover, excessive absenteeism and accidents reduce Training programmes are no doubt expensive; but their worth to a growing concern cannot be over-emphasised.

Training in general areas is given in such subjects as general and home economics, basic English, instruction in better writing and report drafting, reading using gauges, the operation of machines, fire-fighting and safety devices on the job, shop practices and secretarial practices, elementary mathematics, sociology, industrial psychology, time study, personal hygiene, public speaking and public relations, selling and communication with people.

So far as women employees are concerned, they are given training in telephone etiquette, personal hygiene, good grooming, sales talk and handling of sales and courtesy.

SUPPORT MATERIAL FOR TRAINING

A variety of equipments is utilized to impart effective training. These are:

(*a*) Lectures (learning by hearing supplemented by reading assignments); conferences, seminars and staff-meetings (learning by participation); demonstrations (learning by seeing); and short courses, through coaching.

(*b*) Role-playing (learning by doing) and job rotation (learning by experience).

(*c*) Case or Project studies and problem-solving sessions (learning by personal investigation).

(*d*) Use of pamphlets, charts, brochures, booklets, handbooks, manuals, etc.

(*e*) Graphs, pictures, books, slides, movie projectors, film strips, tape recorders, etc.

(*f*) Posters, displays, notice and bulletin boards.

(*g*) Reading rooms and libraries where specified books and journals are maintained for reference and use.

(*h*) Under-study and visits to plants.

(*i*) Correspondence courses under which knowledge about business law, statistics, industrial management, marketing, office procedures, retailing and many other similar subjects may be imparted.

(*j*) Teaching machines.

(k) Membership of professional or trade associations, which offer new techniques and ideas to their members.

Training material has to be prepared with great care and distributed among the trainees so that they may come well-prepared to a session and are able to understand the operations and/or demonstrations quickly and correctly.

TRAINING PERIOD

The duration of a training varies with the skill to be acquired, the complexity of the subject, a trainee's aptitude and ability to understand, and the training media used.

Generally, a training period should not be unduly long; if it is, trainees may feel bored, uninterested. The ideal session should not go beyond 2 to 3 hours at a stretch, with a break in between two sessions. If convenient, employees may be trained for a week or a fortnight for an hour or two, every day after work hours.

The training period may extend from 3 weeks to 6 months or even more, depending upon job requirements.

The physical location of the programme should be in pleasant surroundings away from the noise and tension of the work place.

TRAINING FOR DIFFERENT EMPLOYEES

Employees at different levels require training. *Unskilled workers* require training in improved methods of handling machines and materials to reduce the cost production and waste and to do the job in the most economical way. Such employees are given training on the job itself; and the training is imparted by their immediate superior officers, *sardars* or foremen. The training period ranges from 3 weeks to 6 weeks.

Semi-skilled workers require training to cope with the requirements of an industry arising out of the adoption of mechanisation, rationalisation and technical processes. These employees are given training either in their own sections or departments, or in segregated training shops where machines and other facilities are usually available. The training is usually imparted by the more proficient workers, bosses or inspectors, and lasts for a few hours or weeks, depending upon the number of operations, and the speed and accuracy required on a job. Training methods include instruction in several semi-skilled operations because training in one operation only creates difficulties in adjustments to new conditions, lends the colour of specialisation to a job and makes work somewhat monotonous for an individual.

Skilled workers are given training through the system of apprenticeship, which varies in duration from a year to three or five years. Such training is also known as *tradesmen* or *craftsmen training,* and is particularly useful for such trades in industry which require highly sophisticated skills — as in carpentry, drilling, boring, planing and host of other industrial jobs and operations. While the mass production in industry has considerably reduced the proportion of employees who must be skilled tradesmen, the design, the construction and maintenance of new machines have increased to such an extent that a very high level of skill and capacity is required to become a skilled tradesman. Any apprentice programme usually takes into consideration the facts of individual differences in abilities and capacities. Such programmes are usually conducted in training centres and industry itself.

Besides the above types of employees, others — typists, stenographers, accounts clerks, and those who handle computers — need training in their particular fields; but such training is usually provided outside an industry.

Salesmen are given training so that they may know the nature and quality of the products, and the routine involved in putting through a deal; they are trained in the art of salesmanship, and in handling customers and meeting their challenges.

The supervisory staff need training most, for they form a very important link in the chain of administration. The training programmes for supervisors must be tailor-made to fit the needs of an undertaking. Their training enables supervisors to cope with the increasing demands of the enterprise in which they are employed and to develop team spirit. Supervisory training aims at:

(i) Helping the present supervisors to improve their performance;

(ii) Helping them to prepare for the greater responsibilities of the higher levels of management;

(iii) Building up the security and status of supervisors; and

(iv) Ensuring their technical competence with a view to enabling them to know and understand all about the processes and operations in which their workers participate.

The courses for supervisors concentrate upon those areas which are closely related to their day-to-day jobs. Accordingly, they are generally given training in:

(a) The organisation and control of production, in maintenance and materials handling at the departmental level;

(b) Planning, allocation and control of work and personnel;

(c) Impact of methods study, time study, job evaluation, and the supervisors' responsibilities and functions in connection therewith;

(d) Company policies and practices for the purchase of stores, the preparation of requisitions, inventories, cost analysis, cost control and shop rules and the preparation of reports and other standard operating procedures;

(e) Personnel procedures, policies and programmes;

(f) Training of subordinates and grievance handling; and techniques of disciplinary procedures.

(g) Communication, effective instruction, report writing;

(h) Appraisal of employees and their rating, and the maintenance of personnel records;

(i) Dealing with the problem of absenteeism, tardiness, indiscipline and subordination.

(j) The handling of human problems — i.e., maintaining good interpersonal relations and morale of the employees;

(k) Evaluating the effects of industrial legislation at the department level;

(l) Leadership qualities;

(m) Industrial law; standing orders, and trade union organisation; and

(n) Principles of administration, safety, health, and welfare regulations.

Supervisors' training may include the supply of necessary reading material, job rotation to give them a wide inplant experience, holding of staff meetings, visits to other industrial units, participation in the work of other departments, lectures and teaching, role-playing, case studies and conferences.

In India, such training is provided by the National Productivity Council, New Delhi and the Central Labour Institute at Mumbai and Delhi.

TRAINING METHODS/TECHNIQUES

The forms and types of employee training methods are inter-related. It is difficult, if not impossible, to say which of the methods or combination of methods is more useful than the other. In fact, methods are multifaceted in scope and dimension, and each is suitable for a particular situation. The best technique for one situation may not be best for different groups or tasks. Care must be used in adapting the technique/method to the learner and the job. An effective training technique generally fulfils these objectives; provide motivation to the trainee to improve job performance, develop a willingness to change, provide for the trainee's active participation in the learning process, provide a knowledge of results about attempts to improve (i.e., feedback), and permit practice where appropriate.

Chart 8.2 gives the techniques mostly used for training of employees.

CHART 8.2

Classification of Training Methods

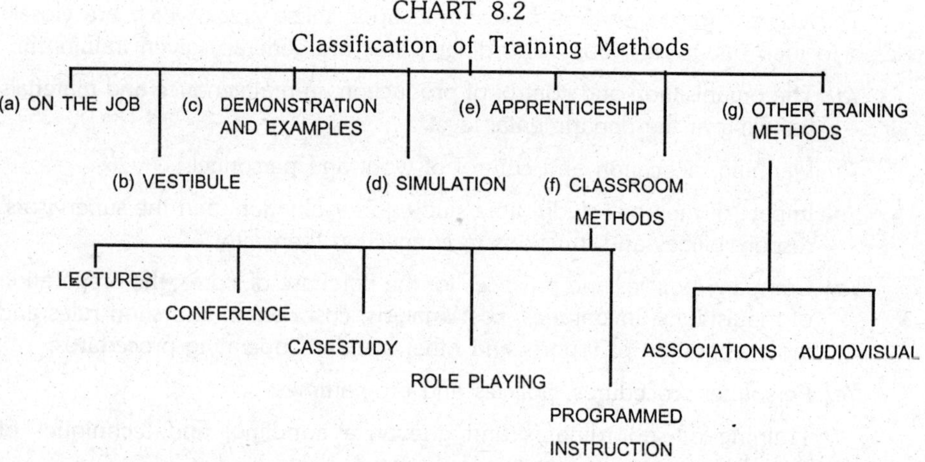

ON-THE-JOB-TRAINING (OJT)

Virtually every employee, from the clerk to company president, gets some "on-the-job-training," when he joins a firm. That is why William Tracly calls it, "the most common, the most widely used and accepted, and the most necessary method of training employees in the skills essential for acceptable for job performance."

Trainees earn as they learn under the watchful eyes of a master mechanic or craftsman, receive immediate feedback, practise in the actual work environment, and associate with the same people they will work with after training. Under this technique, an employee is placed in a new job and is told how it may be performed. It is primarily concerned with developing in an employee a repertoire of skills and habits consistent with the existing practices of an organisation, and with orienting him to his immediate problems. It is mostly given for unskilled and semi-skilled jobs — clerical and sales jobs.

Employees are coached and instructed by skilled co-workers, by supervisors, by the special training instructors. They learn the job by personal observation and practice as well as occasionally handling it. *It is learning by doing,* and it is most useful for jobs that are either difficult to stimulate or can be learned quickly by watching and doing.

There are a variety of OJT methods, such as "coaching" or "understudy"; job rotation; and special assignments. Under *coaching* or *understudy method* (which is also known as 'internship' and 'apprenticeship' method) the employee is trained on the job by his immediate superior. 'Internship' is usually applied to managerial personnel and provide wide variety of job experience, often involving job rotation, or an "assistant to" type of position. '*Apprenticeship*' is generally used to impart skills requiring long periods of practice as found in trade, crafts and other technical fields.

In *job rotation,* a management trainee is made to move from job to job at certain intervals. The jobs vary in content.

Special assignments or *committees* are other methods used to provide lower-level executives with first hand experience in working on actual problems. Executives from various functional areas serve on "boards" and are required to analyse problems and recommend solutions to top management. On-the-job training is made more effective by the use of a variety of training aids and techniques, such as procedure charts, lecture manuals, sample problems, demonstrations, oral and written explanations, tape-recorders and other aids.

Merits: The main advantage of on-the-job training is that the trainee learns on the actual equipment in use and in the true environment of his job. He, therefore, gets a feel of the actual production conditions and requirements. In this way, a transfer from a training centre or school to the actual production conditions following the training period is allowed. *Secondly,* it is highly economical since no additional personnel or facilities are required for training. *Thirdly,* the trainee learns the rules, regulations procedures by observing their day-to-day applications. He can, therefore, be easily sized up by the management. *Fourthly,* this type of training is a suitable alternative for a company in which there are almost as many jobs as there are employees. *Finally,* it is most appropriate for teaching the knowledge and skills which can be acquired in a relatively short period, say, a few days or weeks.

Demerits: The principal disadvantage of on-the-job training is that instruction is often highly disorganised and haphazard and not properly supervised. This is due to such reasons as the inability of the experienced employee to impart skills to the trainee, the breakdown of the job for the purpose of instructions, and the lack of motivation on the part of the trainee to receive training. Moreover, learners are often subjected to distractions of a noisy shop or office. Further, the other drawback is the low productivity, especially when the employee is unable to fully develop his skills.

However, this training is generally given in a large number of organisations, and is suitable for all levels of operatives, supervisors and executives, for it needs no schools, and the employee's contribution adds to the total output of the enterprise.

JOB INSTRUCTION TRAINING (JIT)

This method is very popular in the States for preparing supervisors to train operatives. The JIT method requires skilled trainers, extensive job analysis, training schedules, and prior assessment of the trainee's job knowledge. This method is also known as "training through step-by-step learning." It involves listing all necessary steps in the job, each in proper sequence. These steps show *what* is to be done. Along side each step is also listed a corresponding "Key point," which show *how* it is to be done and *why*.

The actual training follows a four-step process, beginning with *(i) the preparation of the trainee for instruction.* This includes putting him at ease, emphasising the importance of the task and giving a general description of job duties and responsibilities; *(ii) presentation of the instructions*, giving essential information *in a clear manner*. This includes positioning the trainee at work site, telling and showing him each step of the job, stressing why and how each step is carried out as it is shown; *(iii)* having the trainee try out the job to show that he has understood the instructions, if there are any errors they are corrected; and *(iv)* encouraging questions and allowing the trainee to work along and the trainer follows up regularly.

The JIT method provides immediate feedback on results, quick correction of errors, and provision of extra practice when required.

However, it demands a skilled trainer and can interfere with production and quality.

VESTIBULE TRAINING (OR TRAINING-CENTRE TRAINING)

This method attempts to duplicate on-the-job situations in a company classroom. It is a classroom training which is often imparted with the help of the equipment and machines which are identical with those in use in the place of work. This technique enables the trainee to concentrate on learning the new skill rather than on performing an actual job. In other words, it is geared to job duties. Theoretical training is given in the classroom, while the practical work is conducted on the production line.

It is a very efficient method of training semi-skilled personnel, particularly when many employees have to be trained for the same kind of work at the same time. It is often used to train clerks, bank tellers, inspectors, machine operators, testers, typists, etc. It is most useful when philosophic concepts, attitudes, theories and problem-solving abilities have to be learnt.

Training is generally given in the form of lectures, conferences, case studies, role-playing and discussion.

Merits: This method has several merits. *First,* as training is given in a separate room, distractions are minimised. *Second,* a trained instructor, who knows how to teach, can be more effectively utilised. *Third,* the correct method can be taught without interrupting production. *Fourth,* it permits the trainee to practise without the fear of supervisors'/co-workers' observation and their possible ridicule.

Demerits: First, the splitting of responsibilities leads to organisational problems. *Second,* an additional investment in equipment is necessary, though the cost may be reduced by getting some productive work done by trainees while in the school. *Third,* this method is of limited value for the jobs which utilise equipment which can be duplicated. *Finally,* the training situation is somewhat artificial.

However, when the number of trainees is large, vestibule schools are generally utilised; but when the number is small, on-the-job training is preferred.

TRAINING BY EXPERIENCED WORKMEN

By this method, training is imparted by experienced senior fellow-workers. It is particularly adaptable where experienced workmen need helpers. It is useful for departments in which workmen advance through successive jobs to perform a series of operations.

TRAINING BY SUPERVISORS

Such training is imparted on the job by the workers' immediate supervisors. It provides to the trainees opportunities for getting acquainted with their bosses. The bosses, too, have an opportunity to judge the abilities and possibilities of trainees from the point of view of their job performance.

The success of both these methods depends upon the fact that:

(a) The experienced supervisors must be good teachers;

(b) They should have incentives and sufficient time for carrying out the training programmes; and

(c) They should be provided with an accurate account of the training needs of the trainees they are to teach.

DEMONSTRATIONS AND EXAMPLES (OR LEARNING BY SEEING)

In the demonstration method, the trainer describes and displays something, as when he teaches an employee how to do something by actually performing the activity himself and by going through a step-by-step explanation of "why" and "what" he is doing.

Demonstrations are very effective in teaching because it is much easier to show a person how to do a job than to tell him or ask him to gather instruction from the reading material. Demonstrations are often used in combination with lectures, pictures, text materials, discussions, etc.

Teaching by example is effective in mechanical operations or interpersonal relationships, for job duties and responsibilities, for informal group standards, supervisory expectations, and the like.

Demonstrations are particularly effective in the training for the acquisition of skills; but their usefulness is limited when it is a question of training management personnel. In a demonstration, the emphasis is primarily on know-how, the principles and theory of a job must, therefore, be taught by some other method.

SIMULATION

Simulation is a technique which duplicates, as nearly as possible, the actual conditions encountered on a job. The vestibule training method or the business-game method are examples of business simulations. Simulation techniques have been most widely used in the aeronautical industry.

Trainee interest and employee motivation are both high in simulation exercise because the actions of a trainee closely duplicate real job conditions. This training is essential in cases in which actual on-the-job practice might result in a serious inquiry, a costly error, or the destruction of valuable materials or resources. It is for this reason that the technique is a very expensive one.

APPRENTICESHIP

For training in crafts, trades and in technical areas, apprenticeship training is the oldest and most commonly used method, especially when proficiency in a job is the result of a relatively long training period of 2 years to 3 years for persons of superior ability and from 4 years to 5 years for others. The field in which apprenticeship training is offered are numerous and range from the job of a draughtsman, a machinist, a printer, a tool-maker, a pattern designer, a mechanic, carpenters, weavers, fitters, jewellers, die-sinkers, engravers, and electricians. A major part of training time is spent on-the-job productive work. Each apprentice is given a programme of assignments according to a pre-determined schedule, which provides for efficient training in trade skills.

The merits of this method are: *(i)* A skilled workforce is maintained; *(ii)* Immediate returns can be expected from training; *(iii)* The workmanship is good; *(iv)* The hiring cost is lower because of reduced turnover and lower production costs; *(v)* The loyalty of employees is increased and opportunities for growth are frequent.

CLASS-ROOM OR OFF-THE-JOB METHODS

CLASS-ROOM OR OFF-THE-JOB METHODS

"Off-the-job training" simply means that training is not a part of everyday job activity. The actual location may be in the company class-rooms or in places which are owned by the company, or in universities or associations which have no connection with the company.

These methods consist of:

1. Lectures;
2. Conferences;
3. Group Discussions;
4. Case Studies;
5. Role-playing;

1. Lectures (or Class-Room Instruction): Lectures are regarded as one of the most simple ways of imparting knowledge to the trainees, especially when facts, concepts, or principles, attitudes, theories and problem-solving abilities are to be taught. Lectures are formal organised talks by the training specialist, the formal superior or other individual specific topics.

The lecture method can be used for very large groups which are to be trained within a short time, thus reducing the cost per trainee. It can be organised rigorously so that ideas and principles relate properly. Lectures are essential when it is a question of imparting technical or special information of a complex nature. They are usually enlivened with discussions, film shows, case studies, role-playing and demonstrations. Audio-visual aids enhance their value. "The lecture method is not dead as some would believe." In the hands of able lecturers, and for certain kinds of purposes and participants, it may turn out to be more interesting and effective than any other methods.

In training, the most important uses of lectures include:

(1) Reducing anxiety about upcoming training programmes or organisational changes by explaining their purposes.

(2) Introducing a subject and presenting an overview of its scope.

(3) Presenting basic material that will provide a common background for subsequent activities.

(4) Illustrating the application of rules, principles; reviewing, clarifying and summarising.

The main advantage of the lecture system is that it is simple and efficient and through it more material can be presented within a given time than by any other method.

However, the lecture system suffers from some limitations:

(i) The learners are passive instead of active participants. The lecture method violates the principle of learning by doing. It is a one-way communication. There is no feedback from the audience.

(ii) A clear and vigorous verbal presentation requires a great deal of preparation for which management personnel often lack the time. Moreover, it calls for a substantial speaking skill.

(iii) The attention span of even a well-motivated and adequately informed listener is only from 15 minutes to 20 minutes so that, in the course of an hour, the attention of listeners drifts.

(iv) It is difficult to stimulate discussion following a lecture, particularly if the listener is uninformed or awestruct by the lecturer.

(v) The untrained lecturer either rambles or packs far too much information in the lecture, which often becomes unpalatable to the listener.

(vi) The presentation of material should be geared to a common level of knowledge.

(vii) It tends to emphasise the accumulation and memorisation of facts and figures and does not stress on the application of knowledge.

(viii) Though a skilful lecturer can adapt his material to the specific group, he finds it difficult to adjust it for individual differences within a group.

According to the conclusions reached at the Conference on Management Education and Training (held from January 22 to 24, 1964) at Pune, the essential pre-requisites for a successful lecture method are:

(i) Group interest should be motivated and adapted to its needs;

(ii) A lecture should be well-planned as to purpose; the main ideas and organisation should be clear and the development interesting;

(iii) It should be presented by an enthusiastic and animated speaker who has his listener's needs and interest in mind at all times;

(iv) It should not last less than 30 minutes and not more than an hour;

(v) A lecture should be made interesting and enlist the active participation of the learners with the aid of guided discussion; the lecturer should pose leading questions, instead of giving out knowledge and information, to which the listeners should provide answers.

2. The Conference Method: In this method, the participating individuals 'confer' to discuss points of common interest to each other. A conference is basic to most participative group-centered methods of development. It is a formal meeting, conducted in accordance with an organised plan, in which the leader seeks to develop knowledge and understanding by obtaining a considerable amount of oral participation of the trainees. It lays emphasis on small group discussions, on organised subject matter, and on the active participation of the members involved. Learning is facilitated by building up on the ideas contributed by the conferees.

There are three types of conferences. In the *directed discussion,* the trainer guides the discussion in such a way that the facts, principles or concepts are explained. In the *training conference,* the instructor gets the group to pool its knowledge and past experience and brings different points of view to bear on the problem. In the *seminar conference,* answer is bound to a question or a solution to a problem. For this, the instructor defines the problem, encourages and ensures full participation in the discussion.

Merits: The conference is ideally suited for the purpose of analysing problems and issues and examining them from different viewpoints. It is an excellent method for the development of conceptual knowledge and for reducing dogmatism and modifying attitudes because the participants develop solutions and reach conclusions, which they often willingly accept.

Demerits: However, the conference method suffers from certain limitations:

(i) It is limited to a small group of 15 to 20 persons, because larger groups often discourage the active participation of all the conferees;

(ii) The progress is usually slow because all those desiring to speak on a point are generally allowed to do so. Consequently irrelevant issues easily creep in.

If the method is to be effective: *(a)* The conferees should have some knowledge of the subject to be discussed at the conference. *(b)* Good and stimulating leaders are needed, for it is they who summarise material at appropriate times during a discussion and think along with the group to help it analyse and reach decisions; adopt a permissive point of view which encourages members to express themselves without fear to censure or ridicule; control the more verbose members and bring out the more reserved; develop sensitivity to the thoughts and feelings of individuals and finally, ensure a general consensus on points without forcing agreement or side-stepping disagreement. *(c)* The size of the group should be small enough to allow each individual to participate and become personally involved in the deliberations of the group. *(d)* Training issue must involve a problem or need each individual is currently facing or interest in the conference results will wane.

3. Seminar or Team Discussion: This is an established method for training. A seminar is conducted in many ways:

(i) It may be based on a paper prepared by one or more trainees on a subject selected in consultation with the person in charge of the seminar. It may be a part of a study or related to theoretical studies or practical problems. The trainees read their papers, and this is followed by a critical discussion. The chairman of the seminar summarises the contents of the papers and the discussions which follow their reading.

(ii) It may be based on the statement made by the person in charge of the seminar or on a document prepared by an expert, who is invited to participate in the discussion.

(iii) The person in charge of the seminar distributes in advance the material to be analysed in the form of required readings. The seminar compares the reactions of trainees, encourages discussion, defines the general trends and guides the participants to certain conclusions.

(iv) Valuable working material may be provided to the trainees by actual files. The trainees may consult the files and bring these to the seminar where they may study in detail the various aspects, ramifications and complexities of a particular job or work or task.

4. Case Studies (or Learning by Doing): This method was first developed in the 1800s by Christopher Langdell at the Harvard Law School to help students to learn for themselves by independent thinking and by discovering in the ever-tangled skein of human affairs, principles and ideas which have lasting validity and general applicability. A collateral object is to help them develop skills in using their knowledge.

"The case study is based upon the belief that managerial competence can best be attained through the study, contemplation, and discussion of concrete cases. The 'case' is a set of data (real or fictional), written or oral miniature description and summary of such data that present issues and problem calling for solutions or action on the part of the trainee. When the trainees are given cases to analyse, they are asked to identify the problem and recommend tentative solutions for it. This method offers to the trainees matter for reflection and brings home to them a sense of the complexity of life as opposed to theoretical simplifications of, and practices in the decision-making process. It diagnoses and deals with real-life situations. The case study is primarily useful as a training technique for supervisors and is specially valuable as a technique of developing decision-making skills and for broadening the perspective of the trainee.

The person in charge of training, makes out a case, provides the necessary explanations, initiates the discussion going; and then, once the discussion gets going, he intervenes as little as possible. *In the incident method,* a full detailed description of a situation is not given. The trainer merely presents an outline, often in the form of a complaint from a customer or a severe conflict in the management of a business. The trainee arrives at the facts in issue by asking questions from the trainer or finding out a solution by "acting out" the situation in which a trainee plays a role. In the *live method,* trainers from a particular business describe its development and some of its problems. After discussions and detailed studies, the trainees prepare a report which contains an analyses of the situation and their recommendations on the corrective action to be taken.

In case study method, the trainee is expected to: *(i)* master the facts, become acquainted with the content of the case; *(ii)* define the objectives sought in dealing with the issues in the case, *(iii)* identify the problems in case and uncover their probable causes; *(iv)* develop alternative courses of action; *(v)* screen the alternatives using the objectives as the criteria; *(vi)* define the controls needed to make the action effective; and *(viii)* to 'role play' the action to test its effectiveness and find conditions that may limit it.

Merits: The merits of this method are: *First,* it promotes analytical thinking and develops a person's problem-solving ability. *Second,* it encourages open mindedness and serves as a means of integrating the knowledge obtained from different basic disciplines. *Third,* although trainees quickly learn that there is no single answer to, or solution of, a case problem, they are nevertheless expected to arrive at useful generalisations and principles. *Fourth,* since cases are usually based upon real problem situations the trainees' interest in them tends to be very great. *Fifth,* the method is accepted by everyone, for it deals with detailed descriptions of real-life situations. *Finally,* if the problems faced by managers are described, the trainees become increasingly aware of obscurities, contradictions and uncertainties they encounter in their business careers and the need for remedial action.

Demerits: The method has been criticised on many grounds.

First, it may degenerate into a mere dreary demonstration of dusty museum-pieces, if it is taught only from books at developing centres of learning. *Second,* instruction in the methods of analysis may not be given due importance. It may suppress the critical faculties of mediocre trainees, and the habit of bunking by analogies may develop. *Third,* the cases become permanent precedents in their minds and may be used indiscriminately. *Finally,* the preparation of cases is difficult, for it needs money and time, and it is not quite certain that the outcome of this method would be worth the expenditure in money and men incurred on it.

The method is extensively used in professional schools of law and business administration, in supervisory and executive training programmes in industry, and in teaching personnel management, human relations, labour relations, marketing, production management, business policy and other disciplines. In India, cases are prepared by the Administrative Staff College at Hyderabad and other 18 institutes of higher learning in management.

For an effective use of this method, it is essential that:

(i) The group of learners should be of such persons as are fairly well advanced in understanding the different concepts of management;

(ii) The case should be a faithful representation of the issues involved as objectively as possible without any observations and comments from the case writer;

(iii) It should be comprehensive and well-documented with a proper history, facts and figures, thus enabling students to see the organisation and the historical setting in which the reported events took place;

(iv) The case report should be realistic and based on first-hand information. It should not contain opinions discussed as factual information;

(v) The case situation should be reproduced in full and should be of the Harvard School type or a part of it may be presented in a film, or on television or on tape or recreated through role-playing;

5. *Role-playing:* This method was developed by Moreno, a Venetian psychiatrist. He coined the terms "role-playing," "role-reversal," "socio-drama," "psychodrana," and a variety of specialised terms, with emphasis on learning human relation skills through practice and insight into one's own behaviour and its effect upon others. It has been defined as "a method of human interaction which involves

realistic behaviour in the imaginary situations." As Norman Major has pointed out, a "role-playing experience soon demonstrates the gap between 'thinking' and 'doing.' The idea of role-playing involves action, doing and practice."

In role-playing, trainees act out a given role as they would in a stage play. Two or more trainees are assigned parts to play before the rest of the class. These parts do not involve any memorisation of lines or any rehearsals. The role-players are simply informed of a situation and of the respective roles they have to play. Sometime after the preliminary planning, the situation is acted out by the role-players.

Role-playing primarily involves employee-employer relationships — Hiring, firing, discussing a grievance procedure, conducting a post-appraisal interview or disciplining a subordinate or a salesman making a representation to a customer.

The *merits* of the role-playing method are:

(i) Learning by doing is emphasised;

(ii) Human sensitivity and interactions are stressed;

(iii) The knowledge of results is immediate;

(iv) Trainee interest and involvement tend to be high;

(v) It is a useful method to project the living conditions between learning in the classroom and working on a job and creating a live business situation in the classroom;

(vi) It develops skills and ability to apply knowledge, particularly in areas like human relations; and

(vii) It brings about desired changes in behaviour and attitudes.

Thus, role playing is especially useful in providing new insight and in presenting the trainee with opportunities to develop interactional skills. Unless the trainer engages in coaching or unless someone states the criteria for behaviour, however, role playing may not adhere to the objectives of the training programme and the reinforcement of the desired behaviour may be somewhat lacking. In other words, it is conceivable that the practice the trainee gets in interpersonal relations could be faulty.

Retraining: Retraining programmes are generally arranged for employees who have long been in the service of an organisation. The retraining programme may be necessitated by the following facts:

(i) Some employees are engaged in a confined phase of a particular task and lose their all-round skills in a particular trade. Hence, to keep them active in all-round skills, such training is needed.

(ii) During prolonged lay-off periods, employees on certain highly skilled jobs are given retraining when they are called back to work.

(iii) Technological changes may make a particular job, on which an employee is working, unnecessary, and the company may desire to retrain him rather than discharge him.

(iv) An employee, because of illness, accident or incapacity due to age, may no longer be able to do his share of the work he performed when he was in normal health.

(v) Economic depression or cyclical variations in production create conditions in which employment stabilisation may be achieved by having a versatile work-force capable of performing more than one job.

IMPLEMENTATION OF TRAINING

Once the training programme has been designed, it needs to be implemented. Implementation is beset with certain problems. Firstly, most managers are action-oriented and frequently say no to training efforts. Secondly, there is problem of locating suitable trainers within an organisation. Any training programme implementation involves action on the following lines:

(1) Deciding the location and organising training and other facilities.

(2) Scheduling the training programme.

(3) Conducting the programme.

(4) Monitoring the progress of trainees.

TRAINING EVALUATION

Objectives of training evaluation is to determine the ability of the participant in the training programme to perform jobs for which they were trained, the specific nature of training deficiencies, whether the trainees required any additional on the job training, and the extent of training not needed for the participants to meet job requirements.

PRINCIPLES OF EVALUATION

Evaluation of the training programme must be based on the following principles:

(1) Evaluation specialist must be clear about the goals and purposes of evaluation.

(2) Evaluation must be continuous.

(3) Evaluation must be specific.

(4) Evaluation must provide the means and focus for trainers to be able to appraise themselves, their practices, and their products.

(5) Evaluation must be based on objective methods and standards.

(6) Realistic target dates must be set for each phase of the evaluation process. A sense of urgency must be developed, but deadlines that are unreasonably high will result in poor evaluation.

There are various approaches to training evaluation. To get a valid measure of training effectiveness, the personnel manager should accurately assess trainee's job performance two to four months after completion of training.

Two writers have suggested that four basic categories of outcomes can be measured.

1. Reaction: Evaluate the trainee's reaction to the programme. Did he like the programme? Did he think it worthwhile?

2. Learning: Did the trainee learn the principles, skills and fact that the supervisor or the trainer wanted him to learn?

3. Behaviour: Whether the trianee's behaviour on the job changed because of the training programme?

4. Results: What final results have been achieved? Did he learn how to work on machine? Did scrappage costs decrease? Was turnover reduced? Are production quotas now being met? etc.

Questionnaires or structured interviews with the immediate supervisor of the trainees are acceptable methods for obtaining feedback on training. The supervisor is asked to rate the former trainee on job proficiency directly related to the training objectives.

Another approach is to involve the use of experimental and control groups. Each group is randomly selected, one to receive training (experimental) and the other not to receive training (control). The random selection helps to assure the formation of groups quite similar to each other. Measures are taken of relevant indicators of success (e.g., words typed per minute, units of work produced per hour, reduction in wastage and turnover, etc.), before and after training for both groups. If the results shown by the experimental group are significantly greater than those of the control group, the training can be considered as successful.

Another method involves longitudinal or time series analysis. A series of measurements are taken before the programme begins and continues during and after the programme is completed. The results obtained are plotted on a group to determine whether changes have occurred and remain as a result of the training effort.

Besides, pre-and-post tests be administered to the training groups. Prior to the training, a test related to the training material is applied, and the results of this pre-test are compared with results on the same or similar test administered after the programme has been completed.

WHY TRAINING FAILS?

The following factors have been regarded as the main reasons for failure of training programmes:

(1) The benefits of training are not clear to the top management.

(2) The top management hardly rewards supervisors for carrying out effective training.

(3) The top management rarely plans and budgets systematically for training.

(4) The middle management, without proper incentives from top management, does not account for training in production scheduling.

(5) Without proper scheduling from above, first line supervisors have difficulty in production norms if employees are attending training programmes.

(6) Behavioural objectives are often imprecise.

(7) Training external to the employing unit sometimes teaches techniques on methods contrary to practices of the participants' organisation.

(8) Timely information about external programmes may be difficult to obtain.

(9) Trainers provide limited counselling and consulting services to the rest of the organisation.

IMPROVING EFFECTIVENESS OF TRAINING

The training programmes can be made effective and successful if the following hints are considered:

1. Specific training objectives should be outlined on the basis of the type of performance required to achieve organisational goals and objectives. An audit of

personal needs compared with operational requirements will help to determine the specific training needs of individual employees. This evaluation should form a well-defined set of performance standards towards which each trainee should be directed.

2. Attempt should be made to determine if the trainee has the intelligence, maturity, and motivation to successfully complete the training programmes. If deficiencies are noted in these respects, the training may be postponed or cancelled till improvements are visible.

3. The trainee should be helped to see the need for training by making him aware of the personal benefits he can achieve through better performance. He should be helped to discover the rewards and satisfactions that might be available to him through changes in behaviour.

5. Attempts should be made to create organisational conditions that are conducive to a good learning environment. It should be made clear why changes are needed. Any distractions, in the way of training environment, should be removed. The support of the upper levels of management should be obtained before applying training at lower levels.

6. If necessary, a combination of training methods should be selected so that variety is permitted and as many of the senses as possible are utilised.

7. It should be recognised that all the trainees do not progress at the same rate. Therefore, flexibility should be allowed in judging the rates of progress in the training programme.

8. If possible, the personal involvement or active participation of the trainee should be got in the training programme. He should be provided with opportunity to practise the newly needed behaviour norms.

9. As the trainee acquires new knowledge, skills or attitudes and applies them in job situations, he should be significantly rewarded for his efforts.

10. The trainee should be provided with regular, constructive feedback concerning his progress in training and implementation of the newly acquired abilities.

11. The trainee should be provided with personal assistance when he encounters learning obstacles.

MANAGEMENT DEVELOPMENT

All those persons who have authority over others and are responsible for their activities and for the operations of an enterprise are managers. In a business organisation, the co-ordination and direction of the efforts of others is a major part of the management job. The manager has to deal not only with the staff but also with others outside his own group, and has a decided influence on the organisation. In any organisation, each supervisor, foreman, executive is a manager in the area of his responsibility. Even the corporate chairman, departmental head, personnel administrator, planner or co-ordinator is, in fact, a manager, although many of them do not supervise others but are on the Board of Management. The titles of managers are not standardised; but, in a broad sense, all supervisors, foremen, executives and administrators and managers. These terms are used interchangeably.

The manager is the dynamic life-giving element in a business. The calibre and performance of managers will largely determine the success of a business. If the business wants to improve the quality of its managers, it must expend money and effort and introduce imaginative and systematic development schemes for them — in which managers themselves play a crucial role. All enterprises need to devote great attention to the continuous supply of their future managers, both functional and general.

Management development is any attempt to improve managerial performance by importing knowledge, changing attitudes or increasing skills. It includes programs conducted in the company and external programs conducted outside the company by external trainers.

A manager's task includes certain skills which can be improved, even perfected or nearly so. The major and more elusive task of management development is to mould and fashion the behaviour component into a virile and unmixed weapon of enterprise achievement. The secret of effective management lies in vitality, a conceptual attitude of mind concerned with profitable results matched by determination and integrity in management and managers.

MANAGERIAL FUNCTIONS

Managerial functions consist of three key tasks, viz.,

(i) The maintenance and operation of the organisational communication with a view to translating the broad organisational goals into detailed working purposes and providing feedback on progress on the problems of achievement.

(ii) The maintenance of the organisation.

(iii) The maintenance of faith in the *superiority* and *desirability* of achieving the organisational aims.

For the discharge of these functions, it is essential and appropriate that men with certain qualities are appointed. These qualities may be broadly identified as:

(a) *Domination by organisational personality,* i.e., surrender of personal predilections and desires while executing organisational action.

(b) *Adherence to corporate morality and code of conduct* in official actions under conditions of powerful contrary urges, i.e., *a high sense of responsibility.*

(c) *Possession of general abilities* such as persistence and determination, flexibility of mind and in leadership.

(d) *Specialised knowledge and ability* which are pertinent to a particular vocation or discipline.

KNOWLEDGE AND SKILLS OF THE MANAGER

In analysing the skills of a manger, Katz speaks of three types: technical, human and conceptual.

(a) Technical skills are those that enable a manager to use effectively techniques, methods, processes and equipment in performing specific jobs. To a large extent, these skills are developed through experience and education. Technical skills are most important for operating managers because many of the jobs they are called upon to perform require them to have some knowledge of "*how things work,*" i.e., they should have the ability to operate complex machinery, and have knowledge to interpret meaningful financial data. In every type of organisation, managers at the

lower levels have to understand the mechanics of their jobs if they are to supervise their subordinates effectively. However, as they move up the hierarchy, technical skills become less important than other skills.

(b) Human skills refer to the ability to work effectively with others on a person-to-person basis, and to build up co-operative group relations to accomplish the organisational goals. Such skills include the ability to communicate, motivate and lead. These skills are also referred to as *human relations abilities*, which enable a manager to handle human resources in such a way that not only personal satisfaction is achieved but organisational goals are also easily attained.

(c) Conceptual skills are those which make it possible for a manager to consider an enterprise as a whole and evaluate the relationships which exist between various parts or functions of a business. Top managers in particular need these skills because they are of the maximum importance in long-range planning. Such skills are concerned with the realm of ideas and creativity. The higher one rises in the

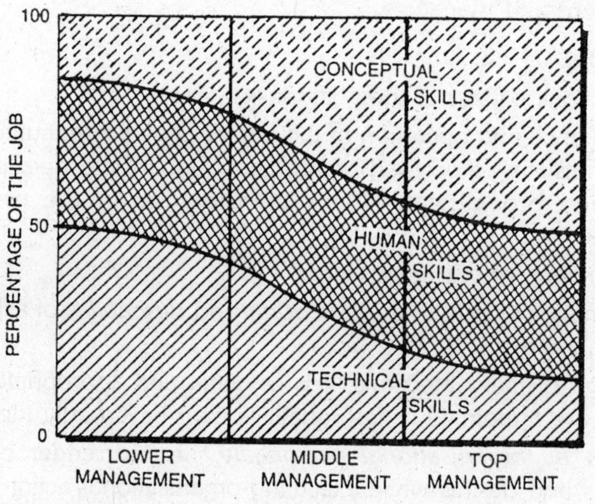

Fig. 8.2 Management Skills

management hierarchy, the greater the need of conceptual skills. For example, members of the Board of Directors have to rely heavily on their conceptual abilities in making decisions. On the other hand, supervisors and foremen have little need for conceptual skills and abilities, for their prime interest is in using technical and human skills.

In sum, *it may be said that technical skill is an essential ingredient in low-level management: human skills are important at all levels of the management: and conceptual skill is essentially critical in top executive positions.*

CHARACTERISTICS OF MANAGERS

The management development process would be better understood if the main characteristics of managers are noted. The successful manager in a large firm has the following characteristics:

(i) He moves rapidly from job to job. "It now takes 20 years on an average to rise from the first level manager to president, during which time there are seven geographical moves, 11 positional ones, and countless numbers of special and project

assignments." More than before, the successful manager's career may include moving from one company to another.

(ii) He is flexible, realistic and sensitive to the complexities of his work environment. Compared with less successful managers, he is both challenged by, and comfortable in, situations filled with high risk and ambiguity.

(iii) He earns his spurs by handling critical assignments, which are more important than routine work done well.

(iv) Very often, he has a "sponsor", someone from the higher management who is impressed by his abilities, finds him useful to have around, and who looks after his interests. It helps if the sponsor is himself moving up rapidly.

(v) He engages in "anticipatory socialization"; at each stage he copies the values of those who are a step above him.

(vi) He is not necessarily an "organisation conformist." High level managers tend to be more "inner directed" and less "outer directed" and less concerned with pleasing others than are those at lower levels.

Executive or management development activities are used inter-changeably. They are that part of the enterprise function which aim at full development of mangers at whatever level they are. Executive development is a systematic process of training and management development is a systematic process of training and growth by which managerial personnel gain and apply skill, knowledge, attitude and insights to manage the work in their organisations effectively and efficiently. In other words, "management development is an educational process utilising a systematic and organised procedure by which nmanagerial personnel learn conceptual and theoretical knowledge for general purposes." These purposes concern: *(i)* Productivity; *(ii)* Quality; *(iii)* Human resource planning; *(iv)* Morale; *(v)* Indirect compensation; *(vi)* Health and safety; *(vii)* Obsolescence prevention; and *(viii)* Personnel growth.

PURPOSE AND OBJECTIVE OF MANAGEMENT DEVELOPMENT

Executive development is an attempt at improving an individual's managerial effectiveness through a planned and deliberate process of learning. For an individual this means a change through a process of planned learning. This should be the common and significant aim of development attempts from the point of view of the trainer and the trainee in an organisational setting.

"All development is self development. It must be generated within the man himself. Development is highly individual. The development of an individual is due to his day to day experience on a job. Hence, emphasis should be on experiences from day to day work. Any activity to designed to improve the performance of existing managers and to provide for a planned growth of managers to meet future organisational needs is management development.

The change in the individual must take place in those crucial areas which can be considered as *output variables:*

(i) Knowledge change;

(ii) Attitude change;

(iii) Behaviour change;

(iv) Performance change; and

(v) End-operational results (the last two changes being the result of the first three changes).

The success of development effort, to be marked as effective depends upon the following *inputs:*

(i) Trainee's personal characteristics, such as his intelligence and motivation to learn;

(ii) His actual learning efforts.

These two variables are influenced by: *(i)* Formal organisation; *(ii)* Leadership climate; and *(iii)* Cultural factors, such as attitudes and norms of the small group of which an individual is a member.

The organisational aims of management development are to secure the following valuable end-results:

(i) Improvement in technical performance;

(ii) Improvement in supervision and leadership at each level;

(iii) Improvement in inter-departmental co-operation;

(iv) Highlighting an individual's weaknesses;

(v) Attracting good men;

(vi) Facilitating sound "promotion-from-within" policies and practices;

(vii) Ensuring that the qualifications of key personnel become better known;

(viii) Creating reserves in management ranks;

(ix) Marking an organisation more flexible by an increased versatility of its members;

(x) Improving organisational structure;

(xi) Stimulating junior executives to do better work;

(xii) Keeping the company abreast of technical and economic conditions; and

(xiii) 'Broadening' key men in the middle cadre.

In sum, *management development aims at securing management improvement in the short-run.*

The department of Industrial Administration and Business Management, Delhi University, Delhi, is of the view that management objectives should be:

(i) To create an understanding of the methods and problems of management;

(ii) To enable candidates to understand the problems of a business organisation in so far as they arise out of its policies and system of control; and

(iii) To indicate how to apply to practical problems the knowledge of the physical and social aspects of business problems and management.

On the basis of the survey undertaken by M. N. Basavaraj, the objectives of management development are:

(i) To develop managers to perform better on their present assignments;

(ii) To prepare them for higher assignments;

(iii) To provide a steady source of competent persons at all levels to meet future organisational needs;

(iv) To help them grow fast;

(v) To prevent obsolescence of managers;

(vi) To replace elderly executives, who have risen from the ranks, by highly competent and academically qualified processionals; and

(vii) To create conditions and a climate which contribute to the growth process.

Noting the practices in the U.S.A., Prof. A. Das Gupta has given the level-wise objectives of the management development thus:

(a) TOP MANAGEMENT

(i) To improve thought processes and of analytical ability in order to uncover and examine problems and take decisions in the best interests of the country;

(ii) To broaden the outlook of the executive in regard to his role, position and responsibilities in the organisation and outside;

(iii) To think through problems which may confront the organisation now or in the future:

(iv) To understand economic, technical and institutional forces in order to solve business problems; and

(v) To acquire knowledge about the problems of human relations.

(b) MIDDLE LINE MANAGEMENT

(i) To establish a clear picture of executive functions and responsibilities;

(ii) To bring about an awareness of the broad aspects of management problems, and an acquaintance with, and appreciation of, inter-departmental relations;

(iii) To develop the ability to analyse problems and to take appropriate action;

(iv) To develop familiarity with the managerial uses of financial accounting, psychology, business law and business statistics;

(v) To inculcate knowledge of human motivation and human relationships; and

(vi) To develop responsible leadership.

(c) MIDDLE FUNCTIONAL EXECUTIVE AND SPECIALISTS

(i) To increase knowledge of business functions and operations in specified fields in marketing, production, finance, personnel;

(ii) To bring about an awareness of the broad aspects of management problems, and an acquaintance with, and appreciation of, inter-departmental relations;

(iii) To develop familiarity with the managerial uses of financial accounting, psychology, business law and business statistics;

(iv) To inculcate knowledge of human motivation and human relationships; and

(v) To develop responsible leadership.

He concludes: "for the top management, the objectives are mostly general and aim at developing the ability to understand and to decide, although a few functional areas like personnel, marketing and finance are also included. For middle line executives, the objectives may be of two types: *one* to develop intellectually, and the *other* to broaden the outlook and improve the ability to make decisions along with some knowledge of specialised fields. In other words, the personnel development of an executive is a very important aim of management education; so is the need for preparing future executives in business.

It may be summed up that the primary objectives of executive development are: *(i)* to provide adequate leaders; *(ii)* to increase the efficiency of performance of existing executives; *(iii)* to serve as a means of control in operations; *(iv)* to train managers for higher assignment who show potential for growth greater than those of their colleagues; *(v)* to prepare them for adaptation to changes, environmental, ideological and technological; and *(vi)* to develop a unity of purpose and improve morale.

The need for management development has been keenly felt since the beginning of this century. Earlier, only a few chosen persons were picked up to fill the key posts, and these were the "crown princes" and "fair-haired boys" of an organisation; but now business and industry concentrate on the development of all those who are in management positions, or who are fresh from management institutions and have the potential for development. Since no two persons are alike in capacity, ability, experience and temperament, "tailor-made" programmes have been evolved to meet individual needs.

The causes of, or factors which bring about, management development programmes may be stated thus:

1. The rapid rate of technological and social change in society has necessitated the training of managers so that they may cope with these developments.

2. The introduction of automation, intense market competition from foreign countries, the growth of new markets in the under developed countries, enlarged participation of labour in management, and greater interest by the public and the government in the actions of businessmen have all led to the need for the development of managerial personnel.

3. Increased recognition by business and industrial leaders of the social and public responsibilities of management has necessitated the development of managerial personnel.

4. The increased size and complexity of most organisations — governmental, industrial, commercial, non-profit public services — require trained managers.

5. The frequent labour-management strifes have necessitated the services of trained personnel.

6. The changes in socio-economic forces, including changes in public policy and the concepts of social justice, industrial democracy, problems of *ecology* (smog or pollution), *ekistics* (the problems of human settlements), *ergonomics* (the problem of working environment), and *cultural anthropology* (the problem of fitting machines to men) — all these demand increasing attention of the management for decisions in diverse fields. If management development programmes are not evolved, the managerial personnel would become "obsolete." Managerial obsolescence may be due to redundancy, mergers and take-overs, reorganisations, changes in technology, products and trade and individual causes. Such obsolescence may lead to lay-off, which may cause a great emotional trauma and disturbance.[16] David Ewing has rightly said: "The managerial personnel must realise that they will not survive unless they keep pace with modern management education, research theory, principles and practices."

NEED FOR MANAGEMENT DEVELOPMENT IN THE INDIAN CONTEXT

There is growing need for the development of an efficient managerial pool to meet the challenges of industry. Realising this, many management institutes and training organisations have geared up their training and development activities to a great extent. However, there is a certain imbalance in the spread of management education. A concentration of management training is found in the industrial sector mostly in traditional industries and public sector enterprises. Therefore, India requires:

1. Techno-managers in such sectors as engineering and steel, coal, fertilizer, oil and cement industries. Personnel in these industries need training not only in the functional areas of management but also need to acquire a thorough knowledge of the sector.

2. Management resource mobilisation towards professionalising such public utilities as water supply, power distribution, transport and communications, for agriculture and industry are dependent on the efficient functioning of these utilities.

3. Government and civic offices organised to render public services, including municipal services, housing, insurance, mass media, police, medical services and education, have been untouched by the management movement. The "managerialisation" of these services needs immediate attention.

4. Management principles and techniques need to be introduced in other areas of national economy — managerial services for agriculture and rural development, irrigation, co-operation and animal husbandry, fisheries, forestry and marketing. Management know-how also needs to be brought to bear on production processes at the farm level with a view to increasing efficiency in the tertiary or service sector in rural areas.

5. Public administration is a vast sector which needs management attention, because this segment has a direct relevance to economic and social activity, for it brings functionaries into contact with the citizenry and the entrepreneurial class.

6. Management development programmes for all those who are engaged in positions above the supervisory level of operations — whether as Deans of hospitals, the Vice-Chancellors of Universities, Superintendents of Police or Collectors of districts. Their job calls for the use of a management component which is concerned with such skills as leadership and communication. For them, training in management, productivity and human relations would be very valuable.

MANAGEMENT DEVELOPMENT CONCEPTS

A number of development concepts have evolved over the past quarter of a century. These concepts were nurtured by modest experimentation and a vast amount of empirical findings. They now form the basis of sound programmes of management development. Some of these important concepts are:

(i) There is no time limit for learning. Management training is not a "one-shot" affair but continues throughout an executive's whole professional career.

(ii) There always exists some gap between actual performance and capacity, which provides considerable opportunity for improvement. A large number of employees do operate below a pre-determined standard which their training aptitude desires of them. If they get further training and acquire additional technical knowledge in management, in communication and in organisational affairs, they are bound to work faster and more efficiently, actively, and productively.

(iii) Increased understanding of others, their behavioural attitude and of oneself definitely aid in managing and contributing to personal development, which is needed to increase and expand managerial effectiveness.

(iv) There are certain forces which may retard further growth but these may be offset or the direction of their movement changed. For example, interests tend to become restricted with age; habits fixed; motivation is reduced; and one may not like to move on to another job or place because of the effort and cost involved in this move, which one may not be willing to provide for.

(v) Development seldom takes place in a completely peaceful and relaxed atmosphere. Growth involves stresses and strains. "Adversity is the mother of invention." Growth is possible when one is willing to meet new, more difficult and more challenging situations. Growth, moreover, is almost always accompanied by errors and some failures. It is because of the errors and failures that one is impelled to try and succeed in one's mission.

(vi) Development requires a clear-cut setting of the objectives and goals which are to be achieved or attained, and the ways and methods of achieving these.

(vii) Participation is essential for growth. Active learning and effort are needed. *Spoon-feeding seldom brings significant or long-lasting improvement.*

(viii) Feedback from a superior to a subordinate, and from a group to an individual *is necessary* for the recognition of shortcomings and for keeping oneself in touch with the progress that has been achieved.

(ix) An important responsibility in the management of personnel is that of development. Management is a major factor in organisational efficiency.

It is on the basis of these concepts that programmes of development *must be* constructed, for it is *through* these concepts that an organisation itself grows.

COMPONENTS OR INGRADIENTS OF MANAGEMENT DEVELOPMENT PROGRAMME

The essential components or steps of a comprehensive management development programme are discussed below under the following heads:

(i) Looking at organisation's objectives;

(ii) Ascertaining development needs;

(iii) Appraisal of present management talents;

(iv) Preparation of Manpower Inventory;

(v) Planning of individual development programmes;

(vi) Establishment of training and development programmes;

(vii) Programme evaluation.

Diagramatically the model for developing executives may be shown as in Fig. 8.3.

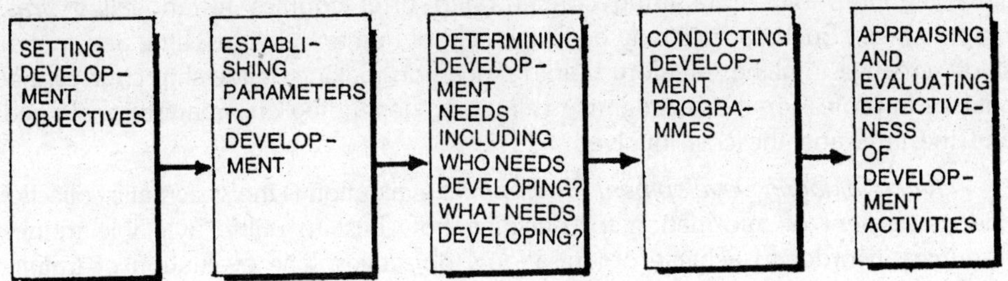

Fig. 8.3 Model for Developing Executives

(i) Looking at Organisations' Objectives: this is the first step in executive development programme. The objects tell "where we are going" and will develop a framework from which the executive need can be determined.

(ii) Ascertaining Development Needs calls for organisational planning and forecast of its needs for present and future growth. This is generally based upon a comprehensive job description, job specification and job analysis — with particular reference to the kind of management work performed, the kind of executives needed, and the kind of education, experience, training, special knowledge, skills, personal traits, etc., required for such work. Most companies train their own executives, except when they experience a critical shortage of specialised high-level talent. In the latter case, executives are hired from outside.

(iii) An Appraisal of Present Management Talent is made with a view to determining qualitatively the type of personnel that is available within an organisation itself. The performance of a management individual is compared with the standard expected of him. His personal traits are also analysed so that a value judgment may be made of his potential for advancement.

(iv) A management Manpower Inventory is prepared for the purpose of getting complete information about each management individual's biodata and educational qualifications, the results of tests and performance appraisal. It may also be maintained on *replacement tables or charts.* From these, it can be known that several capable executives are available for training for higher positions.

An analysis of the information will bring to the attention of the management the potential obsolescene of some of the present executives, the inexperience or shortage of managers in certain functions, and skill deficiencies relative to the future needs of the organisation.

(v) The Planning of Individual Development Programmes is undertaken to meet the needs of different individuals, keeping in view the differences in their attitudes and behaviour, and in their physical, intellectual and emotional qualities. The weak and strong points of an individual are known from his performance appraisal reports; and, on the basis of these, tailor-made programmes are framed and launched. Such programmes give due attention to the interests and goals of the subordinates as well as the training and development opportunities which exist within an organisation.

(vi) Establishment of Training and Development Programmes this job is done by the personnel department. A comprehensive and well-conceived programme is generally prepared, containing concentrated brief courses (often called *crash programmes).* Such courses may be in the field of human relations, time and motion study, creative thinking, memory training, decision-making, leadership courses, and courses in professional or academic institutions, depending on organisational needs and the time and the cost involved.

(vii) Evaluating Development Programmes evaluation is the systematic collection and assessment of information for deciding how best to utilise available training resources in order to achieve organisational objectives. The evaluation of training has been defined by Hamblin as "any attempt to obtain information (feedback) on the effects of a training programme and to assess the value of training in the light of that information." According to him, the objectives of evaluating development programmes are:

(a) *Reactions objectives,* that is, objectives intended to "stimulate a high level of involvement and interest."

(b) *Learning objectives,* that is those objectives which are concerned with acquiring knowledge, skills and attitudes.

(c) *Job behaviour objectives,* which are concerned with achieving over-all results.

Other authorities are of the opinion that an evaluation of training is helpful because:

(a) It discloses the relevance of programmes to an organisation's needs, i.e., what changes are to be made in existing programmes to make them more effective;

(b) It reveals whether programmes have contributed to the effectiveness of an organisation; and

(c) It tells us whether programmes need to be continued or replaced by other relevant activities, which might aid in the achievement of an organisation's goals.

According to Tracey, the most important means of evaluating development programmes are:

(a) *Observation,* that is, observing the behaviour of people. Such observation must be specific, systematic, quantitative, recorded and expert;

(b) *Ratings,* under which various elements of the training system should be rated independently by several raters. The elements of rating are the trainees, instructors, equipment, materials, training aids and facilities;

(c) *Trainee surveys,* concerned with knowing the opinion of the trainees about the programmes;

(d) *Trainee interviews,* at which ideas and views of the trainees are elicited.

Two other methods may be added to this test. *One,* measuring the score secured by a trainee in tests and examination; *two,* measuring changes that might have taken place in such areas as costs, quality, quantity of work, grievances.

SHORT-TERM MEASUREMENT OF RESULTS

When programmes are designed to meet critical current needs, the results may be measured in terms of the success in meeting those needs — for safety, grievance reduction, quality, cost reduction, and improvement in report writing. The employee opinion survey can be useful as a measuring tool when it indicates deficiencies which are then attacked by the management. A second survey can show how much progress has been made in eliminating specific problem areas.

When the question is *how much* has been learned, objective tests may be arranged. Where specific goals have been established for an individual as result of appraisal, a review of such goals in subsequent conferences or appraisals will give an indication of the progress that has been achieved.

LONG-TERM MEASUREMENT OF RESULTS

The indices in determining the effectiveness of an entire programme of development are general. It is possible to use certain criteria — for example, the nature of problems confronted and how they are met, the general feeling or morale of an organisation, its progress, pace of operating, and the quality of decisions.

The final test is a judgement as to what extent a programme hampers or helps in the achievement of the basic goals of an enterprise.

ORGANISATIONAL CLIMATE FOR MANAGEMENT DEVELOPMENT

Management development cannot take place unless a favourable climate for it is created at the top which extends down through each level of the organisation. It may come to a standstill if encouragement is not available to the persons concerned. If the growth stops at the middle management, it is impeded at that level; and then the first line management and non-supervisory employees, too, suffer. Therefore, the creation of a proper organisational climate is a "must" for the success of any development programme.

By "organisational climate" is meant the circumstances or conditions in which the management guides the development and growth of the people at all levels by training, counselling, delegation and communication. The growth process is largely influenced in the home environment of a company by the manner in which superiors and peers manage the affairs, the manner in which they treat people, how they delegate authority, how they encourage ideas, initiative and enterprise, how they provide opportunities to experiment and test new concepts, tools and techniques, and how they project company goals, policies and philosophy.

In order that a proper development climate is created, it must be borne in mind that;

First, development is a learning rather than a teaching process; the burden for final growth rests on the individual.

Second, growth takes place through a striving process in which sights (objectives) are set high and tasks involve "stretching."

Third, development takes place largely by building on the strength of the people rather than by a concentration on the elimination of weakness.

Fourth, a feeling of confidence in, and approval of, the process of development must be generated among those who are to be affected by it. This is seldom possible when the superior has a negatively critical point of view.

Fifth, at all levels, a genuine faith in development is necessary, a belief that people *can* and *will,* with proper goals and encouragement, do better.

Finally, all concerned must, with an open heart and mind, be willing to welcome and accept any change in a point of view.

To develop a proper management climate, it is vital to pay a vigorous and constant attention to the administration of a development programme. There must be a comprehensive and co-ördinated planning, and the plan should apply first to the top so that management at that level may, by its own efforts, set an example for personnel development.

In our view, the management development programme should be based on a definite strategy, which should spell out the type, coverage and objectives of the programme. The multi-tier supervisory and management development programme should start from the first line supervisor and go all the way up to the top management.

A management programme should not only be looked upon as something meant for the "limping horses" in the organisation; it should be for the "high fliers" as well. In view of knowledge explosion and the consequent threat of managerial obsolescence, such programmes should be meant for everyone in an organisation and not just for the "weak ones."

The training division should not be a dumping ground for people found to be unsuitable for other jobs; it should be manned by a group of smart and successful executives drawn from various functional areas and disciplines. A multi-disciplinary approach should be emphasised in training programmes rather than the purely personal flavour that is often found in them.

For the development of management, it is essential for the top management to promote a culture:

(i) For learning and gaining knowledge;

(ii) For the quest of excellence;

(iii) For tolerance of mistakes;

(iv) For striving to maintain a balance and an equity;

(v) Which enables a subordinate to become aware of his superiors' interest in his development and mental growth; and

(vi) For the discovery of self and of others.

The programme should be prepared well in advance and should contain decisions about instructional methods and development approached to be used and have a provision of expertise and the necessary support system, and should be based on the policy of promoting a proper utilisation of trained executives, their knowledge and techniques in the improvement of the operations of an organisation.

Management development programmes may be made fruitful by circulating the following materials among the participants:

(i) Newsletter conveying information about corporate affairs;

(ii) Copies of talks given by management personnel;

(iii) Excerpts from well-written and informative articles;

(iv) Copies of minutes of meetings distributed among those who were not present.

When this material is discussed by a group, new plans and improved procedures often result.

PEDAGOGICAL APPROACHES TO AND TECHNIQUES OF MANAGEMENT DEVELOPMENT

A large number of management development methods and techniques are used. These include: lectures, conferences, seminars or group discussions, case studies, films and slides, outside reading and private study panels, forums, role playing and workshop. These have been discussed in a previous chapter. The other techniques used are: Under-study, job-rotation, coaching and counselling, position, professional classes, membership in professional and technical associations, committee assignments, management course in colleges, and professional institutes and universities, multiple management syndicate incident process, project management, or in basket, business game and sensitivity training.

Observe Yoder and others that "the multiplicity of these methods and techniques is because of their applications for different groups and jobs." However, with respect to particular management development methods, it has been suggested that no one technique is most effective: "Lectures, discussion techniques, role playing, case analysis and T-groups have been shown to have an impact. Comparative studies have indicated some superiority for certain procedures in specific instances."

Chart 8.3 gives as inventory of teaching methods, training techniques, development media etc.

CHART 8.3

Range of Management Development

(A) Leader-Centred Instruction (Structure and controlled by the instructor: a more or less authoritarian directive).	Traditional lecture, chart lecture, slipboard lecture, slide-lecture, indirect lecture, dinner meeting lecture, etc.
(B) Student-Centred Instruction (Permissive and democratic).	*(a)* Discussion-guided or directed. *(b)* Case discussion. *(c)* Problem-solving conferences work-shops, syndicates, seminars, brain-storming, buzz sessions. *(d)* Role-playing, socio-drama. *(e)* Stimulated group activities: *(i)* Business games; *(ii)* In-basket games; *(iii)* Exercises; and *(iv)* Workshops. *(f)* Sensitivity training or T-Groups.

(C) Student-on-his-own (Self-teaching, but structured/ controlled by the instructor).	*(i)* Planned reading; *(ii)* Correspondence courses; *(iii)* Programmed instruction(PI); *(iv)* Computer-aided instruction (CAI); *(v)* New-letters, manuals, handouts; and *(vi)* T.V. lessons;
(D) Individual off-the-job (mid-stream education, different methods).	*(i)* Night School/College on leave to attend short-term programmes.
(E) Individual on the job (Guided and controlled experience under line managers, etc).	*(i)* Coaching and counselling; *(ii)* Job rotation, assistant to positions; *(iii)* Under study; *(iv)* Task force assignment; *(v)* Junior Board or Committee members.

The methods of management development have been classified in two broad categories, viz., the leader-centred method and the student centred method.

Under the *leader-centred method:*

(a) Suggestions are evaluated by the instructor who advises or leads the class to correct their conclusions;

(b) Techniques and steps for activities are given by the instructor.

(c) The instructor, rather than the student, considers and handles questions and individual problems; and

(d) The instructor is the focus of attention. Student to student attention happens rarely or very occassionally.

Lecture and lecture-cum-discussion methods are typical examples of the leader-centre method.

Under the student-centred method:

(a) The instructor encourages suggestions from students and uses this procedure to stimulate the class to carry out class activities.

(b) Techniques and steps for activities emerge from group discussions;

(c) Group consideration of individual problems is encouraged by the instructor, and

(d) Students direct their attention to one another. The instructor becomes the focus of their attention only when discussion or activity required guidance.

Group discussion, decision-making, group activities (including case method, role-playing, T-Group training, etc.) are examples of this method.

Powel has shown the comparative value of different methods thus: Some very popular and frequently used training methods and techniques are:

CHART 8.4
Comparative Value of Different Methods

Primary Purposes	*Method*
1. Explaining facts and procedures, expounding general principles	Lecture, guided discussion
2. Developing analytical skills and ability to ask oneself questions	Case method, incident process
3. Developing awareness of oneself and one's impact on others	Sensitivity training (T-Group). Role-playing
4. Carrying over from class to job	Problem-solving conference
5. Inducing change in behaviour	Role-playing, T-Groups, Problem-solving conference
6. Opportunity for emotional catharsis	T-Groups, case method, problem-solving conference
7. Insuring good training with skilled trainers	Lectures, incident process

ON-THE-JOB TECHNIQUES

Where the object of managers' development is improving on-the-job behaviour, this method of training and education has its own value. It is inexpensive and saves productive hours. But the main drawback is that neither the trainer nor the trainee is free from the daily chores and the pressure of their respective routine jobs. A senior has seldom the time and patience to impart training to the person.

Most popular techniques under this type are:

1. The coaching or guided method,
2. Job rotation method, and
3. Participation in deliberations of the Boards and Committees.

1. THE COACHING METHOD

Coaching is a method which is used in developing managerial thinking processes as well as operative skills. In coaching, the superior plays the role of the guide and the instructor. The coach sets some mutually agreed upon goals and tells the trainee what he wants to be done, suggests how it might be done, follows up suggestions, and corrects errors. He helps the trainee live up to those goals through periodic reviews of the trainee's progress and by suggesting modifications in his behaviour where needed. The objective of coaching is not only to teach and guide a subordinate in the performance of his immediate assignments but also provide him with deversified work so that he may grow and progress.

The coaching method enjoys certain advantages: *(i)* It requires the least centralised staff co-ordination, for every executive can coach his men even if no management development programme exists. *(ii)* Periodic feedback and evaluation are also a part of coaching, which yield immediate benefits to an organisation, to the coach and to the subordinate. *It is learning by doing.*

However, *(i)* the coaching technique is authoritarian, for an executive tends to familiarise his subordinates with his own work habits and beliefs, even though these may be faulty. In other words, it has the tendencies to perpetuate the current managerial styles and practices in the organisation. *(ii)* It heavily relies on the coaoh's ability to be good teacher, which he may not necessarily be. *(iii)* The training atmosphere, free from worries of the daily duties, is not available.

To be effective, coaching demands that the superior should render assistance when the subordinate seeks or needs it. The superior should have the ability to communicate and to stimulate, and should have patience to help his subordinates. He should also set aside time for scheduling sessions. He should avoid being too dominant in the performance process, so that the trainee can experience things for himself and does not become completely dependent upon the coach for decisions.

"Coaching will work well if the coach provides a good model with whom the trainee can identify; if both can be open with each other; if the coach accepts his responsibility fully; and if he provides the trainee with recognition of his improvement and suitable rewards."

2. JOB ROTATION METHOD OF DEVELOPMENT

Job rotation represents an excellent method for broadening the manager or potential manager, for turning specialists into generalists. It refers to the transfer or movement of executives from one job to another and from one plant to another on some planned basis for educational learning purposes. "Job rotation is often designed for beginning level managers while planned progression is more likely to occur at higher managerial levels." Such rotation may continue for a period ranging from 6 months to 24 months. This method provides a great deal of job experience for those who are potential executives who need broadening of outlook and an increased understanding of the various aspects of management. The emphasis is on diversified instead of specialised skills and knowledge.

Under this method, the trainees are rotated over various routine jobs in a department, division or unit before they are due for promotion as managers. The idea is to impart an overall knowledge and familiarity with the different sectional jobs (such as billing, issuing challans, preparing inspection notes, settling railway claims, handling customer accounts, etc. in the sales department) before they are posted as Managers in the department. This secures a compromise between over-specialisation even from the lowest most routine level, and a minimum of special skills and expertise necessary for middle level managers. These persons are moved from one job to another according to a schedule of rotation. It also includes moving people between line and staff positions.

Job rotations are mostly *horizontal or lateral.* Such rotations can be instituted *(i) on a planned basis,* i.e., by means of a training programme whereby the worker spends 2 or 3 months in an activity and is then moved on; or *(ii) on a situational basis,* i.e., by moving the person to another activity when the first is no longer challenging to him, or to meet the needs of work scheduling.

Merits: The merits of this method are:

(i) It breaks down departmental provincialism for everyone is moved from one to another. It rather develops inter-departmental co-operation.

(ii) Boredom, monotony are reduced and since job rotation permits a greater understanding of other activities within the organisation people are prepared more rapidly to assume greater responsibility, especially at the upper echelons.

(iii) Job rotation injects new ideas into the older departmental personnel who may otherwise fall in a rut. New concepts are infused into them and they are diffused throughout an enterprise.

(iv) Through this system, a man does not end up in just one place. He gets a chance to step into a higher position. In this way, an organisation gains management strength in depth.

(v) Job rotation ensures the avoidance of the problem which arises when a newly promoted manager is required to supervise his former peers.

(vi) It makes it possible for the management to compare one man with another, and gives everyone an equal chance for advancement.

(vii) It does not develop "specialists" but produces "generalists," that is, men who take a broad, company-wide point of view, men whose chief ability is to handle people and make decisions.

(viii) Awareness of what is happening elsewhere and familiarity with other task-centres helps a balanced and informed attitude to enterprise goal and activities.

(ix) Each manager's abilities and talents are best tested in a variety of jobs, so the enterprise can secure his best utilisation in the ultimate assignment.

Demerits: Job rotation suffers from certain defects. There are:

(i) It upsets family and home life, because many a time transfers are effected to different geographical areas.

(ii) It undermines organisational morale, efficiency since "executives may have little inducement to sink their teeth deeply into as assignment." Established operations are disturbed and the manager is prone to error in a new seat.

(iii) It becomes difficult for a subordinate to adjust himself to his new bosses. Interpersonal relationship takes time for adjustment and employees, with frequent moves, are apt to feel insecure.

(iv) The new incumbent is likely to bring in a zeal for change; while sound changes are good, ill-conceived and hasty innovations may lead to costly experimentations.

(v) Job rotation can demotivate intelligent and aggressive trainees who seek specific responsibility in their chosen speciality.

(vi) It develops sharp cleavages, friction, jealously and other non-co-operative and dysfunctional forms of human behaviour;

(vii) The system is like a highly competitive game of "musical chairs." Whenever there are promotions and transfers, some people are left behind. Therefore, smart young people avoid taking risks.

(viii) Rotation sometimes leads to subtle class distinctions. Men who are not rotated tend to develop defensive reactions. This leads to misunderstanding and poor communication.

(ix) The system may easily become over-centralised, inflexible and "closed."

For rotation to be effective, those moved to different positions should be helped to understand the new task thoroughly, view the change as an opportunity for a genuine learning experience and identify themselves with the new position so that they may exercise full responsibility to achieve results and job improvement.

3. UNDERSTUDY ASSIGNMENT OR ATTACHMENT METHOD

An 'understudy' is a person who is under training to assume, at a future time, the full duties and responsibilities of the position currently held by his superior. In this way, it is ensured that a fully trained person is available to replace a manager during his long absence or illness, or on his retirement, transfer or promotion.

An understudy may be picked up by a manager from amongst a large number of subordinates, or several individuals. Such an understudy learns the complexities of the problems and how to solve them, learns also the process of decision-making and investigation and making written recommendations to his superior. He is generally assigned a project which is closely related to the work in his section. He is deputed to attend executive meetings as a representative of his superior, at which he makes a presentation and proposals. The essence is that the senior routes much of the departmental work through the junior; discusses problems with him and allows him to participate in the decision-making process as often as possible.

Merits: The understudy method enjoys certain advantages, viz.:

(i) It is practical and quick in training persons for greater responsibility for it lays emphasis on learning by doing.

(ii) The learners' interest and motivation are high and the superior is relieved of his heavy work load.

(iii) The trainee manager is also not overburdened with work and responsibility; at the same time he secures full participation in the running of the function and insight into the job-content.

(iv) The trainee is able continuously to obtain guidance of the senior. The work that passes through him opens up windows for him to appreciate different angles and view-points related to the job. He receives an opportunity to see the job in total.

(v) It ensures continuity of management facilities even when the superior leaves his position.

(vi) The chances of costly mistakes or upsetting relationship within the group are eliminated.

Demerits: But the method suffers from some defects as well, such as:

(i) Since the understudy is picked up by the superior often on the basis of favouritism, he tends to perpetuate the existing practices of in-breeding.

(ii) The motivation of all the employees in the unit may decrease since the incentive to get ahead is partially destroyed when one particular subordinate is identified in advance as one who will be the next occupant of a higher-level managerial position.

(iii) Under a competent senior, the Junior trainee might lose his independence and his critical appraisal of the way of job is performed.

(iv) The subordinate employees might ignore him and withhold cooperation; they might tend to treat him as an intruding appendage to the function without authority and accountability.

While there are opportunities for sizeable errors, this technique is used predominantly in situations where major or critical decisions can be delayed till the manager returns or can be made in close consultation with the manager next up in line.

4. PARTICIPATION IN DELIBERATIONS OF THE JUNIOR BOARD AND COMMITTEES OR THE MULTIPLE-MANAGEMENT TECHNIQUE

It is a technique whereby juniors are assigned to Board or Committees, by the chief executive. They are asked to participate in deliberations of these Board and Committees. In these sessions, real life actual problems are discussed, different views are debated and decisions are taken. The juniors get an opportunity to share in managerial decision-making, to learn by watching others and to delve into specific organisational problems. When Committees are of "ad hoc" or temporary nature, they often take a task force activities designed to delve into a particular problem, ascertain alternative solutions, and make a recommendation for implementing a solution. These temporary assignments can be both interesting and rewarding to the employees' growth. On the other hand, appointment to permanent committees increases the employees' exposure to other members of the organisation, broadens his understanding, and gives him an opportunity to grow and make reommendations under the scrutiny of other committee members.

Merits: This technique has several advantages:

(i) It gives Board members an opportunity to gain knowledge on various issues.

(ii) It helps identify those who have executive talent. Multiple judgements are obtained on each individual through the Board rating system.

(iii) The members gain practical experience of group decision-making and of team-work. As a result of the interaction process, they develop respect for the rights and view of their associates.

(iv) It is relatively inexpensive method of development.

(v) It permits a considerable number of managers to participate in certain activities within a reasonable period of time. Besides, the Boards do make important contributions to efficiency, productivity, and a better human relations climate. In fact, they assist in a better administration in the organisation.

Demerits: The demerits or limitations of the method are:

(i) It is only suitable for middle and senior level managers.

(ii) It does not permit any specific attention to training needs of the manager.

(iii) The debates in these committees often tend to be discursive lacking purposiveness or authority. The deliberations often degenerate into academic discussions without the participants feeling committed to the conclusions.

5. SYNDICATE

The purpose of the syndicate technique is to "expose a participant to a milieu in which he is persuaded into reflecting upon his experiences as an executive, updating his knowledge, improving his executive skills and developing a greater insight into human behaviour." In other words, this method enables an executive to acquire a proper perspective on his job in relation to the activities in areas other than his own, and to give him practice in skills, techniques and procedures which he has to use in his day-to-day work as he rises higher up the ladder of management.

By this methods, a team of persons of mature judgement and proved ability is set up with different functional representations so that there is an interchange of ideas and experiences. The syndicate is given a task properly spelt out in terms of briefs and background papers. Large groups are split into small ones (consisting of 7 to 10 persons), and discussions are supplemented by short lectures. The teacher acts as a "resource person" rather than as a lecturer. Both the organisation and participants must understand the machanics of the utilisation of this method; otherwise it would result in a lot of waste of time and frustration. Each syndicate prepares a report which is presented to the other groups of executives. An opportunity is provided for discussion, suggestions, criticism, comments and recommendations for action.

This method is used as a device not only for the study of a specific problem but also for other tasks.

OFF-THE-JOB TECHNIQUES

Although, as stated above, a number of on-the-job management development programmes are in vogue, they are considered inadequate for a number of reasons. And, hence, the need for off-the-job techniques. The limitations of on-the-job techniques are:

(i) The management process has become complex, but on-the-job training does not allow adequate facilities, environment and teaching expertise.

(ii) Though the main objective of management development is to improve behaviour of the managers in different environment, in actual practice, this objective is not well achieved.

(iii) Modern tools and techniques of managers' development are more sophisticated and highly developed and their handling needs specialised field instructions.

(iv) Technological developments demand that managers need to be placed in a highly manoeuvred and stimulated atmosphere to derive the maximum from training techniques. This is not possible on the job training.

(v) In a group of participants from different spheres of management and drawn from different enterprise cultures, the participants are exposed to new ideas, new ways of analysis and divergent experiences of members of the group. This provokes introspection and generates impulses to behaviour change.

There are a wealth of management development techniques that managers can partake in off-the-job. Of these, the more popular ones are:

1. The Case Study;
2. Incident Method;
3. Role Playing;
4. In-Basket Method;
5. Business or Management Game;
6. Sensitivity Training;
7. Simulation;
8. Grading Training;
9. Team Building;
10. Conferences; and
11. Lectures.

1. THE CASE STUDY

Case method is an excellent medium for developing analytical skill. It was started by Harvard Business School. This method is increasingly being used by many other prestigious and not so prestigious management institutes in India. What is a case? A case is "a written description of an actual situation in business which provokes in the reader the need to decide which is going on, what the situation really is or what the problems are and what can and should be done." A case is an objective description of a "real life" business situation in which executives are required to take action and are responsible for results.

In this method, an actual business situation is described, in writing, in a comprehensive manner. The trainees are asked to appraise and analyse the problem-situation and suggest solutions. The actual decision taken in the subject case is known only to the executive and is disclosed only at the end of the session when it is compared with the various solutions offered by the group.

Case study can provide stimulating discussions among participants as well as excellent opportunities for individuals to defend their analytical and judgemental abilities. It is rather an effective method for improving decision-making abilities within the constraints of limited information.

This method represents a dynamic and powerful approach to learning. Sometime the case discussion, takes place in a small syndicate before they are called upon to discuss before the whole class.

The case study method accomplishes several objectives of the management development programmes *(i)* It distributes knowledge and facts *(ii)* It improves participants' skills in problem analysis.

This method has already been discussed in the previous chapter and hence, need not be reiterated here.

2. INCIDENT METHOD

This method was developed by Paul and Faith Pigors. "The central aim of this method is to stimulate self-development in a blend of understanding that is essential for productive interaction. This blend combines *intellectual ability* (power to think clearly, incisively and reasonably about specific facts and also about abstractions); *Practical judgement* (capacity to modify conclusions arrived at intellectually, so that they meet the test of common sense); and *social awareness* (being able to appreciate the force of other people's feelings and willing to adjust or implement a decision so that it can be more acceptable to persons who are affected by it). Group work of each of 'these cases' begins when a group meets. Each member, working along for a couple of minutes, studies a written incident. He asks himself; What seems to be going on in this incident? What lead can I find here toward facts of the case and issues that stirred people up? Appended to each incident is an invitation to make short-term decisions in the role of a person who had to cope with the incident when it actually happened."

Under this method, group members address questions to the discussion leader. The general trend of questioning is to find out about the *what, when, where* and *how* of the situation in which an incident developed, and *who* was present there at the time. Clues are also tracked down if they seem to offer reliable insight into the *why* of behaviour. After the collection of data, it is necessary to isolate the most important items for decision-making.

Project: A project is a planned undertaking, a proposed scheme, a definitely formulated piece of research or a mental projection. This is an excellent method of learning. Students are assigned a specific problem area, depending on their specialisation and professional work. Each student studies a problem of the organisation, studies the facts and makes recommendations in the light of his theoretical learning in the classroom and his experience in business. He prepares a report, which is evaluated in a *viva voce* examination to test the depth of his understanding. This method is useful in reinforcing learning and in exposing students to various problems of business organisation, and teaches them how to tackle them.

3. ROLE PLAYING

Role playing is the concept of creating a more realistic situation, usually one of human problems and conflicts, and then acting out the various parts. The role assuming closely approximate a real situation and affords the participants the vicarious experiences that enhance their sensitivity, growth and development.

The value of role playing are:

(i) It requires the person to carry out a thought or decision he may have reached.

(ii) It permits the practice of carrying out an action and makes it clear that good human relations require skill.

(iii) Attitudinal changes are effectively accomplished by placing persons in specified roles. It becomes clear in role play that a person's behaviour is not only a function of his personality but also of the situation in which he finds himself.

(iv) It makes person aware of the feeling of others.

(v) It helps in developing a fuller appreciation of the important part played by feelings.

(vi) Each person gets an opportunity to discover his own personal faults.

(vii) It permits training in the control of feelings and emotions. Four types of learning can take place through role play *(a)* Learning by practice of deserted skill *(b)* learning through imitation of desirable behaviour *(c)* learning through observations and feedback about their effectiveness and weakness *(d)* Learning through analysis and conceptualisation.

The pros and cons of this method have been discussed in the previous chapter.

4. IN-BASKET METHOD

In this method, each team of the trainees is given a file of correspondence bearing on a functional area of management. Each individual studies the file and makes his own recommendations on the situation. If further information is required by him, it is supplied by the members of the team. Later, the observations of each individual member are compared and conclusions on different functional areas reached; and these are put down in the form of a report. For this purpose, such teaching methods as the incident process, role-playing, the syndicate method, and the conference method are used.

Merits: This method has the following advantages:

(i) Decisions are rapid, feedback is objective, and further decisions are based on the feedback of earlier decisions.

(ii) The consequences of many possible alternatives in a situation can be evaluated over a period of time.

(iii) The participants pay for the consequences of their decisions.

(iv) Because of emotional involvement without any strain, the participants play for hours with sustained interest.

(v) Decision-making is by a group which consists of managers and specialists from different departments. Each member, therefore, gets an opportunity to participate in it.

(vi) An abstract and complex situation is given the semblance of a real world situation, and this illusion facilitates the learning process.

(vii) Teachers welcome management games since student participation is excellent.

(viii) By mixing with managers from different functional areas, managers get a better appreciation of other functional areas.

(ix) The effect of long-term policies can be domonstrated in the game.

(x) The efficiency of planning and systematic approach can be demonstrated.

(xi) Team co-operation can be fostered and departmental conflicts softened down and/or eliminated.

(xii) Promising young managers get a perspective on the company as a whole when they work with their senior colleagues in the game.

(xiii) The specified time limit imposes the time constraint on the trainees which stimulates reality.

(xiv) The method is inexpensive and can be organised easily.

Demerits: The main demerits are:

(i) It sometimes discourages originality for teams have to adopt themselves to rigid situations.

(ii) The logical solutions suggested by the team to be abstracted from compulsions against which it had to be tackled in the actual situation.

5. BUSINESS OR MANAGEMENT GAME

Business games are classroom simulation exercises in which teams of individuals compete against one another or against an environment in order to achieve a given objective. These games are designed to be representative of real life conditions. Under these, an atmosphere is created in which the participants play a dynamic role, and enrich their skills through involvement and simulated experience. Most business games are expressed in the form of a mathematical model controlled and manipulated by an electric computer; while others can be played manually. In the former case, quicker feedback is available; clerical work is avoided and time is controlled. Some games are interacting types of games, while others are non-interacting types. The interacting types of games are like a game of tennis: the decisions of one team influence or affect the performance of the other teams. In the non-interacting types of games, each team is independent, and its performance entirely depends upon its own competence; the decisions of one team do not affect others.

Usually, management games consist of several teams which represent competing companies. Each team consists of 2 to 6 members. Teams take decisions regarding production, prices, research expenditure, marketing, advertising, and attempt to maximise hypothetical profits in this simulated environment. The decisions of a team are fed into a computer which has been programmed according to a particular model of the market. The game continues for 6 to 12 periods. At the end of that period, the final results are worked out by each team and compared with those of others.

Business games are intended to teach trainees how to take management decisions in an integrated manner. The participants learn by analysing problems and by making trial-and-error decisions. Such games illustrate the existence of various group processes, including communication, the resolution of conflicts, the emergence of leadership, and the development of ties of friendship.

Merits: This method enjoys following advantages:

(i) There is usually a great sense of excitement and enjoyment in playing the game. This helps to develop problem-solving skills; and helps focus attention on the need for planning than on "putting out fires."

(ii) As the companies elect their own officers and develop their own organisation structures, they can, therefore, be useful for developing leadership skills and for fosterning cooperation and team-work.

(iii) It helps to analyse and select the significant and relevant data from a mass of information; and also helps ability to decide with incomplete data and amid conditions of uncertainty.

(iv) It helps in changing attitudes. The participant becomes more tolerant.

Demerits:

(i) A major problem with games is that they can be very expensive to develop and implement particularly when the game itself is computerised.

(ii) Management games usually force decision maker to choose his alternatives from a "closed" list; in real life managers are more often rewarded for creating new alternatives.

(iii) Though games may be accurate simulations, they are never totally realistic; for no evidence is available which may indicate that those who are successful in business games will also be successful in a real job.

On the whole, the trainees almost always react favourably to a well-run game and it is a good technique for developing problem-solving and leadership skills.

6. SENSITIVITY, LABORATORY OR T-GROUP TRAINING

This method was originally developed by Kurt Lewin and popularised by the National Training Laboratories, U.S.A. under Leland Bradford. It is known by several names such as 'sensitivity training', 'T-Group training', 'action training,' 'Group dynamics', 'Confrontation Groups', 'Awareness expertises', 'human capacity movement', 'sensitivity retreats', 'encounter sessions' and so forth.

According to Chris Argyris, "sensitivity training is a group experience designed to provide maximum possible opportunity for the individuals to expose their behaviour, give and receive feedback, experiment with new behaviour and develop awareness of self and of others."

Objectives: Sensitivity training involves the use of development techniques which attempt to increase or improve human sensitivity and awareness. The goal of laboratory training is broadly defined as "helping trainees to improve in quality and participation in human affairs." In other words, it tries to provide:

(i) managers with increased awareness of their own behaviour and of how others perceive them;

(ii) greater sensitivity to be behaviour of others, and increased understanding of group process;

(iii) a clarification and development of personal values and goals consonant with a democratic and scientific approach to problem of social and personal decision and action;

(iv) development of concepts and theoretical insights that will serve as tools in linking personal values, goals and intentions to actions that are consistent with these inner factors and with the situation requirements; and

(v) achievement of greater behavioural effectiveness in transactions with one's various environments.

According to the two internationally known behavioural scientists, below is represented the objectives of most programmes.

1. Increased *awareness* of own feelings and reactions and of own impact on others.
2. Increased *awareness* of feelings and reactions of others and their impact on self.
3. Increased *awareness* of dynamics of group action.
4. *Changed attitudes* toward self, others and groups, i.e., more respect for tolerance of and faith in self, others and groups.
5. Increased *interpersonal competence,* i.e., skill in handling interpersonal and group relationships toward more productive and satisfying relationships.
6. Increased *awareness* of own organisational role, organisational dynamics, dynamics of larger social systems, and dynamics of the process of change in self, small groups and organisations.
7. *Changed attitudes* toward own role, role of others and oranisational relationships, i.e., more respect for and willingness to deal with others whom one is inter-dependent, greater willingness to achieve collaborative relationships with others based on mutual trust.
8. Increased *interpersonal competence* in handling relationships of own organisation role with superiors, peers and subordinates.
9. Increased awareness of changed attitudes toward, and increased *interpersonal competence* about specific organisational problems existing in groups or units which are inter-dependent.

10. *Organisational improvement* through the training of relationships or groups rather than isolated individuals.

Thus, it will be observed that the objectives of sensitivity training include an understanding of oneself and sensitivity to others; an ability to listen to others and to communicate diagnostic understanding of group problem, and ability to contribute effectively and properly to the work of the group; and an understanding of the complexities of inter-group and intra-organisation problems. The specific results sought include increased ability to empathize with others, improved listening skills, greater openness, increased tolerance for individual differences, and improved conflict resolution skills.

THE PATTERN OR OUTLINE OF A TYPICAL SENSITIVITY TRAINING PROGRAMME

The basic pattern of such a programme is to organise trainees into small unstructured group consisting of 10 to 15 persons in which inter-action will occur regularly throughout the training programme. Usually there is no leader, no planned agenda and no stated goal. The trainees may be given case, role playing situations or other training assignments as a spring board for group interaction. The discussion focuses on "here and now", i.e., the participants, are encouraged to openly discuss each participant's attitudes, reactions and other behavioural patterns. The participants are also encouraged to be introspective and at the same time to be more empathetic toward the feeling of others. The feedback process is all important. The trainees have to feel secure enough to inform each other truthfully on their personal feelings and reactions to one another's behaviour. *The emphasis is on a "face to face" interaction and confrontation.*

T-group may be used to help participants:

(i) Learn more about themselves, especially their own weaknesses and emotions;

(ii) Develop insights into how they react to others and how others react to them;

(iii) Discover how groups work and how to diagnose human relations problems;

(iv) Find out how to behave more effectively in inter-personal relations and how to manage people through means other than power;

(v) Develop more "competent" and "authentic" relations in which feelings are expressed openly;

(vi) Confront inter-personal problems directly, so that they may be solved, and not try to avoid them; rather smooth them over, or seek a compromise.

After training the trainees usually do become more sensitive to others and more open, such training can also result in increased company performance and profits.

The *demerits* of the system are:

(i) The trainers often create stress situations. At times, groups are "converted into psychological nudist camps which end up mainly as self-flagellation societies." There is a danger that training of this sort may do a better job of tearing apart people than of bringing them together.

(ii) Whatever changes occur in the trainees tend to fade out when they return to an unsympathetic environment in which company policy and their boss's attitude may inhibit the exercise of their newly learned skills.

(iii) This type of training makes the management trainee so sensitive to the feelings of others that he is unwilling to take hard decisions.

(iv) T-group training, when applied to technical professional is often less effective as a training method than more conventional methods such as the lecture method and conferences.

(v) Such training is not only capable of inducing anxiety but it is very likely to do so. The anxiety may have an unrewarding effect, such as causing the people to be highly frustrated, unsettled and upset. In other cases, high levels of depression, rejections and other disruptive influences are also visible.

Sensitivity training is a very controversial development technique. The reason is the depth of emotional involvement required of trainees. They laterally need to bare their souls in training session and so the training is, thus, very personal in nature. Sensitivity training has, therefore, been widely criticised. The critics have observed:

- Sensitivity training based on creating stress *situations* for their own sake.
- The participants are often unaware of what the *outcome* of a session will be.
- Its ultimate goals and techniques are often *inconsistent* with the business and economic world in which we live.
- Such a training has been known to result in nervous *breakdown* of trainees.
- Anybody with a registration fee can attend.

In the light of the above criticisms, some hints for setting a T-group programme may be somewhat like this:

1. T-group training is more appropriate for developing "organic" organisations. When this type of openness and flexible organisation structure is not appropriate, such a training is not appropriate.
2. The leader-trainer must be carefully selected on the basis of his ability to lead effectively so that emotional situations can be translated into constructive rather than destructive consequences.
3. The participants for such training should be selected for their emotional stability and their tolerance for anxiety.
4. Programme should be strictly *voluntary.*
5. All trainees should know *ahead of time* what sort of training they are going to get.
6. A great deal of attention should be given to building in mechanisms for *transferring the learning* back to the organisation.

7. SIMULATION

It is a training technique which indicates the duplication of organisational situations in a learning environment. *It is a mock-up of a real thing.* This technique has been used for developing technical and interpersonal skills.

In simulation, the following procedure is usually adopted:

1. Essential characteristics of a real-life organisation or activity are abstracted and presented as a case — not to be studied and analysed as in the usual case study method but to be experienced by the trainee as a realistic, life-like circumstance.
2. Trainees are asked to assume various roles in the circumstance and to solve the problem facing them. They are asked to be themselves, not to act.
3. A simulation often involves a telescopic or compressing of time events; a single hour may be equated with a month or a quarter of a year in real life, and many events are experienced in a relatively brief period of time.
4. Trainees are required to make decision that have a real effect in the simulation and about which they receive rapid feedback.
5. The simulation is followed by a critique of what went on during the exercise.

The advantages to simulation are the opportunities to attempt to "create an environment" similar to real situations the managers incur, without high costs involved should the action prove undesirable. The disadvantages are that it is difficult to duplicate the pressures and realities of actual decision-making on the jobs, and individuals often act differently in real life situations when they do in acting out a simulated exercise.

8. TEAM BUILDING

Team building is one of the OD (organization development) techniques aimed at improving the effectiveness of teams at work. In this technique stress is laid on action learning, i.e., on letting the trainees scheme the problem. Data concerning teams performance are collected and then feedback to the member of the team. The participants examine explain and anlayse the data and develop specific action plans for solving the team's problems.

The team building program begins with the consultant (an outsider) interviewing each of the team members and the leader of the team prior to a group meeting — asking them what their problems are, how they think the group functions and what obstacles are in the way of the group performing better. The consultant then categorises the interview data into topics or themes and presents these themes to the group at the beginning of the group meeting. The schemes are ranked by the group in terms of their importance. The most important themes from the agenda for the meeting. The group examines and discusses the issues and examines the underlying causes of the problem and begins work on a solution to the problems.

9. GRID TRAINING

The "managerial grid" is an organisational development technique, developed by Robert R. Blake and Jane S. Mouton. The grid represents several possible leadership, "styles." Each style represents a different combination of two basic orientations — concern for people (1.9) and *concern for production* (9.1).

The management training programme is built around this managerial grid. It aims at developing open confrontation of organisational problems and *high-people-high-production* (9.9) leaders.

Such a programme lasts for 3 to 5 years and usually involves the following steps:

1. *Phase* 1 involves a week-end conference, where trainees are taught the fundamental of grid-training.
2. *Phase 2* comprises the discussion, analysis and solution of the units' problems and practices by the management and the subordinates.
3. *Phase 3* involves meeting with various groups with the aim of working out company-wide problems and setting some development targets for the company as a whole.
4. *Phase 4* involves outlining specific procedures for accomplishing the company's development targets.
5. *Phase 5* includes evaluation of the units' accomplishments and beginning work on any remaining or new problems.

Various methods of management development have been discussed above. However, it is difficult to suggest which of the training methods/techniques will prove better, for the success of each method largely depend on:

(a) How it is employed;

(b) The instructor's ability and personality;

(c) The trainee's maturity, background and willingness to learn; and

(d) Company atmosphere and the extent to which there is an opportunity and encouragement to the trainee to apply to the job what he learn in the class or the programme.

It may only be said that some methods may suit some training objective or group of participants better than others; but the acceptance and adoption of one or other of these methods will have to be done with caution and after careful thinking.

ADMINISTERING A MANAGEMENT DEVELOPMENT PROGRAMME

While administering the programme, due consideration should be given to the following points:

1. *An M.D.P. should support a systematic career planning for managerial personnel,* otherwise the frustrated trainees might seek opportunities elsewhere and the whole investment made in training programmes would go waste.
2. *Management development does not comprise involvement in a series of structured courses,* but there should also be an active interaction between the trainee and the management.
3. *Training programme should cover, as far as possible, every manager, capable of showing potential for growth,* i.e., "the crown prince or heir apparent"

approach should not be adopted in the selection of the trainees. As Peter Drucker puts it, "The eight men out of every ten who were not included in the programme will understandably, feel slighted. They may end of by welcoming less effective, less productive, less willing to do new thing."

4. *The entire programme should be properly planned.* The trainees should take part in it. An individual may stay out, but it should be made clear that he does so at some risk to his future promotion. The company should not normally allow any manager to opt out of a training programme.

COURSES FOR MANAGEMENT DEVELOPMENT

Although foremen, department heads, plant managers, and vice-presidents are all members of management, the nature of their duties and responsibilities differ greatly. There are certain areas in which development courses may be regarded as essential for all levels of management (such courses as on the company, on management principles and techniques, on economic social and political environment, on personal skills and human relations). However, certain areas are more appropriate for one level than another. For example, foremen are not directly involved in the economic, social and political environment of a corporation; but the executives are. Further, in some areas, not only the content but also the depth of knowledge and skill varies with the personnel involved.

Courses for members of the middle management contain elements of both top and lower level management programmes. Middle level managers, however, devote a considerable time to human relations and personnel management principles because these are essential at all levels of management. They should have a solid grounding in such management techniques as cost analysis and control, data processing, production planning and control, wage and salary administration, work study, PERT/CPM, value engineering, etc.

Courses for first level supervisors concentrate upon the technical processes of the business, human relations and personal skills, for they are immediately practicable and are closely related to a supervisor's day-to-day job. According to Prof. Beach, the subject matter of a course for management development may comprise:

I. COMPANY OR ORGANISATION

(i) Objectives and philosophy.

(ii) Policies, procedures and practices.

(iii) Products and services.

(iv) Organisational structure and organisation dynamics.

(v) Plant facilities.

(vi) Financial aspects (investment planning, financial planning and control, capital budgeting).

(vii) Labour-management and non-management relations (industrial relations, human relations, and personnel administration).

II. MANAGEMENT TECHNIQUES AND PRINCIPLES

(i) Organisation principles.

(ii) Financing, planning, and management.

(iii) Management and administrative principles and practices.

(iv) Production planning and control.

(v) Methods analysis, work assignment, work study, materials handling, value engineering.

(vi) Cost analysis and control.

(vii) Statistics, management information system, computer applications.

(viii) Operations research and data processing.

(ix) Marketing management, Marketing research.

(x) Decision-making.

III. HUMAN RELATIONS

(i) Understanding human behaviour.

(ii) Motivation.

(iii) Group dynamics.

(iv) Attitudes, training and development.

(v) Leadership.

(vi) Introducing changes.

(vii) Participation programmes.

(viii) Supervisory responsibilities.

(ix) Selection methods and procedures.

(x) Job evaluation and performance appraisal.

(xi) Communication.

(xii) Counselling and suggestion schemes.

(xiii) Complaints and grievances.

(xiv) Discipline.

(xv) Labour economics.

(xvi) Collective bargaining.

(xvii) Industrial relations.

IV. TECHNICAL KNOWLEDGE AND SKILLS

(i) Adequate understanding of technology, products, processes.

(ii) Linear programming.

(iii) PERT/CPM.

(iv) Computer technology.

(v) Basic mathematics.

(vi) Materials handling.

(vii) Inventory control.

V. ECONOMIC, SOCIAL AND POLITICAL ENVIRONMENT

(i) Business.

(ii) Economic system.

(iii) Relations with the state.

(iv) Community relations.

(v) Social responsibilities of the corporation and business.

(vi) Legal framework of business.

(vii) Political systems.

VI. PERSONNEL SKILLS

(i) Speaking.

(ii) Report writing.

(iii) Conference leadership.

(iv) Learning through listening.

(v) Reading improvement.

ADMINISTRATION OF MANAGEMENT DEVELOPMENT PROGRAMMES

The management development prgramme must be launched by the chief executive officer of an organisation or by a committee consisting of the chief executive because this programme involves fundamental policy issues, decisions of far-reaching importance, and an expenditure of considerable sum of money. The ultimate responsibility for chalking out these programmes is that of the personnel department, which should carefully study the development needs of the organisation and prepare a specific programme for the consideration of the top executive. Adequate records should be kept to audit and control management development activities throughout the organisation.

Since effective administration often makes all the difference between the success and failure of development courses, it is well to take a good look at plans, co-ordination, arrangements, operation and continuation. The very conception of development eliminates the thought of a single, isolated course in development.

In planning course, it is necessary to think in terms of at least the coming year so that development may be well-rounded, covers different groups, and does not involve too many courses running consecutively or simultaneously.

There should be a substantial number of sessions if a course is to have a lasting impact. If it runs too long, the group taking the course gets fed up, and attendance begins to drop sharply. This is equally true if too many courses are run one after the other for the same persons. The time at which a course will be conducted during the day is worth considering, the most difficult periods being just before lunch, just after lunch, and at the end of the day. Evening meetings, after dinner, are likely to have drowsy participants in the course.

Further, matters such as temperature, ventilation, blackboards, seating arrangements (square, V or U for conferences), provision of lavatories, name plates (where the members do not know each other or the leader) and freedom from noise and interruptions need to be given a careful consideration.

Incentive must be there. A powerful motivator is the realisation that the top management is interested in the courses, considers them valuable and follows their progress closely. To indicate the boss's interest, a memorandum from him may be circulated in advance of a course's inauguration; the top management may have a preview of the course; the president or general manager may introduce topics and persons at the first session; the top management may keep track of the attendance record, talk with members about the course, and be present at the final session or for the award of certificates. The following incentives would be found to be valuable:

Granting certificates after a successful completion of the course; taking attendance; requiring a minimum of 75 per cent or higher attendance for certification; making a notation on personal records about courses taken and completed; and checking on those who have missed sessions.

No programme can be effective unless it is aided by proper support systems. In a survey of 12 organisations, it was "found that 6 organisations (aluminium, tobacco, steel, engineering, cosmetics and chemicals) have their own management training and development centres at which company programmes are organised. Another 50 per cent do not have this facility, and use out-company premises. Some organisations have their own training hall or conference rooms for in-company training programmes, while others hire these in top hotels.

"Films, slides, projectors, movies, stills, graphs, charts, flash cards, flannel boards, pamphlets, brochures, exhibits, posters, displays, notice boards, bulletin boards, stationery, library and reading rooms are the various support systems provided by these organisations.

"Facilities such as course or tuition fees, hotel expenses, travel, transport, time off, leave facilities, and participation in conferences, seminars, symposia organised by professional associations are provided by all the sample organisations. They also provide membership fees for professional associations, and subscription allowance for obtaining management journals and periodicals."

SUMMARY

1. Management development is aimed at preparing young managers for future jobs in the organisation or resolving existing bottlenecks or obstacles with the organisation.
2. In house on-the-job experience is most useful form of management development. However, other techniques are also used depending on the organisation needs.
3. Managerial responsibility on the job training methods include job rotation, coaching, action, learning. Basics of the job techniques include case studies, management gains outside seminars, role playing, behaviour modelling.
4. Organisation development (OD) is an approach to bring about a change in which the employees (participants) themselves play a major role in the

change process. They provide data, feedback on problems and team building solutions.

5. Grid training and other intergroup team buildings efforts aim at developing better problem solving process.
6. Successful development programs require CEO involvement, a clear development policy, succession planning and development and time responsibility.

HR can contribute to building the learning organisation — through systematic problem solving, experimentation, learning from experience transferring knowledge.

❑ ❑ ❑

9

Performance Appraisal

Once the employee has been selected, trained and motivated, he is then appraised for his performance. Performance appraisal is the step where the management finds out how effective it has been at hiring and placing employees. If any problems are identified, steps are taken to communicate with the employee and to remedy them. A "performance appraisal" is a process of evaluating an employee's performance of a job in terms of its requirements. Heyel observes; "It is the process of evaluating the performance and qualifications of the employees in terms of the requirements of the job for which he is employed, for purposes of administration including placement, selection for promotions, providing financial rewards and other actions which require differential treatment among the members of a group as distinguished from actions affecting all members equally." Others regard it as a "process of estimating or judging the value, excellence, qualities or status of some object, person or thing." Individually and collectively, it is a part of all the other staffing processes, viz., recruitment, selection, placement and indoctrination.

Performance appraisal may be defined as any procedure that involves: (*i*) setting work standards; (*ii*) assessing the employee's actual performance relative to these standards; (*iii*) providing feedback to the employee with the aim of motivating that person to eliminate his deficiencies and/or continue to perform better.

Performance appraisal contains three steps: (*i*) Define the jobs; (*ii*) Appraise performance; (*iii*) Provide feedback to the employee.

TERMINOLOGY USED

Employee appraisal techniques are said to have been used for the first time during the First World War, when, at the instance of Walter Dill Scott, the US Army adopted the "Man-to-man" rating system for evaluating military personnel. During the 1920-30 period, rational wage structures for hourly paid workers were adopted in industrial units. Under this system, the policy of giving grade wage increments on the basis of merit was accepted. These early employee plans were called *merit rating programmes,* which continued to be so called up to the mid-fifties. By then, most of these plans were of the rating-scale type, where emphasis was given to factors, degrees and points. In the early fifties, however, attention began to be devoted to the performance appraisal of technical, professional and managerial personnel. Since then, as a result of experiments and a great deal of study, the philosophy of performance appraisal has undergone tremendous changes. Consequently, a change has also taken place in the terminology used. Now, the older phrase *merit rating* is largely restricted to the rating of hourly paid employees, and is used frequently in developing criteria for salary adjustments, promotions, transfers, etc. The later phrase, *personnel appraisal,* places emphasis on the development of the individual as and widely used to evaluate technical, professional and managerial personnel.

Prof. Beach has provided a useful chart, showing the changes in the terminology of employee appraisal which have taken place since 1920.

CHART 9.1

Trends in Employee Appraisal

Item	*Former Emphasis*	*Present Emphasis*
Terminology	Merit Rating	Employee Appraisal Performance Appraisal
Purpose	Determine qualifications for wage increase, transfer, promotion, lay-off	Development of the individual; improved performance on the job; and provide emotional security
Application	For hourly-paid workers	For technical, professional, and managerial employees
Factors Rated	Heavy emphasis upon personal traits	Results, accomplishments, performance
Techniques	Rating scales with emphasis upon scales, Statistical manipulation of data for comparison purposes	Mutual goal-setting, critical incidents; group appraisal; Performance standards; less quantitative
Post-Appraisal Interview	Superior communicates his rating to employee and tries to sell his evaluation to him; seeks to have employee con form to his view	Superior stimulates employee to analyse himself and set own objectives in line with job requirements; superior is helper and counsellor

The appraisal of individuals in an employment has been labelled and described by experts over the years in different ways. Common descriptions include *performance appraisal, merit rating, behavioural assessment, employee evaluation, personnel review, progress report, staff assessment, service rating and fitness report.* Some personnel authorities use such concepts interchangeably, while others interpret some of these appraisal phrases differently. However, the term *performance appraisal or evaluation* is most widely used.

IMPORTANCE AND PURPOSES

Performance appraisal has been considered as a most significant and indispensable tool for an organisation, for the information it provides is highly useful in making decisions regarding various personal aspects such as promotions and merit increases. Performance measures also link information gathering and decision-making processes which provide a basis for judging the effectiveness of personnel sub-divisions such as recruiting, selection, training and compensation. Accurate information plays a vital role in the organisation as a whole. They help pinpoint weak areas in the primary systems (e.g., marketing, finance and production). It is easier for managers to see which employees need training or counselling, because jobs are grouped by categories (e.g., production foreman, sales manager, financial analyst). These categories can be broken into smaller and smaller groups, if necessary. If valid performance data are available, timely, accurate, objective, standardised and relevant, management can maintain consistent promotion and compensation policies throughout the total system.

McGregor says: "Formal performance appraisal plans are designed to meet three needs, one of the organisation and the other two of the individual, namely:

(i) They provide systematic judgements to back up salary increases, transfers, demotions or terminations.

(ii) They are means of telling a subordinate how he is doing, and suggesting needed changes in his behaviour attitudes, skills, or job knowledge. They let him know "where he stands" with the boss.

(iii) They are used as a base for coaching and counselling the individual by the superior.

According to Roland Benjamin, a "performance appraisal determines who shall receive merit increases; counsels employees on their improvement; determines training needs; determines promotability; identifies those who should be transferred. Moreover, it improves employee job performance; encourages employees to express their views or to seek clarification on job duties; broadens their outlook, capacity and potential; promotes a more effective utilization of manpower and improves placement; facilitates selection, reward and promotion of the best qualified employee; prevents grievances and increases the analytical abilities of supervisors."

Levinson has given three functions of performance appraisal: *(i)* It seeks to provide an adequate feedback to each individual for his or her performance. *(ii)* It purports to serve as a basis for improving or changing behaviour toward some more effective working habits. *(iii)* It aims at providing data to managers with which they may judge future job assignments and compensation. He stresses the fact that the existing systems of performance appraisal do not serve any of these functions effectively but focus on 'outcome of behaviour.'

According to Cummings, "the overall objective of performance appraisal is to improve the efficiency of an enterprise by attempting to mobilise the best possible efforts from individuals employed in it. Such appraisals achieve four objectives including the salary reviews, the development and training of individuals, planning job rotation and assistance promotions."

On the basis of merit rating or appraisal procedures of various companies in India, the main objectives of employee performance appraisal are:

(i) To enable an organisation to maintain an inventory of the number and quality of all managers and to identify and meet their training needs and aspirations;

(ii) To determine increments rewards, and provide a reliable index for promotions and transfers to positions of greater responsibility;

(iii) To maintain individual and group development by informing the employee of his performance standard; by giving feedback.

(iv) To suggest ways of improving the employee's performance when he is not found to be up to the mark during the review period;

(v) To identify training and development needs of the employees and to evaluate effectiveness of training and development programmes;

(vi) To plan career development, human resources planning based on potentialities.

It will, thus, be seen that performance appraisal is an important tool of personnel management. It is a judgement of the characteristics, traits and performance of employees and has a wide range of utility. For example:

(i) It unifies the appraisal procedure so that all employees are rated in the same manner, utilising the same approach so that the ratings obtained of separate personnel are comparable.

(ii) It provides information which is useful in making and enforcing important decisions about selection, training, promotions, pay increases, transfers, lay-offs, discharges, salary adjustments, etc. The information is supplied well in advance so that spot judgements may be avoided.

(iii) It provides information in the form of records about ratings which may be produced as evidence when decisions on ratings are challenged in a court of law. Even arbitrators accept these in the course of grievance handling procedures as authentic records.

(iv) It serves to stimulate and guide employee development. Appraisal programmes provide information on the weaknesses of employees and enable them to gauge their own value and accomplishments and to know what they are doing. The weaknesses provide the basis for an individual development programme. If used properly, such periodical appraisals will establish an atmosphere in which criticism can be taken without resentment and can be used constructively for self-improvement.

(v) By finding out an employee's qualifications, and his work and comparing it with job requirements, inefficient employees and those whose views are not in harmony with the company's objectives or management philosophy can be weeded out or persuaded to adjust themselves.

(vi) A periodic and accurate appraisal constrains a supervisor to be alert and competent in his work, i.e., it improves the quality of supervision by giving him an incentive to do the things that he should normally be doing anyway.

(vii) It gives supervisors a more effective tool for rating their personnel, enables them to make a careful analysis of their men and gives them a better knowledge and understanding of them.

(viii) It makes for better employer-employee relations through mutual confidence, which comes as a result of frank discussions between a supervisor and his men.

In short, the main purpose of performance appraisal is to provide the 'deadlock' and research data for improving the overall personnel information system.

CHART 9.2

Differences Between Administrative and Employee Development Appraisal

Criteria	*Purpose of Employee Performance Appraisal*	
	Employee Development	*Administrative*
1. Definition of Purpose	Performance improvement by advising employees what is expected of them	Information for decision: salary adjustments, transfers, promotions, reductions in work force
2. Basis for Comparison	Performance relative to pre-determined standards of performance (absolute standard)	Performance relative to other similar employer
3. Technique of Appraisal	Results-oriented appraisal	Employee ranking
4. Role of Supervisor	Counsellor	Judge
5. Distribution of Evaluation Information	Employee and supervisor	Employee, supervisor, personnel folders, others involved in administrative actions listed above.

WHAT SHOULD BE RATED?

The seven criteria for assessing performance are:

1. Quality: The degree to which the process or result of carrying out an activity approaches perfection.

2. Quantity: The amount produced, expressed in monetary terms, number of units, or number of completed activity cycles.

3. Timeliness: The degree to which an activity or a result produced.

4. Cost Effectiveness: The degree to which the use of the organisation's resources (e.g. human, monetary, technological, material) is maximised in the sense of getting the highest gain.

5. Need for Supervision: The degree to which a job performer can carry out a job function without supervisory assistance.

6. Interpersonal Impact: The degree to which a performer promotes feelings of self-esteem, goodwill and co-operation among co-workers and subordinates.

7. Training: Need for training for improving his skills knowledge

The above criteria relate to past performance and behaviour of an employee. There is also the need for assessing the potential of an employee for future performance, particularly when the employee is tipped for assuming greater responsibilities.

APPROACHES TO PERFORMANCE APPRAISAL

Generally speaking three approaches are used in making performance appraisal:

(a) A causal, unsystematic, and often haphazard appraisal : This method was commonly used in the past, but now it has given place to a more formal method, the main basis being seniority or quantitative measures of quantity and quality of output for the rank-and-file personnel.

(b) The traditional and highly systematic measurement of (i) employee characteristics, and *(ii)* employee contributions, or both. It evaluates all the performances in the same manner, utilising the same approach, so that the ratings obtained of separate personnel are comparable.

(c) The behavioural approach, emphasising mutual goal-setting: According to McGregor, in the traditional approach, the supervisor is placed in the position of "Playing Gods." He judges and at times criticizes the personal worth of his men. Therefore, emphasis has been laid upon providing mutual goal-setting and appraisal of progress by both the appraiser and the appraisee. This approach is based on the behavioural value of fundamental trust in the goodness, capability and responsibility of human beings.

THE EVALUATION PROCESS

Stolz observes that "the process of performance appraisal follows a set pattern, viz., a man's performance is periodically appraised by his superiors. Questions are raised — Is his potential the greatest as a manager or as a staff specialist? What are his strengths and weaknesses? Where can he make his great contribution? Next, sometimes in consultation with the man himself, tentative decisions are made on what might be done to advance his development.

"Usually, the resulting plan is then reviewed at a higher echelon of management, where it may be challenged, changed or added to. But out of the discussion and debate emerges a development plan tailored to the individual's unique needs."[12]

Broadly speaking, the process of evaluation begins with the establishment of 'performance standards.' At the time of designing a job and formulating a job description, performance standards are usually developed for the position. These standards should be clear and not vague, and objective enough to be understood and measured. These standards should be discussed with the supervisors to find out which different factors are to be incorporated, weights and points to be given to each factor and these then should be indicated on the Appraisal Form, and later on used for appraising the performance of the employees.

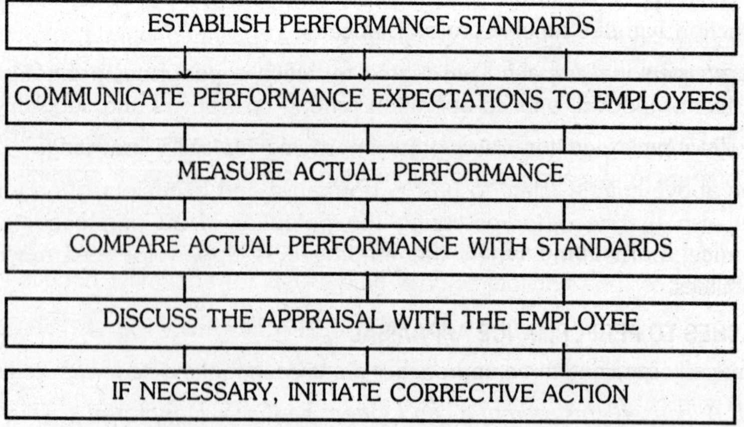

Fig. 9.1: The Evaluation Process

The *next step* is to communicate these standards to the employees, for the employees left to themselves, would find it difficult to guess what is expected of them. To make communication effective, 'feedback' is necessary from the subordinate to the manager. Satisfactory feedback ensures that the information communicated by the manager has been received and understood in the way it was intended.

The *third step* is the 'measurement of performance.' To determine what actual performance is, it is necessary to acquire information about it. We should be concerned with *how* we measure and *what* we measure. Four sources of information are frequently used to measure actual performance: personal observation, statistical reports, oral reports, and written reports.

The *fourth step* is the comparison of actual performance with standards. The employee is appraised and judged of his potential for growth and advancement. Attempts are made to note deviations between 'standard performance' and 'actual performance.'

At the *next stage,* the results of appraisal are discussed periodically with the employees, where good points, weak points, and difficulties are indicated and discussed so that performance is improved. The information that the subordinate receives about his assessment has a great impact on his self-esteem and on his subsequent performance. Conveying good news is considerably less difficult for both the manager and the subordinate than when performance has been below expectations.

The *final step* is the initiation of corrective action when necessary; immediate corrective action can be of two types. One is immediate and deals predominantly with symptoms. The other is basic and delves into causes. Immediate corrective action is often described as "putting out fires," whereas basic corrective action gets to the source of deviation and seeks to adjust the difference permanently. Coaching and Counselling may be done or special assignments and projects may be set; persons may be deputed for formal training courses, and decision-making responsibilities and authority may be delegated to the subordinates. Attempts may also be made to recommend for salary increases or promotions, if these decisions become plausible in the light of appraisals.

The details given above may vary from or organisation to organisation, but these steps usually form the principal steps/features of a sound evaluation programme.

TYPICAL APPRAISAL SUMMARY

An appraisal summary is a brief synopsis of the description of an individual employee. According to Miner and Miner, this summary generally covers the following data:

CHART 9.3

Typical Appraisal Summary

1. Personal Background

Age

Family Background

Marital status

Children

Education:

(a) Specialisation and degrees

(b) Extra-curricular activities and offices held

Work History

Employees Position, titles and duties

Social accomplishments

Honours and awards

Professional or trade organisation membership

Publications, if any

Special limitations, if any

Health

Family problems

Hobbies and recreational activities.

2. Nature of Work

A generalised statement based on organisation planning and job analysis data.

Committee assignments.

Number and titles of people supervised.

3. Job Performance and Personal Qualification

A general statement of an employee's value to the company and his probable future contribution.

Technical Performance: Evaluation against expectations in each of the key areas noted in the job description. Specific achievements in each of the key duties.

Motivation in Current Position: Attitude towards the company, superiors, and job acceptance of, and desire for, responsibility. Personal desire for accomplishment and drive. Self-reliance in making decisions. Degree and fairness of competition. Loyalty to the Company.

Intelligence as Manifested on the Job: Selection of realistic goals and methods of goal attainment.

Ability to learn new techniques. Resourceful in new and trying conditions. Quality of, and speed in, thinking. Organisational and planning ability and judgement. Thoroughness and accuracy. Ability to sell ideas. Flexibility in dealing with the ideas of others' creativity.

Emotional Stability: Ability to make adjustments in the face of frustrations and constraints. Capacity to take calculated risks. Ability to get along with others. Reaction to criticism and pressure; objectivity and freedom form prejudices. Excessive emotionally. Impairment caused by off-the-job problems.

Leadership Skills: Ability to win co-operation from subordinates. Ability to criticise and give orders, if necessary. Skill as a team worker with other organisational units. Development of subordinates. Delegation of power and use of controls. Capacity to establish and publicise performance standards. Types of subordinates sought and ability to appraise them.

The accomplishments in the present job which indicate what an employee's srtrength and weaknesses are.

4. Overall Performance Rating

Individual rating relative to what is expected. Ranking among others at the same level doing similar work.

Potentially: Promotability and expected rate of progress. Actual job types qualified for long-range potential.

5. Recommended Action

Changes in placement.

Ideal duration of current placement.

Development needs plans based on a comparison with the following list of management knowledge and skills:

Knowledge of: Technical information bearing on the job; related specialists and jobs; labour relations; business economics, company and departmental objectives; job evaluation and payment policies; safety; employee benefits and privileges; company organisational structure; legal constraints industry practices and competitive picture.

Skills: Delegation of authority to subordinates; coaching subordinates; setting performance standards; establishing controls and indicating follow-up action; long-range planning; decision-making; selling ideas; negotiation; evaluation of individuals and groups; taking disciplinary action; maintaining morale; communications; analysing accounting reports and other data cost control; discussion leadership; report and letter writing; public speaking; interviewing and meeting people framing budgets; reading (speed and comprehension).

METHODS, TECHNIQUES OR TOOLS FOR APPRAISING PERFORMANCE

Several methods and techniques of appraisal are available for measurement of the performance of an employee. The methods and scales differ for obvious reasons. *First,* they differ in the sources of traits or qualities to be appraised. The qualities may differ because of differences in job requirements, statistical requirements and the opinions of the management. *Second,* they differ because of the different kinds of workers who are being rated, viz., factory workers, executives or salesmen. *Third,* the variations may be caused by the degree of precision attempted in an evaluation. *Finally,* they may differ because of the methods used to obtain weightings for various traits.

There is little agreement on the best method to evaluate managerial, professional or salaried performance. Different authors have suggested different approaches. For example:

Rock and Lewis have classified the methods into two broad categories, viz., the narrow interpretation and broad interpretation of appraisal. The former is considered as "a post-mortem of a subordinate's performance by his superior during a pre-determined period of time, often, the preceding year. It involves assessment of performance vis-a-vis such as the traits or characteristics' rating scale, the ranking method, the employee comparison method and performance standard method are included under this category." The latter, "also known as *accountability management, management by objectives or management by end-results,* involves a broad purview, and aims at improving the entire managing process and the individual managers on a year round basis."

Robbins gives three categories, viz., *(i)* Single-trait, single subject, in which subjects are not compared with any other person and each trait is measured alone. The check-list, the numerical and graphic scale methods are more popular of such category. *(ii)* Single-trait, multiple-subject, in which the subjects are compared with other subjects. Group order ranking, individual ranking and pair comparison methods belong to this category. *(iii)* Multiple-trait, single-subject, in which force choice rating is done by either the subject himself or the evaluation, into traits offered for evaluation.

The widely used categorisation is that given by Strauss and Sayles. They have classified performance appraisal methods into traditional, and newer or modern methods. The traditional methods lay emphasis on the rating of the individual's personality traits, such as initiative, dependability, drive, responsibility, creativity, integrity, leadership potential, intelligence, judgement, organising ability, etc. On the other hand, newer methods place more emphasis on the evaluation of work results — job achievements — than on personality traits. Results oriented appraisals tend to be more objective and worthwhile, especially for counselling and development purposes.

CHART 9.4

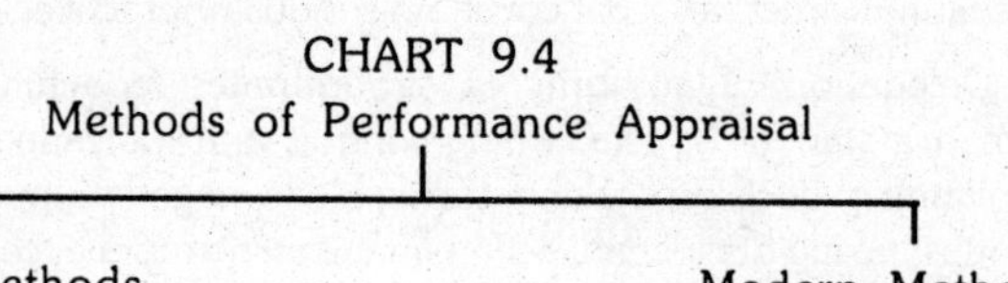

Traditional Methods

1. Straight Ranking Method
2. Man-to-man Comparison Method
3. Grading
4. Graphic Rating Scales
5. Forced Choice Description Method
6. Forced Distribution Method
7. Check Lists
8. Free Form Essay Method
9. Critical Incidents
10. Group Appraisal
11. Field Review Method

Modern Methods

1. Assessment Centre
2. Appraisal by Results or Management by Objectives (MBO)
3. Human Asset Accounting Method
4. Behaviourally Anchored Rating Scales (BARS)

TRADITIONAL METHODS

Straight Ranking Method: It is the oldest and simplest method of performance appraisal, by which the man and his performance are considered as an entity by the rater. No attempt is made to fractionalize the ratee or his performance; the "whole man" is compared with the "whole man"; that is, the ranking of a man in a work group is done against that of another. The relative position of each man is tested in terms of his numerical rank. It may also be done by ranking a person on his job performance against that of another member of a competitive group by placing him as number one or two or three in total group, i.e., *persons are tested in order of merit and placed in a simple grouping.*

This is the simplest method of separating the most efficient from the least efficient; and relatively easy to develop and use. But the greatest limitation of this method is that in practice it is very difficult to compare a single individual with human beings having varying behaviour traits. *Secondly,* the method only tells us how a man stands in relation to the others in the group but does not indicate how much better or worse he is than another. *Thirdly,* the task of ranking individuals is difficult when a large number of persons are rated. *Fourth,* the ranking system does not eliminate snap judgements, nor does it provide us with a systematic procedure for determining the relative ranks of subordinates. To remedy this defect, the paired comparison technique has been evolved.

Paired Comparison Technique: By this technique, each employee is compared every trait with all the other persons in pairs one at a time. With this technique, judgement is easier and simpler than with the ordinary ranking method. The number of times each individual is compared with another is tallied on a piece of paper. These numbers yield the rank order of the entire group. For example, if there are five persons to be compared, then A's performance is compared to B's, and a decision is arrived at as to whose is the better performance. Then A is compared to C, D and E... in that order. Next B is compared with all the others individually. Since he has already been compared with A, he is compared only with C, D and E. A similar comparison is made in respect of other personnel. Thus, by this method, we arrive at ten decisions, and only two are involved in each decision. The number of decisions is determined by the formula N(N-2), where N represents the number of persons to be compared.

The results of these comparisons are tabulated, and a rank is assigned to each individual.

This method is not suitable when a group is large because, in that case, the number of judgements becomes excessively large.

FOR THE TRAIT "QUALITY OF WORK"

PERSON RATED

AS COMPARED TO	A	B	C	D	E
A		+	+	–	–
B	–		–	–	–
C		+		+	–
D	+	+	–		+
E	+	+	+		–

FOR THE TRAIT "CREATIVITY"

PERSON RATED

AS COMPARED TO	A	B	C	D	E
A		–	–	–	–
B	+		–	+	+
C	+	+		–	+
D	+	–	+		–
E	+	–	–	+	

Fig. 9.2: Ranking Employees by Paired Comparison Method

Man-to-Man Comparison Method: This technique was used by the USA army during the First World War. By this method, certain factors are selected for the purpose of analysis (such as leadership, dependability and initiative), and a scale is designed by the rater for each factor. A scale of man is also created for each selected factor. The each man to be rated is compared with the man in the scale, and certain scores for each factor are awarded to him. In other words, instead of comparing a "whole man" to a "whole man," personnel are compared to the *key man* in respect of one factor at a time. This method is used in job evaluation, and is known as the *factor comparison method.* In performance appraisal, it is not of much use because the designing of scales is a complicated task.

Grading Method: Under this system, the rater considers certain features and marks them accordingly to a scale. Certain categories of worth are first established and carefully defined. The selected features may be analytical ability, co-operativeness, dependability, self-expression, job knowledge, judgement, leadership and organising ability, etc. They may be: A — outstanding; B — very good; C — good or average; D — fair; E — poor; and — B (or B —) very poor or hopeless.

The actual performance of an employee is then compared with these grade definitions, and he is allotted the grade which best describes his performance. Such type of grading is done in semester examinations and also in the selection of candidates by the public service commissions.

Graphic or Linear Rating Scale: This is the most commonly used method of performance appraisal. Under it, a printed form, one for each person to be rated. According to Jucius, these factors are: employee characteristics and employee contribution. In *employee characteristics* are included such qualities as initiative, leadership, co-operativeness, dependability, industry, attitude, enthusiasm, loyalty, creative ability, decisiveness, analytical ability, emotional ability, and co-ordination. In the *employee contribution* are included the quantity and quality of work, the responsibility assumed, specific goals achieved, regularity of attendance, leadership offered, attitude towards superiors and associates, versatility, etc. These traits are then evaluated on a *continuous scale,* wherein the rather places a mark. Somewhere along a continum. For example:

CHART 9.5

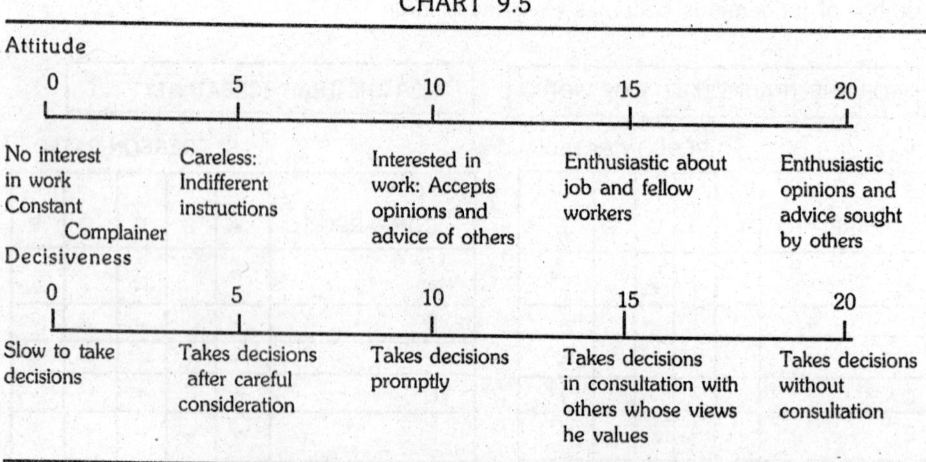

Sometimes a *discontinuous or multiple type of scale* is used, wherein one factor is used along a discontinuous scale, consisting of appropriate boxes or squares which are to be ticked off. The scale may be represented by, and broken down into 3, 7, 10 or more parts and points. Often, the number of factors used varies from 9 to 12; in some methods, they are as many as 30.

CHART 9.6

	☐	☐	☐	☐	☐
Attitude	No interest	Indifferent	Interested	Enthusiastic	Very enthusiastic
Job knowledge	Serious gaps	Satisfactory knowledge	Well informed	Good knowledge	Exceptional expertise
Contact with others	Very little	Departmental only	Several departments	Multi-dimensional internally	Multi-dimensional, internally & externally

The rating-scale method is easy to understand and easy to use, and permits a statistical tabulation of scores. A ready comparison of scores among the employees is possible. These scores indicate the worth of every individual. It is the most common evaluation tool in use today.

Besides, when ratings are objectively given, they can provide useful feedback.

However, this method suffers from a serious disadvantage, for it is arbitrary, and the rating is generally subjective. Often, the rating clusters on the high side when this method is used. Another severe limitation is that it assumes that each characteristic is equally important for all jobs. Perhaps, worst of all, it assumes everyone's definition of 'dependable' is the same.

This method was introduced by Walter D. Scott to get the judgement of superiors on subordinates. The two important features of this system are:

(a) The person who is making the judgement is freed from direct "quantitative" terms in making his decision of merit on any quality; and

(b) The person who is making the judgement can make as fine a discrimination of merit as he chooses.

These two facts eliminate the restrictions on natural judgements which other rating methods impose.

To ensure the success of this method, one should:

(a) Obtain the descriptions of persons at two extremes of the performance scale;

(b) Analyse these descriptions into simple behavioural qualities and present these either as a statement or as trait names;

(c) Establish the discrimination value (i.e., the index of the extent to which a quality is valued);

(d) Pair the statement or trait names and preference value;

(e) Pair high and low preference values forming an item;

CHART 9.7

Graphic Rating Scale

Employee .... Job Title .... Date ....

Department .... Job No. .... Rater ....

Factor	*Score Rating*				
	Unsatisfactory So definitely inadequate that it justifies release	*Fair* Minimal; Barely adequate to justify retention	*Good* Meet basic requirements for retention	*Superior* Definitely above norm and basic requirement	*Exceptional* Distinctly and consistently outstanding
Quality Accuracy, thoroughness, appearance, and acceptance of output					
Quantity Volume of output and contribution					
Attention Regularity dependability and promptness					
Required Supervision Need for advice, direction or correction					
Conservation Prevention of wage, spoilage, protection of equipment					

Reviewed by...(Reviewer's comments on the Reverse)

Employee Comment

Date .... Signature or Initial ....

(Note: In this form, the supervisor checks the appropriate box)

(*f*) Prefer instructions for the rater, asking him to choose one "best fit" and one "least appropriate" statement for the employees;

(*g*) Validate the technique, determine discriminating responses, and assign weights;

(*h*) Prepare a scoring key on the basis of responses and weights.

Forced Choice Description Method: This method was evolved after a great deal of research conducted for the military services during World War II. It attempts to correct a rater's tendency to give consistently high or consistently low ratings to all the employees. The use of this method calls for objective reporting and minimum subjective judgement. Under this method, the rating elements are several sets of pair phrases or adjectives (usually sets of four phrases two of which are positive, two negative) relating to job proficiency or personal qualifications. The rater is asked to indicate which of the four phrases is most and least descriptive of the employee.

The following statements are illustrative of the type of statements that are used:

(a) Makes little effort and individual instruction;

(b) Organises the work well;

(c) Lacks the ability to make people feel at ease;

(d) Has a cool, even temperament;

(e) Is punctual and careful;

(f) Is a hard worker and co-operative;

(g) Is dishonest and disloyal;

(h) Is ove-bearing and disinterested in work.

In each illustration above, two of the above phrases are relatively favourable terms, while the other two are relatively unfavourable. The favourable terms earn a plus credit, while unfavourable terms get no credit. The employee also gets plus credit if one of the negative phrases is checked as being least characteristic.

The method has certain drawbacks such as while choosing two statements from each series, the rater is unable to introduce personal bias or halo effect, as only one of the favourable and of the unfavourable phrases in each series is related to success or failure on the job. Further, he also does not know how 'high' or 'low' he is evaluating the individual because he has no access to the scoring key. This increases the overall objectivity of this method.

However, this method is not clearly superior to traditional rating methods. Trained technicians are required to prepare sets of series for each occupational group. And most managers do not like to "rate in the dark." Further, such tests are expensive to develop, because of the particular job and company. Again, most of the raters become irritated with the tests because they are not being trusted. Finally, the results of evaluation do not prove useful for counselling and training purposes because the rater is ignorant of how he is evaluating the individual.

Forced Distribution Method: This method was evolved by Joseph Tiffin after statistical work. This system is used to eliminate or minimise raters' bias, so that all personnel may not be placed at the higher end or at the lower end of the scale. It requires the rater to appraise an employee according to a pre-determined distribution scale. Under this system, it is performance and promotability. For this purpose, a five-point performance scale is used without any descriptive statement. Employees are placed between the two extremes of 'good' and 'bad' job performances; for example, 10 per cent are placed at the top end of the scale, given *superior or outstanding merit;* 20 per cent given good rating (i.e., *above the average)*; 40 per cent satisfactory (or *average*); 20 per cent fair; and 10 per cent unsatisfactory (or *below average* or *poor*). This forced distribution method assumes that, of the total personnel, 10 per cent must go to the *top grade*, 20 per cent to the *second grade*, 40 per cent to the *middle grade,* 20 per cent to the *grade next to the lowest end* of the scale, and 10 per cent of the *lowest grade.*

In addition to job performance, employees are rated for promotability. A three-point scale is often used for this purpose:

(a) Very likely promotional material;

(b) May or may not be promotional material; and

(c) Very unlikely to be promotional material.

The good point of this system is that by forcing the distribution in this manner, the problem of different appraisers using different parts of the scale is avoided. *Second,* this method tends to eliminate or reduce bias; but its use in wage administration leads to low morale and low productivity. *Third,* the method is highly simple to understand and very easy to apply in organisations.

Checklist: Under this method, the rater does not evaluate employee performance; he supplies reports about it and the final rating is done by the personnel department. A series of questions are presented concerning an employee to his behaviour. The rater, then, checks to indicate if the answer to a question about an employee is positive or negative. The value of each question may be weighed equally or certain questions may be weighed more heavily than others. An example of a checklist is given below:

(1) Is the employee really interested in his job? yes/no
(2) Is he regular on his job? yes/no
(3) Is he respected by his subordinates? yes/no
(4) Does he show uniform behaviour to all? yes/no
(5) Does he keep his temper? yes/no
(6) Is he always willing to help other employees? yes/no
(7) Does he follow instructions properly? yes/no
(8) Does he give recognition and praise to employees for work done well? yes/no
(9) Is the equipment maintained in order? yes/no
(10) Does he ever make mistakes? yes/no

This method suffers from bias on the part of the rater because he can distinguish positive and negative questions. Secondly, a separate checklist must be developed for different classes of jobs. This process can be expensive and time consuming. *Thirdly,* it is difficult to assemble, analyse, and weigh a number of statements about employee characteristics and contributions.

FREE ESSAY METHOD

Under this method, the supervisor makes a free form, open-ended appraisal of an employee in his own words and puts down his impressions about the employee. He takes note of these factors:

(a) Relations with fellow supervisors and personnel assigned to him;

(b) General organisation and planning ability;

(c) Job knowledge and potential;

(d) Employee characteristics and attitudes;

(e) Understanding and application of company policies and procedures;

(f) Production, quality and cost control;

(g) Physical conditions; and

(h) Development needs for future.

The description is always as factual and concrete as possible. No attempt is made to evaluate an employee in a quantitative manner.

There are several advantages of this method. An essay can provide a good deal of information, especially if the supervisor is asked, for instance, to give two or three examples of each judgement he makes. The explanations will give specific information about the employee, and can reveal even more about the supervisor.

However, there are certain drawbacks too: *(i)* It contains a subjective evaluation of the reported behaviour of an individual and may affect such employment decisions as promotion, lay-off, etc. There is no common criterion for evaluation. *(ii)* Some appraisers may be good at narrative appraisal, while others may not have the facility to write a descriptive report. *(iii)* The appraisal may be loaded with a flowery language about the quality of the ratee than with the actual evaluation of performance. *(iv)* Under this system, the supervisor is required to devote considerable time and thought to the procedure. He has to be critical. The appraisal depends more on the appraiser's literary skills than on an employee's abilities and performance. *(v)* Rater bias is easily introduced into such ratings, since the essay is in the supervisor's own words.

CHART 9.8

Specimen of Staff Assessment Form (Descriptive Essay Type)

Staff Appraisal

Name...Job Title ....

Department ....Date of Review ....

Age...Years in present job ....

Section I *Appraisal of Performance*

Notes to Appraiser

1. This appraisal must cover the period of the preceding 12 months
2. Consideration must be given to every function and responsibility of the job, and the standard of performance of each element must be analysed.
3. It must include specific examples of duties carried out to illustrate your comments on an.

   employee's strength and weaknesses.
4. An objective factual assessment of an employee's improvement or deterioration in perfor-mance since the last appraisal must be given and commented upon.
5. The employee should not only be assessed for those personnel traits which have a significant influence on the performance of his work.

   (A full-page is allotted to this section of assessment)

   Overall performance (a) Outstanding

   Rating (b) Very satisfactory

   (c) Satisfactory

   (d) Unsatisfactory

   (e) Very unsatisfactory

   (f) Unproved.

Section II *Promotability and Potential*

Promotability

Assess the promotability of the employees under review under one of the following headings.

1. Ready for promotion now.
2. Ready for promotion within 2 years.
3. Ready for promotion within 5 years.
4. Unlikely to qualify for promotion.

Potential

Assess the specific level of responsibility to which you believe the employee can rise in the forseable future.

Section III *Career Development*

Specify plans for the future development of the employee — these may include:

(a) Further development in the present post;

(b) Transfer to another type of work or place;

(c) Special assignment;

(d) Further training or re-training;

Was last year's plan for employees' career development carried out in full or in part"?

Section IV *Notes on Interview with Employee*

A brief account of the interview, including the employee's comments and suggestions.

Date of Interview:.............................. Interviewed by:..............................

Section V *Comments on, and Endorsement by the Reviewing Authority*

Signature of Appraiser ....Date ....

Comments of the reviewing authority, giving evidence in support of any significant divergence in opinion.

Signature of the Reviewing ....

Authority ....

Designation:...

Date: ....

Critical Incident Method: This method was developed following research conducted by the armed forces in the United States during World War II. The essence of this system is that it attempts to measure workers' performance in terms of certain 'events' or 'episodes' that occur in the performance of the ratee's job. These events are known as *critical incidents*. The basis of this method is the principle that "there are certain significant acts in each employee's behaviour and performance which make all the difference between success and failure on the job."

The supervisor keeps a written record of the events (either good or bad) that can easily be recalled and used in the course of a periodical or formal appraisal. Feedback is provided about the incidents during performance review session. Various behaviours are recorded under such categories as the type of job, requirements for employees, judgement, learning ability, productivity, precision in work, responsibility and initiative. To give an illustration, a materials manager may be trained to look for and recognise the following critical incidents in a purchasing agent's performance:

(i) He treated a salesman in a markedly discourteous fashion;

(ii) He helped a buyer to prepare an unusually difficult purchase order;

(iii) He persuaded a local vendor to stock a particularly important material needed by the firm;

(iv) He rejected a bid that was excessively over-priced;

(v) He failed to return an important phone call; and

(vi) He improved the design of the internal material requisition form.

These critical incidents are discovered after a thorough study of the personnel working on a job. The collected incidents are then ranked in order of frequency and importance.

This method provides an objective basis for conducting a discussion of an individual's performance. Vague impressions and general remarks are avoided, for the supervisor is trained to record accurately the actual incidents from the daily activities of an employee. This approach reduces the "recency" effect (most recent incidents get too much emphasis) of most performance ratings.

However, this method has significant limitations. These include: *(i)* Negative incidents are generally more noticeable than positive ones. *(ii)* The recording of incidents is a chore to the supervisor and may be put off and easily forgotten. *(iii)* Very close supervision may result, which may not be to the liking of an employee. *(iv)* Managers may unload a series of complaints about incidents during an annual performance review session. The feedback may be too much at one time and appear as a punishment.

CHART 9.9

Sample Items from a Managerial Critical Incident Check List

- Refused to take an unpleasant decision or administer a reprimand in his own name: named his supervisor as the responsible one.
- Resisted pressure to start a job without sufficient advance thought and planning.
- Refused to accept job instructions without a prolonged discussion or argument.
- Reported findings on a problem in a fashion which expedited an effective solution.
- Failed to consider alternative ways of performing a job when available information indicated that he should.
- Apologised to a subordinate when he was in the wrong.
- Performed ineffectively on a project because of failure to plan properly.
- Demonstrated the ability to give first priorities to jobs.
- Planned for long-range requirements and future developments with unusual effectiveness.
- Acquired a thorough knowledge of the equipment for which he was not responsible, but which was related to his job.
- Made unrealisitc demands of his group in terms of time and effort.

- Studied a current operating procedure and made effective recommendations for improvement.
- Needed prodding on jobs outside of his major responsibilities.
- Displayed ingenuity in cutting corners to meet a deadline.
- Put the blame for his own mistakes on his subordinates.
- Demonstrated an inability to get along with other employees having the same level of responsibility.
- Misinformed his superior concerning an important matter.
- Failed to prepare a report on time when specifically requested to do so.
- Recognised the abilities and weaknesses of his subordinates and made job assignments accordingly.
- Insisted on using equipment which was not justified on economic grounds.
- Failed to keep superiors informed about important job developments affecting other departments or divisions.
- Refused to accept sub-standard work from subordinates who were capable of better performance.
- Refused to follow instructions even though they were clearly given.
- Made excellent and reliable contribution on important matters.
- Performed a difficult task which was outside his regular duties without being told to do so.
- Ignored the results of a study revealing defects in a proposal he submitted.
- Appropriated the good ideas of subordinates as his own.
- Ignored important facts when recommending merit increases or promotions.
- Instituted an effective procedure for the control of expenses in his department,
- Failed to communicate clearly the duties and responsibilities of a job to his subordinates,

CHART 9.10

Excerpts from a Critical-Incident Rating Form Performance Record of an Employee Work Habits and Attitudes

Response to Departmental Needs

(a) Tried to get others to slow down; refused to work:

(b) Unnecessarily criticised facilities, equipment and facilities, methods;

(c) Was unwilling to work beyond his assignment or responsibility;

(d) Refused to pass along his idea for an improvement;

(e) Tried to get other workers to accept a new rate-job;

(f) Increased his efficiency despite the resentment of other workers;

(g) Accepted extra work inspite of inconvenience;

(h) Accepted more difficult jobs;

(i) Suggested improved production procedures.

Getting Along with Others

(a) Became upset or angry because of the kind of work he was called upon to do;

(b) Quarrelled with fellow-employees;

(c) Criticised and annoyed other workers;

(d) Bossed over other workers;

(e) Tinkered at the equipment of another worker;

(f) Refused to help another worker;

(g) Remained calm under stress;

(h) Kept his temper under provocations;

(i) Helped another worker at some inconvenience to himself;

(j) Avoided friction by tact and consideration;

(k) Assisted fellow-employee needing help.

Initiative

(a) Failed to plan work when necessary;

(b) Failed to obtain tools until need arose;

(c) Failed to point out defective parts of operation;

(d) Failed to take action in an emergency;

(e) Planned efficient ways of doing work;

(f) Stocked materials and tools ahead to time;

(g) Prepared work area and machine in advance;

(h) Volunteered for more responsible tasks;

(i) Voluntarily did work in addition to what was expected of him;

(j) Pointed out defects in time.

Responsibility

(a) Passed up the chance for additional training;

(b) Passed up the chance to learn more about the job;

(c) Gave misleading, incorrect instructions;

(d) Poorly directed work in the foreman's absence;

(e) Got additional information on the job or department;

(f) Took additional information on the job or department;

(g) Took additional outside training;

(h) Got information on improving work;

(i) Planned a scheme for others;

(j) Trained and instructed other employees;

(k) Ensured co-operation among employees.

Group Appraisal Method: Under this method, employee are rated by an appraisal group, consisting of their supervisor and three or four other supervisors who have some knowledge of their performance. The supervisor explains to the group the nature of his subordinates' duties. The group then discusses the standards of performance for that job, the actual performance of the job-holder, and the causes of their particular level of performance, and offers suggestions for future improvement, if any.

The advantage of this method is that it is thorough, very simple and is devoid of any bias, for it involves multiple judges. But it is very time-consuming.

Field Review Method: Under this method, a trainer employee from the personnel department interviews line supervisors to evaluate their respective subordinates. The appraiser is fully equipped with definite test questions, usually memorised in advance, which he puts to the supervisor. The supervisor is required to give his opinion about the progress of his subordinates, the level of the performance of each subordinate, his weaknesses, good points, outstanding ability, promotability, and the possible plans of action in cases requiring further consideration. The questions are asked and answered verbally. The appraiser takes detailed notes of the answers, which are then approved by the supervisor and placed in the employee's personal folder. The success of this system depends upon the competence of the interviewer. If he knows his business, he can contribute significantly to a reasonably accurate appraisal. Moreover, he keeps the supervisor on his toes by this evaluation and minimises bias and prejudice on his part.

This system is useful for a large organisation, and does not suffer from the weaknesses which are evident in other systems. The over-all ratings are obtained by largely using a three-way categorisation, viz., *outstanding, satisfactory* and *unsatisfactory*. It relieves the supervisor of the need for filling out appraisal forms. The main defect is that it keeps two management representatives busy with the appraisal.

GENERAL DEMERITS OF TRADITIONAL TECHNIQUES

Many of the above traditional performance evaluation techniques have internal weaknesses. For example,

1. Managers generally are not qualified to assess personality traits, and most managers are even not properly trained to conduct evaluation and performance interviews. They have very vague notions of the purpose of evaluations. Hence, they do a poor job.
2. Some managers discourage good performance by over-emphasising shortcomings and almost neglecting good work. Others have little effect on poor workers because they tend to sugar-coat their criticisms. Consequently the real message is lost.
3. Rater's personality also plays an important part in the effectiveness of evaluation programmes. Some raters are by temperament, overtly harsh and give low ratings to all subordinates. Others are too lenient and give everyone a good rating; some raters play favourites, some are victims of 'halo' effect.
4. The relative status of raters in their organisation is a factor that is important to the validity of performance appraisal. Using more raters or endorsements by a superior reduces rater bias and increases validity of appraisals.

NEWER OR MODERN METHODS OF APPRAISAL AND CAREER DEVELOPMENT

As we have seen, most traditional methods emphasise either on the task or the worker's personality, while making an appraisal. In order to bring about a balance between these two, modern methods have been developed. Of such methods, the most important are:

1. Appraisal by Results or Management by Objectives.
2. Assessment Centre Method.
3. Human Asset Accounting Method.
4. Behaviourally Anchored Rating Scales.

1. APPRAISAL BY RESULTS OR MANAGEMENT BY OBJECTIVES (MBO)

This method has been evolved by Peter Drucker. MBO is potentially a powerful philosophy of managing and an effective way for operationalising the evaluation process. It seeks to minimise external controls and maximise internal motivation through joint goal setting between the manager and the subordinate and increasing the subordinate's own control of his work. It strongly reinforces the importance of allowing the subordinate to participate actively in the decisions that affect him directly.

Management by objectives can be described as "a process whereby the superior and subordinate managers of an organisation jointly identify its common goals, define each individual's major areas of responsibility in terms of results expected of him and use these measures as guides for operating the unit and assessing the contributions of each of its members."

From another point of view, MBO has been defined as: (1) a system approach to managing and organisation, where those accountable for directing the organisation first determine where they want to take the organisation; (2) a process requiring and encouraging all key management personnel to contribute their maximum to achieving the overall objectives; (3) an effort to blend and balance all the goals of all key personnel; and (4) an evaluation mechanism.

Objectives of MBO: MBO has an objective in itself. The objective is to change behaviour and attitudes towards getting the job done. In other words, *it is results-oriented; it is performance that counts.* It is management system and philosophy that *stress goals rather than methods.* It provides responsibility and accountability and recognises that employees have needs for achievement and self-fulfillment. It meets these needs by providing opportunities for participation in goal-setting process. Subordinates become involved in planning their own careers.

MBO Process: Although MBO has something of an aura of mystery about it, it really is fairly simple procedure. It consists of five basic steps as follows:

1. Set organisation goals, i.e., establishment of an organisation — wide strategy and goals. Such goals are expressed clearly and concisely and can be measured accurately. They have to be periodically revised. They should be challenging: high enough to provide motivation, but not so high that they are out of reach. Otherwise they might result in frustration among the employees and lead to defensive behaviour.

Clear attainable goals help channel energies in specific directions, and let the subordinate know the basis on which he will be rewarded.

2. Joint goal setting, i.e., establishment of short-term performance targets between the management and the subordinate in a conference between them. The individual manager must clarify in his own mind the responsibilities of their subordinates. *Organisation Charts* and *Job Descriptions* may be used. The manager may ask each subordinate to write down his personal goals, while in turn the manager writes out the goals he thinks subordinates should have. The manager and subordinate then discuss them reach an agreement about them, and put them in writing.

The manager may ask his subordinates how he personally can help achieve these goals, and request suggestions. The goals set should be flexible enough to accommodate new ideas, and they should stress individual responsibility. The goals should be specific, and clear and should be quantified for easier measurement; for example:

- to prepare, process, and transfer to the office superintendent, all accounts payable vouchers within three working days from the receipt of the invoice;
- to cut each day, 350 meters of wire to standard three-meter lengths, with a maximum scrap of 10 metres;
- to use programme evaluation and review technique (PERT) for all new plant layouts;
- to hold weekly meetings with all subordinates, etc.

3. Performance reviews, i.e., frequent performance review meetings between the managers and the subordinate. During the initial stages of the MBO programme, monthly reviews may be used and then extended to quarterly reviews. For maximum effectiveness, reviews probably should be made more often than once each year.

4. Set checkposts, i.e., establishment of major checkposts to measure progress. The quirk of human nature demands that the manager be constantly alert and exercise sound judgement. However, as subordinate learns to establish objectives and direct activities towards their goals, the rate of control and amount of checking gradually can be decreased.

5. Feedback: The employees who receive frequent feedback concerning their performance are more highly motivated than those who do not feedback that is specific, relevant, and timely helps satisfy the need most people fell about knowing where they stand.

Thus, under MBO programme, an employee and his supervisor meet and together define, establish, and set certain goals or objectives which the employee would attempt to achieve within the period of prescribed time. They also discuss the ways and methods of measuring employee progress. The goals which are set are work-related and career-oriented. The employee periodically meets his supervisor to evaluate the employee's goal progress. If necessary, these goals may be revised. Frequent feedback and supervisor-subordinate interaction are the other key features of this method. The supervisor plays supportive, counselling and coaching roles.

In sum, the three foundations of MBO are: (1) goal-setting; (2) feedback; and (3) participation — all these enhance performance.

This method emphasises the value of the present and the future instead of that of the past, and focuses attention on the results that are accomplished and not on personal traits or operational methodology. An employee is not judged in terms of operational methodology, or in terms of 'initiative, co-operativeness, attitude, emotional stability, or any other human quality, but on the basis of the achievement of the targets that have been set. This method is largely applied to technical, professional, supervisory or executive personnel, and not to the hourly-paid workers because their jobs are usually too restricted.

CHART 9.11
Pattern of Questions and Answers for Performance Review (or Goal Setting) Interviews

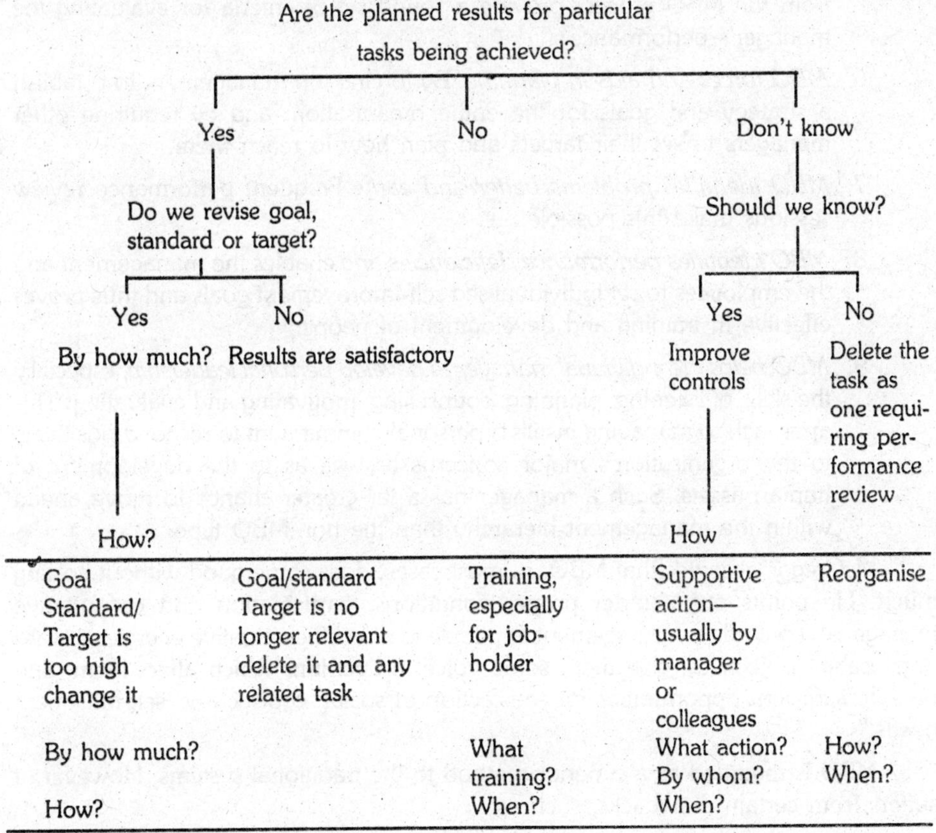

BENEFITS OF MBO PROGRAMME

Management by objectives is an important performance tool. It has certain advantages.

1. *MBO helps and increases employee motivation* because it relates overall goals to the individual's goals; and helps to increase an employee's understanding of where the organisation is and where it is heading.

2. *Managers are more likely to compete with themselves than with other managers.* This kind of evaluation can reduce internal conflicts that often arise when managers compete with each other to obtain scarce resources.
3. *MBO results in a "means ends" chain.* Management at succeedingly lower levels in the organisation established targets which are integrated with those at the next higher level. Thus, it can help insure that everyone's activity is ultimately aimed toward organisation's goals.
4. *MBO reduces role conflict and ambiguity.* Role conflict exists when a person is faced with conflicting demands from two or more supervisors; and role ambiguity exists when a person is uncertain as to how he will be evaluated, or what he has to achieve. Since MBO aims at providing clear targets and their order or priority, it reduces both these situations.
5. *MBO provides more objective appraisal criteria.* The targets that emerge from the MBO process provide a sound set of criteria for evaluating the manager's performance.
6. *MBO forces and aids in planning.* By forcing top management to establish a strategy and goals for the entire organisation; and by requiring other managers to set their targets and plan how to reach them.
7. *MBO identifies problems better and early.* Frequent performance review sessions make this possible.
8. *MBO identifies performance deficiencies and* enables the management and the employees to set individualised self-improvement goals and thus proves effective in training and development of people.
9. *MBO helps the individual manager to develop personal leadership,* especially the skills of listening, planning, counselling, motivating and evaluating. This approach to managing instills a personal commitment to respond positively to the organisation's major concerns as well as to the development of human assets. Such a manager has a far greater chance to move ahead within the management hierarchy than the non-MBO type.

McGregor observes that MBO, in most cases, does some good without costing much. He points out, "under proper conditions, participation and consultative management provide encouragement to people to direct their creative energies toward organisation objectives, give them some voice in decisions which affect them, and provide sufficient opportunities for satisfaction of social, egoistic and self-fulfillment needs."

MBO is regarded as a superior method to the traditional systems. However, it suffers from certain drawbacks, such as:

1. MBO programme takes a great deal of time, energy and form — completing on the part of managers. An individual becomes so enmeshed in performing assigned functions that he often loses sight of the goal, the reason for performance. It has been called "the activity trap" by Odiorne. It requires a great deal of investment of the top management's time and effort before it arrives at realistic targets and reviews the performance.
2. MBO is far from panacea. Those executives who have been involved very often find it difficult to apply MBO concepts to their own work habits. They

find it hard to think about the results of work rather than the work itself. They tend to over emphasize goals that are easy to quantify, sometimes forgetting that workers often behave almost like children at play — when the game no longer challenges, interest is soon lost.

3. In some areas, such as cutting costs or increasing sales, measuring performance is a straight forward and more or less objective matter. But in many other areas, such as subordinate development, appraising performance can be an acute problem.
4. Many times neither the managers know the rationale and value of MBO, nor the subordinates are clear about the goals. This unnecessarily becomes more exasperating.
5. There is sometimes a "tug of war" in which the subordinate tries to set the lowest targets possible and the supervisor the highest.

A number of pitfalls have been indicated, by the researchers, in the way of effective working of MBO programmes. The reasons for failure in the MBO process are: hasty implementation, unknowledgeable users, lack of top management follow through, and support, over emphasis on structure, treatment as another gimmick, failure to carefully monitor and encourage the MBO process during hard initial years of implementation.

The most important reason why MBO fails is that many managers are unconcerned with performance, and they reward other criteria (e.g., reward people for "looking productive," rather than for "being productive"). More concern is given to how actions look than the effect of these actions. Instead of rewarding good performance, managers frequently reward other characteristics: things like getting along with people, good work habit, physical appearance, and personality. Further, organisations offer a narrow differentiation in the awards that are offered. As a result of community wage patterns, union contracts, and organisational policies, salaries for similar jobs tend to bunch quite closely, irrespective of the performance that individuals exhibit on these jobs. This undermines the concept of MBO.

MBO can be effective technique for performance evaluation and for motivating subordinates, by developing communication between executives at all levels. Those at the bottom must be willing to listen to the voice of experience, and those at the top willing to accept fresh ideas from lower-echelon employees. Similarly, executives must keep abreast of new programmes, especially the modern ideas that have been developed in the academic circles.

2. ASSESSMENT CENTRE METHOD

The Assessment centre concept was initially applied to military situations by Simoniet in the German Army in the 1930s and the War Office Selection Board of the British Army in the 1960s. The purpose of this method was and is to test candidates in a social situation, using a number of assessors and a variety of procedures. The most important feature of the assessment centre is job-related simulations. These stimulations involve characteristics that managers feel are important to the job success. The evaluators observe and evaluate participants as they perform activities commonly found in these higher level jobs.

Under this method, many evaluators join together to judge employee performance in several situations with the use of a variety of criteria. It is used mostly to help select employees for the first level (the lowest) supervisory positions. Assessments are made to determine employee potential for purposes of promotion. The assessment is generally done with the help of a couple of employees and involves a paper-and-pencil test, interviews and situational exercises. Some of the other features of this system are:

(i) The use of situational exercises (such as an in-basket exercise, business game, a role-playing incident and leaderless group discussion);

(ii) Evaluators are drawn from experienced managers with proven ability at different levels of management;

(iii) They evaluate all employees, both individually and collectively, and each candidate is given one of the three categories: more than acceptable, less than acceptable and unacceptable;

(iv) A summary report is prepared by the members, and a feedback on a face-to-face basis is administered to all the candidates who ask for it.

Purpose of Assessment Centres: Assessment centres are used for the following purposes:

1. To measure potential for first level supervision, sales and upper management positions; and also for higher levels of management for development purposes.
2. To determining individual training and development needs of employees.

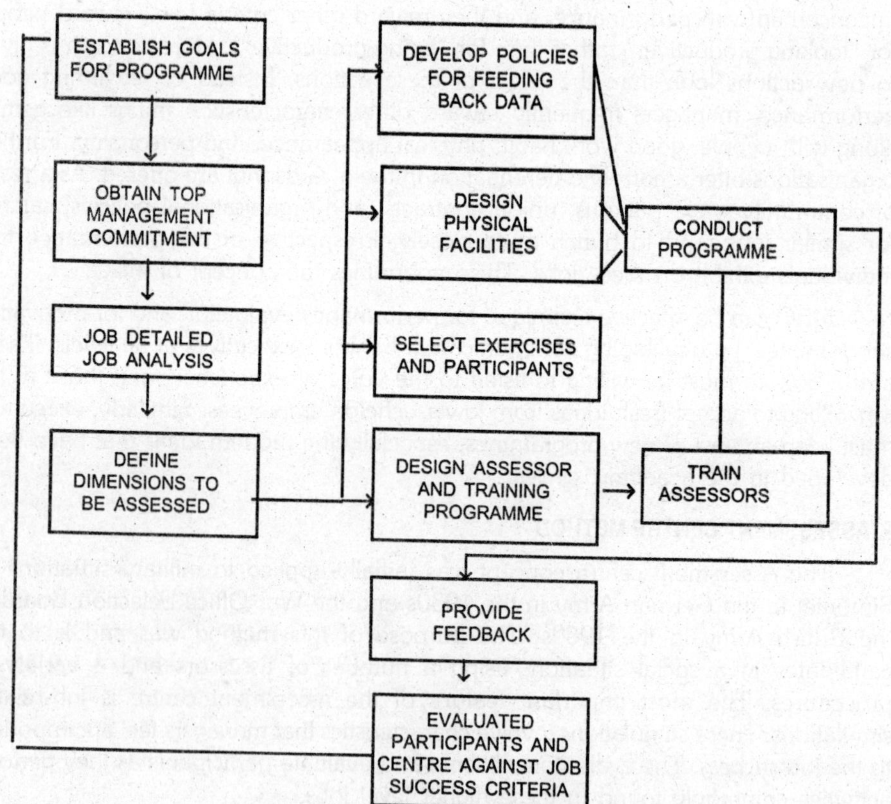

Fig. 9.3 An Assessment Centre Model

3. To select recent college students for entry level positions.
4. To provide more accurate human resource planning information.
5. To make an early determination of potential.
6. To assist in implementing affirmative action goals.

The Assessment Centres generally measure interpersonal skills and other aspects such as: organising and planning; interpersonal competence (getting along with others), quality of thinking, resistance to stress, orientation (motivation) to work, dependence on others, other community communication and creativity. The ability to organise, plan and make decisions, as in basket simulations and scores obtained on paper and pencil, psychological tests, are important to the overall assessment score.

Procedure: The Assessment centre programme commonly used follows. This procedure. First, a leadership group is established; each member supporting a predefined position, but the group must arrive at consensus. Then a task force is used with an appointed leader, who decides on a course of action. Simulation games and in basket exercises are used to test organisational and planning abilities. Oral report is made by the candidate, which tests his communication skills and straight into his present position. Personal interviews, and projective tests are used to assess work motivation, career orientation, and dependence on others. Paper and pencil tests measure intellectual ability.

The duration of Assessment centre programme varies with the persons. For example, centres designed for selection of firstline supervisors, sales personnel, and management trainees generally last for a day or less; while those used for higher-level managers may run for two or three days or longer if used for developmental and not for selection purposes.

Problems: Assessment centre ratings are said to be strongly influenced by the participant's interpersonal skills, judges tend to evaluate the quality of the individual's social skills rather than quality of the decisions themselves. Further, the organisation and decision-making abilities are measured by in-basket exercises, verbal ability and personal traits. Thus, the relatively inexpensive paper-and-pencil tests for measuring potential may be as accurate as the high-cost high-stress assessment centre.

The Assessment Centre approach, therefore, suffers from many real hazards. One of the most obvious is the exam-taking. Solid performers in day-to-day operations suddenly choke in simulated environment. Another drawback is the potential bad effects on those not selected to participate in the exercise. The cost of assessing an individual in a particular job level is prohibitive. Many Assessment Centres have one particular weakness: immediate supervisors nominate participants. Employees who are curious, independent, aggressive, and intelligent may never be selected because such traits, though important at higher levels, are not accepted by lower-level supervisors. Further, employees who receive a poor report from the centre may react in negative ways and might demoralise an employee who was once an asset.

To make Assessment Centre Programme successful it is necessary that heavy emphasis must be placed on clear statement of goals, the obtaining of top management commitment, job analysis, assessor training and programme audit and evaluation.

3. 360 DEGREE PERFORMANCE APPRAISAL

Some organisations have expanded the idea of upward feedback into what they call 360 degree feedback. Performance information is collected "all round" an employee, from his supervisors, subordinates, peers, and internal and external customers. The feedback is generally used for training and development rather than for pay increase.

Most 360 degree feedback system contain several common features. The employee's supervisors, peers, subordinates, customers complete the survey questionnaires on the individual. These feedbacks are there complied and presented to the person being rated. Then they meet their supervisor and subordinates and share the information they feel is pertinent for their own self improvement plan.

The appraiser may be any person who has thorough knowledge about the job done by contents to be appraised, standards of contents and who observes the employee while performing a job. The appraiser should be capable of determining what is more important and what is relatively less important. He should assess the performance without bias. The appraisers are supervisors, peers, subordinates employees themselves, users of service and consultants. Performance appraisal by all these parties is called "360°" appraisal.

4. HUMAN ASSET ACCOUNTING METHOD

The human asset accounting method refers to activity devoted to attaching money estimates to the value of a firm's internal human organisation and its external customer goodwill. If able, well-trained personnel leave a firm, the human organisation is worthless; if they join it, its human assets are increased. If distrust and conflict prevail, the human enterprise is devalued. If teamwork and high morale prevail, the human organisation is a very valuable asset.

The current value of a firm's human organisation can be appraised by developed procedures, by undertaking periodic measurements of "key causal" and "intervening enterprise" variables. The *key causal variables* include the structure of an organisation's management policies, decisions, business leadership, strategies, skills and behaviour. The *intervening variables* reflect the internal state and health of an organisation. They include loyalties, attitudes, motivations, and collective capacity for effective interaction, communication and decision-making. These two types of variable measurements must be made over several years to provide the needed data for the computation of the human asset accounting.

This method is not yet very popular.

5. BEHAVIOURALLY ANCHORED RATING SCALES (BARS)

This is a new appraisal technique which has recently been developed. Its supporters claim that it provides better, more equitable appraisals as compared to other techniques. The procedure for BARS is usually five stepped.

1. *Generate Critical Incidents:* Persons with knowledge of the job to be appraised (job holders/supervisors) are asked to describe specific illustrations (critical incidents) of effective performance behaviour.

2. *Develop Performance Dimensions:* These people then cluster the incidents into a smaller set (or say 5 or 10) of performance dimensions. Each cluster (dimension) is then defined.

3. *Reallocate Incidents:* Any group of people who also know the job then reallocate the original critical incidents. They are given the cluster's definitions, and

critical incidents, and asked to redesign each incident to the dimension it best describes. Typically a critical incident is retained if some percentage (usually 50 to 80%) of this group assigns it to the same cluster as the previous group did.

4. Scale of Incidents: This second group is generally asked to rate (7 or 9 point scales are typical) the behaviour described in the incident as to how effectively or ineffectively it represents performance on the appropriate dimension.

5. Develop Final Instrument: A subset of incidents (usually 6 or 7 per cluster) are used as "behaviour anchors" for the performance dimensions.

Performance	Scale	Behaviour anchors
Extremely Good Performance	7	
Good Performance	6	You can expect this Checker to be aware of items that constantly fluctuate in price. You can expect this checker to know the various sizes at cans —No...., No...., No.....
Slightly Good Performance	5	When in doubt this checker would ask the other clerk if the item is taxable. This checker can be expected to verify with another checker a discripancy between the shell and the marked price before ringing up that item.
Neither Good Nor Poor Performance	5	When operating the quick check, the lights are flashing, this checker can be expected to check out a customer with 15 items.
Slightly Poor Performance	3	You could expect this checker to ask the customer the price of an item that he does not know. In the daily course of personal relationships, may be expected to linger in long coversations with a customer or another checker.
Poor Performance	2	In order to take a break, this checker can be expected to block off the checkstand with people in line.
Extremely Poor Performance	1	

Fig. 9.4: A 'Bars' for "Knowledge and Judgement"

Below is given an example of how the method works in practice, based upon the research done on grocery clerks in a large grocery chain store in USA. A number of critical incidents were collected there and these were then clustered into eight performance criteria, viz:

1. Knowledge and Judgement.
2. Conscientiousness.
3. Skill in Human Relations.

4. Skill in Operation of Register.
5. Skill in Bagging.
6. Organisational Ability of Check-stand work.
7. Skill in monetary transactions.
8. Observational ability.

In the chart is given the BARS for one of these critieria, viz., "knowledge and Judgement." The scale ranges, from one to seven, for rating performance from "extremely poor" to "extremely good."

Though BARS technique is more time-consuming and expensive than other appraisal tools, yet it has got certain advantages, such as:"

1. *A more accurate gauge*, since BARS is done by persons expert in the technique, the results are sufficiently accurate.
2. *Clear Standards.* The critical incidents along the scale help to clarify what is meant by "extremely good" performance, "average" performance and so forth.
3. *Feedback.* The use of critical incidents may be more useful in providing feedback to the people being appraised.
4. *Independent dimensions. Systematically clustering the critical* incidents into 5 or 6 performance dimensions, helps in making the dimensions more independent of one another.
5. *Rater — Independence.* The technique is not biased by the experience and evaluation of the rater.

COMPONENTS OF APPRAISAL EVALUATION

As we have seen, performance evaluations can be made for a variety of reasons — counselling, promotion, research, salary, administration or a combination of these. So it is necessary to begin by stating very clearly the objectives of the evaluation programme. Having done this, the personnel evaluation system should address the questions *who, what, when, where, how?* of performance appraisal.

So, the first question involved is *who?* and this issue states "who should be rated, and who should do the rating." The answer to the first issue is that all employees of an organisation should be appraised, from the operator to the top-level management need be appraised for one reason or the other. Regarding the second issue, it may be said that personnel experts assist and advise the top and line management, who should participate in the appraisal programme; and the line management should actually do the evaluation work. The personnel officer obtains the ratings of different raters and analyses and determines the realiability and validity of such ratings. Such validity can be checked against certain objective evidence such as production quantities, quality, absenteeism, and by comparing the results of one system with those of another. The ratings should not be changed by the personnel expert. However, he has the obligations to point out inconsistencies to the rater.

"WHO" OF THE APPRAISAL?

As Ruderman observes, "the appraisal can be accomplished by one or more individuals involving a combination of the immediate supervisor, other managers acquainted with the assessee's work, a higher level manager, a personnel manager, the assessee's peers, the assessee himself and the assessee's subordinates."

Usually the immediate supervisor must be entrusted with the task of rating the assessee because he is most familiar with his work; and because he is also responsible for recommending or approving personnel actions based on the performance appraisal; and for providing a feedback of performance appraisal to the subordinate. Because of these reasons supervisors' ratings are regarded as the best possible assessment; and they are often considered as the "heart of the most appraisal systems." This is so because getting supervisor's appraisal is relatively easy and also makes sense. Therefore, most appraisal systems rely heavily on the supervisor's evaluation. In such rating hierarchical control is maintained over the appraisal process.

Appraisal is also done, by the staff specialists, i.e., the personnel officers. They may advise the supervisor while evaluating their subordinates stressing the need for evidence for making specific appraisal judgements and comparing a particular subordinate's evaluation with those of others.

The appraisal of an individual may also be done by his peers. Such appraisal proves effective in predicting future management success. Researchers have verified that ratings made by peers have been quite accurate in predicting which persons would be promoted and which would not.

Sometimes self-evaluation is also employed for evaluating performance. Self-rating emphasizes human relations, which supervisors focus on technical knowledge and initiative. Flippo observes: "The major value lies in the development and motivation areas, it being claimed that this approach (1) results in a superior upward flow of information, (2) forces the subordinate to become more personally involved and, to some extent constrains him to think about himself and his work, (3) improves communication between superior and subordinate, in that each is given more information by the other when disagreements are discovered, and (4) improves motivation as a result of great participation." But this approach has its disadvantage that the individual may rate himself excessively high than it would be if he was rated by his superior. Because of this fairly consistent upward bias in self-appraisals, the best thing would be to use these appraisals for counselling and developing subordinates. They are not as useful for making salary and promotion decisions.

Many companies use Rating Committees to evaluate employees. These committees consist of supervisors, peers, and subordinates. Everyone on the Committee is a person who is able to intelligently evaluate some aspect of the employee's performance. Many discrepancies in the ratings may occur — such as "very strict" or "very lenient" ratings — when evaluations are done by individuals. It has, therefore, been felt that "the combined use of several rates" can help "cancel out" problems like 'bias' as 'halo' effect on the part of the individual rates. Second, the raters at different levels in the organisation usually observe different facets of an employee's job performance and the appraisal by a group reflect these differences.

Last, in many companies, subordinates and superiors jointly establish goals and periodically evaluate the subordinate's performance with respect to these goals.

"WHAT" OF APPRAISAL

The "what" of the performance appraisal consists in appraising non-supervisory employees for their current performance, and managers for future potential. It also includes evaluation of human traits.

THE "WHY" OF APPRAISAL

The 'why' of an appraisal is concerned with:

(a) Creating and maintaining a satisfactory level of performance of employees in their present jobs;

(b) Highlighting employee needs and opportunities for personal growth and development;

(c) Aiding in decision-making for promotions, transfers, lay-offs and discharges; and

(d) Promoting understanding between the supervisor and his subordinates.

(e) Providing a useful criterion for determining the validity of selection and training methods and techniques and forming concrete measures for attracting individual of higher calibre to the enterprise.

THE "WHEN" OF APPRAISAL

The 'when' answers the query about the frequency of appraisal. It has been suggested informal counselling should occur continuously. The manager should discuss an employee's work as soon as possible after he has judged it. *He should use good work as an opportunity to provide positive reinforcement and use poor work as a basis for training.*

In most organisations employees are formally evaluated once a year, in others twice a year. New employees are rated more frequently than the older ones. The ideal thing is that each employee should be rated three months after being assigned to a job, after six months on the job, and every six months thereafter. The time of rating should not coincide with the time of salary reviews, for if the two occur

CHART 9.12

Traits Used in Appraising Personnel

Ability to delegate	Habits	Personal appearance
Ability to sell ideas	Health	Personality
Acceptability	Human relations	Physical energy
Accuracy	—	Planning
Adaptability	Imagination	Poise
Ambition	Industriousness	Product knowledge
Analytical ability	Initiative	
Attitude	Integrity	Quality of work
	Intelligence	Quantity of work
Ability to learn		
Ability to supervise	Job Knowledge	Reliability
Character	Job performance	Resourcefulness
Commands confidence and respect	Judgement	Responsibility
Co-operativeness	Leadership	Self-confidence
Co-ordination	Loyalty	Sense of humour
Creative ability	Maturity	Tactfulness
Decisiveness		Thoroughness
Dependability	Oral Expression	Training of personnel
Educational level	Organising ability	
Emotional stability	Originality	Vision
Enthusiasm	Perseverance	Written expression
Foresight		

together constructive evaluation and considerations of self-development will probably take second place to the pressures of pay.

THE "WHERE" OF APPRECIATION

The 'where' indicates the location where an employee may be evaluated. It is usually done at the place of work or office of the supervisor.

Informal appraisals may take anywhere and everywhere, both on-the-job in work situations and off-the-job.

CHART 9.13

Characteristics Used by Selected Companies in U.S.A.

Large Bank	*Manufacturing Concern*	*Meta Manufacturing Concern*	*Department Store*	*Manufacturing Plant*
	Machine Operator	Salesman	Supervisor	
1. Output	1. Job Knowledge	1. Work	1. Appearance	1. Employee relationship
2. Accuracy	2. Quantity of work	2. Quantity of work	2. Job knowledge	2. Meeting quality requirements
3. Promptness	3. Quality of work	3. Adaptability	3. Knowledge of merchandise	3. Meeting cost requirements
4. Neatness	4. Acceptance of responsibility	4. Job knowledge	4. Customer contact	4. Meeting schedules
5. Thoroughness	5. Co-operation	5. Depend-ability	5. Speed in setting	5. Maintenance
6. Industriousness	6. Initiative	6. Attitude		6. Leadership
7. Supervision required				7. Job Knowledge
	Set-up man			
8. Knowledge of own work	1. Accuracy			8. Dependability and Judge-ment
9. Ease in learning	2. Job Knowledge			
10. Memory	3. Ability to instruct			
11. Co-operation	4. Speed			
12. Self-control	5. Safety			
13. Persistence				
14. Attitude towards job				
15. Personal appearance				
16. Health				
17. Punctuality				

THE "HOW" OF APPRAISAL

Under 'how,' the company must decide what different methods are available and which of these may be used for performance appraisal. On the basis of the comparative advantages and disadvantages it is decided which method would suit the purpose best.

Chart 9.14 depicits such advantages and disadvantages.

CHART 9.14

Important Advantages and Disadvantages of Appraisal Tools

Appraisal Tool	*Advantages*	*Disadvantages*
1. Graphic Rating Scales	(i) Simple to use; (ii) provides a quantitative rating for each employee	(i) Standards may be unclear; (ii) Halo effect, central tendency; leniency, bias can be the main problems.
2. Alternatives Ranking	(i) Simple to use. (ii) Avoids central tendency and other problems of rating scales.	Ratings may still not be precise.
3. Paired Comparison Method	Results in more precise ranking than does alternative ranking.	More difficult than ranking.
4. Forced Distribution Method	Results in predetermined number of people in each group.	Appraisal results depend on the adequacy of original choice of cut-off points.
5. Critical Incident Method	(i) Helps specify what is "right" and "wrong" about the employee's performance; (ii) forces managers to evaluate subordinates on an ongoing basis.	Difficult to rate or rank employees relative to one another.
6. BARS	(i) Participation of employees in developing the BARS leadsto more accurate gauge; (ii) the Critical incidents help "anchor" and Clarify the scale.	Very difficult to develop.

In the Chart 9.15 Sikula has very succinctly given the tabular information about different components of appraisal evaluation.

FACTORS DETERRING OBJECTIVE EVALUATION OR PROBLEMS OF APPRAISAL

The ideal approach to performance evaluation is that in which the evaluator is free from personal biases, prejudices, and idiosyncrasies. This is because when an evaluation is objective, it minimizes the potential capracious and dysfunctional behaviour of the evaluator which may be detrimental to the achievement of the organisational goals. However, a single foolproof evaluation method is not available. Inequities in evaluation often destroy the usefulness of the performance system — resulting in inaccurate, invalid appraisals, which are unfair too.

There are many significant factors which deter or impede objective evaluation. These factors are:

1. The Halo Effect or Error: The "halo effect" is a "tendency to let the assessment of an individual one trait influence the evaluation of that person on other specific traits." There is this effect in appraisal when the appraiser assigns the same rating to all traits regardless of an employee's actual performance on these traits. The 'halo' effect refers to the tendency to rate an individual consistently high or low or average on the various traits, depending upon whether the rater's over-all impression of the individual is favourable or not. This means that the halo effect allows one

CHART 9.15
Appraisal Questions

WHO?

Appraisal: *All Appraisers: employees*	1. Immediate supervisor	5. Subordinates
	2. Other supervisors	6. Personnel Manager
	3. Peers or colleagues	7. External consultant
	4. Self	8. Group combination

WHAT

Object: Human beings *Time frame*
1. Current performance
2. Future potential

Specifics
1. Personal traits
2. Achieved results

WHY?

1. Maintain work force
2. Improve performance
3. Determine organisational training needs.
4. Determine personnel development opportunities
5. Basis for promotions, transfers, lay-offs, discharges, etc.
6. Basis for pay increase, and in recruitment, selection, placement and indoctrination processes
7. Feedback and communication mechanism

WHEN?

Formal	*Informal*
1. Annually	1. Weekly
2. Semi-annually	2. Daily
3. Quarterly	3. Continuously

WHERE?

On-the-Job	*Off-the-job*
1. Boss's office	1. Consultant's office
2. Subordinate place of work	2. Social or recreational setting
3. Everywhere	3. Everywhere

HOW?

Methods

Traditional

Rating scale, employee comparison, check lists, free from essays interviews, critical incidents

Modern

Assessment centres, M.B.O.
Human asset accounting

Problems
1. Halo effect
2. Leniency or strictness
3. Central tendency
4. Personal bias.

characteristic, observation or occurrence (either good or bad) to influence the rating of all performance factors. The halo effect arises when traits are unfamiliar, ill defined and involve personal relations. This often occurs when an employee tends to be more conscientious and dependable, that the appraiser might become biased toward that individual to the extent that the appraiser rates him high on many desirable attributes; or when the employee is more friendly or unfriendly toward the appraiser. In such cases, a very high rate may be given to a favoured employee, whereas a low rating may be given to an unfriendly employee so that he may be bypassed even though he is a very capable one, when the question of a promotion arises.

Another example may be of the students who tend to rate a faculty member as 'outstanding' on all criteria when they are particularly appreciative of a few things he does in the class room. Similarly a few bad habits like coming late for lectures, being slow in returning papers, or assigning an extremely demanding reading requirement — might result in student's evaluating the lecturer as "lousy" across-the-board.

The halo effect problem can be alleviated by: *(i)* providing a five to ten minutes training programme to the evaluators; *(ii)* restructuring the questions by requiring the evaluator to consider each question independently; and *(iii)* having the evaluator appraise all rates on each dimension before going to the next dimension.

2. Leniency or Strictness Tendency or Constant Errors: Every evaluator has his own value system which acts as a standard against which he makes his appraisals. Relative to the true or actual performance an individual exhibits, some supervisors have a tendency to be liberal in their ratings, i.e., they consistently assign 'high values' to their employees, while at other times they may have a tendency to assign consistently 'low ratings.' The former tendency is known as *'positive leniency error';* while the latter as *'negative leniency error.'* When an evaluator is positively lenient in his appraisal, an individual's performance becomes overstated, i.e., rated higher than it actually should. Similarly, under the negative tendency, performance is understated than what it should be. Both these trends usually arise from varying standards of performance observed by supervisors and from different interpretations of what they evaluate in employee performance. The tendency can be avoided by holding meetings or training sessions for raters so that they may understand what is required of them in rating.

3. The Central Tendency Problem: It is the most commonly found error. It assigns "average ratings" to all the employees with a view to avoiding commitment or involvement; or when the rater is in doubt or has inadequate information or lack of knowledge about the behaviour of the employee, or when he does not have much time at his disposal. Such tendency seriously distorts the evaluations, making them most useless for promotion, salary, or counselling purposes. The ranking tools discussed earlier are aimed at avoiding this problem.

4. Similarity Error: This type of error occurs when the evaluator rates other people in the same way he perceives himself. For example, the evaluator who perceives himself as aggressive may evaluate others by looking for aggressiveness. Those who show this characteristic may be benefited while others may suffer. This error also washes out if the same evaluator appraises all the people in the organisation.

5. Miscellaneous Biases: Bias against employees on ground of sex, race, religion or position is also a common error in rating. For example, a higher rating may be assigned to a senior employee. The rater may also be influenced by organisational influence and give higher ratings to those holding higher positions. Besides these, there may be opportunity bias, group characteristic bias and knowledge-of-predictor bias. Beach observes: "Actual experience with rating has demonstrated that supervisors will rate their people near the middle of the spectrum (average) if their bosses put pressure on them to correct the sub-par performers (or get rid of them) and if they are called upon to really justify an outstanding rating. In other words, they will follow the path of least resistance, because they know that the 'Big Boss' will question them about those rated low or very high."

6. *Social Differentiation:* Rating is sometimes impeded by the evaluator's style of rating behaviour. Pigou has classified raters as: "*high differentiators*" — i.e., using all or most of the scale; or *"low differentiators"* — i.e., using a limited range of the scale. He observes: "Low differentiators tend to ignore or suppress difference, perceiving the universe as more uniform than it really is. High differentiators, on the other hand, tend to utilise all available information to the utmost extent and, thus, are better able to perceptually deny anomalies and contradictions than low differentiators."

Social differentiation makes evaluations using 'trait' criteria unreliable.

WHY APPRAISAL TECHNIQUES PROVE FAILURE?

Performance appraisal techniques have often failed to give a correct assessment of the employee. According to Zavala, the causes of such failures are:

(a) The supervisor plays dual and conflicting role of both the judge and the helper.

(b) Too many objectives often cause confusion.

(c) The supervisor feels that subordinate appraisal is not rewarding.

(d) A considerable time gap exists between two appraisal programmes.

(e) The skills required for daily administration and employee development are in conflict.

(f) Poor communication keeps employees in the dark about what is expected of them.

(g) There is a difference of opinion between a supervisor and a subordinate, in regard to the latter's performance.

(h) Feedback on appraisal is generally unpleasant for both supervisor and subordinate.

(i) Unwillingness on the part of supervisors to tell employees plainly how to improve their performance.

HOW APPRAISALS MAY BE MADE SUCCESSFUL?

The rater must be thoroughly well-versed in the philosophy and nature of the rating system. Factors and factor scales must be thoroughly defined, analysed, and discussed.

The success of an appraisal programme depends upon:

(a) The existence of an atmosphere of confidence and trust so that both supervisor and employee may discuss matters frankly and offer suggestions which may be beneficial for the organisation and for an improvement of the employee.

(b) The supervisor must very thoroughly evaluate the employee's performance so that he is capable of meeting challenges about his ratings of his subordinate.

(c) The results of performance rather than personality traits should be given due weight. Suggestions for improvement should be directed towards the objective facts of the job (such as work schedules, output, reports completed, sales made, losses incurred, profits earned, accomplishments, etc.). Plans for the future must be developed jointly after consultation with subordinates. The individual as a person should never be criticised.

(d) The supervisor should try to analyse the strengths and weaknesses of an employee and advise him on correcting the weaknesses.

(e) The appraisal programme should be less time-consuming and less costly. At the same time, it should bring the maximum benefit.

(f) Which particular technique is to be adopted for appraisal should be governed by such factors as the size, financial resources, philosophy and objectives of an organisation.

(g) The results of the appraisal, particularly when they are negative, *should be immediately communicated to the employees,* so that they may try to improve their performance.

(h) A post-appraisal interview should be arranged so that employees may be supplied with feedback and the organisation may know the difficulties under which employees work, so that their training needs may be discovered.

Norman Maier suggests three such interviews: *(a) Tell-and-Sell Method,* to communicate to the employee information about his performance, gain his acceptance of it, and draw up a plan for future improvement, if necessary. *(b) The-Sell-and-Listen Method,* to communicate the evaluation results to the employee and get his reactions to them. *(c) Problem-solving Approach,* under which the ratee and the rater sit together and find out alternative solutions for improving performance.

(i) The standards of performance appraisal can be improved by training of the evaluators. It has been indicated that appraisers who are trained in how to evaluate subordinates tend to be more effective appraisers than those who had not undergone such training.

(j) Lastly, many of the problems or hindrances can be minimised if *right appraisal tools are chosen.*

ETHICS OF APPRAISAL

In any performance appraisal, due consideration must be given to the ethics of appraisal, failing which many organisational problems may crop up and the very purpose of appraisal may be defeated. In this connection, M.S. Kellog has suggested the following *do's and don'ts:*

(i) Don't appraise without knowing why the appraisal is needed;

(ii) Appraise on the basis of *representative information;*

(iii) Appraise on the basis of *sufficient information;*

(iv) Appraise on the basis of *relevant information;*

(v) Be honest on your assessment of all the facts you have obtained;

(vi) Don't write one thing and say another;

(vii) In offering an appraisal, make it plain that this is only your personal opinion of the facts as you see them;

(viii) Pass on appraisal information only to those who have good reason to want it;

(ix) Don't imply the existence of an appraisal that has not been made;

(x) Don't accept another's appraisal without knowing the basis on which it was made.

Kellog maintains that these "ethical standards are most certain to be met if appraisals are accomplished by such qualifiers as:

(i) The fact on which an appraisal is based;

(ii) The time period covered;

(iii) The purpose for which an appraisal is made;

(iv) The situational factors which shed light on the facts presented;

(v) The nature of the appraiser's working relationship with the appraised; and

(vi) An explanation of how and where the facts were obtained."

SUMMARY

1. Employees want feedback regarding how they are performing and appraisal provides an opportunity to give them that feedback.
2. Employer needs to know the performance to enable him to: *(a)* reward an employee; *(b)* provide training and development for his betterment, progression; *(c)* to make the employee aware of his deficiencies which he can improve.
3. The employee should be given a complete idea of what is expected of him and should he told how often he will be rated, apprised and on what criteria (items) he will be rated.
4. Appraisals should be fair, free from bias and opportunity should be given to him for improvement. Appropriate appraisal method should be used for each category of employee. Appraisal methods may differ from one level Category) of employee to another.
5. Appropriate follow up action should be intiated after the appraisal. Recourse of previous appraisals should be maintained for future references.

❑❑❑

10

Wage Salary Administration, Incentives, Fringe Benefits and Services

WAGES AND SALARY ADMINISTRATION

'Wage and Salary Administration' refers to the establishment and implementation of sound policies and practices of employee compensation. It includes such areas as job evaluation, surveys of wage and salaries, analysis of relevant organisational problems, development and maintenance of wage structure, establishing rules for administering wages, wage payments incentives, benefits including health insurance, profit sharing, wage changes and adjustments, supplementary payments, control of compensation costs and other related items.

NATURE AND PURPOSE

The basic purpose of wage and salary administration is to establish and maintain an equitable wage and salary structure. Its secondary objective is the establishment and maintenance of an equitable labour-cost structure, i.e., an optimal balancing of conflicting personnel interests so that the satisfaction of employees and employers is maximised and conflicts minimised. The wage and salary administration is concerned with the financial aspects of needs, motivation and rewards. Managers, therefore, analyse and interpret the needs of their employees so that reward can be individually designed to satisfy these needs. For it has been rightly said that "people do what they do to satisfy some need. Before they do anything, they look for a reward or pay-off." Steven Kerr observes: "Whether dealing with monkeys, rats, or human beings, it is hardly controversial to state that most organisms seek information concerning what activities are rewarded, and then seek to do those things, often to the virtual exclusion of activities not rewarded. The extent to which this occurs of course will depend on the perceived attractiveness of the reward offered...." The reward may be money or promotion, but more likely it will be some pay-off-a smile, acceptance by a peer, receipt of information, a kind word of recognition etc.

A sound wage and salary administration tries to achieve these objectives:

(a) For employees: (i) Employees are paid according to requirements of their jobs, i.e., highly skilled jobs are paid more compensation than low skilled jobs. This eliminates inequalities.

(ii) The chances of favouritism (which creep in when wage rates are assigned) are greatly minimised.

(iii) Job sequences and lines of promotion are established wherever they are applicable.

(iv) Employees' morale and motivation are increased because a wage programme can be explained and is based upon facts.

(b) To employers: (i) They can systematically plan for and control their labour costs.

(ii) In dealing with a trade union, they can explain the basis of their wage progamme because it is based upon a systematic analysis of job and wage facts.

(iii) A wage and salary administration reduces the likelihood of friction and grievances over wage inequities.

(iv) It enhances an employee's morale and motivation because adequate and fairly administered wages are basic to his wants and needs.

(v) It attracts qualified employees by ensuring and adequate payment for all the jobs.

According to Beach, wage and salary programmes have four major purposes:

(i) To recruit persons for a firm;

(ii) To control payroll costs;

(iii) To satisfy people, to reduce the incidence of quitting, grievances, and fractions over pay; and

(iv) To motivate people to perform better.

COMPENSATION, REWARD, WAGE LEVELS AND WAGE STRUCTURES

Compensation may be defined as money received in the performance of work, plus the many kinds of benefits and services that organisations provide their employees. 'Money' is included under *direct compensation* (popularly known as *wages,* i.e., gross pay); while benefits come under *indirect compensation,* and may consist of life, accident, and health insurance, the employer's contribution to retirement, pay for vacation or illness, and employer's required payments for employee welfare as social security.

A *'wage'* (or *pay)* is the remuneration paid, for the service of labour in production, periodically to an employee/worker. "Wages" usually refer to the hourly rate or daily rate paid to such groups as production and maintenance employees (*"blue-collar workers").* On the other hand, *'Salary'* normally refers to the weekly or monthly rates paid to clerical, administrative and professional employees *("white-collar workers").* The *'wage levels'* represent the money an average worker makes in a geographic area or in his organisation. It is only an average; specific markets or firms and individual wages can vary widely from the average. The term *wage structure'* is used to describe wage/salary relationships within a particular grouping. The grouping can be according to occupation, or organisation, such as wage structure of craftsman (carpenters, mechanics, bricklayers, etc.)

The wage structure or *'grade'* is comprised of jobs of approximately equal difficulty or importance as determined by job evaluation. If the *'point'* method of job evaluation is used, the *'pay-grade'* consists of jobs falling within a range of points. If the *'factor comparison'* plan is used, the grade consists of a range of evaluated wage rates (or points, if the wage rates are converted to points). If the *'ranking'* plan is used, the grade consists of a specific number of ranks. If *'classification'* system is used, the jobs are already categorised into 'class' or 'grades.'

THE WAGE DETERMINATION PROCESS

Usually, the steps involved in determining wage rates are: performing job analysis, wage surveys, analysis of relevant organisational problems forming wage structure, framing rules of wage administration, explaining these to employees, assigning grades and price to each job and paying the guaranteed wage.

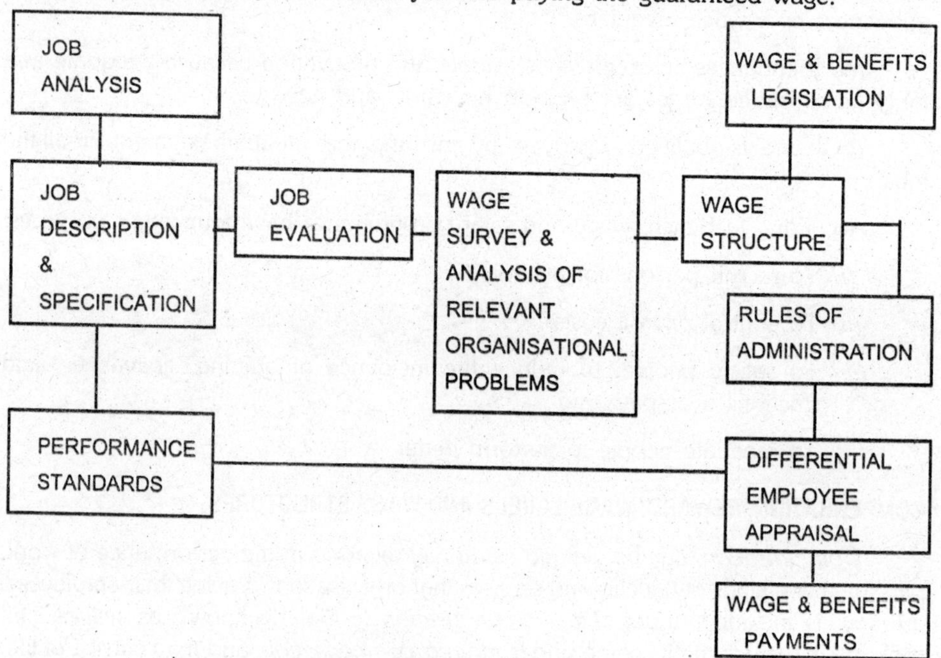

Fig. 10.1 Steps Involved in Determination of Wage Rate

The Process of Job Analysis: Results in job descriptions lead to job specifications. A job analysis describes the duties, responsibilities, working conditions and inter-relationships between the job as it is and the other jobs with which it is associated. It attempts to record and analyse details concerning the training, skills, required efforts, qualifications, abilities, experience, and responsibilities expected of an employee. After determining the job specifications, the actual process of grading, rating or evaluating the job specifications, the actual process of grading, rating or evaluating the job occurs. A job is rated in order to determine its value relative to all the other jobs in the organisation which are subject to evaluation. The next step is that of providing the job with a price. This involves converting the relative job values into specific monetary values or translating the job classes into rate ranges.

Wage Surveys: Once the relative worth of jobs has been determined by job evaluation, the actual amounts to be paid must be determined. This is done by making wage or salary surveys in the area concerned. Such surveys seek to answer questions like what are other firms paying? What are they doing by way of social insurance? What is the level of pay offered by other firms for similar occupations? etc., by gathering information about '*benchmark jobs*', which are usually known as good indicators.

There are various ways to make such a survey. Most firms either use the results of "*packaged surveys*" available from the research bodies, employer's associations, Government Labour Bureaus, etc., or they participate in wage surveys and receive copies of results, or else they conduct their own. These surveys may be carried out by mailed questionnaire, telephone, or personal interviews with other managers and personnel agencies.

A wage survey to be useful, must satisfy these points:

(a) Frequency — affected by rapidity of changes, current and contemplated. Once per year is common. *(b) Scope* (number of firms) — influenced by the geographic area from which people are drawn, the number of units competing for this labour, accuracy requirements, and willingness of organisations to share information. *(c) Accuracy* — the diversity in job titles and specific job duties is staggering. The greater the accuracy and detail needed, the greater the requirements for careful description and specification and surveyor's reliance on person-to-person interviewing rather than mailed questionnaires.

Such wage surveys provide many kinds of useful information about differences in wage levels for particular kinds of occupations. This can have a great influence on an organisation's compensation policy.

Relevant Organisational Problems: In addition to the results of job analysis and wage surveys, several other variables have to be given due consideration in establishing wage structure. For example, whether there exists well-established and well-accepted relationships among certain jobs which can upset job evaluation, whether the organisation would recruit new employees after revised wage structure; are the prevailing rates in industry or community inconsistent with the results of job evaluation? What will be the result of paying lower or higher compensation; and what should be the relationship between the wage structure and the fringe benefit structure? Belcher has listed 108 variables which can affect levels of compensation and the wage structure.

Preparation of Wage Structure: The next step is to determine the wage structure. For this, several decisions need be taken, such as: *(a)* whether the organisation wishes, or is able, to pay amounts above, below, or equal to the average in the community or industry; *(b)* whether wage ranges should provide for merit increases or whether there should be single rates: *(c)* the number and width of the 'pay grades' and the extent of overlap; *(d)* which jobs are to be placed in each of the pay grades; *(e)* the actual money value to be as signed to vaious pay grades; *(f)* differentials between pay plans; and *(g)* what to do with salaries that are out of line once these decisions have been made.

It is a standard practice to establish 'pay grades' or equal width or 'point spread,' i.e., each grade might include all those jobs falling between 50 to 100 points, 100 to 150 points, 150 to 200 points, and so forth. Since each grade is of the same width, it is necessary to determine how many grades there should be. In an industry, the number varies from as few as five to as high as thirty. Two points need consideration when deciding the number of grades. *First,* the size of the organisation, i.e., if there are 1,000 jobs to be graded, more 'pay grades' will be needed, than where the jobs are few, say 100. *Second,* the broadness of the grades. For instance, in the case of hourly jobs, the maximum of individual pay grades may vary from 10 to 20% above the minimums; while in case of salaried employees the maximum of pay grades may vary from 15 to 75% above the minimum.

Some authorities feel that there should be only one comprehensive 'pay grade' for each organisation. But it is probably more realistic to have several pay grades/ranges. Several wage structures are developed — one for each type of job or "job cluster." Dunlop describes the cluster concept as follows:

"A job cluster is defined as a stable group of job classifications or work assignments within a firm... which are linked together by (1) technology, (2) the administrative organisation of the production process, including policies of transfer, lay-off, and promotion, or (3) social custom that they have common wage-making characteristics....

"Thus, the employees on a furnace or a mill and the crew of a train or a plane can constitute a job cluster *(technology);* so also may employees in a department *(administrative organisation),* or the sales girls in a department store or the stenographers in an office *(social custom)....* Certain job clusters may be more closely related to some rather than to other clusters. In this sense, clerical rates as a whole may be closely related to other clerical rates than to managerial or factory rates..."

Livernash described that: "Broad groups may be illustrated within manufacturing as: (1) *managerial* — executive, administrative, professional, and supervisory; (2) *clerical;* and (3) *factory,* within each broad group, narrower groups are obvious. Within the factory group are maintenance, inspection, transportation and production. Within production are certain smaller groups, varying with the nature of the industry."

This indicates the need for having several pay ranges for each organisation. Such a range usually has several advantages: *(i)* The management can take a more flexible stance with respect to the labour market. *(ii)* It makes it easier to attract experienced employees from other organisations. *(iii)* It helps to ensure that there is an overlap between the pay rates and those prevailing in the labour market. *(iv)* It also allows the management to provide for performance differences between employees. While determining pay ranges the following consideration should be attended to:

1. It is important to keep in mind that there is an adequate differential between superiors and subordinates — whether they are paid under the same pay plan or under different ones.
2. When the pay-range of one group is changed, equal attention must be given to the pay-level of the other.
3. Because of the continuous rise in wage and salary levels, a rise resulting from a variety of environmental pressures, considerable attention must be given to handling upward changes in wage-structure. Some firms give general percentage or "across the board" pay increases shortly after wage increases are negotiated. Others give increases based on merit or length of service. The sound thing is to make general adjustments in wage structure according to the price index number.

4. The existing pay structure should be regularly reviewed and revised. This will make job evaluation programme more acceptable to employees.
5. Regional differences in wages should invariably be maintained. Forces that favour regional differences are: low mobility; lower skill jobs; major cost of living differences between areas; added sources of income; or characteristics (rural versus urban or industrial); seasonal occupations as in agriculture versus stable occupations.

WAGE ADMINISTRATION RULES

The development of rules of wage administration has to be done, after the rate ranges have been determined. Rules have to be developed to determine to what degree advancement will be based on length of service rather than merit; with what frequency pay increases will be awarded; how controls over wage and salary costs can be maintained; what rules will govern promotion from one pay grade to another, etc.

At the next stage, the employees are to be informed of the details of wage and salary programme. Although most hourly-paid workers are informed through the wage contract about the details of wage programme, a substantially smaller number of salaried employees have such information about their jobs. It is considered advisable, in the interest of the concern and the employees, that the information about average salaries and ranges in the salaries of group should be made known to the employees concerned; for secrecy in this matter may create dissatisfaction; and it may also vitiate the potential motivating effects of disclosure.

FACTORS INFLUENCING WAGE AND SALARY STRUCTURE AND ADMINISTRATION

The wage policies of different organisations vary somewhat. Marginal units pay the minimum necessary to attract the required number and kind of labour. Often, these units pay only the minimum wage rates required by labour legislation, and recruit marginal labour. At the other extreme, some units pay well above the going rates in the labour market. They do so to attract and retain the highest calibre of the labour market. They do so to attract and retain the highest calibre of the labour force. Some managers believe in the economy of higher wages. They feel that, by paying high wages, they would attract better workers who will produce more than the average worker in the industry. This greater production per employee means greater output per man hour. Hence, labour costs may turn out to be lower than those existing in firms using marginal labour. Some units pay high wages because of a combination of favourable product market demand, higher ability to pay and the bargaining power of a trade union. But a large number of them seek to be competitive in their wage programme, i.e., they aim at paying somewhere near the going rate in the labour market for the various classes of labour they employ. Most units give greater weight to two wage criteria, viz., job requirements and the prevailing rates of wages in the labour market. Other factors, such as changes in the cost of living, the supply and demand of labour, and the ability to pay are accorded a secondary importance.

A sound wage policy is to adopt a job evaluation programme in order to establish fair differentials in wages based upon differences in job contents. Besides the basic factors provided by a job description and job evaluation, those that are usually taken into consideration for wage and salary administration are:

(i) The organisation's ability to pay and the sustaining strengths;

(ii) Supply and demand of labour and levels of skills;

(iii) The prevailing market rate — government legislation on wages;

(iv) The cost of living — inflation rate;

(v) Living wage concept;

(vi) Productivity;

(vii) Trade Union's Bargaining power and judicial directions;

(viii) Job requirements, working conditions;

(ix) Managerial attitudes; and

(x) Psychological and Sociological factors.

(xi) Levels of Skills available in the market.

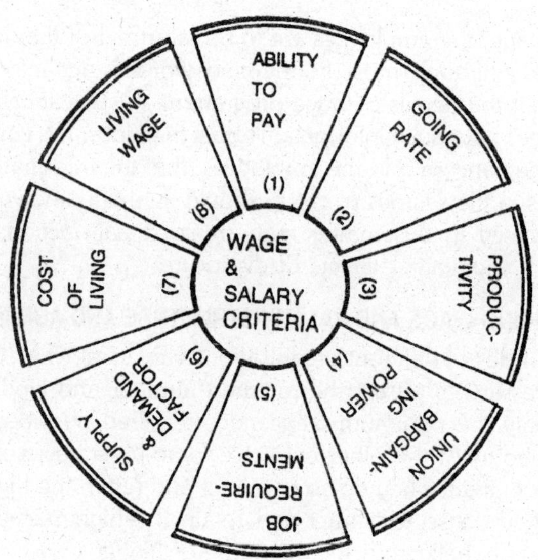

Fig. 10.2 Criteria for Wage Fixation

(i) The Organisation's Ability to Pay: Wage increases should be given by those orgnisations which can afford them. Companies that have good sales and, therefore, high profits tend to pay higher wages than those which are running at a loss or earning low profits because of the high cost of production or low sales. In the short run, the economic influence on the ability to pay is practically nil. All employers, irrespective of their profits or losses, must pay no less than their competitors and need pay no more if they wish to attract and keep workers. In the long run, the ability to pay is very important. During the time of prosperity, employers pay high wages to carry on profitable operations and because of their increased ability to pay. But during a period of depression, wages are cut because funds are not available. Marginal firms and non-profit organisations (like hospitals and educational institutions) pay relatively low wages because of low or no profits.

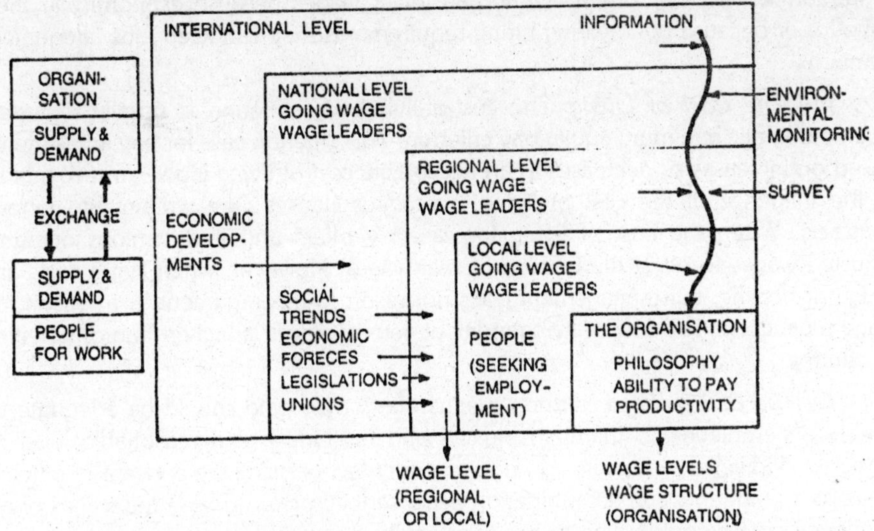

Fig. 10.3 Factors Affecting Compensation Plans

(ii) Supply and Demand of Labour: The labour market conditions or supply and demand forces operate at the national, regional and local levels, and determine organisational wage structure and level.

If the demand for certain skills is high and the supply is low, the result is a rise in the price to be paid for these skills. When prolonged and acute, these labour-market pressures probably force most organisations to "reclassify hard-to-fill jobs at a higher level" than that suggested by the job evaluation. The other alternative is to pay higher wages if the labour supply is scarce; and lower wages when it is excessive. Similarly, if there is great demand for labour expertise, wages rise; but if the demand for manpower skill is minimal, the wages will be relatively low. Mescon says: "The supply and demand compensation criterion is very closely related to the prevailing pay, comparable wage and on-going wage concepts since, in essence, all of these remuneration standards are determined by immediate market forces and factors."

(iii) Prevailing Market Rate: This is also known as the '*comparable wage*' or *'going wage rate'*, and is the most widely used criterion. An organisation's compensation policies generally tend to conform to the wage-rates payable by the industry and the community. This is done for several reasons. *First,* competition demands that competitors adhere to the same relative wage level. *Second,* various government laws and judicial decisions make the adoption of uniform wage rates an attractive proposition. *Third,* trade unions encourage this practice so that their members can have equal pay, equal work and geographical differences may be eliminated. *Fourth,* functionally related firms in the same industry require essentially the same quality of employees, with the same skills and experience. This results in a considerable uniformity in wage and salary rates. *Finally,* if the same or about the same general rates of wages are not paid to the employees as are paid by the organisation's competitors, it will not be able to attract and maintain a sufficient quantity and quality of manpower. Belcher and Atchison observe: "Some companies pay on the

high side of the market in order to obtain goodwill or to insure an adequate supply of labour, while other organisations pay lower wages because economically they have to, or because by lowering hiring requirements they can keep jobs adequately manned."

(iv) The Cost of Living: The cost-of-living pay criterion is usually regarded as an automatic minimum equity pay criterion. This criterion calls for pay adjustments based on increases or decreases in an acceptable cost of living index. In recognition of the influence of the cost of living, "escalator clauses" are written into labour contracts. When the cost of living increases, workers and trade unions demand adjusted wages to offest the erosion of real wages. However, when living costs are stable or decline, the management does not resort to this argument as a reason for wage reductions. The cost of living index at certain places is higher than other cities or centres.

(v) The Living Wage criterion means that wages paid should be adequate to enable an employee to maintain himself and his family at a reasonable level of existence. However, employers do not generally favour using the concept of a living wage as a guide to wage determination because they prefer to base the wages of an employee on his contribution rather than on his need. Also, they feel that the level of living prescribed in a worker's budget is open to argument since it is based on subjective opinion.

(vi) Productivity is another criterion, and is measured in terms of output per man-hour. It is not due to labour efforts alone. Technological improvements, better organisation and management, the development of better methods of production by labour and management, greater ingenuity and skill by labour are all responsible for the increase in productivity. Actually, productivity measures the contribution of all the resource factors — men, machines, methods, materials and management. No productivity index can be devised which will measure only the productivity of a specific factor of production. Another problem is that productivity can be measured at several levels — job, plant, industry or national, economic level. Thus, although theoretically it is a sound compensation criterion, operationally many problems and complications arise because of definitional measurement and conceptual issues.

(vii) Trade Union's Bargaining Power: Trade unions do affect rate of wages. Generally, the stronger and more powerful the trade union, the higher the wages. A trade union's bargaining power is often measured in terms of its membership, its financial strength and the nature of its leadership. A strike or a threat of a strike is the most powerful weapon used by it. Sometimes trade unions force wages up faster than increases in productivity would allow and become responsible for unemployment or higher prices and inflation. However, for those remaining on the pay roll, a real gain is often achieved as a consequence of a trade union's stronger bargaining power.

(viii) Job Requirements: Generally, the more difficult a job, the higher are the wages. Measures of job difficulty are frequently used when the relative value of one job to another in an organisation is to be ascertained. Jobs are graded according to the relative skill, effort, responsibility, and job conditions required.

(ix) Managerial Attitudes: These have a decisive influence on the wage structure and wage level since judgement is exercised in many areas of wage and

salary administration — including whether the firm should pay below average, or above average rates, what job factors should be used to reflect job worth, the weight to be given for performance or length of service, and so forth, both the structure and level of wages are bound to be affected accordingly. These matters require the approval of the top executives. Lester observes "Top management's desire to maintain or enhance the company's prestige has been a major factor in the wage policy of a number of firms. Desires to improve or maintain morale, to attract high-caliber employees, to reduce turnover, and to provide a high living standard for employees as possible also appear to be factors in management's wage-policy decisions."

(x) Psychological and Social Factors: These determine in a significant measure how hard a person will work for the compensation received or what pressures he will exert to get his compensation increased. Psychologically, persons perceive the level of wages as a measure of success in life; people may feel secure; have an inferiority complex, seem inadequate or feel the reverse of all these. They may not take pride in their work, or in the wages they get. Therefore, these things should not be overlooked by the management in establishing wage rates. Sociologically and ethically, people feel that "equal work should carry equal wages," that "wages should be commensurate with their efforts," that "they are not exploited, and that no distinction is made on the basis of caste, colour, sex or religion." To satisfy the conditions of equity, fairness and justice, a management should take these factors into consideration.

(xi) Skill Levels Available in the Market: with the rapid growth of industries, business trade, there is shortage of skilled resources. The technological development, automation have been affecting the skill levels at a faster rates. Thus the wage levels of skilled employees are constantly changing and an organisation has to keep its level upto suit the market needs.

ADMINISTRATION OF WAGES AND SALARIES

Wage and salary administration should be controlled by some proper agency. This responsibility may be entrusted to the personnel department or to some job executive. Since the problem of wages and salary is very delicate and complicated, it is usually entrusted to a Committee composed of highranking executives representing major line organisations. The major functions of such Committee are:

(i) Approval and/or recommendation to management on job evaluation methods and findings;

(ii) Review and recommendation of basic wage and salary structure;

(iii) Help in the formulation of wage policies; from time to time;

(iv) Co-ordination and review of relative departmental rates to ensure conformity; and

(v) Review of budget estimates for wage and salary adjustments and increases.

This Committee should be supported by the advice of the technical staff. Such staff committees may be for job evaluation, job description, merit rating, wage and salary surveys in an industry, and for a review of present wage rates, procedure and policies.

Alternatively, the over-all plan is first prepared by the Personnel Manager in consultation and discussions with senior members of other departments. It is then submitted for final approval of the top executive. Once he has given his approval, for the wage and salary structure and the rules for administration, its implementation becomes a joint effort of all heads of the departments. The actual appraisal of the performance of subordinates is carried out by the various managers, who in turn submit their recommendations to higher authority and the latter, in turn, to the personnel department. The personnel department ordinarily reviews recommendations to ensure compliance with established rules of administration. In unusual cases of serious disagreement, the president makes the final decision.

PRINCIPLES OF WAGES AND SALARY ADMINISTRATION

The generally accepted principles governing the fixation of wages and salary are:

(i) There should be definite plan to ensure that differences in pay for jobs are based upon variations in job requirements, such as skill effort, responsibility or job or working conditions, and mental and physical requirements.

(ii) The general level of wages and salaries should be reasonably in line with that prevailing in the labour market. The labour market criterion is most commonly used.

(iii) The plan should carefully distinguish between jobs and employees. A job carries a certain wage rate, and a person is assigned to fill it at that rate. Exceptions sometimes occur in very high-level jobs in which the job-holder may make the job large or small, depending upon his ability and contributions.

(iv) Equal pay for equal work, i.e., if two jobs have equal difficulty requirements, the pay should be the same, regardless of who fills them.

(v) An equitable practice should be adopted for the recognition of individual differences in ability and contribution. For some units, this may take the form of rate ranges, with in-grade increases; in others, it may be a wage incentive plan; in still others, it may take the form of closely integrated sequences of job promotion.

(vi) There should be a clearly established procedure for hearing and adjusting wage complaints. This may be integrated with the regular grievance procedure, if it exists.

(vii) The employees and the trade union, if there is one, *should be informed about the procedure used to establish wage rates.* Every employee should be informed of his own position, and of the wage and salary structure. Secrecy in wage matters should not be used as a cover-up for haphazard and unreasonable wage programme.

(viii) The wage should be sufficient to ensure for the worker and his family reasonable standard of living. Workers should receive a guaranteed minimum wage to protect them against conditions beyond their control.

(ix) The wage and salary structure should be flexible so that changing conditions can be easily met.

(x) Prompt and correct payments of the dues of the employees must be ensured and arrears of payment should not accumulate.

(xi) For revision of wages, a Wage Committee should always be preferred to the individual judgement, however unbiased, or a manager.

(xii) The wage and salary payments must fulfil a wide variety of human needs, including the need for self-actualisation. It has been recognised that "money is the

only form of incentive which is wholly negotiable, appealing to the widest possible range of seekers.... Monetary payments often act as motivators and satisfiers interdependently of other job factors."

WAGES

Wages in the widest sense mean any economic compensation paid by the employer under some contract to his workers for the services rendered by them. Wages, therefore, include family allowance, relief pay, financial support and other benefits. But, in the narrower sense wages are the price paid for the services of labour in the process of production and include only the performance wages or wages proper. Thy are composed of two parts — the basic wage and other allowances. The *basic wage* is the remuneration, by way of basic salary and allowances, which is paid or payable to an employee in terms of his contract of employment for the work done by him. *Allowances,* on the other hand, are paid in addition to the basic wage to maintain the value of basic wages over a period of time. Such allowances include holiday pay, overtime pay, bonus and social security benefits. These are usually not included in the definition of wages.

However, in India, different Acts include different items under wages, though all the Acts include basic wage and dearness allowance under the term wages. For example, under the Workmen's Compensation Act, 1923, Section 2 (m), "wages for leave period, holiday pay, overtime pay, bonus, attendance bonus, and good conduct bonus" form part of wages.

Under the Payment of Wages Act, 1936, Section 2 (vi), "any award of settlement and production bonus, if paid, constitutes wages."

But under the Payment of Wages Act, 1948, "retrenchment compensation, payment in lieu of notice and gratuity payable on discharge constitute wages."

The following type of remuneration, if paid, do not amount to wages under any of the Acts:

(i) Bonus or other payments under a profit-sharing scheme which do not form a part of the contract of employment.

(ii) Value of any house accommodation, supply of light, water, medical attendance, travelling allowance, or payment in lieu thereof or any other concession.

(iii) Any sum paid to defray special expenses entailed by the nature of the employment of a workman.

(iv) Any contribution to pension, provident fund, or a scheme of social security and social insurance benefits.

(v) Any other amenity or service excluded from the computation of wages by a general or special order of an appropriate governmental authority.

A *wage level* is an average of the rates paid for the jobs of an organisation, an establishment, a labour market, an industry, a region or a nation. A *wage structure* is a hierarchy of jobs to which wage rates have been attached.

MINIMUM, FAIR AND LIVING WAGE

Statutory Minimum Wage: It is the wage determined according to the procedure prescribed by the relevant provisions of the Minimum Wages Act, 1948. Once the rates of such wages are fixed, it is the obligation of the employer to pay them, regardless of his ability to pay. Such wages are required to be fixed in certain employments where "sweated" labour is prevalent, or where there is a great chance of exploitation of labour.

Bare or Basic Minimum Wage: It is the wage which is to be fixed in accordance with the awards and judicial pronouncements of Industrial Tribunals, National Tribunals and Labour Courts. They are obligatory on the employers.

Minimum wage, and *fair wage* and *living wage* are the terms used by The Report of the Committee on Fair Wages, set up by the Government in 1948 to determine the principles on which fair wages should be based and to suggest how these principles should be applied. According to this Committee, the minimum wage should represent the lower limit of a fair wage. The next higher level is the *fair wage,* and the highest level of the fair wage is the *living wage.*

A Minimum Wage: It has been defined by the Committee as "the wage which must provide not only for the bare sustenance of life, but for the preservation of the efficiency of the worker. For this purpose, the minimum wage must provide for some measure of education, medical requirements and amenities." In other words, a minimum wage should provide for the sustenance of the worker's family, for his efficiency, for the education of his family, for their medical care and for some amenities.

The question of determining the minimum wage is a very difficult one for more than one reason. Conditions vary from place to place, industry to industry and from worker to worker. The standard of living cannot be determined accurately. What then should be the quantum of the minimum wage? What is the size of the family it should support? Who should decide these questions? These issues are very difficult to decide. Moreover, since the cost of living varies with the price level, it follows that this index should be periodically reviewed and modified.

However, the principles for determining minimum wages were evolved by the Government and have been incorporated in the Minimum Wages Act, 1948, the important principle being that minimum wages should provide not only for the bare sustenance of life but also for the preservation of the efficiency of the workers by way of education, medical care and other amenities.

Living Wage: This wage was recommended by the Committee as a fair wage and as ultimate goal in a wage policy. It defined a Living Wage as "one which should enable the earner to provide for himself and his family not only the bare essentials of food, clothing and shelter but a measure of frugal comfort, including education for his children, protection against ill-health, requirements of essential social needs and a measure of insurance against the more important misfortunes, including old age." In other words, a living wage was to provide for a standard of living that would ensure good health for the worker, and his family as well as a measure of decency, comfort, education for his children, and protection against misfortunes. This obviously implied a high level of living.

Such a wage was so determined by keeping in view the national income and the capacity to pay of an industry. The Committee was of the opinion that although the provision of a living wage should be the ultimate goal, the present level of national income did not permit of the payment of a living wage on the basis of the standards prevalent in more advanced countries.

The goal of a living wage was to be achieved in three stages. *In the first stage,* the wage to be paid to the entire working class was to be established and stabilised. *In the second stage,* fair wages were to be established in the community-cum-industry. *In the third stage,* the working class was to be paid the living wage. The living wage may be somewhere between the lowest level of the minimum wage and the highest limit of the living wage, depending upon the bargaining power of labour, the capacity of the industry to pay, the level of the national income, the general effect of the wage rise on neighbouring industries, the productivity of labour, the place of industry in the economy of the country, and the prevailing rates of wages in the same or similar occupations in neighbouring localities.

Fair Wage: According to the Committee on Fair Wages, "it is the wage which is above the minimum wage but below the living wage." The lower limit of the fair wage is obviously the minimum wage; the upper limit is set by the "capacity of the industry to pay." Between these two limits, the actual wages should depend on considerations of such factors as: *(a)* The productivity of labour; *(b)* The prevailing rates of wages in the same or neighbouring localities; *(c)* The level of the national income and its distribution; and *(d)* The place of industry in the economy of the country.

The Need-Based Minimum Wage: The Indian Labour Conference, at its 15th session held in July 1957, suggested that minimum wage fixation should be *need-based,* and should meet the minimum needs of an industrial worker. For the calculation of the minimum wage, the Conference accepted the following norms and recommended that they should guide all wage-fixing authorities, including the Minimum Wage Committee, Wage-Boards, and adjudicators:

(i) The standard working class family should be taken to consist of 3 consumption units for the earner; the earnings of women, children and adolescents should be disregarded;

(ii) The minimum food requirements should be calculated on the basis of the net intake of 2,700 calories, as recommended by Dr. Akroyd, for an average Indian adult of moderate activity.

(iii) The clothing requirements should be estimated at a per capita consumption of 18 yards per annum, which would mean, for an average worker's family of four, a total of 72 yards;

(iv) In respect of housing, the norms should be the minimum rent charged by the Government in any area for houses provided under the Subsidised Housing Scheme for low-income groups; and

(v) Fuel, lighting and other miscellaneous items of expenditure should constitute 20 per cent of the total minimum wage.

Ever since the I.L.C. made its recommendations on the need-based minimum wage, attempts were made by several government and private agencies and trade union organisations to work out is monetory equivalent. These estimates have varied considerably.

BASIC KINDS OF WAGE PLANS

There are two major kinds of wage and salary payment plans: those under which remuneration does not vary with output or the quality of output, but depends on the time unit consumed in performing work. These are known as *time wage plans.* The time unit may be the day, week, fortnight or month. Time plans are non-incentive in the sense that earnings during a given time period do not vary with the productivity of an employee during that period.

The *second kind* is concerned with the output or some other measure of productivity during a given period of time. To earn more, an employee is required to put in more labour and produce more. This kind is known as the *piece* or *output wage plan.* It is a direct financial incentive plan.

Thus, the "time" and the "output" wage plan are the two basic systems. All the other plans are simply variations of these two.

ELEMENTS OR INGREDIENTS OF A GOOD WAGE PLAN

Before we discuss these two plans, it would be fruitful to know the ingredients of a good wage plan. These are:

(i) It should be easily understandable, i.e., all the employees should easily understand what they are to get for their work. They should be instructed in how the wage plan works.

(ii) It should be capable of easy computation, i.e., it should be sufficiently simple to permit quick calculation. Mathematical tables may be supplied, be reference to which calculations can be quickly made.

(iii) It should be capable of effectively motivating the employees, i.e., it should provide an incentive for work. If both the quality and quantity of work are to be stressed at the same time, a plan should be selected that will not unduly influence the worker to work too fast or to become careless of quality.

(iv) It should provide for remuneration to employees as soon as possible after the effort has been made. Daily or weekly payment of wages would be preferable to induce employees to work.

(v) It should be relatively stable rather than frequently varying so that employees are assured of a stable amount of money.

TYPES OF WAGES

Time Rate: This is the oldest and the most common method of fixing wages. Under this system, workers are paid according to the work done during a certain period of time, at the rate of so much per hour, per day, per week, per fortnight or per month or any other fixed period of time. The essential point is that the production of a worker is not taken into consideration in fixing the wages; he is paid at the settled rate as soon as the time contracted for is spent.

Merits: The merits of the system are:

(i) It is simple, for the amount earned by a worker can be easily calculated.

(ii) As there is no time limit for the execution of a job, workmen are not in a hurry to finish it and this may mean that they will pay attention to the quality of their work.

(iii) As all the workmen employed for doing a particular kind of work receive the same wages, ill-will and jealousy among them are avoided.

(iv) Due to the slow and steady pace of the worker, there is no rough handling of machinery, which is a distinct advantage for the employer.

(v) It is the only system that can be used profitably where the output of an individual workman or groups of employees cannot be readily measured.

(vi) The day or time wage provides a regular and stable income to the worker and he can, therefore, adjust his budget accordingly.

(vii) This system is favoured by organised labour, for it makes for solidarity among the workers of a particular class.

(viii) It requires less administrative attention than others because the very basis of the time wage contract is good faith and mutual confidence between the parties.

Demerits: The main drawbacks of this system are:

(i) It does not take into account the fact that men are of different abilities and that if all the persons are paid equally, better workmen will have no incentive to work harder and better. They will therefore be drawn down to the level of the least efficient workman. Halsey observes: "Matters naturally settle down to an easy-going pace in which the workmen have little interest in their work and the employer pays extravagantly for his product." Taylor says: "The men are paid according to the position which they fill and not according to their character, energy, skill and reliability."

(ii) The labour charges for a particular job do not remain constant. This puts the authorities in a difficult position in the matter of quoting rates for a particular piece of work.

(iii) As there is not specific demand on the worker that a piece of work needs to be completed in a given period of time, there is always the possibility of a systematic evasion of work by workmen.

(iv) This system permits many a man to work at a task for which he has neither taste nor ability, when he might make his mark in some other job.

(v) As the employer does not know the amount of work that will be put in by each worker, the total expenditure on wages for turning out a certain piece of work cannot be adequately assessed.

(vi) As no record of an individual worker's output is maintained, it becomes difficult for the employer to determine his relative efficiency for purposes of promotion.

Piece Rate: Under this system, workers are paid according to the amount of work done or the number of units completed, the rate of each unit being settled in advance, irrespective of the time taken to do the task. This does not mean that a worker can take any time to complete a job because if his performance far exceeds the time which his employer expects he would take, the overhead charge for each unit of article will increase. There is indirect implication that a worker should not take more than the average time. If he consistently takes more time than the average time, he does it at the risk of losing his job.

Under this plan, a worker, working in given conditions and with given machinery, is paid exactly in proportion to his physical output. He is paid in direct promotion to his output, the actual amount of pay per unit of service being approximately equal to the marginal value of his service in assisting to produce that output.

This system is adopted generally in jobs of a repetitive nature, where tasks can be readily measured, inspected and counted. It is particularly suitable for standardised processes, and it appeals to skilled and efficient workers who can increase their earnings by working to their full capacity. In weaving and spinning in the textile industry, the raising of local in the mines, the plucking of leaves in plantations, and in the shoe industry, this system can be very useful. But its application is difficult where different shifts are employed on the same work or where a great variety of different grades of workers are employed on different and immeasurable services, as in the gas and electricity industries.

A worker's earnings can be calculated on the basis of the following formula:

$WE=NR$, where WE is the worker's earning, N stands for the number of pieces produced and R for the rate per piece.

Merits: This system has many advantages:

(i) It pays the workman according to his efficiency as reflected in the amount of work turned out by him. It satisfies an industrious and efficient worker, for he finds that his efficiency is adequately rewarded. This gives him a direct stimulus to increase his production.

(ii) Supervision charges are not so heavy, for workers are not likely to while away their time since they know that their wages are dependent upon the amount of work turned out by them.

(iii) Being interested in the continuity of his work, a workman is likely to take greater care to prevent a breakdown in the machine or in the workshop. This is a point of considerable gain to the management, for it reduces plant maintenance charges.

(iv) As the direct labour cost per unit of production remains fixed and constant, calculation of costs while filling tenders and estimates becomes easier.

(v) Not only are output and wages increased, but the methods of production too are improved, for the worker demands materials free from defects and machinery in perfect running conditions.

(vi) The total unit cost of production comes down with a larger output because the fixed overhead burden can be distributed over a greater number of units.

Demerits: The demerits of the system are:

(i) In spite of the advantages accruing to the management as well as to the workmen, the system is not particularly favoured by workers. The main reason for this is that the fixation piece rate by the employer is not done on a scientific basis. In most cases, he determines the rate by the rule-of-thumb method, and when he finds that the workers, on an average, get higher wages compared to the wages of workers doing the same task on a day-rate basis, pressure is brought to bear upon the workers for a cut in the piece rate. Halsey observes: "cutting the piece price is simply killing the goose that lays the golden eggs. Nevertheless, the goose must be killed. Without it, the employer will continue to pay extravagantly for his work; with it he will stifle the rising ambition of his men."

(ii) As the workers wish to perform their work at breakneck speed, they generally consume more power, overwork the machines, and do not try to avoid wastage of materials. This results in a high cost of production and lower profits.

(iii) There is a greater chance of deterioration in the quality of work owing to over-zealousness on the part of workers to increase production. This over-zealousness may tell upon their health, resulting in a loss of efficiency.

(iv) It encourages soldiering; and there "arises a system of hypocrisy and deceit, because to escape further cuts they begin to produce less and also regard their employers and their enemies, to be opposed in everything they want."

(v) Excessive speeding of work may result in frequent wear and tear of plant and machinery and frequent replacement.

(vi) Trade unions are often opposed to this system, for it encourages rivalry among workers and endangers their solidarity in labour disputes.

Balance or Debt Method: This is a combination of *time* and *piece* rates. The worker is guaranteed an hourly or a day-rate with an alternative piece rate. If the earnings of a worker calculated at the piece rate exceed the amount which he would have earned if paid on time basis, he gets credit for the balance, i.e., the excess piece rate earnings over the time rate earnings. If his piece rate earnings are equal to his time rate earnings, the question of excess payment does not arise. Where piece rate earnings are less than time rate earnings, he is paid on the basis of the time rate; but the excess which he is paid is carried forward as a debt against him to be recovered from any future balance of piece work earnings over time work earnings. This system presupposes the fixation of time and piece rates on a scientific basis.

Let us suppose that the piece rate for a unit of work is Re. 1.00 and the time rate is Rs. 0.37½ an hour, the weekly work hours are 40 and the number of units to be completed during these 40 hours is 16.

It will be seen that the debit during the second week completely eliminated the credit of Re. 1.00 obtained during the first week. The worker will be paid his guaranteed time rate, in this case Rs. 15.00, in the first week and the same amount in the second week, although his earnings during the first week are Rs. 16.00 and during the second week they are Rs. 14.00. An adjustment will be made periodically to find out the balance to be paid to him.

The obvious merit of this system is that an efficient worker has an opportunity to increase his wages. At the same time, workers of ordinary ability, by getting the guaranteed time wage, are given a sufficient incentive to attain the same standard, even though the excess paid to them is later deducted from their future credit balance.

Table 10.1
Balance Method

Name of Worker	*Units of Completed*	*Total Earnings Under Piece Rate*	*Total Earnings Under-time Rate*	*Credit*	*Debit*	*Balance*
Sohan (First week)	16	Rs. 16/-	Rs. 15/-	Rs. 1/-	Nil	Rs. 1/-
Sohan (Second week)	14	Rs. 14/-	Rs. 15/-	Rs. Nil	Nil	Rs. 1/-

WAGE DIFFERENTIALS

Wages differ in different employments or occupations, industries and localities, and also between persons in the same employment or grade. One therefore comes across such terms as *occupational wage differentials, inter-industry, inter-firm, inter-area* or *geographical differentials* and *personal differentials.* Wage differentials has been classified into three categories:

First, the differentials that can be attributed to imperfections in the employment markets, such as the limited knowledge of workers in regard to alternative job opportunities available elsewhere; obstacles to geographical, occupational or inter-firm mobility of workers; or time lags in the adjustment of resource distribution and changes in the scope and structure of economic activities. Examples of such wage differentials are inter-industry, inter-firm, and geographical or inter-area wage differentials.

Second, the wage differentials which originate in social values and prejudices and which are deeper and more persistent than economic factors. Wage differentials by sex, age, status or ethnic origin belong to this category.

Third, occupational wage differentials, which would exist even if employment markets were perfect and social prejudices were absent.

In other words, wage differentials may be:

(i) Occupational differentials or differentials based on skill;

(ii) Inter-firm differentials;

(iii) Inter-area or regional differentials;

(iv) Inter-industry differentials; and

(v) Differentials based on sex.

(i) Occupational Differentials: These indicate that since different occupations require different qualifications, different wages of skill and carry different degrees of responsibility, wages are usually fixed on the basis of the differences in occupations and various degrees of skills. The basis functions of such differentials are:

(a) To induce workers to undertake "more demanding," "more agreeable or dangerous" jobs, or those involving "a great chance of unemployment, or wide uncertainty of earnings."

(b) To provide an incentive to young person to incur the costs of training and education and encourage workers to develop skills in anticipation of higher earnings in future.

(c) To perform a social function by way of determining the social status of workers.

In countries adopting a course of planned economic development, skill differentials play an important role in manpower and employment programmes, for they considerably help in bringing about an adequate supply of labour with skills corresponding to the requirements of product plans.

Inter-occupational differentials may comprise skilled, unskilled and manual wage differentials; non-manual and manual (white and blue-collar); and general skill differentials. *Occupational wage differentials* generally follow the changes in the relative supplies of labour to various occupations.

(ii) Inter-firm Differentials: Inter-firm differentials reflect the relative wage levels of workers in different plants in the same area and occupation. The main causes of inter-firm wage differentials are:

(a) Difference in the quality of labour employed by different firms;

(b) Imperfections in the labour market; and

(c) Differences in the efficiency of equipment, supervision and other non-labour factors.

Differences in technological advance, managerial efficiency, financial capacity, age and size of the firm, relative advantages and disadvantages of supply of raw materials, power and availability of transport facilities — these also account for considerable disparities in inter-firm wage rates. Lack of co-ordination among adjudication authorities, too, are responsible for such anomalies.

(iii) Inter-area or Regional Differentials: Such differentials arise when workers in the same industry and the same occupational group, but living in different geographical areas, are paid different wages. Regional wage differentials may be conceived in two senses. In the first sense, they are merely a part of inter-industry differentials in a particular region. "The industry mix varies from one area to another, and for this reason alone, the general average of wages would be expected to vary." In the second sense, they may represent real geographical differentials, resulting in the payment of different rates for the same type of work. In both cases, regional differentials affect the supply of manpower for various plants in different regions.

Such differentials are the result of living and working conditions, such as unsatisfactory or irksome climate, isolation, sub-standard housing, disparities in the cost of living and the availability of manpower. In some cases, regional differentials are also used to encourage planned mobility of labour.

(iv) Inter-industry Differentials: These differentials arise when workers in the same occupation and the same area but in different industries are paid different wages. Inter-industry differentials reflect skill differentials. The industries paying higher wages have mostly been industries with a large number of skilled workers, while those paying less have been industries with a large proportion of unskilled and semi-skilled workers. Other factors influencing inter-industry differentials are the extent of unionisation, the structure of product markets, the ability to pay, labour-capital ratio, and the stage of development of an industry.

(v) Personal Wage Differentials: These arise because of differences in the personal characteristics (age or sex) of workers who work in the same plant and the same occupation. "Equal pay for equal work" has been recommended by the I.L.O. Convention (No. 100), as also by Industrial Courts, Labour Tribunals, the Minimum Wages Committee and the Fair Wage Committee. But in practice this principle has not been fully implemented because in occupations which involve strenuous muscular work, women workers, if employed, are paid less than men workers. Lack of organisation among women employees, less mobility among them, their lower subsistence and their weak constitution are other reasons which bring them lower wages than their male counterparts receive.

IMPORTANCE OF WAGE DIFFERENTIALS

Wage differentials have a great economic and social significance, for they are directly related to the allocation of the economic resources of a country, including manpower, growth of the national income, and the pace of economic development. Social welfare activity depends, in a large measure, on such wage differentials as will:

(a) Cause labour to be allocated among different occupations, industries and geographical areas in the economy in such a manner as to maximise the national product;

(b) Enable full employment of the resources of the economy to be attained; and

(c) Facilitate the most desirable rate of economic progress.

Wage differentials reflect difference in the physical and mental abilities of workers, differences in productivity, in the efficiency of management and in consumer preferences, and act as sign posts for labour mobility. By providing an important incentive for labour mobility, they bring about a re-allocation of the labour force under changing circumstances. Under competitive conditions, wages are determined by conditions of demand (which reflect the productivity of workers) and conditions of supply (which reflect the attractiveness of jobs). The level of wages would depend upon the relative scarcity of supply in relation to demand. Scarcity differentials (which may be due to specific skills and mental abilities) produce wage differentials; and as long as the former as inevitable, the latter, too, would be so. In other words, wage differentials reflect the different degrees of scarcity of the different categories of labour; and since different categories cannot be reduced to the same degree of scarcity in the market, wage differentials are inevitable.

Wage differentials arise because of the following factors:

(a) Differences in the efficiency of the labour, which may be due to inborn quality, education, and conditions under which work may be done.

(b) The existence of non-competing groups due to difficulties in the way of the mobility of labour from low paid to high paid employments.

(c) Differences in the agreeableness or social esteem of employment.

(d) Differences in the nature of employment and occupations.

The nature and the extent of wage differentials are conditioned by a set of factors such as the conditions prevailing in the market, the extent of unionisation and the relative bargaining power of the employers and workers. The rate of growth in productivity, the extent of authoritarian regulations and the centralisation of decision-making, customs and traditions, the general economic, industrial and social conditions in a country, and a host of other subjective and objective factors operating at various levels. The prevailing rates of wages, the capacity of an industry to pay, the needs of an industry in a developing economy, and the requirements of social justice also directly or indirectly affect wage differentials.

WAGE DIFFERENTIALS IN INDIA

Due to the paucity of relevant data on wage differentials, it is not possible to analyse them in India; yet the main features of the Indian wage structure may be stated thus: "As a characteristic of the unorganised labour market, personal differentials because of job selling, individual bargaining and wage discrimination have tended to persist in India, especially in the unorganised sector of the economy, and even in the organised and unorganised sections in industry."

The tendency appears to be towards the elimination of wage differentials because of government interference through the fixation of the minimum wages and, of late, through the appointment of Wage Boards and pressures from trade unions. Wage differentials by sex are quite common. Despite the fact the Constitution of India enjoins upon the State to direct its policy towards securing "equal pay for equal work" for men and women, awards of some industrial Tribunals provide for "different wages for men and women workers, not on the ground that the work done is unequal but on the ground that the wages of women workers support a smaller family, that the cost of employing women workers is higher."

As regards inter-firm and inter-industry differentials in India, the former were quite important and frequent in the past, particularly in the jute mill industry. Of late, however, there has been a tendency towards the elimination of inter-firm differentials. The forces which tend to eliminate inter-personal differentials in the country operate in this case as well.

EXECUTIVE COMPENSATION

For the higher management, salaries are influenced by the size of a company performance of the company, by the specific industry, and in part by the contribution of the incumbent to the process of decision-making. The more profitable the organisation is the firm, the better is the compensation paid to the executives. The industries that are more highly constrained by governmental regulation (banks, life insurance, railroads, public utilities) pay relatively less than those that are more free to carry on their business (private firms).

Executive remuneration has certain unique features, such as:

(1) It cannot be compared to the wage and salary schemes meant for other employees in organisations.

(2) Executives are denied the privilege of having unionised strength.

(3) Secrecy is maintained in respect of executive remuneration.

(4) Executive pay is not supposed to be based on individual performance measure but rather on unit or organisational performance.

(5) Executive remuneration includes a portion based on performance.

COMPONENTS OF REMUNERATION

Executive remuneration generally comprises four elements: *(i)* salary and allowance, *(ii)* bonus *(iii)* incentives *(iv)* perquisites. Salary is the first component of executive remuneration. Salary is supposed to be determined through evaluation and serves as the basis for other types of benefits. Bonus plays an important role in today's competitive executive payment programmes. There are almost as many bonus systems as there are companies using this form of executive remuneration. If bonus constitutes short-term benefit, stock options are long-term benefits offered to executives. Stock options are attractive to shareholders too. Perquisites contribute a major source of income for executives.

Straight salaries, bonuses, stock purchase plans and profit-sharing are used to compensate major executives. Of these, the straight salary is the most common method. The salary is determined by mutual agreement between the individual and the employer. The sales effected, the cost of production, reduction in expenses and the profits made are also taken into account.

Bonuses related to performance are also aid to executives at a certain percentage of the profits. The bonuses may average from 30 per cent to 50 per cent of the basic salary. These bonuses operate most effectively in increasing motivation when the following conditions exist:

(i) The amount paid is closely related to the level of individual performance;

(ii) The amount paid after taxes represents a clearly noticeable rise above the base salary level;

(iii) The amount paid is closely related to the level of company performance;

(iv) The amount paid is tied into the base salary in such a way that the combined earnings are equitable both in relation to internal and external standards;

(v) The amount paid is reduced drastically whenever an individual experiences a real and continuing decrease in performance effectiveness;

(vi) The amount paid is based on an easily understandable system of allocation, and the individual is provided with complete information on the relationship between bonus and performance.

Moreover, executives are compensated for the various expenses incurred by them, for taxation takes away a major portion of their salary. Such payments are in the form of —

(a) Medical care;

(b) Counsel and accountants to assist in legal, tax and financial problems;

(c) Facilities for entertaining customers and for dining out; entertainment expenses holiday expenses;

(d) Company recreational area, holiday homes, leave travel allowance, membership of clubs;

(e) The cost of the education and training of executives, scholarships for their children, and allowances for business magazines and books; and

(f) Free well-furnished accommodation, conveyance and reimbursement for servants. All these go under the head of *perquisites.*

Based upon his research findings on managerial pay, Megginson offers the following generalisations:

(i) Satisfaction with pay is a function of comparison with another's pay, with downward comparisons having the greatest impact.

(ii) A manager's satisfaction with his income and its motivational effect appear to be directly related to anticipated pay raises.

(iii) Those managers who expect large increases in future apparently are less satisfied with their existing level of income; those expecting little or no increases are more satisfied.

(iv) The choice of merit, as opposed to seniority, as the basis for determining salary rates tends to increase with education and position. The actual determinants of pay differentials seem to be job level supervisory experience and professional experience.

(v) Managerial incentive compensation has tended to become flexible. If the various compensation media are to be used to motivate managers, there must be a return to a greater flexibility.

INCENTIVES

MEANING AND FEATURES

An 'incentive' or 'reward' can be anything that attracts a employees' attention and stimulates him to work. In the words of Burack and Smith, "An incentive scheme is a plan or programme to motivate individual or group performance. An incentive programme is most frequently built on monetary rewards (incentive pay or monetary bonus), but may also include a variety of non-monetary rewards or prizes."

On the other hand, French says, the term "*incentive system* has a limited meaning that excludes many kinds of inducements offered to people to perform work, or to work up to or beyond acceptable standards. It does not include: (i) wage and salary payments and merit pay; (ii) over-time payments, pay for holiday work or differential according to shifts, i.e., all payments which could be considered incentives to perform work at undesirable times; and (iii) premium pay for performing danger tasks. *It is related with wage payment plans which tie wages directly or indirectly to standards of productivity or to the profitability of the organisation or to both criteria.*"

The use of incentives assumes that people's actions are related to their skills and ability to achieve important longer-run goals. Even though many organisations, by choice, or tradition or contract, allocate rewards on non-performance criteria, rewards should be regarded as a "pay off" for performance.

An Incentive Plan has the following important features:

1. An incentive plan may consist of both 'monetary' and 'non-monetary' elements. Mixed elements can provide the diversity needed to match the needs of individual employees.
2. The timing, accuracy and frequency of incentives are the very basis of a successful incentive plans.
3. The plan requires that it should be properly communicated to the employees to encourage individual performance, provide feedback and encourage redirection.

DETERMINANTS OF INCENTIVES

These feature are contingencies, which affect the suitability and design of incentives to varying degrees. The effective use of incentives depends on three variables — the individual, work situation, and incentive plan.

(i and iii) The Individual and the Incentives: Different people value things differently. Enlightened managers realise that all people do not attach the same value to monetary incentives, bonuses, prizes or trips. Employees view these things differently

because of age, marital status, economic need and future objectives. However, even though employee reaction to incentives vary greatly, incentives must have some redeeming merits. For example, there might be a number of monetary and non-monetary incentive programmes to motivate employees. Money, gift certificates, praises, or merit pay are of the continuous parade of promotions.

(ii) The Work Situation: This is made up of four important elements: (a) *Technology,* machine or work system, if speed of equipment operation can be varied, it can establish range of the incentive. (b) *Satisfying job assignments,* a workers' job may incorporate a number of activities that he finds satisfying. Incentives may take the form of earned time-off, greater flexibility in hours worked, extended vacation time and other privileges that an individual values. (c) *Feedback,* a worker needs to be able to see the connection between his work and rewards. These responses provide important reinforcement. (d) *Equity,* worker considers fairness or reasonableness as part of the exchange for his work.

Incentives, in general, are important motivators. Their effectiveness depends upon three factors: drives, preference value, and satisfying value of the goal objects. Misra says: "Beyond subistence level, becoming needs (self-actualisation needs) possess greater preference value and are more satisfying than deficiency needs (which are necessary for survival). Below the subsistence level, however, the reverse holds true." He makes the following generalisations:

(i) Incentives, whether they are monetary or non-monetary, tend to increase the level of motivation in a person.

(ii) Financial incentives relate more effectively with basic motivation or deficiency needs.

(iii) Non-financial incentives are linked more closely with higher motivation, or becoming needs.

(iv) The higher the position of a person in an organisation's hierarchy, the greater is his vulnerability to non-financial incentives.

"While budgetary restrictions and temporary improvements in performance place a limit on the potency of money as a motivator, non-financial incentives involve only human ingenuity as investment and also insure a relatively stable acceleration in output. Monetary incentive imply external motivation, non-monetary incentives involve internal motivation. Both are important. It is a judicious mix-up of the two that tends to cement incentives with motivation."

CLASSIFICATION OR TYPES OF INCENTIVES

Incentives can be classified into: (i) direct compensation, and (ii) indirect compensation.

Direct compensation includes the basic salary or wage that the individual is entitled to for his job, overtime-work and holiday premium, bonuses based on performance, profit sharing and opportunities to purchase stock options, etc.

Indirect compensation includes protection programmes (insurance plans, pensions), pay for time not worked, services and perquisites. But these are maintenance factors rather than reward components. Since they are made available to all employees, irrespective of performance, they will tend to retain people in the organisation but not stimulate them to greater effort and higher performance.

Sometimes, the rewards are also termed as *'Intrinsic'* rewards and *'Extrinsic'* rewards. The former are those that an individual receives for himself. They are largely a result of the job that the worker does. The techniques of job enrichment, shorter work weeks, flexible work hours, project structures, and job rotation can offer intrinsic rewards through providing interesting and challenging jobs, and allowing the worker greater freedom.

On the other hand, the latter rewards refer to direct compensation, indirect compensation, and non-financial rewards. Fig. 10.4 gives structure of rewards.

Controversy prevails over the issue of 'money' only motivates the individual. The supporters of the view say that money is potentially an effective motivation. For example:

"Money may potentially be an effective motivator, regardless of the level one has attained and the organisation or the amount of money he is earning."

"Money does appear to have a good deal of symbolic value, and it does mean different people having differing biographics or backgrounds of training and experience."

"For some people, money can be instrumental in satisfying esteemed and recognition need as well basic physical needs. Motivating people with financial rewards is not a picker's game. A company must be willing and able to give certain employees very large raises and/or bonuses if pay is to motivate performance. If a company cannot afford to do this, or is not willing to do so, it should probably forget about using pay to motivate performance."

"Pay in one form or another is certainly one of the main-springs of motivation in our society. The most evangelical human relationist insists it is important while protesting that other things are too (and are perhaps in his view) nobler. It would be unnecessary to belabour the point if it were not for a tendency for money drives to slip out of focus in a miasma of other values and other practices. As it is, it must be repeated: *Pay is the most important single motivator used in our organised society*".

Contrary to these observations, Allen Port observes: "Money incentives alone do not bring the desired motivation. Employees in an industry are not 'economic men' so much as they are 'ego men.' What they want, above all else, is credit for work done, interesting tasks, appreciation, approval and congenial relations with their employers and fellow-workers. These satisfactions they want even more than high wages or job security." "Workers will normally respond to monetary incentives only to a certain point. Beyond that point money becomes ineffective as an inciter of action. This is for two reasons: (i) Money is not foreseen as having the ability to satisfy an urgent need. (ii) The worker may respond to money as a motivator if he believes the benefits will be greater than the expenses incurred by him. If the benefits perceived are less than the personal cost he will not respond to money as an incentive any further. In effect, a break-even point is reached in which additional money earnings become marginal or even undesirable because of the efforts and conditions demanded to earn the added income."

"Using money as a motivator may decrease intrinsic motivation. To use money and other extrinsic reward as effective motivators, they must be made contingent upon performance."

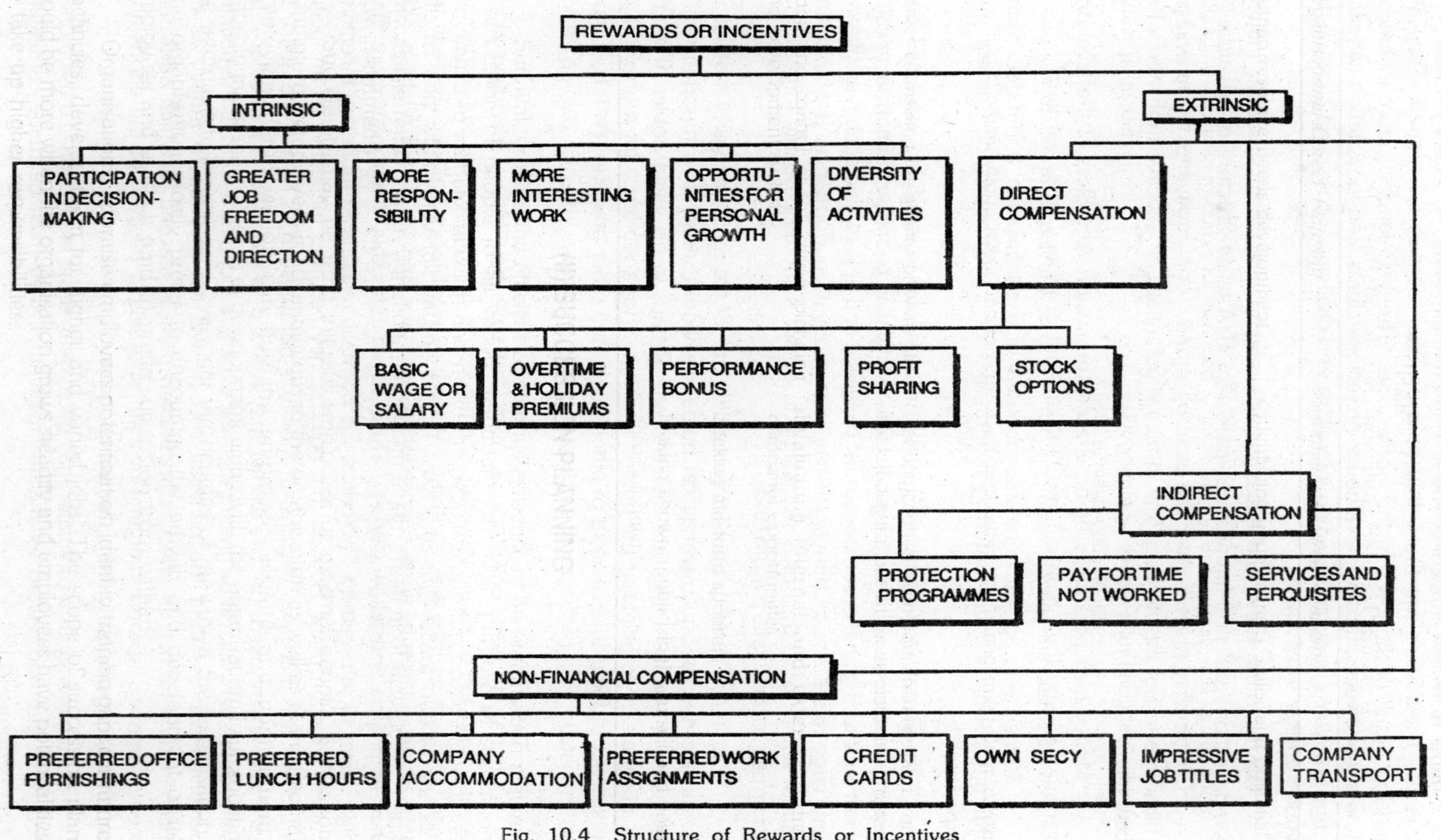

Fig. 10.4 Structure of Rewards or Incentives

It may be summed up that a more reasonable interpretation would be that intrinsic motivation is *increased* by money if two conditions are met: (i) the monetary reward closely follows performance so as to be reinforcing, and (ii) the monetary reward is perceived by the employee to be a function of his work behaviour. Further, it may be fair to conclude that *pay holds motivational properties.* However, the issue is considerably more complex than merely stating that "money motivates."

INCENTIVE PAYMENTS

Incentive are monetary benefits paid to workmen in recognition of their outstanding performance. The International labour organisation (ILO) refers to incentives as "payment by results." But it is appropriate to call them "incentive systems of payments" emphasising the point of motivation, that is, the imparting of incentives to workers for higher production and productivity.

The primary advantage of incentives is the inducement and motivation for higher efficiency and greater output. But with fixed remuneration, it is difficult to motivate employees. Increased earnings would enable the employees to improve their standard of living and help the organisation to improve their production capacity. They also help in reduced supervision, better utilisation of equipment, reduced scrap, reduced lost time, reduced absenteeism and turnover and increased output.

ILO classifies incentive schemes into four categories: (1) schemes in which earnings vary in proportion to output, (2) schemes where earnings vary proportionately less than output, (3) schemes where earnings vary proportionately more than output, and (4) schemes where earnings differ at different levels of output.

WAGE INCENTIVES

The term *wage incentives* has been used both in the restricted sense of *participation* and in the widest sense of *financial motivation.* It has been defined differently by different authors. We give below a few of these definitions.

"It is a term which refers to objectives in the external situation whose function is to increase or maintain, some already initiated activity, either in duration or in intensity." According to Hummel and Nickerson: "It refers to all the plans that provide extra pay for extra performance in addition to regular wages for a job." Florence observes: "It refers to increased willingness as distinguished from capacity. Incentives do not create but only aim to increase the national momentum towards productivity."

In the words of Scott, "it is any formal and announced programme under which the income of an individual, a small group, a plant work force or all the employees of a firm are partially or wholly related to some measure of productivity output."

According to the National Commission on Labour, "wage incentives are extra financial motivation. They are designed to stimulate human effort by rewarding the person, over and above the time rated remuneration, for improvements in the present or targeted results."

"A wage incentive scheme is essentially a managerial device of increasing a worker's productivity. Simultaneously, it is a method of sharing gains in productivity with workers by rewarding them financially for their increased rate of output."

According to Suri, this definition is based on the principle that "an offer of additional money will motivate workers to work harder and more skilfully for a greater part of their working item, which will result in a stepped-up rate of output."

We may define a wage *incentive as a system of payment under which the amount payable to a person is linked with his output.* Such a payment may also be called *payment by results.* The term *incentive* has gradually acquired a wide connotation and includes all the possible factors, besides economic gains, which can possibly motivate human beings towards better and greater performance.

OBJECTIVES OF WAGE INCENTIVE SCHEMES

Wage incentive schemes aim at the fulfillment of one or more of the following objectives:

(i) To improve the profit of a firm through a reduction in the unit costs of labour and materials or both;

(ii) To avoid or minimise additional capital investment for the expansion of production capacity;

(iii) To increase a worker's earnings without dragging the firm into a higher wage rate structure regardless of productivity; and

(iv) To use wage incentives as a useful tool for securing a better utilisation of manpower, better production scheduling and performance control, and a more effective personnel policy.

MERITS OF WAGE INCENTIVE SCHEMES

Such schemes are regarded as beneficial to both employers and workers. They are accepted as a sound technique for the achievement of greater production on the ground that workers would work at their best if they are offered monetary rewards for good performance. For employers, the need for a vigorous supervision is reduced, and consequently there is a cut in the expenditure on supervision. The position of the supervisors changes from that of being "watch dogs" to that of managers of "machines and materials." On the other hand, workers have the advantage of working in a relatively calm atmosphere to the extent to which supervision over their activities is relaxed. Moreover, incentives may be regarded as a step in the direction of linking a worker's compensation with his productivity — an important prerequisite of economic development.

The experience gained in India and elsewhere indicates that wage incentives have resulted in gains in productivity."In a majority of cases, the existence of payment by results was related to increased output, higher earnings, and lower costs." In India, in a survey conducted by it, the National Productivity Council (NPC) pointed out that about 70 per cent of the reporting companies had wage incentive plans. On an average, the schemes seemed to have achieved increases in output which ranged between 30 per cent and 50 per cent and increases in earnings which were between 25 per cent and 45 per cent. The increase in productivity has also been reported in other cases too; for example, in the National Coal Development Corporation, the group productivity index improved from 30 per cent to 50 per cent in the pre-incentive period to 60 per cent to 75 per cent in the post-incentive period. Because of this scheme, the Corporation was able to achieve 80 per cent rated capacity.

According to Suri, "in majority of the jobs investigated, wage incentive schemes succeeded in raising productivity, increasing earnings and reducing direct labour costs." The National Commission on Labour has reached the conclusion that, "under our conditions, wage incentive is the cheapest, quickest, and surest means of increasing productivity." In support of this, its Report indicates that productivity has been progressively increasing and costs falling in the Chittaranjan Locomotive Works, where incentive schemes have been in operation since 1954.

DEMERITS OF INCENTIVE SCHEMES

Despite this rosy picture, the experience with the working of incentives in the highly industralised countries of the West is not quite happy. Some studies on the subject show that incentive schemes have a dubious value for increase in output. Even where an incentive scheme yields an increased output, it may generate tensions among the different parts of an organisation. Such tensions often create difficult managerial problems and may eventually affect output. A sound and effective administration of incentive schemes would depend upon an understanding of the problems of human relations as well as those of engineering.

WAGE INCENTIVE SCHEMES IN INDIA

In a country like India, the role of financial incentives as a primary tool for motivating workers cannot be over-emphasised. Besides, the necessity of raising the productivity of Indian labour is also getting due attention. In this context, the First Plan recommended the introduction of incentive schemes to promote a more efficient working of industries with due safeguards for the interests of workers through the guarantee of a minimum wage and protection against fatigue and undue speed-up. The Second Plan recommended that the earnings beyond the minimum wage should be related to results, and that workers should be consulted before a system of payment by results was introduced in an establishment.

The Third Plan emphasised the need for higher productivity and reduction in the unit cost of production. It put the responsibility on management to provide the most efficient equipment, correct conditions and methods of work, impart training and create suitable psychological and material incentives for workers. The Study Group of the National Commission on Labour has recommended that "under our conditions, a wage incentive is concerned with an effective utilisation of manpower which is the cheapest, quickest and surest means of increasing productivity. The only practicable and self-sustaining means of improving manpower utilisation is to introduce incentive schemes and stimulate human efforts to provide a positive motivation to greater output."

The need for introducing wage incentive schemes in India has been felt on the following grounds:

(i) The efficiency of the Indian worker is very low, and needs to be raised. Wage incentives can play an important part improving his efficiency.

(ii) The average Indian worker is financially very poor. Financial incentives therefore are likely to tempt him to work better.

(iii) India is at a low level of technology, and wage incentives can help in promoting the use of electronic devices.

(iv) A proper application of wage incentive schemes can so affect the prices that the community would be benefited.

(v) In the national interest, it is felt that wage incentive schemes should be applied to all economic activity.

TYPES OF WAGE INCENTIVE PLANS

Wage Incentive Plans may be discussed as *(i)* plans for blue-collar workers; *(ii)* plans for white-collar workers; and *(iii)* plans for managerial personnel — because each of these categories of employees have separate and distinct needs and specific plans tailored for each category may prove beneficial.

1. INCENTIVE PLANS FOR BLUE-COLLAR WORKERS: FOR INDIVIDUALS

(A) SHORT-TERM PLANS

These systems may be broadly classified into three categories:

(a) Systems under which the rate of extra incentive is in proportion to the extra output;

(b) Systems under which the extra incentive is proportionately at a lower rate than the increase in output; and

(c) Systems under which the rate of incentives is proportionately higher than the rate of increase in output.

Every employer wants his workmen to do the maximum work they are capable of doing. On the other hand, there is a feeling among the workers that an increase in effort benefits only the employer even when they are employed on a piece-rate basis. The result is that they never produce to their full capacity, and, in most cases, put in the minimum necessary work. This feeling on the part of workers may be removed either through fear or through expectation of gain. It has been found that fear can never produce the desired effect; but a hope of earning a bonus does induce them to work harder and produce more. Incentive plans are, therefore, known as premium plans because they offer a premium for outstanding performance.

All bonus of premium plans relate to two factors: *one,* they set a standard time for the completion of a definite output or piece of work for a fixed wage; *two,* the fixing of a rate of percentage by which bonus would be earned by a worker over and above his set wage, if the standard time is saved or the standard output is exceeded.

Merits: The chief advantages of an incentive-wage plan are:

(i) When well-designed and properly applied, payment by results may generally be relied upon to yield increased output, lower the cost of production, and bring a higher income to the workers.

(ii) A works study associated with payment by results is a direct stimulus to workers to improve the organisation of work and to eliminate lost time and other waste.

(iii) Labour and total costs per unit of output can be estimated more accurately in advance.

(iv) Less direct supervision is needed to keep output up to a reasonable level.

(v) The conflicting interests of employers and employees are unified. Increased efficiency and smooth working can therefore be promoted and sustained.

Demerits: The plan suffers from the following defects:

(i) Quality tends to deteriorate unless there is a stricter system of checking and inspection.

(ii) Payment by results may lead to opposition or restriction on output when new machines and methods are proposed or introduced. This is because of the fear that the job may be restudied and earnings reduced.

(iii) When paid by result, workers tend to regard their highest earnings as norms, and, therefore, press for a considerable higher minimum wage.

(iv) The amount and cost of clerical work increases, if done manually.

(v) There is a danger of disregarding safety regulations and thereby increasing the rate of accidents.

(vi) Jealousies may arise among workers because some are able to earn more than others or because fast workers are dissatisfied with the slower or older workers in the group.

(vii) It is difficult to set piece or bonus rates accurately. If they are too low, workers may be under pressure to work too hard and become dissatisfied; and if too high, they may slacken their efforts to avoid a revision of rates.

A successful wage incentives plan should consist of the following key points:

(i) The management should recognise that the effectiveness of an incentive depends on the total situation, which includes worker-management confidence, relations with the trade union, the quality of communication and of supervision and the traditions in an industry.

(ii) Management should not introduce an incentive system until it has taken action to ensure full understanding of what is involved. This may call for procedures for the participation of employees and negotiations with the trade union.

(iii) The management should avoid any action that may be interpreted *unfair*. There must be a proper machinery for handling grievances. The management should avoid action that resemble "rate cutting" because of the need to change method and rates from time to time.

(iv) It is essential that the management pay in proportion to output, once this output has risen above that required amount for guaranteed pay.

(v) The management should train supervisors all the way down the line so that foremen and department managers are able to deal with problems within their own departments.

(vi) Great care should be taken in setting up standards to avoid rates that are too loose or too right.

SOME IMPORTANT WAGE INCENTIVE PLANS

The chief incentive plans are:

(i) Halsey Premium Plan.

(ii) Halsey Weir Premium Plan.

(iii) Rowan Premium Plan.

(iv) The 100 Per cent Premium Plan.

(v) The Bedeaux Point Plan.

(vi) Taylor's Differential Piece Rate Plan.

(vii) Merric's Multiple Piece Rate Plan.

(viii) Gnatt Task Plan.

(ix) Emerson Efficiency Plan.

(x) Co-Partnership System.

(xi) Accelerating Premium Systems.

(xii) Profit Sharing.

(i) Halsey Premium Plan: This is a time-saved bonus plan which is ordinarily used when accurate performance standards have not been established. Under this plan, it is optional for a workman to work on the premium plan or not. His day's wage is assured to him whether he earns a premium or not, provided that he is not so incompetent as to be useless. A standard output within a standard time is fixed on the basis of previous experience. The bonus is based on the amount of time saved by the worker. He is entitled to a bonus calculating on the basis of $33^1/_3$ per cent of the time saved. He thus gets wages on the time rate basis. If he does not complete the standard output within the stipulated time, he is paid on the basis of a time wage. The plan is a combination of the day wage and the piece wage in a modified form.

Example: Suppose the standard time is 20 hours, the number of units to be completed is 10, and the hourly rate is 25 paise. Then, the working of the scheme will be:

Time taken (hrs)...	14
No. of hrs saved...	6
Amt. of wages recd...	Rs. 3.50
Amt. of bonus...	Re. 0.75
Total earnings...	Rs. 4.25

Example: If 8 hours is the standard time of a job, and Re. 0.50 is the guaranteed wage per hour, the worker, if he takes 8 hours to perform the work, receives Rs. 4.00. If he performs the task in less than 8 hours he receives an extra premium on the time saved (i.e., for 2 hours).

Table 10.2

	Premium (Half of the Time Saved)	*Total Wages Rs.*
If the work is completed	in 6 hours 0.66	4.66
-do-	in 4 hours 2.00	6.00
-do-	in 2 hours 6.00	10.00
-do	in 1 hour 14.00	18.00

Formula: $\text{Bonus} = \frac{1}{2} \text{ of } \frac{\text{Time saved}}{\text{Time taken}} \times \text{Daily wage.}$

Merits: The merits of this plan are:

(a) It guarantees a fixed time wage to slow workers and, at the same time, offers extra pay to efficient workers.

(b) The cost of labour is reduced because of the percentage premium system; the piece rate of pay gradually decreases with increased production.

(c) The plan is simple in design and easy to introduce.

(d) As the wages are guaranteed, it does not create any heartburning among such workers as are unable to reach the standard.

Demerits: The disadvantages of the plan are:

(a) It depends upon past performance instead of making new standards.

(b) The workers can beat the game by spurting on certain jobs to capture a premium and soldiering on other jobs to rest under the protection of the guarantee of day wages.

(c) From the point of view of the administration, the policy is one of drift, for, in this plan, the worker is left alone to decide whether or not to produce more after the standard has been reached.

(ii) Halsey-Weir Premium Plan: This plan is similar to the Halsey Premium Plan except that 50 per cent of the time saved is given as premium to worker.

Bonus = ½ × Time Saved × Hourly Rate

(iii) Rowan Premium Plan: This plan differs from the Halsey Plan only in regard to the determination of the bonus. In all other respects, the two are the same. In the Rowan Plan, the time saved is expressed as a percentage of the time allowed, and the hourly rate of pay is increased by that percentage so that total earnings of the worker are the total number of hours multiplied by the increased hourly wages. The plan aims at ensuring the permanence of the premium rate, which is often cut by the employer when the worker's efficiency increase beyond a certain limit. The premium is calculated on the basis of the proportion which the time saved bears to standard time.

Example: If 8 hours are the standard time for doing a job and Rs. 4.00 per day wage, the premium and total wages would be as follows:

Table 10.3

		Premium	*Total Wages*
		Rs.	*Rs.*
If the job is completed	in 5 hours	1.00	5.00
-do-	in 4 hours	2.00	6.00
-do-	in 3 hours	3.00	7.00
-do-	in 1 hours	3.50	7.50

Formula: $\text{Bonus} = \frac{\text{Time Saved}}{\text{Time Allowed}} \times \text{Time taken} \times \text{Hourly Rate}$

The Rowan Plan has all the merits and demerits of the Halsey Plan except that, because of the limitation on earnings, it does not provide an incentive for maximum productivity. Moreover, the complex method of premium calculation is generally unintelligible to the worker. He cannot, therefore, be expected to take much interest in the plan.

These premium plans may be classified as differential piecework systems and have been evolved with a view to giving the benefit to both parties. They are based on the fundamental principle that a worker's earning should increase when his production rises above a pre-determined target. As his extra earning is not in proportion to his usual wage rate, the overall production cost per piece falls when the output increases. The bonus paid and the total earnings under each of these three schemes are given in Table 10.4.

Table 10.4

Plan	Bonus (B)	Total Earnings (E)
Halsey	$B = 1/3\ (Hs - Ha)\ Rh$	$E = Ha.\ Rh + 1/3\ (Hs - Ha).\ Rh.$
		$= 1/3\ (Hs + 2\ Ha)\ Rh.$
Halsey-Weir	$B = 1/2\ (Hs - Ha)\ Rh$	$E = Ha.\ Rs + 1/2\ (Hs - Ha).\ Rh.$
		$= 1/2\ (Hh + Ha)\ Rh.$
Rowan	$B = \frac{(Hs - Ha)}{Hs} \times Ha.\ Rh$	$E = Ha - Rh + \frac{(Hs - Ha)}{Hs}\ Ha.\ Rh.$
		$= \frac{Ha}{Hs}\ (2\ Hs\ Ha)\ Rh.$

Hs = the hour allowed or standard time.

Ha = the actual time taken on a job.

Rh = the worker rate per hour.

It will be seen that, for a little time saving Rowan Plan gives more bonus than the Halsey or the Halsey-Weir Plans. Up to 50 per cent of the time saved, the bonus earned under the Halsey-Weir or the Rowan Plan is equal; but above 50 per cent of the time saved, the Rowan Plan pays more than the Halsey Plan. However, under, the Rowan Plan a worker gets his maximum bonus when he completes the task in half the standard time allowed. If he saves more than 50 per cent of the time, the bonus he earns decreases, and his increase in wage is at a diminishing rate. But under the Halsey and Halsey-Weir Plan, it is progressively higher.

(iv) The 100 Per Cent Premium Plan: Under this plan, task standards are set by time study or work sampling, and rates are expressed in time rates rather than in money (e.g., 0.20 hour per piece). A definite hourly rate is paid for each task-hour of work performed. The plan is identical with the straight piece-rate plan except for its higher guaranteed hourly rate and the use of task time as a unit of payment instead of a *price* per piece. The worker is paid the full value of the time saved. If he completes the tasks of 10 hours and if the hourly rate is Re. 0.50, his total earnings will be Rs. 8 × 0.50 + (10 – 8) × 0. 50 = Rs. 4.00 + 100 = Rs. 5.00.

(v) The Bedeaux Point Plan: This plan is used when careful assessed performance standards have been established. It differs from the 100 per cent plan in that the basic unit of the time is the minute termed as B. Every job is expressed in terms of Bs (after Bedeaux), which means that a job should be completed in so

many minutes. If a particular work is rated at 60 Bs (or one B hour), the worker is allowed one hour for its completion and receives a bonus of 75 per cent for the number of Bs, i.e., time, saved. Suppose a worker earns 600 Bs in a day; if the rate per point is Re. 0.01, his total earnings would be:

Rs. 4.80 × 0.01 + 3/4 (600 – 480) × .01.

= Rs. 480 + Re. 0.90 = Rs. 5.70.

The chief advantage of this plan is that it can be applied to any kind of a job. It is particularly suitable for plants in which workers are assigned diverse kinds of jobs, shifted from one job or department to another. All the points which a worker earns in a day are recorded, and the bonus is calculated on that basis.

(vi) Taylor's Differential Piece-Rate Plan: This system was introduced by Taylor with two objects: *First,* to give sufficient incentive to workmen to induce them to produce up to their full capacity; and *second,* to remove the fear of wage cut. There is one rate for those who reach the standard; they are given a higher rate to enable them to get the bonus. The other is the lower rate for those who are below the standard, so that the hope of receiving a higher rate (that is, a bonus) may serve as an incentive to come up to the standard. Workers are expected to do certain units of work within a certain period of time. This standard is determined on the basis of time and motion studies. Such scientific determination ensures that the standard fixed is not unduly high and is within the easy reach of workers. On a proper determination of the standard depends the success of the scheme.

This system is designed to encourage the specially efficient worker with a higher rate of payment and to penalise the inefficient by a lower rate of payment. In practice, this plan is seldom used now.

Example: Let the standard time for the completion of 10 pieces of a job be 8 hours and the piece rate be Re. 1.00. Then the basic hourly rate comes to 12.5 paise. The one who completes the work within the allotted time is paid wages at a rate which is 320 per cent higher than the basic one.

Table 10.5

(Amount in Rs.)

Worker	*No. of Units Completed in Allotted Time*	*Percentage of Efficiency*	*Total Amt. Received*	*Basic Piece Rate*	*Effective Piece Rate*
A	10	100	1.20	0.1	0.12
B	9	90	0.90	0.1	0.10
C	8	80	0.80	0.1	0.10
D	11	110	1.32	0.1	0.12
E	12	120	1.44	0.1	0.12

It is evident that workers A, B and C are better off, and for them the system is good; but for D and E, who are more than 100 per cent efficient, the effective piece rate remains the same when compared with that of A, who is just 100 per cent efficient.

(vii) Merrie's Multiple Piece Rate System: This system, too, is based on the principle of a low piece rate for a slow worker and a higher piece rate for higher production; but the plan differs from Taylor's Plan in that it offers three graded piece rates instead of two. (i) Up to, say 83% of standard output a piece-rate + 10% of time rate as bonus; (ii) Above 83% and up to 100% of standard output — same piece rate + 20% of time rate; and (iii) Above 100% of standard output — same piece rate but no bonus.

Such a scheme is usually introduced in an organisation where the performance level is already high and management is aiming at 100% efficiency. Management has some discretion in distributing the 20% of time rate over 17% of production above 83%.

(viii) The Gnatt Task and Bonus Plan: This plan has been devised by H.L. Gnatt and is the only one that pays a bonus percentage multiplied by the value of standard time. Under this system, fixed time rates are guaranteed. Output standards and time standards are established for the performance of each job. Workers completing the job within the standard time or in less time receive wages for the standard time plus a bonus which ranges from 20 per cent to 50 per cent of the time allowed and not time saved. When a worker fails to turn out the required quantity of a product, he simply gets his time rate without any bonus.

Under this plan, there are also three stages of payment: (i) *Below the standard performance*, only the minimum guaranteed wage is to be paid; (ii) *at the standard performance*, this wage + 20% of time-rate will be paid as a bonus; and (iii) *when the standard is exceeded*, a higher piece rate is paid but there is no bonus.

Example: If the standard task for a day is 8 units and the day wage is Rs. 4, the bonus at 50 per cent and the total wages would be:

Table 10.6

Units of Work	*Task Wages (Rs.)*	*Bonus (Rs.)*	*Total Wages (Rs.)*
If 6 units are completed in a day	4.00	Nil	4.00
If 8 units are completed	4.00	2.00	6.00
If 10 units -do-	4.00	2.50	7.50
If 12 units -do-	4.00	3.00	9.00

This system is most profitable for workers whose efficiency is very high. The basic wages rise proportionately as under ordinary piece wage system, and the bonus is allowed on the increased wage. In addition to this workers with lower efficiency are not penalised, as they are in Taylor's Differential Piece Rate.

(ix) Emerson Efficiency Plan: Under this system, a standard time is established for a standard task. The day wage is assured. There is no sudden rise in wages on achieving the standard of performance. The remuneration based on efficiency rises gradually. Efficiency is determined by the ratio between the standard time fixed for a performance and the time actually taken by a worker. Thus, if the period of 8 hours is the standard time for a task and if a worker performs it in 16 hours, his efficiency is 50 per cent. He who finishes the task in 8 hours has 100 per cent efficiency, at which stage he receives a nominal bonus. This bonus goes on increasing

till, when he achieves 100 per cent efficiency, the bonus comes to 20 per cent of the guaranteed wage. At 120 per cent efficiency, a worker receives a bonus of 40 per cent and at 140 per cent efficiency the bonus is 60 per cent of the day wage.

(x) Co-Partnership System: This system tries to eliminate friction between capital and labour. Under this system, not only does a worker share in the profits of the undertaking but he also takes part in its control and, therefore, shares responsibilities. There are different cases; but in a complete co-partnership system, the following factors are present:

(a) The payment of the existing standard wages of labour;

(b) The payment of a fixed rate of interest on capital;

(c) The division of the surplus profit between capital and labour in an agreed proportion;

(d) The payment for a part of the worker's labour by the allotment of a share in the capital;

(e) The sharing in the control of the business by the representatives of labour.

The system arouses and sustains the interests of the workers in their work. By giving them a voice in the management of the factory it raises their status as well. As they have become partners in the business, they try to make it a very profitable enterprise.

(xi) Accelerating Premium Systems: There are the system which provide for a guaranteed minimum wage for output below standard.

For low and average increases in output above the standard, small increment in earnings are allowed. Increasingly large earnings are conceded for above average output, the increment being different for each 1% increase in output. Very significant increases in earnings are given for really high output.

In this system, the production is pushed up higher and higher by discouraging low output and rewarding at an increasingly effective rate higher outputs.

Such schemes are generally adopted when much higher outputs than what are currently obtained are to be achieved.

(B) LONG-TERM WAGE INCENTIVE PLANS

Under such plans, each member of the group receives a 'bonus' based on the output of the group *as a whole.* There are several reasons for adopting such a plan. Sometimes (as on assembly lines) several jobs are *inter-related.* Here one worker's performance reflects not only his own effort but that of his co-workers too. In such cases, group incentive plans are advantageous. *Secondly,* such plans also encourage *co-operation* among group members. There tends to be less bickering among group members as to who has "tight" production standards and who has "loose" ones. *Thirdly,* the groups can bring pressure to bear on their members (through badgering, ostracism, etc.) and help keep *shrinkers in line.* This, in turn, can help elminate some of the need for close supervision. *Fourthly,* group production levels tend to be *more stable* than individual ones, and group incentive payments vary less than individual ones. *Finally,* group incentive plans also facilitate *on-the-job training,* since each member of the group has a vested interest in getting a new group member trained as well as quickly as possible.

The chief disadvantages of the group plans are: (i) each worker's rewards are no longer based soley or directly on his own efforts. To the extent that person does not see his effort leading to the desired reward, a group plan is probably not as effective as an individual plan. (ii) There is uneveness of performance of different members of the group and this may have resentment of active members against mere 'passengers.' (iii) Ill-feeling may be generated among the groups themselves where the technology is such that one group's earnings depend on the performance of another group.

Group incentive plans are usually applied to small work groups, for example, 5 or 6 people who must assemble a component together. The incentives usually take three forms.

1. *(a) A standard output,* i.e., target production, may be laid down for a month or a larger period and bonuses are paid if this is achieved; and (b) *A standard output per man-hour* is laid down for a department or for the plant as a whole, and the bonus is paid in proportion to which the actual output per man-hour exceeds the standard, the other conditions of work remaining the same.

2. *The 'Value added' by manufacturer* at factory cost leading to cost reduction forms the basis for calculating the bonus. If the actual cost of production is lower than the 'standard cost' to the extent the workers are able to influence such reduction — by harder working, saving in materials, fuels, lubricants, etc. — a bonus whose money value is a percentage to the cost reduction is paid.

3. *Bonus can also be calculated on the increased value of sales* where this result is obtained by increased production.

The Group Incentive Plans are usually:

(i) The Profit-sharing schemes, and

(ii) The Scanlon Plan.

(I) PROFIT-SHARING

Profit-sharing is regarded as a stepping stone to industrial democracy. Prof. Seager observes: "Profit-sharing is an arrangement by which employees receive a share, fixed in advance of the profits." The International Co-operative Congress held in Paris in 1889 considered the issue and defined profit-sharing as "an agreement (formal or informal) freely entered into, by which an employee receives a share fixed in advance of the profits."

Profit-sharing usually involves the determination of an organisation's profits at the end of the fiscal year and the distribution of a percentage of the profits to workers qualified to share in the earnings. The percentage to be shared by the workers is often predetermined at the beginning of the work period and is communicated to the workers so that they have some knowledge of their potential gains. To enable the workers to participate in profit-sharing, they are required to work a certain number of years and develop some seniority. The theory behind profit-sharing is, that management feels its workers will fulfill their responsibilities more diligently if they realise that their efforts may result in higher profits, which will be returned to the workers through profit-sharing. In India, the law relating to profit-sharing is known as the Payment of Bonus Act and this sharing of profit is not linked to performance but to the level of profits made by the company.

Features of Profit-sharing: The main features of the profit-sharing schemes are:

(a) The agreement is voluntary and based on joint consultation made freely between the employers and the employees.

(b) The payment may be in the form of cash, stock of future credits of some amount over and above the normal remuneration that would otherwise be paid to employees in a given situation.

(c) The employees should have some minimum qualifications, such as tenure or satisfy some other condition of service which may be determined by the management.

(d) The agreement on profit-sharing having been mutually accepted, is binding and there is no room on the part of the employer to exercise discretion in a matter which is vital to the employees.

(e) The amount to be distributed among the participants is computed on the basis of some agreed formula, which is to be applied in all circumstances.

(f) The amount to be distributed depends on the profits earned by an enterprise.

(g) The proportion of the profits to be distributed among the employees is determined in advance.

It should be noted that profit-sharing is not a system of wage payment as such; it is something else. Profit-sharing and bonus (also known as *profit-sharing bonus)* are two different things, for the former sharing implies sharing on an equal footing rather than yielding on the part of a management to a persistent demand. Profit-sharing bonus on the other hand refers to the distribution of profits on the basis of a certain percentage of one's monthly wages. Moreover, it is not voluntary and is not based on agreement.

Profit-sharing is a distinctly progressive measure towards industrial harmony. It may be considered as a step short of joint consultation or co-partnership schemes. Wage-business affairs are managed and shared on a footing of equality. Essentially this means "the creation of a mental climate in which a strong sense has to grow that the business is the business of all, since it is the joint effort of the workers and the management and since the one cannot carry on a business without the help of the other. This is the inner essence of profit-sharing which has often been overlooked."

There are three main characteristics of labour remuneration in the form of profit-sharing, which distinguish it from *gain-sharing* and from an *ordinary system of wage payment.* These features are:

(a) A share in profits is payable at long intervals when the final accounts of a firm are prepared and its profit or loss ascertained.

(b) The payment is of an uncertain nature because of the uncertainty of profits. Sometimes there may be no profits or very high profits; in other cases, there may actually be some losses.

(c) The payment is not based on individual work, efficiency or merit, but is a remuneration for collective effort, the total remuneration due to workers being equally divided among them or in some agreed proportion.

(d) The payment is sometimes regarded as *windfall gain* or as something to which a worker is entitled and not as something in recognition of his efficiency.

Types of Profit-Sharing: Employee profit-sharing is often regarded by employers as a supplementary benefit programme.

Although plans differ widely as to specific details, three basic types of profit-sharing plans are in use:

(a) *Current* (cash) profits are paid directly to employees in cash or by cheque or in the form of stock as soon as profits are determined (e.g., monthly, quarterly, biannually or annually).

(b) *Deferred* profits are credited to employee accounts to be paid at the time of retirement or in particular circumstances (i.e., disability, death, severance or under withdrawal provisions during employment).

(c) *Combination* by which a part of the profits is paid in cash and a part is deferred and placed in the employee's account in a trust fund.

Objectives of Profit-Sharing: Profit-sharing is more than just another employee benefit. It may be the most important part of a progressive personnel policy. It may incorporate incentive features and produce results not possible by the implementation of other programmes. Companies which offer this incentive have realised higher profits and increased efficiency, and have created a climate for better employee relations.

The critical ingredient in profit-sharing is the desire of the employees and the management to ensure the success of a programme. The programme is formulated at the top because profit-sharing is first and foremost, a principle and technique of leadership.

The real objective of profit-sharing is to foster "the unity of interest and the spirit of co-operation." From the point of view of the employees, profit-sharing may serve a multiple of objectives, depending upon the type of plan which is adopted. A cash plan contributes directly to an employee's immediate economic gain. Deferred plans and combination plans contain features very similar to benefit plans which provide for retirement benefits and against loss of income following disability, for benefits to dependants in the event of the death of an employee, and for other related benefits. From the view point of the organisation, employee productivity is the overriding objective of profit-sharing. At the same time, it may contribute to employee satisfaction because profit-sharing provides for rewards which are related to employee needs.

A profit-sharing scheme is generally introduced to achieve the following objectives:

(a) To promote industrial harmony and stabilisation of the work force;

(b) To eliminate waste in the use of materials and equipments;

(c) To instil a sense of partnership among employees and employers and to increase employee interest in the company in which he works;

(d) To attract desirable employees and retain them, thereby reducing the rate of turnover;

(e) To encourage employee thrift;

(f) To provide a group incentive for a larger output;

(g) To ensure employee security; and

(h) To demonstrate some measure of social justice to employees.

The purpose of profit-sharing is the achievement of industrial harmony.

Forms of Profit-Sharing: Profit-sharing may be on —

(a) Industry Basis: Here the profit of a number of industrial units in the same industry may be pooled together to determine the share of labourers. Such a scheme has the advantage of putting the whole labour force in a particular industry on a uniform basis. Moreover, if a certain industrial unit somehow shows a loss in a particular year, its workers are not deprived of their remuneration because other units have made a good profit.

(b) Locality Basis: Industrial units in a particular locality may pool their profits to determine labour's remuneration by way of profit-sharing. However, if there are heterogeneous industrial units in a locality, where labour's work is for a widely divergent nature, there may be great difficulties in bringing about an adjustment in their share.

(c) Unit Basis: This is the simplest way of giving a labourer a share in the profits of the individual undertaking in which he is employed. This mode of profit-sharing establishes a close relationship between the efforts of labour and rewards it receives. In the first two schemes, the reward of workers depends on the combined efforts of all in a number of units.

(d) Department Basis: Sometimes the various departments of an industrial unit may have their separate profit-sharing schemes. The workers in a particular department share in the profits made by that department. This aims at bringing about an even closer relationship between a worker's efforts and the reward he receives.

(e) Individual Basis: A worker receives a proportion of the profit which may have been earned by a business through the efforts of that particular worker. This aims at bringing about a direct and most intimate relationship between individual effort and reward. In practice, it is impossible to determine such profits.

Requisites for Profit-Sharing: To be effective, profit-sharing schemes should be based on the following considerations:

(a) Profitability of Industrial Units: Industrial units should be profitable for, without profitability the profit-sharing scheme would not succeed. No scheme should be launched until business conditions are favourable. A business or any industry may be stabilised by an expansion in production, by the adoption of sound distribution methods and by keeping constant vigilance over its functioning. In other words, there should be compreshensive and flexible schemes for incentives and other kind of bonus which promote productivity. Until these essentials have become permanent features in an industry, unless working conditions in a business have been stabilised, the purchasing power of the people has considerably increased, and profits are sufficiently high to ensure their distribution between workers and shareholders, no profit-sharing scheme would be sound or anything more than a paper scheme.

(b) Computation of Surplus Profit: The computation of surplus profit for distribution should be arrived at by deducting from it normal and additional depreciation and initial or development rebate, so that the replacement or modernisation cost of plant and equipment is properly provided for. Losses, when they occur, should also be deducted before the profits for the subsequent year are declared. If additional bonus is to be paid, its payment will have to be made out of the balance left over after the above deductions. The margin of profits should be adequate and substantial so that, after providing for all these expenses, there must be a surplus of a sizable amount to be distributed among the workers.

(c) Fair Return on Capital: The return on the capital invested in an enterprise should be that which would encourage partnership investment. It should be at least 6 per cent on paid-up capital, with a charge of 10 per cent to be made for reserves.

(II) THE SCANLON PLAN

This plan was developed in 1937 by Joseph Scanlon a Lecturer at the Massachusetts Institute of Technology and a trade union leader in a steel mill. The plan was designed to involve the workers in making suggestions for reducing the cost of operation and improving working methods and sharing in the gains of increased productivity.

The plan has two basic features: *one,* financial incentives aimed at cutting cost and thereby increasing efficiency are installed. Two, a network of departmental and plan screening committees are set up to evaluate employee and management cost-cutting suggestions. *The plan is essentially a suggestion system and assumes that efficiency requires company-wise/plant-wise co-operation.*

Usually all employees in the plant participate in the plan. Workers, supervisors, and managers make cost-cutting suggestions that are screened and evaluated by the various screening committees. If a suggestion is implemented and successful, all employees usually share in 75% of the savings, and the rest 20% is set aside for the months in which labour costs exceed the standard.

The Scanlon plan has been successful where adopted. It tends to encourage a sense of partnership and sharing among workers, less over-time and employee insistence on efficient management.

Certain conditions need be fulfilled to make the plan successful:

(i) They are more effective where there is a relatively small number of participants, generally less than 1,000.

(ii) It is more successful where there are stable product lines and costs.

(iii) There should be good supervision and healthy labour relations.

(iv) There should be a strong commitment to plan on the part of management — particularly during the confusing phase in period.

THE PREVALENT SYSTEMS IN INDIA

The most widely prevalent incentive scheme in Indian industries is the piece-rate system. In industries like iron, steel and chemicals, however only a small percentage of workers are paid on piece-rate basis.

Another incentive system that is prevalent in Indian industries is the payment of production bonus usually at a differential rate for the output produced in excess of the normal output for a unit of time. The norms are generally fixed on the basis of job anaylsis and/or time studies. The incentive scheme operates on a group or individual basis, depending on the measurability of the work of individual workers and the inter dependence of their output performance. Engineering and chemicals have mostly the group system, while textiles have mainly the individual system of incentives. The group incentive system is more widely prevalent in the Indian industry than the system of individual incentive or a combination of both.

Wage incentive plans, other than the piece-rate system, bristle with some problems in their operation.

First, incentive earnings, as a percentage of the total wages of workers covered under the incentive plans, are very low. In 1961, it was 10.9 per cent. There may be several reasons for this situation: either the norms of standard work are fixed high and it is not possible for a worker to exceed them by a sizable percentage; or the fall-back on time rate wage is sufficiently high and workers do not have much inducement to put in greater effort beyond the standard norms; or the rate structure of incentive wage is not adequately progressive. In any case, this situation reflects the relative ineffectiveness of incentive plans. Moreover, the percentage of workers paid by results is around 31 in India as compared to 42 per cent in the U.K., 45 per cent in the U.S.A. and 77 per cent in USSR for iron and steel industry. For cotton textiles, the percentage of workers paid on piece-rate in India is 70 against Britain's 63, America's 36, and Russia's 87.

Second, a number of units may have unnecessarily complex incentive plans, probably transplanted from European firms, which are not easily comprehensible to illiterate or semi-literate workers on the one hand, and which do not have a direct relationship between effort and wages on the other. In addition to numerous slabs in the rate structure, there are often changing bases of calculation and distinctions between different types of employees — permanent, temporary staff, workmen, etc.

Third, in cases where group incentive plans are in vogue, a system becomes difficult to operate effectively, for the direct link between effort and earnings is lost.

Fourth, while there is no need for the rate structure of incentive wages to be progressive from the beginning, it needs to be so when workers show high levels of productivity. Some of the incentive plans actually turn out to be regressive in practice in these final stages. These maladies of the incentive plans betray a lack of wage to make them an effective tool of increasing productivity.

PRECAUTIONS AGAINST ILL-EFFECTS OF INCENTIVE SYSTEMS

Experience has shown that incentive schemes are not an unqualified blessing in themselves. They are fraught with some dangers that have to be guarded against during the course of their evolution and implementation. *First,* there is a tendency amongst workers to sacrifice quality for quantity. This calls for a strict system of checking and inspection. *Second,* incentive schemes bring about a certain fixity in the operations and undermine flexibility, which is an essential requirement in view of the rapid progress in technology. Such changes in technology, methods, machines and materials involve a revision of norms and rates. The incentive schemes should, therefore, be adequately provided with such revision in case of significant changes.

Thirdly, there is a danger that safety regulations would be disregarded by workers and this may result in higher accident rates. This may be solved by greater vigilance on the part of workers concerned. *Fourthly,* there is a danger that workers would tend to overwork and undermine their health. This may be checked by fixing a ceiling on incentive earnings. *Finally,* incentive schemes sometimes lead to jealousies and misunderstanding among the workers because of the difference in their earnings. However, differences in earning will differ for workers according to the differences in their abilities and efforts. Moreover, trade unions discourage ill feelings or jealousies amongst its members.

PRE-REQUISITIES OF A GOOD WAGE INCENTIVE SCHEME

The installation of an incentive scheme presupposes the existence of certain pre-requisities, which are, more often than not, ignored. Quite often, incentive payments are just taken to be necessary part of the total wage packet, and hastily conceived schemes are introduced primarily because of pressures from workers and trade unions. such schemes naturally result in a number of personnel problems which may, in fact, be impediments to improve productivity. It is, therefore, advisable to ensure that a proper climate exists for the introduction of such schemes. Some important considerations, which should ordinarily be taken into account while choosing a particular type of wage incentive scheme, are:

(i) The management should strive to create a proper climate by adopting sound policies of recruitment, promotion, trading etc., right from the inception of an enterprise. Unless there is mutual understanding and concern for improving productivity, even a well-conceived incentive scheme may not yield the optimum results. Therefore, the management must concentrate on creating a proper industrial relations climate before introducing incentive schemes.

(ii) The objectives of the scheme must be clear, and these should be well understood at the levels of management and of workers. Certain specific factors may be selected as the basis for a scheme. Too many factors selected at a time may make it complicated. The scheme should suit both the particular enterprise and its workers. At every stage, right from the conception of the scheme to conducting studies, etc., all the workers and supervisors should be consulted so that they understand the objectives and benefits of the scheme and may contribute to its success.

(iii) Incentive schemes should be installed only when production has reached 60 per cent of the rated capacity. Care should be taken to provide a suitable gestation mechanism in the scheme on a time-bound basis so that incentive payments at a lower level of the performance are allowed only for limited time periods. The quantum of incentive paid at the low levels of production and efficiency should be such as to ensure that earnings continuously increase when the targets are raised.

(iv) The scheme chosen should be one which would result in overall economy for the establishment. Incentives should not only increase production but also result in higher productivity and lower cost per unit; and the gains of increased productivity should be shared both by the employer and the employed.

(v) The scheme should not be very costly in operation, i.e., it should not involve the maintenance of very elaborate records, complicated calculations, and too much material handling.

(vi) The scheme should be based on a work study, and the work contents of various jobs should be stabilised.

(vii) In principle, each individual or group should be paid according to effort and productivity, for disparity in earnings may create discontent. Unless the scheme is well-defined, it may turn out that indirect groups may receive higher incentive earnings than the main production group.

(viii) The scheme should have elasticity to take care of technological and other changes taking place from time to time and rectify errors that may have crept in at the time of its initial introduction.

(ix) The scheme should not undermine co-operation amongst the workers. It should rather stimulate co-operation with a view to achieving the common objective of increasing the well-being of the business and, therefore, of the workers in general.

(x) Performance standards and norms for incentive payments should be set up at the average performance level of the employees, i.e., they should not be too high nor too low. Such performance standards should be set as are within the control of employees. The adoption of objective assessment procedures and the use of functional responsibility are to be advocated in addition to such indices of productivity as wage cost per unit sale, salary savings on inventory, etc.

(xi) To make the scheme effective, a climate should be created in which the employees feel that the management is fair and just in its dealings with them on wage incentive matters. For this purpose, mutual discussions and appropriate management action would be called for.

(xii) Incentive payment should be made as soon as possible after a job is completed.

Any hastily conceived or haphazardly introduced incentive scheme does more harm than good. Therefore, it should be introduced after a proper consideration of the various preparatory measures.

2. INCENTIVE PLANS FOR WHITE COLLAR WORKERS/SALESMEN

The salesmen are usually given incentives in the form of sales commissions. One study reported that almost 75% of the organisations surveyed paid salesmen on some type of incentive basis. This is due to three factors: (i) the unsupervised nature of most sales work; (ii) tradition in the market and (iii) the assumption the incentives are needed to motivate salesmen.

The are several incentive plans, each appropriate for different markets, products, etc., but all plans are basically variations of three types of plans: straight salary, straight commission, and combination plans.

Table 10.7
Firms Using Incentive Plans for Salesmen

Incentive Plan	Percentage of Companies			
	Consumer Products	Industrial Products	Other Commerce and Industry	All Industries
1. Straight salary	20.1	25.6	56.5	27.6
2. Straight commission	2.1	1.3	2.2	1.5
3. Draw straight commission	7.5	1.3	—	20.1
4. Salary + commission	19.2	21.1	13.0	17.7
5. Salary + Individual bonus	21.3	10.8	8.7	17.7
6. Salary + group bonus	8.5	4.4	6.5	5.4
7. Salary + commission + individual bonus	7.5	5.3	2.2	5.4
8. Salary + commission + group bonus	1.1	0.6	–	0.6
9. More than one method of payment	12.7	22.4	10.9	19.3
Total	100.0	100.0	100.0	100.0

(a) Straight Salary Method: Is not an incentive plan; the salesman is simply paid on weekly, monthly, or on yearly basis. The *advantages* of this method are that: (i) The salesmen know in advance what their income will be; and (ii) the expenditure on salesmen is known beforehand. The *disadvantage* are: (i) This method tends to shift salesman's emphasis to just making the sale rather than prospecting and cultivating long-term customer; and (ii) pay is not related to results. This lack of relationship reduced salesmen's performance.

(b) Straight Commission Basis: Under this method the salesmen are paid on the basis of sales effected, i.e., *they are paid for results and only for results.* Therefore, high performance salesmen are generally attracted. But the *disadvantages* are: (i) Salesman focusses on making a sale on high volume items. Cultivating dedicated customers and working to "push" hard-to-sell items are often neglected, (ii) Salesmen tend to be less company-oriented and more money-oriented, and the company has less control over them; (iii) Salesmen's income generally fluctuates widely.

(c) Combination Method of Salary and Commission Basis: Under this, salesman not only get a fixed salary but also a commission in proportion to the sales effected. The *advantages* of this method are: (i) Since salesmen are assured of minimum earnings, they are relieved of financial worries. (ii) The company has more control over its salesmen, as there is sizable salary component in most combination plans. So that it can direct salesman's activities by detailing what services and salary component is being paid for. But the main *disadvantage* is that salary is not related to performance; only incentive value of money is being traded off for its security value. Such plans also tend to become very complicated, and misunderstanding often results in frustration. In spite of these disadvantages, these plans are widely used with several basic variations, like:

(d) Salary Plus Commission: Commission Plus Drawing Account where not only commission is paid but the salesman is also allowed to draw on future earnings to get him through low sales period; *commission plus bonus,* where salesmen are paid primarily on the basis of commission but they are also given a bonus for activities like "slow moving" items; and *salary plus bonus,* wherein salesmen are paid a basic salary; and also given a bonus for carrying out specified activities.

3. INCENTIVES FOR MANAGEMENT EMPLOYEES

In many orgnisations, the managers are paid bonus. There are two types of bonus plans: *one* determined by formula (i.e., some criteria like increased sales) and *two,* determined by some discretion used in allocation of bonus (i.e., paid on more or less permanent basis). The bonus plans are generally reviewed annually to make them more effective.

For top level management, bonuses are generally tied to overall corporate results. The size of bonus is much higher for top level executives, and lower for the lower level executives.

Failure of Incentive Plans: Many of the incentive plans, aimed at increasing the motivation of employees, often fail to have their desired impact. This is due to several reasons, most of which become apparent when it is considered that for motivation to take place, the worker must believe that his effort will lead to rewards and that he must want that reward. In most cases incentives plans fail because one or both of these facts are not met.

The principal reasons of failure are:

1. *Unfair Standards* are a great hindrance in the way of motivating employees. In order to motivate them, *the standards must be viewed as fair and attainable.*

2. *Fear of Rate Cut:* There is fear in the minds of the employees that standards will be raised high or rates will be cut if they earn too much.

3. *Group Restrictions: Peer pressure is a double-edged sword when it comes to incentive plans.* If the group views the plan as fair, it can keep "Loafers" in line and maintain high production. If the group feels that plan is not in its interest it will — through education, ostracism, or punishment — see that production levels of group members is kept at a minimum.

4. *Employees do not Understand the Plan:* This happens when either the details of the plans are not communicated to employees or if communicated, the employees do not clearly understand them. If employees cannot understand how performance will lead to rewards, the plans would not prove fruitful in motivating them.

5. *Lack of Require Tools, Training, Equipment etc:* The lack of required machines and tools, equipment and absence of a sound organisation structure often break the effort — reward link; and without that link, incentive plan fails.

6. *Other Causes:* The inequitable wage structure with the organisation and the inter-group conflict also lead to non-cooperation of the employees.

WHEN TO USE 'TIME' OR 'OUTPUT' BASIS AS AN INCENTIVE PLAN?

The employees may be paid on a 'time' basis under following circumstances:

1. When units of output are difficult to measure;
2. When employees have little control over the quantity of the output, such as on much-paced assembly lines;
3. When there is no clear direct relationship between the worker's effort and his output, such as when jobs are highly interrelated;
4. When delays in the work are frequent and beyond employee's control;
5. When quality is a primary consideration as with engineering and other professional personnel; and
6. When precise advance knowledge of unit labour costs is not required by competitive conditions.

On the other hand, payment on 'output' basis would be preferable if:

1. Units of output can be measured.
2. There is a clear relationship between employee effort and quantity of output.
3. The job is standardised, the work-flow is regular, and delays are few or consistent.
4. Quality is less important than quantity or, if quality is important, it is easily measured.
5. Competitive conditions require that unit labour costs be definitely known and fixed in advance of production.

REQUISITES OR GUIDELINES FOR EFFECTIVE INCENTIVE PLANS

Monetary incentive plans do motivate employees. Robert Opsahl and Marvin Dunnettee have concluded: "There is considerable evidence that installation of such plans usually results in greater output per man hour, lower unit cost, and higher wages in comparison with outcomes associated with the straight payment systems."

But these plans will not be effective unless a careful planning is done and the plans properly implemented. Several authors have suggested a list of requisites that monetary incentive plans should meet if the incentive method is to be attractive to the employee; and at the same time administratively sound. Some of the more important requisites/specific guidelines for developing effective incentive plans are:

1. *Insure that Efforts and Rewards are Directly Related:* The incentive plan should reward employees *in direct proportion* to their performance and increased productivity. Employees must also perceive that they can *actually do the tasks required.* This standard set has to be attainable; necessary tools, equipment, training etc. *should be timely provided* and the employee should have *adequate controls* over the work process.

2. *The Reward Must be Valuable to the Employees:* Increased *monetary earnings must have the potential to satisfy* the existing needs of the worker if the worker is to be attracted to them. In other words, the *monetary incentives offered must be relative to current or visible future needs.*

3. *The Reward Must be Clearly Identifiable:* Individual's or groups' contributions and efforts must be clearly identifiable, if rewards are to be given for specific performance.

4. *Methods and Procedures Must be Carefully Studied:* Since effective incentive plans are generally based on a meticulous work methods study, the services of an Industrial Engineer or other Methods' expert should be obtained who may, through careful observation and measurement, define fair performance standards on which the plan is to be based.

5. *The Plan Must be Understandable and Easily Calculable by the Employees:* The incentive plan should be easily understood by the workers so that they can easily calculate personal cost benefit for various levels of effort put by them.

6. *Effective Standard Must be Set:* The standards of which the plan is to be based should be effective, i.e., they should satisfy these conditions: (i) standards are viewed as *fair* by the subordinates; (ii) they should be set high, but reasonable (i.e., there should be about a 50-50 chance at reaching it); (iii) they should be specific; and (iv) they should be complete. "Do not just focus on quantity and disregard quality, unless that is the intention."

7. *Standards Must be Guaranteed:* The standard should be viewed as a contract with the employees. Once the plan is operational, great caution should be used before decreasing the size of the incentive in any way.

8. *An Hourly Base Rate Must be Guaranteed:* At least the plant employees should be guaranteed the base rate. Moreover, there should be *one base rate* for a job regardless of whether or not it is on 'incentives.'

9. *Clear Policies and Rules Must be Developed:* Specific policies and rules concerning how employees will be paid, and the rules for attaining the standard (and incentives) should be clear to both manager and employees.

10. *Rewards Must be Consistent with Government Regulations:* The incentives offered must govern regulations regarding compensation. The level of the reward and the frequency of it must meet minimum wage guidelines.

11. *Rewards Must be Granted Promptly:* The incentive plan should provide for rewards to follow quickly after the performance that justifies the reward.

12. *The Plan Must be within the Financial and Budgetary Capacity of the Organisation:* It must be compatible with the financial resources available.

13. *Additional Reinforcement Must be Provided:* The incentive plan can be more effective if high performance is encouraged and reinforced by management and subordinates. Reinforcement, in terms of points accumulated or incentives given, should be as frequent as possible preferably daily, or (at least) weekly.

14. *It Must Minimise Frictions between Workers:* Ideally, the plan encourages workers to support each other rather than to be non-co-operative.

15. *Employee Participation May be Useful for Increasing the Effectiveness of Incentive Plans:* In sum, it may be said that each incentive method must be weighed to determine its ability to meet the criteria stated above. Some piece-rate methods meet most of these requirements successfully. Others do not. Bonus paid after a period often fails to meet criterion 11 — in many cases there

is a time lag between the performance bonuses. The cause-effect relationship may become muddled and confused, and the desired reinforcement effect can be lost.

Profit sharing programmes also suffer weaknesses at times, particularly in meeting criteria 1, 3, 5 and 11. Often a worker sees little relationship between his own efforts and the rewards he receives. He also feels, that there are many things affecting profits that are outside his realm of control.

NON-MONETARY INCENTIVES

While monetary incentives often appear as important motivators, many factors unrelated to money can also serve as 'attention-getters' and 'encouragers of action.' "The classification of such non-financial incentives tends to a smorgasbord of desirable 'things' that are potentially at disposal of the organisation. The creation of such rewards is only limited by managers' ingenuity and ability to assess 'payoffs' that individuals within the organisation find desirable and which are within the managers' jurisdition." As the old proverb goes: "One man's food is another man's poison" certainly applies to rewards. What one employee views as "something I have always wanted", another finds superfluous. Therefore, care must be taken in providing the "right" reward for each person.

Following are some examples of non-monetary incentives:

The need-motives for affiliation, power and recognition in particular can be appealed to by such incentives. For example:

1. A person with strong need for affiliation may respond readily to *job assignments* that provide with opportunities to relate to socially attractive and satisfying individuals or groups.

2. *The opportunity to communicate with and relate to others is a* factor many workers emphasize and seek.

3. Persons who are very status conscious, can be motivated with the availability of a panelled office, a carpeted floor and wall paintings, a large desk and aristocratic furniture or a private bathroom, impressive job title, their own visiting cards, their own secretary and telephone, or a well located parking place with their name clearly painted underneath the "Reserved" sign — *all of which are status symbols.*

4. An employee with high-level desires for power may *respond easily to opportunity whereby he can gain leadership and administrative responsibilities.* He may be stimulated by *participative or free rein leadership in the decision-making process. The use of job enlargement* provide added incentive to some employees because they feel capable of controlling wider sets of activities than they previously performed.

5. Persons interested in enhancing their reputations and receiving recognition in the eyes of *others may respond to verbal 'praise' or two publicized 'awards.'*

6. Persons proud of their long service may be attracted by *awards recognising their seniority.*

7. Workers in safety minded organisation are often attracted by *competition on awards* for best safety performance records.

8. Individuals proud of their past accomplishments may feel recognised and rewarded if their superiors *extend opportunities for participation* on more complex and more important job assignments.

In short, management may look to many non-monetary incentives for effective motivation of those who are most need-conscious. In many cases, these non-monetary incentives might stimulate even more attention than the monetary ones.

CAFETERIA STYLE COMPENSATION

This type of compensation refers to compensation programmes that allow employees to choose what type and how much of each reward is desired during the coming year. This programme is based upon the assumption that every employee's needs are different and he has flexible arrangements that meet individual needs, and for that he is permitted to select that combination of rewards that is most attractive to him. Under this programme, the employee is told that his total compensation is made of say Rs. 2000/- and that he can choose a mix of salary life insurance, deferred compensation, and other benefits that suit his particular needs. Each of these options carries a price and the employee can select upto Rs. 2000/- of salary — those items that he feels best suit his personal needs.

The philosophy of this approach is that workers will be more highly motivated if they can select those rewards that have the greatest payoff for them. If the organisation's benefit programmes are such because they have been designed for the "average employee" in the organisation, by giving the employee the option to develop his own flexible compensation package, each package should be ideally tailored to the needs of the employee. In other words, *cafeteria compensation can make maintenance items motivators.*

While adopting the programme, the management should remember that the most of younger employees are more concerned with "take-home pay" than with "retirement benefits." On the other hand, older employees are "more concerned about retirement and pension programmes."

One of the major problems with compensation programme is that employees tend to think in the short rather than the long term. Hence, the management may be forced to pressure workers to make a decision that directly affects their"take-home" pay.

Robert Good has observed:

"If an employee selects the 'wrong' benefits package, the motivational purpose for the company is defeated. Moreover, even just a few bad choices can put the company at severe risk. It is a crushing demotivator throughout the company when the news spread that X was laid up for weeks without pay or that Y is destitute because Z choose cash over survivors' benefits. Even though the employees made these choices themselves, the company simply cannot allow such situation to come about. If a company undertakes the heavy and costly administration burden of installing a cafeteria compensation programme, it will be forced to step in and rectify 'inequities' even though the circumstances were created by the employees' own free choice."

For an effective and successful working this programme requires more information to be provided to employees by management so that they will have adequate data with which to make their decision. This might increase administrative cost. Further, each employees' benefits have to be carefully priced out and updated periodically.

This programme has not gained much success even where it has been introduced.

THE PROBLEM OF EQUITY

It is a general practice all over that employees make comparisons between themselves and their co-workers. They perceive what they get from a job situation (outputs) in relation to what they must put into it (inputs). They also compare their output-input ratio with the output-input ratio of their fellow-workers. If a person's ration and that of others are perceived to be equal a state of equity is said to exist. If they are unequal, inequity exists i.e., the individual considers himself as 'under rewarded' or 'over-rewarded' when an employee envisions an equity, he may choose any one or more of five alternatives: (i) distort either his own or other inputs or outputs; (ii) behave in the same way as to induce others to his own inputs or outputs; (iii) behave in some way as to change his own inputs or outputs; (iv) choose a different comparison referent; and (v) leave the job.

Equity approach recognises that individuals are concerned not only with the absolute amount of money they are paid for their efforts but also with the relationship of this amount to what others are paid. They make judgement as to the relationship between their inputs and outputs with those of the others. Based on one's inputs such as effort, education and competence — one compares outputs — such as salary levels, raises and other factors. When people perceive an imbalance in their input output ratio relative to others tension is created. It may result in lower productivity, more absenteeism, etc. This tension provides the basis for motivation, as one strives for what he perceives as equity and fairness. To get relief, the employee may decrease his inputs while holding his output constant, or increase his outputs while holding inputs constant — possibly resulting in fighting the system, increased absenteeism, or other undesirable behaviours.

EMPLOYEE BENEFITS AND SERVICES

INTRODUCTION

Management is concerned with attracting and keeping employees, whose performance meets at least minimum levels of acceptability; and at keeping 'absenteeism' and 'turnover' to tolerable levels. The provision of 'benefits' and services' can be and are important in maintaining the employees and reducing or keeping turnover and absenteeism low.

It is important to note that 'financial' incentives are paid to *specific employees* whose work is above standard. 'Employee benefits and services' on the other hand, are available to *all employees* based on their membership in the organisation. The purpose of such benefits and services is to retain people in the organisation and not to stimulate them to greater effort and higher performance. They foster loyalty and act as a security base for the worker.

TERMINOLOGY AND MEANING

These benefits are usually known as *"fringe benefits"* — as they are offered by the employer to the employee as a "Fringe." Different terms have been used for these benefits, such as *"Fringe Benefits," "Welfare Expenses," "Wage Supplements," "Subwages"* or *"Social Charges," "Perquisites other than Wages,"* or *"Transpecuniary Incentives."* The other terms used are: *"Extra Wages," "Hidden Payroll," "Non-Wage Labour Costs"* or *"Selected Supplementary Compensation Practices."*

It is difficult to define what a fringe benefit is, for there is no agreement among the experts on its precise meaning, significance or connotation. The chief area of disagreement is between "wages" and "fringe" on the one hand and between "fringes" and "company personnel services" on the other. There are also differences on whether the benefits which have been legally provided for should be included among the "fringes."

The *Glossary of Current Industrial Relations and Wage Terms* has defined fringe benefits as "Supplements to wages received by workers at a cost to employers. The term encompasses a number of benefits — paid vacation, pension, health insurance plans, etc. — which usually add up to something more than a "fringe," and is sometimes applied to a practice that may constitute a dubious benefit for workers."

The International Labour Organisation has defined "fringe benefits" as under:

"Wages are often augmented by special cash benefits, by the provision of medical and other services, or by payments in kind that form part of the wage for expenditure on the goods and services. In addition, workers commonly receive such benefits as holidays with pay, low-cost meals, low-rent housing, etc. Such additions to the wage proper are sometimes referred to as 'fringe benefits.' Benefits that have no relation to employment or wages should not be regarded as fringe benefits, even though they may constitute a significant part of the workers' total income. This is fairly obvious in the case of public parks, sanitation services, public and fire protection."

The United States Chamber of Commerce includes five categories of services and benefits under the term *fringe benefits.* These are:

(i) Legally required payments — old-age pension, survivor benefits, disability pension, health insurance, unemployment insurance, separation pay, and payments made under the Workmen's Compensation Act; (ii) Pension and group insurance; and welfare payments; (iii) Paid rest periods, waste-up time, lunch periods; (iv) Payment for time not worked — vacations and holidays, for example; and (v) Christmas bonus.

Belcher defines these benefits as "any wage cost not directly connected with the employees, productive effort, performance, service or sacrifice."

According to the Employers' Federation of India, "fringe benefits include payments for non-working time, profits and bonus, legally sanctioned payments on social security schemes, workmen's compensation, welfare cess, and the contributions made by employers under such voluntary schemes as cater for the post-retirement, medical, educational, cultural and recreational needs of workmen. The term also includes the monetary equivalent of free lighting, water, fuel, etc., which are provided for workers, and subsidised housing and related services."

Cockman views employee benefits as "those benefits which are supplied by an employer to or for the benefits as "those benefits which are supplied by an employer to or for the benefits of an employee, and which are not in the form of wages, salaries and time-rated payments."

We may define fringe benefit thus:

It is a benefit which Supplements the employees' ordinary wages, and which is of value to them and their families in so far as it materially increases their retirement benefit.

Fringe benefits help build up a good corporate image. Schemes like housing, educational institutional and recreational activities bring benefits to the society at large. An organisation with the introduction of Fringes seeks to enhance employee morale, remain cost effective, and introduce changes without much resistance.

SPECIAL FEATURES OF FRINGE BENEFITS

It will be noted that there is some difference between 'wages and fringe benefits.' *Firstly,* wages are directly related to the work done and are paid regularly — usually weekly, fortnightly or monthly. Fringe benefits, on the other hand, are those payments or benefits which a worker enjoys in addition to the wages or salary he receives.

Secondly, these benefits are not given to workers for any specific jobs they have performed but are offered to them to stimulate their interest in their work and to make their job more attractive and productive for them. They boost the earnings of the employees, and put extra spending money in their hands.

Thirdly, fringe benefit represents a labour cost for the employer, for it is an expenditure which he incurs on supplementing the average money rates due to his employees who have been engaged on the basis of time schedules. In the circumstances, everything which a company spends over and above "straight time pay" should be considered a fringe benefit. A labour cost is a "fringe" only when it is an avoidable factor; that is, when it can be replaced by money wages without determent to a worker's productive efficiency. Only the legal or union-imposed or voluntary non-wage costs, which can be computed into money wages, are considered to be fringes.

Fourthly, a fringe is never a direct reward geared to the output, effort or merit of an employee. It is offered, *not* on the basis of the hard work or long hours of work put in by an employee *but* on the basis of length of service, his sickness, sex, the hazards of life he encounters in the course of his work, etc. For example, maternity benefits are offered to female workers who have put in a prescribed period of service with a particular employer. Sometimes, the longer an employee's period of service, the larger the fringe benefits he enjoys. But wages are always fixed and paid regularly.

Fifthly, to be termed a 'fringe benefit,' a labour cost should be intended by an employer as a benefit desired by his staff. It is a fringe benefit when it is enjoyed by all the employees. For example, a fringe benefit — subsidising non-vegetarian meals taken in the factory canteen — is not a fringe benefit for vegetarian employees.

Sixthly, a fringe must constitute a positive cost to the employer and should be incurred to finance an employee benefit. If the benefit increases a worker's efficiency, it is not a fringe; but if it is given to supplement his wages, it is. For example, the expenditure incurred on providing better lighting arrangement with a view to increasing a worker's efficiency is not counted as expenditure incurred on fringe benefits, even though the workers may gain financially as a result of their increased efficiency flowing from the provision of better lighting facilities. Subsidised meals, however, definitely constitute a fringe benefit.

Though these benefits are known as fringes, they are not merely so but are a substantial part of the expenditure incurred on wage and salary administration. They are better known now as 'Benefits and services' rather than as 'Fringe Benefits.' But since the terms are also used interchangeably, they are synonymous.

The word 'Benefit' applies to those items for which a direct monetary value to the employee can be easily ascertained, as in the case of holiday pay, pension, medical insurance or separation pay. The word *'Services,'* on the other hand, refers to such items as athletics, company purchasing service, worker's medical examination, legal aid, housing, etc.

OBJECTIVES OF FRINGE BENEFIT AND SERVICE PROGRAMMES

An organisation designs and establishes a benefit-and-service programme to achieve the following ends:

(a) To keep in line with the prevailing practices of offering benefits and services which are given by similar concerns;

(b) To recruit and retain the best personnel;

(c) To provide for the needs of employees and protect them against certain hazards of life, particularly those which an individual cannot himself provide for;

(d) To increase and improve employee morale and create a helpful and positive attitude on the part of workers towards their employers;

(e) To make the organisation a dominant influence in the lives of its employees with a view to gaining their loyalty and co-operation, encouraging them to greater productive efforts;

(f) To improve and furnish the organisational image in the eyes of the public with a view to improving its market position and bringing about product acceptance by it;

(g) To recognise the official trade union's bargaining strength, for a strong trade union generally constrains an employer to adopt a sound benefits-and-services programme for his employees.

In other words, fringe benefits satisfy three goals, viz.:

1. Social Goal: Human resource is the most precious of all resources. In the words of the Philadelphia Charter, 1944, "Labour is not a commodity. It is entitled to a fair deal as an active participant in any programme of economic development and social reconstruction."

Article 43 of the Constitution of Indian provides:

"... All workers should be given a living wage, conditions of work ensuring decent standard of life and fuller enjoyment to ensure social and cultural opportunities."

The fringe benefits act as a social lever in helping conservation of this precious resource, by guarding against its unnatural erosion and providing the climate for its development in a working environment.

2. Human Relations Goal: The management, through motivation, tries to develop and maintain "human relations", i.e., "mutual interest, individual differences, motivation and human dignity." The management provides with an environment which will reasonably meet the economic, social and psychological needs of the employees so that their co-operation could be obtained and productivity of the organisation enhanced.

3. *Macro-Economic Goal:* For maintaining the growth and stability in the economy of a country, ideal utilization of the non-human and human resources is imperative. Fringe benefits do provide protection, during periods of contingencies of life, for training and development of the employees, and for good working conditions and assistance to supplement their main income, opportunities for social interaction through cultural recreational facilities, etc.

HISTORY AND GROWTH FACTORS

Belcher says that "A Fringe is a catchword attributed to the Regional Director of the War Labour Board (USA) during World War II. The idea caught on and is now widely used in spite of its limited value in describing the present practice." It sprang up as off-shoot of the industrial wage system. In the U.K., fringe benefits germinated as the byproduct of Industrial Revolution. In member countries of the I.L.O., the Philadelphia Declaration did influence the origin of these benefits. In India, the Directive Principles of State Policy enshrined in the Constitution and the subsequent Five Year Plan documents laid considerable emphasis on improvement of wages, social security benefits and other welfare measures, for it was rightly recognised in the words of Peter Drucker, "Larger part of the industrial growth is obtained not from more capital investment but from improvements in men. We get from men pretty much what we invest in them."

Many other factors also influenced the concept of 'fringe benefits.' For instance:

(i) Rising prices and cost of living has brought about incessant demand for provision of extra benefits to the employees.

(ii) Employers too have found that fringe benefits present attractive areas of negotiation when wage and salary increases are not feasible.

(iii) As organisations have developed more elaborate fringe benefits programmes for their employees, greater pressure has been placed upon competing organisations to match these benefits in order to attract and keep employees.

(iv) Recognition that fringe benefits are non-taxable rewards has been a major stimulus to their expansion.

(v) Rapid industrialisation, increasingly heavy urbanisation and the growth of a capitalistic economy have made it difficult for most employees to protect themselves against the adverse impact of these developments. Since it was workers who were responsible for production, it was held that employers should accept responsibility for meeting some of the needs of their employees. As a result, some benefits-and-services programmes were adopted by employers.

(vi) The growing volume of labour legislation, particularly social security legislation, made it imperative for employers to share equally with their employees the cost of old age, survivor and disability benefits.

(vii) The growth and strength of trade unions has substantially influenced the growth of company benefits and services.

(viii) Labour scarcity and competition for qualified personnel has led to the initiation, evolution and implementation of a number of a compensation plans.

(ix) The management has increasingly realised its responsibility towards its employees and has come to the conclusion that the benefits of increase in productivity resulting from increasing industrialisation should go, at least partly, to the employees who are responsible for it, so that they may be protected against the insecurity arising from unemployment, sickness, injury and old age. Company benefits-and-services programmes are among some of the mechanisms which managers use to supply this security.

A "tripartite" concept of individual protection has developed in recent years. *First,* every individual is expected to be at least partially responsible for his own present and future well-being. *Second,* industry is now expected to protect its workers from the hazards of life. *Finally,* the government is involved in supporting and financing worker assistance programmes. The contribution of these three parties varies in accordance with the nature and purpose of the various employee benefits-and-services programmes.

A number of factors influence the decision to set up a particular employee benefits-and-services programme. According to Nielson, the criteria governing such a programme are:

(a) Cost;

(b) The ability to pay;

(c) The needs of the employees and their contribution in improving productivity;

(d) The bargaining strength of the trade union;

(e) Tax considerations;

(f) Public relations;

(g) Social responsibility; and

(h) The reactions of the employees.

The following table summarises the factors, key forces and their potential impact on benefits:

COVERAGE OF BENEFITS

It has been recognised that certain benefits must be supplied by the organisation for its employees, regardless of whether it wants to or not. With few exceptions, the hiring of any employee requires the organisation to pay social security premiums, workmens' compensation, etc. Similarly, the payment of these costs by the organisation provides the employee with financial protection at retirement, termination, or as a result of injury, and it also provides to the workers' dependants in case of the employees' death.

The National Association of Manufacturers has indicated the following classification of fringe benefits:

(a) Premium Payments for the period of time a worker has worked; for example, payment on daily or weekly basis, holidays, overtime pay, shift differentials, the cost of living bonus, bonus in lieu of vacation.

(b) Payment for special duties, such as working on grievance redressal procedures and labour contract negotiations.

(c) Payment for health and security benefits : These include retirement plans, social security payments, savings plans, profit-sharing plans, group life insurance, medical, surgical and hospital insurance, accident and sickness insurance, supplemental employment benefits, payments under the Workmen's Compensation Act, disability insurance, old age and survivor insurance, and unemployment compensation.

(d) Payment for time not worked, which includes payment for sick leave and for time during which an employee is under medical care, payment for holidays, vacations, witness time, voting time, excused absence, lunch periods, rest periods, work-up time, reporting pay, severance pay, payment for call-all-time, call-back time, dressing time, portal-to-portal time and wet-time.

(e) Payment for employee services, including cafeteria subsidies, union credit, house financing, parking space operations, etc.

(f) Other expenditure, such as that incurred on making Christmas gifts or offering Christmas bonus, on educational reimbursements, employee uniforms, work clothes, safety equipment or allowance, laundry allowance, supper money or meal allowance.

The United States Chamber or Commerce classifies benefit items into *five categories.* These are:

(a) Payments that have to be made under any specific legislation;

(b) Pensions and such other payments as have been agreed upon;

(c) Paid rest period, lunch periods, wash-up time, travel time, time taken to change clothing, and get-ready time;

(d) Payments for time during which an employee has not put in any work at all; and

(e) Other items, including profit-sharing payments, bonus, etc.

Cockman, however, has made a two-fold classification of fringe benefits:

(i) Those which are offered on the basis of status — car, entertainment facilities, holiday, foreign travel, telephone, security — insurance and medical benefits, children's educational facilities; and work benefits — office accommodation, secretarial services, management training, company scholarships; and

(ii) Those which are key benefits, that is, share schemes, profit sharing, retirement benefits, counselling services, and house purchase facilities.

On the basis of their identification, however, benefits may be classified as under:

(a) Employee Security Payments: These include:

(i) Employer's contribution stipulated in legal enactments such as: old age, pension, survivor, disability, health and unemployment insurance;

(ii) Payments under the Workmen's Compensation Act;

(iii) Supplemental unemployment benefits;

(iv) Accident insurance;

(v) Pensions, Provident Fund, Gratuity Payments;

(vi) Contributions to saving plans and health and welfare funds.

(b) Payment for Time Not Worked: Under these are included call-back and call-in pay; clean-up time; health-in-the-family leave; family allowance; holiday pay; lay-off pay; medical time; paid lunch periods; portal-to-portal time; pay for religious holidays; reporting pay; pay for rest periods; severance pay; paid sick leave; payment for time spent on collective bargaining and on the redressal of grievances; vacation pay; pay for the time spent in offering evidence in a court of a law or other statutory bodies; and payment for the time spent on casting one's vote at election time.

Rest Period: Among office jobs and those jobs requiring heavy exertion, high repetition, or diligent concentration, certain "breaks" — popularly known as a *'Rest period'* or a *'Coffee break'* — are allowed during the day to allow the worker to rest. The idea is to allow the worker some mental and physical diversion from his job.

Holidays: Certain days in the year are stipulated as paid holidays. In Western Countries like USA, USSR and U.K., Christmas, New Years' Thanksgiving, Labour day, are particularly included, on which the employees are paid and they do not have to work. In India, Independence Day, Republic Day, Gandhi Jayanti, Deepavali, Dashara, Holi, Id, Christmas, Gurunanak Jayanti, Mahaveer Jayanti are gazetted holidays.

Vacations: Paid vacations vary from 15 days to 1 month in a year. These are given to the employee after he has put in a specific period of time. The rationale behind the paid vacation is to provide a break in which the employee can refresh himself.

Sick Leave: provides an employee pay when he is out of work due to illness. Full pay for a specified number of "permissible" sick days are granted to the employees.

Severance Pay: This provides a one-time payment when an employee is terminated. This is done on humanitarian ground.

Leave of Absence: This covers leave of absence for which pay is provided. *Educational leave* is given to managers or management trainees during the training period.

The Government of India has enacted the Employees' Provident Fund Act and the Scheme under the Act requiring employer to contribute certain percentage of employee's wages to the government constituted Provident Fund Scheme. Under this scheme the employee can also contribute equal percentage of his salary to the Provident Fund. The funds of this collection are paid back to the employee with interest on his retirement or earlier after stipulated years of service in the organisation.

Thus, on retirement an accumulated lump sum is available to the employees in addition to certain pension. Pension are a monthly payment made to the retired employee and after his death to his legal heirs like wife which the scheme provides.

The Government of India has also enacted a law known as the Payment of Gratuity Act under which the employee who retires after stipulated age or after rendering service for a stipulated period with the employer is eligible to get a one time Payment known as Gratuity. The amount of gratuity payable is linked to the number of years of service and his last drawn salary or wages.

Thus providing these two legally compulsory retirement benefits to certain category of employees is a cost to the employer while fixing wages or salary payable to the employee.

Pension Programmes: A pension represents a fixed payment, made regularly to a former employee or his surviving dependants, provided an employee has fulfilled specific conditions of employment for a specific length of time.

Insurance: Which may be life, health and accident. It may be for individual or the group.

(c) Bonus and Awards: These consist of such financial amenities and advantages as holiday, over-time and shift premiums; attendance bonus; Diwali bonus; bonus for good quality workmanship; safety awards; profit-sharing bonus and service bonus; suggestion awards; waste elimination bonus; and year-end bonus.

EMPLOYEE SERVICES

In addition to the above fringe benefits, organisations also provide a wealth of services that employees find desirable. These services are usually provided by the organisation at no cost to the employee or at a significant reduction from what might have to be paid without the organisation's support.

These services are provided at the discretion of the management and are generally of some concern to trade unions when they engage in collective bargaining with the employees. These services include:

(i) Services related to the type of work performed, including subsidies for the purchase and upkeep of work clothing and uniforms and of the various types of tools used by a worker in the course of his work;

(ii) Eating facilities, which include the provision of company restaurants, cafeterias, canteens, lunchrooms, vending machines, and fully or partially subsidised food;

(iii) Transportation facilities, including parking lots and bus services;

(iv) Child care facilities, comprising nurseries and day care centres for children;

(v) Housing services, including company-owned housing projects and subsidised housing;

(vi) Financial and legal services, including sponsoring of loan funds, credit unions, income-tax service, legal aid, saving plans, and group insurance plans;

(vii) Purchasing services, such as company-operated stores and discounts on company products and services;

(viii) Recreational, social and cultural programmes, including athletics, beauty parlours, social clubs, recreational areas, orchestras, entertainment programmes, parties, picnics, libraries and reading rooms;

(ix) Educational services, which include sponsorship for off duty courses, educational leave, tuition fee refunds, and scholarships for employees and their children;

(x) Medical services, including plant infirmaries, clinics and hospitals, counselling services and referrals to community social services;

(xi) Outplacement services, which include contacts with other employers in the area, help in writing up resumes, and secretarial assistance.

(xii) Flexitime: The workers are permitted to build up their 'flexible work day' around a core of mid-day hours (such as 11.00 to 2.00). It is called 'flexitime' because the workers themselves determine their own starting and stopping time. For example, they may opt to work from 7.00 to 3.00 or 11.00 to 7.00.

There are certain *special features* of this programme.

(1) Since less time is lost due to tardiness, the ratio of man-hours worked to man-hours paid increases. (2) Absenteeism is reduced and sick-leave cut down. (3) The hours actually worked seems to be more productive, and there is less slowing down toward the end of the work day. (4) It reduces the tedium associated with the timing of the employees' work and democratizes the work. (5) The distinction between the management and professional workers is reduced and more authority is delegated by supervisors.

However, there are certain *drawbacks:* (i) flexitime is complicated to administer and may be impossible to implement where large group of workers must work independently. (ii) It requires the use of time-clocks or other time records, which might irritate the workers.

(xiii) Cafeteria Services: One of the recent developments in this field has been the formulation of the cafeterial compensation concept or what is known as 'smorgasbord.' Depending on their age, their educational and income levels, their life styles and other forms of preference, different categories of employees need and demand different combinations of benefits and services.[11]

It may be pointed out here that no company provides all these benefits and services. Those that are provided are determined by the needs of employees and the preferences of a company. Among the benefits and services which are most commonly offered are life insurance, health insurance, pension, unemployment compensation, protective clothing and equipment, rest periods and vacations. Some benefits, such as holidays, vacation and pension, enable employees to meet their self-actualisation needs; they make it possible for them to be away from their job, participate in other activities and share in other experiences even while they continue to receive their wages or salaries. These benefits, moreover, satisfy one's need for esteem in that they are often looked upon as indicators of one's personal worth.

For example, a typical young man generally desires to have direct wages and educational assistance, while an older employee often opts for pension and health insurance services.[12] The cafeterial compensation concept generally involves the idea that each employee ought to design and tailor his own indirect compensation programme by personally picking and choosing the benefits and services he would desire to have from among the many such benefits and services provided by his company. Choice and decision generally depend upon the discretion of each individual employee and not on a management fiat or a centralised collective bargaining agreement.

FRINGE BENEFITS IN INDIA

When the Employers' Federation of India conducted a study of fringe benefits in this country, it was revealed that, in 1960,981 companies, which were included in the survey, paid a little over Rs. 2,148.3 million in wages and fringe benefits, and that the latter was about 21.3 per cent of their total wage bill in that year. The fringe benefits were high in the mining (24.84 per cent of the wage bill) and plantations industries (24.3 per cent of the wage bill), and were comparatively low in the manufacturing sector (19.99 per cent of the wage bill).

In each of these three sectors, however, variations were considerable. In the mining industry, the percentage of fringe benefits varied from 24.5 to 27.88, while in the manufacturing sector it varied between 13.42 and 32.11, followed by the cigarette industry (31.42) and aluminium, brass and copper industries (30.56). A break-up of fringe benefits by types revealed that, of the total amount paid on fringe benefits, that which was paid for the time not worked and for profits and bonus was the highest, accounting for a little more than 9 per cent of the total wage bill. Payments which had to be made under legislative enactments were between 6.1 per cent and 7.5 per cent of the total, while voluntary welfare schemes accounted for 5.36 per cent of the wage bill. In the plantation industry, however, these welfare schemes formed 9.4 per cent of the wage bill, while in the other two (mining and manufacturing industries), they respectively accounted for 4.12 per cent and 3.4 per cent of the total wage bill.

A considerable proportion of fringe benefits was in the shape of monetary bonus and constituted about 5 per cent of the wage bill. The bonus was of various kinds — profits bonus, attendance bonus, service bonus, gratuity payments, etc. The quantum of the bonus varied from sector to sector.

Payments for Time Not Worked: These payments were fairly substantial in the manufacturing industry (5.35 per cent), the mining industry (4.81 per cent) and plantations (3.24 per cent). In the manufacturing sector, the percentage of expenditure on this item varied between 3.06 and 10.42. Industries which spent a relatively larger sum on this item were cigarette manufacturing and distributing (10.42 per cent), petroleum refining and selling (7.15 per cent), chemicals and allied industries (7.11 per cent) and shipbuilding (6.60 per cent).

Statutory Fringe Benefits: These benefits are generally social security, and include gratuity and pension payments, the employer's contribution to the employees' provident fund account and health insurance scheme.

The employers' contribution to statutory provident fund constitutes by far the largest item of expenditure, accounting for 4.23 per cent of the total wage bill in the plantations, mining and manufacturing industries put together. The expenditure on employees' state insurance contributions by the manufacturing industries was 0.36 per cent, while that on gratuity account was 0.59 per cent.

The "other expenditure" incurred under statutory regulations and tribunal awards was on compensation paid to workers, welfare cess payments in the coal mining industry and on the supply of protective clothing in the plantations industry. The expenditure on maternity clothing in the manufacturing and mining industries.

Voluntary Benefits: Retirement benefits, medical care, compensation for injuries and disablement, subsidised food and housing, educational and cultural facilities, payment on life insurance premia, the maintenance of canteens, cafeterias, assistance to co-operative societies — these are some of the benefits accounted for 9.40 per cent of the total wage bill in the plantations industry against 3.74 per cent and 4.12 per cent in the mining and manufacturing industries respectively. The social security benefits voluntarily provided by companies include provident fund, gratuity and pension.

The medical assistance schemes voluntarily provided by employers were the largest single item of expenditure, and accounted for 1.80 per cent of the total expenditure of 5.36 per cent voluntarily incurred by them. The plantations industry spent 4.78 per cent of its total wage bill on this particular voluntary service against only 0.84 per cent spent by the manufacturing industries. The latter's expenditure on canteens, however, was about 0.70 per cent of its total wage bill against that of 0.07 per cent spent by the mining industries.

In the manufacturing industries, nearly two-thirds of the benefits were in the form of profit and bonus, of payments for time not worked and of contributions by employers to social security benefits. In the plantations and mining industries, however, this percentage was 57 and slightly more than 50 respectively.

Apart from the general fringe benefits for employees, there was a wide range of other benefits as well. Some of these benefits are: Rifle allowance to watchmen, cycle allowance to peons, free driving licences for drivers, compensation for a waiting period of three days, free quarters, water and electricity; free uniforms to certain categories of employees, conveyance allowance when no transport is provided by the company, travel concessions, assistance to buy spectacles, provision of snacks during night shifts, shoe allowance of 20 paise and an allowance of 37 paise per hour if a worker attends education classes; sale of company products at concessional rates, benevolent fund assistance if a worker is struck down by tuberculosis or cancer, scholarships to employees' children; employees' tours of government projects, study leave, gift of a wrist watch after a meritorious service of ten years, presents to employees on the occasion of their marriage, co-operative bank facilities, festival allowance, free libraries and facilities for inpatient hospital accommodations.

BENEFIT PROGRAMMES FOR MANAGEMENT

Special considerations and policies apply to the benefit programmes for the management, for which a different benefit structure is provided because of the fact that many legal considerations do not operate in their case. For example, management personnel do not receive overtime allowance or payment; nor are they governed by trade union considerations or agreements. Managers generally are not entitled to, nor do they expect, many of the benefits and services to which employees in general are entitled. However, management personnel are generally required to contribute in part to their insurance, gratuity, pension and provident fund. Tax exemptions become more important and meaningful for them as they advance in the management hierarchy.

The personnel department is generally responsible for the coordination of the plans for the administration of these benefits and services. For this purpose, it seeks the advice of the various departments, calls for their suggestions and anticipates the emergence of possible problems. The final approval of the plans formulated for the management personnel, however, is the preogative of the top authority of an organisation.

PROBLEMS RAISED BY BENEFIT PROGRAMMES

Many problems arise when these programmes are adopted and administered. These are:

(i) Charge of Paternalism: When too many benefits and services are offered to employees, a feeling develops that employers are playing the role of parents and

the workers are looked upon as their children. Moreover, the latter sometimes develop the feeling that these benefits and services are their "right" — which is not really so.

(ii) Excessive Expenditure: The administration of these benefits and services is a fairly costly affair, involving large outlays of direct and indirect financial expenditure, and often involves a great deal of paper work.

(iii) Fads Become Fashionable: With the introduction of these benefits and services in one company, other concerns vie with one another to introduce them as well. Credit unions and severance pay are examples of benefits which were once considered to be novel but are now commonplace in industry.

(iv) Maintenance of the Least Productive Workers: With an increase in benefits and services, employees, particularly when they are not very productive, tend to stick to their jobs, and are not interested in changing them.

(v) Neglect of Other Personnel Functions: When a management becomes more concerned about the provision and administration of benefits and services, it often pays very little attention to other aspects of personnel programmes. Over-emphasis on these benefits and services may often develop a concern among the employees for their future security rather than for their present productivity.

The relationship between a company's benefits-and-services programmes and employee motivation for increased production is somewhat weak.

ADMINISTRATION OF BENEFITS AND SERVICES

Organisations fumble while administering employee benefits and services. Organisations have seldom established objectives, systematic plans and standards to determine the viability of the programmes. The main problem is the lack of employee participation. Managers, too, take little interest in the benefits programme and trade unions are almost hostile to the schemes. Managers are not even aware of the organisation's policy towards benefits and their contribution to the quality of corporate life. Trade unions entertain a feeling of alleviation as the benefits are likely to erode their base. These problems can be avoided if steps are taken:

(i) to establish benefit objectives;

(ii) to assess environmental factors;

(iii) to assess competitiveness;

(iv) to communicate benefit information;

(v) to control benefit costs and evaluation.

SUMMARY

It may be noted that in India the term "Wage" is applied in relation to blue collar (factory workers) and "Salary" in relation to white collar workers who are engaged in office doing non-manual type of jobs.

Wage determination is an important factor in employment contracts of wages and salary and are fixed taking into consideration various aspects which include, region, type of industry, size of industry, comparable levels in similar industry, government rules in relation to minimum wages, variable allowances linked to cost of living index in inflation related measures, levels of skill, responsibility etc.

In addition to wages, salaries, employer also makes available other monetary benefits like incentive bonus, profit sharing bonus, retiring benefits, pension medical treatment, holiday allowances. Besides these there are non-monetary benefits like, canteen, holiday homes, transport, recreation, counselling.

Financial incentives are usually paid to specific employees whose work is above standards. Employee benefits however are available to all employees in an organisation.

Retirement benefits like provident fund, gratuity, pension are all almost legally available to certain class of employees. The employer is finally concerned with over-all costs on account of employees.

❑ ❑ ❑

11

Human Resource Management

Human Resource Management is a management function involving procurement of suitable human resources, train and develop their competencies, motivate them, reward them effectively and create in them an urge to be part of the management team whose aim should be render, dedicated, committed service for the success and growth of the organisation.

The term human resources spells the total sum of all the components (like skill, creative abilities) possessed by all employees and other persons (like self employed, employees, owners etc.) who contribute their services to attain the organisational objectives and goals. Human resources include human values, ethos. The term Human Resource Management is much more broarder compared to the term personnel management either at the component's level or in coverage at organisation level. The comparison Personnel *vs* Human Resource Management is presented in Fig. 11.1 below.

Personnel Management	*Human Resource Management*
(1) Personnel Management is management of people	(1) HRM is management of employees' skills, knowledge, abilities, talents, aptitude, creative abilities.
(2) Personnel Management views man as economic person	(2) HRM views man not only as economic person but looks at him as a full person — taking social and psychological factors in views.
(3) Employee is treated as cost centre and hence controls cost of "Personnel" in the organisation.	(3) Employees are treated as profit centre and hence they invest in Human Resources Development — and future accrue from this resource.
(4) Employee is viewed as a tool or equipment which can the purchased and used.	(4) Employee is treated as a resource.
(5) Employees are utilised for organisational benefit.	(5) Employees are utilised for mutual benefit — both for organisation and employees' own.

Fig. 11.1

DEFINITION, SCOPE AND OBJECTIVES OF HUMAN RESOURCE MANAGEMENT

(a) Definition: Human Resource Management is concerned with the people who work in the organisation to achieve the objectives of the organisation. It concerns with acquisition of appropriate human resources, developing their skills and competencies, motivating them for best performance and ensuring their continued commitment to the organisation to achieve organisational objectives. This definition applies to all types of organisations, e.g., industry, business, government, education, health or social welfare of the people.

Human Resources Management refers to activities and functions designed and implemented to maximise organisational as well as employees effectiveness.

(b) Scope: The scope of Human Resource Management is vast. All major activities in the working life of the employee from the time of his entry into the organisation until he leaves, retires come under the purview of human resource management.

The most important activities undertaken are (1) Planning, job design, job analysis, procurement, recruitment, selection, induction, placement, training and development (2) Compensation, rewards, benefits, retiral benefits, medical and, health care (3) Motivation - Motivational aids, bonus, incentives, profit sharing non-monetary benefits are esteem satisfaction, career development, growth, decision making, delegation of authority and power, promotion, etc. (4) Employee Relations - Grievance handling, participation, collective bargaining and other aspects of cordial relations conducive to mutual understanding and trust. (5) Employee evaluation and performance improvement, Human Resource, Audit; and Human Resource Accounting.

(c) Objectives : The objectives of human Resource Management are:

(i) To provide, create, utilise and motivate employees to accomplish organisational goals.

(ii) To secure integration of individuals and groups in securing organisational effectiveness.

(iii) To create opportunities, to provide facilities, necessary motivation to individuals and groups for their growth with the growth of the organisation by training and development compensation.

(iv) To provide attractive, equitable, incentives, rewards, benefits, social security measures, to ensure retention of competent employees.

(v) To maintain high morale, encourage value system and create environment of trust, mutuality of interests.

(vi) To provide opportunities for communication expression, participation, appreciation, recognition and provide fair efficient leadership.

(vii) To create a sense and feeling of belongingness team spirit and encourage suggestions from employees.

(viii) To ensure that, there is no threat of unemployment, inequalities, adopting a policy recognising merit and employee contribution, and conditions for stability of employment.

FUNCTIONS OF HUMAN RESOURCES DEPARTMENT

In order to realise the objectives stated above HRM must perform certain functions. The scope and objectives stated above are indicative of functions, a manager in charge of human resources department must perform. The Fig. 11.2 below gives the objectives and the functions which are to be performed to achieve those objectives.

HRM Objectives	*Functions to be Performed*
(1) Social (Towards society)	(1) Legal compliance
	(2) Benefits
	(3) Union Management relations
(2) Organisational Objectives	(1) Human Resource Planning
	(2) Selections Training and Development
	(3) Employee Relations
	(4) Employee Evaluation Assestment, Appraisal
(3) Functional objectives	(1) Appraisal
	(2) Placement
(4) Personal objectives (towards employees)	(1) Training & Development
	(2) Appraisal
	(3) Assesment/Placement
	(4) Compensation

Fig. 11.2

Management of human resources basically aims at contributing human efforts through personnel employed in the organisation towards achieving the objectives of the organisation, and these should come out willingly with dedication and high degree of morale amongst the employees. HRM should be viewed as part of strategic managerial function in the development of business policy in which it plays both a determining and contributory role. HRM represents a wider conception of the employment relationship to incorporate an enabling and development role for the individual employee. HRM is essentially a strategically driven activity which is not only a major contributor to that process but is a determinative part of it. HRM systems are proactive, and are anticipated to bring about a cultural change in the organisation. It seeks power equalisation for trust and collaboration. It opens channels of communication to build trust and commitment. Its policies are goal oriented with participative style.

The following Fig. 11.3 below briefly enunciates the functions of HRM.

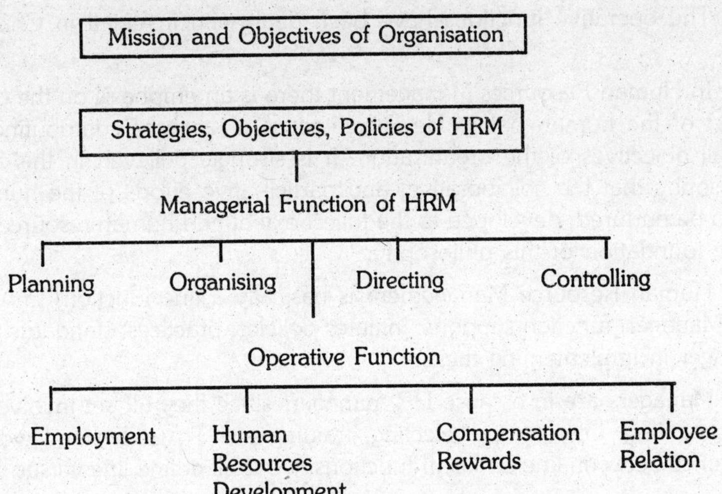

The operative functions can be further subdivided as follows:

Fig. 11.3

OPERATIVE FUNCTIONS OF HRM

Employment	Human Resources Development	Compensation Rewards	Employee Relations
		Remuneration Job	Communication Motivation
Organisational Design	Training & Development	Evaluation Salary & benefits	Morale Job Satisfaction
Job Design	Performance Appraisal	Administration Incentives	Grievances Redrassal
Job Analysis	Performance Improvement	Rewards	Discipline Maintenance
Human Resources Planning Recruitment Selection Induction Placement	Career Planning Management Development		Quality of work life Participation Quality circles.
	Organisation Development Organisation Change		

Fig. 11.4

The operative functions have been dealt with in detail in Chapter 2 of this book.

In Human Resources Management there is an emphasis on the developmental aspect of the human being. He is treated as a resource contributing towards the overall objectives of the organisation. It is strongly believed in this approach and philosophy that the collaborative, and participative efforts of the human resources are to be nurtured, developed to the fullest extent and human resource development is the foundation of this philosophy.

Human Resource Management is basically a line function, to which the staff (HR Manager) function supports, initiates policies, practices, standards and helps line manager in implementing these.

Managers are in a sense HR managers since they all get involved in activities like securiting, interviewing, electing, training etc. To understand work clearly the difference between line and staff functions, we shall define line versus staff authority.

Authority is the right to make decisions, to direct the work of others and to give orders.

Line Managers are authorised to direct the work of subordinates. There is always one boss. Line managers are in charge of accomplishing the organisation's basic goals. (Production and sales managers are line managers generally). Staff managers on the other hand are authorised to assist and advise line managers in accomplishing these basic goals. HR managers are generally staff managers.

LINE MANAGER'S HR MANAGEMENT RESPONSIBILITIES

A Line supervisor's responsibilities for effective human resource management are:

1. Placing right person on the right job.
2. Orientation — starting a new employee on the job.
3. Training employees for jobs that are new to them and improving their performance.
4. Getting cooperation and developing cordial working relationship.
5. Interpreting the company's Policy and Practices.
6. Controlling labour costs.
7. Developing abilities of each employee.
8. Maintaining discipline and morale of employees.

In the figure 11.4 below a division of selected activities illustrating division of HR responsibility between line and staff are shown:

Departmental Supervision Activities	*HR Specialists (Staff) Activities*
1. *Recruitment Section:* Assist in job analysis by listing specific duties and responsibilities of the job. Explain to HR Manager future needs and kinds of people required. Interview candidates and work out final decision in selection.	Write job description, job specification from input by line supervisor. Develop personnel plans indicating promotable employees. Develop promotable employees. Develop sources of qualified applicants and help in securiting qualified employees, by conducting interviews.
2. *Training and Development :* Orient new employees, give them necessary training on the job. Evaluate suitable employees from the department for developmental programs, provide leadership and build effective teams. Apprise employees with the help of Appraisal forms. Assess the future potential of employees and assist and advise them on career profession.	*Prepare training material:* Advise CEO regarding developmental plans for Managers based on present and future needs of the organisation. Work as resource person for providing information an how to commerce and operate programs on quality improvement, team building efforts. Develop performance appraisal tools and maintain records of appraisal.
3. *Wages, salaries, compensation:* Assist HR by providing information regarding the nature and relative worth of each job to serve as basis for wage fixation for different jobs. Decide standards of work to be performed and suggest nature of incentive payments to different categories of employees.	Conduct job evaluation procedures, conduct salary surveys to know how other companies are paying for similar jobs. Serve as resource in advising line management regarding financial incentives. Advise regarding fringe benefits that can be introduced in the company. Develop the services and benefits company can offer to the employees including, medical care, recreational activities, food services and others.
4. *Labour Relations:* Establish the day-to-day climate for mutual trust, respect needed to maintain healthy industrial relations. Ensure that grievance procedure functions. Work with HR in union negotiations on contract terms, discipline and benefits and services.	Analyse causes of labour discontent if any. Train Line Managers on interprertation of contract terms, rules of discipline grievance procedure, Train Line managers in negotations with unions. Anticipate problems that may arise and take preventive actions. Maintain cordial relations with union representatives.
5. Employee security safety, welfare, discipline, education. Keep lines of communciation open between employees and managers to maintain cordial relations. Take care of safety, health of employees. Ensure fair treatment when it relates to discipline, discharge, dismissal and job security. Ensure all amenities under the welfare scheme and maintain properly by assisting HR and educating employees under his control.	Advise Line Manager on Lines of communication and how to maintain these in working order. Encourage upward and downward communciation through various established channels. Develop norms for fair treatment, keep vigil on grievance procedure, ensure safety, health measures. Ensure welfare and amenities measures are in working order and properly maintained. Ensure sufficient means are maintained for safety, accidents, health hazards. Be fair and impartial in disciplinary actions and conflict resolution.

Fig. 11.4

THE CHANGING ENVIRONMENT OF HUMAN RESOURCE MANAGEMENT — TECHNOLOGICAL TRENDS, EFFECT OF GLOBALISATION, NEW TRENDS IN GETTING WORK DONE

Changes in Environment: The human resource management requires new approach due to changes in the Industry, Business Methods, Corporate Policy, Technological impact and trends in Globalisation. This will necessitate the HR manager to understand the winds of change and he will have to orient himself to face new challenges that are coming up due to changes in nature of jobs and work.

Technological Trends: Due to rapid change in technology employment levels will be affected. Applicants for job will have to learn new methods of work and these will be a tremendous demand for knowledge worker than for manual or blue collar works. Manufacturing methods have already undergone vast changes and companies depend on venders, contracts to supply semifinished parts and sometimes finished parts. The another company does only assembly work. Some companies are becoming trading companies with global market. A keen competition makes it necessary for organisation to cut costs in all directions including human resources, Telecommunication, computer aided design, computer aided manufacturing (CAD/CAM) systems are repiacing older method of work. Globalization refers to the tendency of organisations to extend their sales and manufacturing to new markets abroad and for their business expansion everywhere. There is a tremendous rise in Export/Import Trade all over the world. Companies are printing, manufacturing plants where they find it most advantageous. This globalisation of markets and manufacturing has increased international competition. This in turn increases or reduces employment opportunities of employment in the another country or the foreign country. There has been trend in employing qualified foreign nationals due to advantages of costs, taxes and duties. Managing these changes will be a major challenge for HR managers.

Trends in the Nature of Work: The above changes in environment are producing change in the nature of jobs and work. Information Technology, Communication means and new equipment, personal computers, have permitted companies to relocate their operations to locations with lower wages. There is trend to utilise part time workers. The most notable trend is to the service jobs, to knowledge work and stress on human capital. An enormous shift from manufacturing jobs to service jobs is taking place in Western Europe and North America. In USA, itself, today over two-thirds of the work force is employed in producing and delivering services not products. Peter Drucker predicts "the typical business with the knowledge base, an organisation composed largely of specialists who direct and discipline their own performance through organised feedback from colleagues, customers and headquarters." For this reason he calls the modern organisation an information based organisation. The distinguishing characteristic of companies today and tommrow say some experts, is the growing emphasis on Roman capital — the knowledge, education, trainning, skills and expertise of companies workers at the expense of physical capital like equipment, machinery and the physical plant.

These changes and trends have brought in new modes of organising and manufacturing — the traditional, pyramid shaped organisation is giving way to new organisational forms. These include organising stresses, cross functional teams and increasing interdepartmental communication. There in deemphasis on "Sticking to the chain of command" to get decisions. The following trends are entering the business organisations:

(i) Employees are being empowered to make more and more decisions.

(ii) Flatter organisations are emerging in preference to the pyramid shaped organisations.

(iii) Work in factories, offices is being increasingly organised around teams and processes, rather than specialised functions. The multi-function teams will control its own budget and quality of work.

(iv) The base of power are changing in the new organisation, and expert says, position, title and authority are no longer adequate tools for managers to rely on to get their jobs done.

Instead, now the success depends upon tapping the new sources of good ideas, finding out whose collaboration is required to act on those ideas and working with both to produce those results. The new managerial work implies very different ways of obtaining and using power.

(v) Managers today must build commitment — building adoptative, customer responsive organisation means eliciting employees. Commitment and self control is more important than it has been earlier.

(vi) Managers will not manage: Yesterday's managers had derived authority to command and control subordinates from the workers or the CEO. Today, most managers realise that reliance on formal authority is a thing of the post. Peter Drucker says that managers have to learn to manage situations where they do not have command authority, where you are neither controlled or controlling.

The above changes and trends which are taking place at a fast speed, should make the HR manager aware of his new role. This involves his participation in evolving strategic plans and implementing them. Strategic human resource management means linking of HRM with strategic goals and objectives in order to improve business performance and develop organisational culture that cope with faster innovation and flexibility. HR should work as a strategic particular with top management to formulate the company's strategy and execute it formulating a company's overall strategic plan which requires identifying, analysing and balancing two sets of forces — the company's external opportunities and threats on one hand and its internal strengths and weaknesses on the other. HR management can play a role in environmental scanning — i.e., identifiying and analysing external opprotunities and threats that may be crucial to the company's success.

The strengths and weakenesses of a company's human resources can have a determining effect on the viability of a firm's strategic options and hence the HR Manager can play important role in deciding this.

HR today is heavily involved in the execution of many organisation's downsizing and restructuring strategies.

The HR managers have to gear up themselves to these new trends and make themselves useful in implementing the changing plans of the company.

A CHALLENGING TASK

The Personnel (HRM) Manager plays a crucial role in understanding the changing needs of the organisation and society. His task is to attain objective in relation to the employee, organisation and society with the resources available within the organisation. For this he needs to have a good knowledge of such disciplines as Economics, Commerce, Management, Sociology, Psychology, Engineering, Technology and Law. These disciplines and Human Resources Management interact mutually.

❑ ❑ ❑

12

Participative Management

CONCEPT

Within the last three decades in the realm of human resource management, the technique of the workers' participation in management has been regarded as a powerful behavioural tool for managing the industrial relations system. This widely debated concept has evolved from the purely ideological and imaginative plank to an organisational reality. But the form and connotation* of the term varies with the socio-economic goals of a particular country.

For example, earlier in those countries where all or most of the means of production were under public ownership, the term is used in quite a different sense as against those countries where the means of production are in private hands. Again, in a "centrally planned economy," the nature and form of industrial democracy is not the same as in a market economy. It means different things to different people; and most international discussions on the subject suffer from the fact that those who use the term are often thinking of one particular form of workers' participation in management. For management, "It is joint consultation prior to decision-making."The management experts and executives look upon it as "a tool for improving the over-all performance of an enterprise." For them, it means that workers are given an opportunity to take part in those decisions which affect their wages, their working conditions, there very jobs, and this participation paves the way to harmonious industrial relations which are conducive to increasing productivity and efficiency. For labourers, it is just like co-decision or co-determination. The trade unions view the concept as "the harbinger of a new order of social relationship and a new set of power equations within organisations. This does not mean that they are concerned with improving organisational performance; but in terms of relative importance and

---

* A few popular connotations of participation are: 'Labour-management co-operation'; 'Co-determination'; 'Joint consultation'; 'Joint decision-making'; 'Workers' control'; Workers' participation in management'; 'Self-management'; 'Workers' participation in Industry'. All of these connotations are often used interchangeably; in fact, no clear-cut demarcation line can be drawn between them. It would appear that all these connotations represent different forms of participation which differ only in degree but not in nature. By and large, the main idea has always been the same; namely, to increase employees' influence in the management of the enterprise to which they belong.

priorities, they hold the view that the functioning of economic activity is, by its very nature, social. The objective is to gain control over the decision-making process within an enterprise."

The concept of workers' participation in management crystallises the concept of industrial democracy, and indicates an attempt on the part of an employer to build his employees into a team which works towards the realisation of a common objective.

In the words of Davis, "it is a mental and emotional involvement of a person in a group situation which encourages him to contribute to goals and share responsibilities with them."

Sometimes participation is regarded as basically the same thing as Taylor's "scientific management", the aim of which is to secure the maximum prosperity of employers and the employed. However, the approach is somewhat different, for "scientific management" lays emphasis on the technical aspect of work, whereas the "participation" lays primary emphasis on the human element and rests on the assumption that a worker is more than a pair of hands. He is a human resource. The worker's technical knowhow and an ingenuity, properly utilised, may make, more significant contribution to the effectiveness and economic welfare of an organisation than any improvement in his physical effort alone, although that is not unimportant. When operationalised, the term *workers' participation* implies "a formal method of providing an opportunity for every member of the organisation to contribute his brain and ingenuity as well as his physical efforts to the improvement of organisational effectiveness" as well as enhancing his own economic welfare.

Kenneth Walker says: "Workers' participation in management is a resounding phrase, bridging the past and the future. It echoes the millennial vision of nineteenth century thinkers while heralding the evolution of new forms of industrial organisation under twentieth century pressures. The word 'workers' participation' is plentifully supplied with ideas, institutions and opinions." He adds that "there are two basic ideas in the concept of workers' participation in management: that there are two groups of people in an undertaking (managers and workers) and that there are two separate sets of functions to be performed (managerial and operative). The managerial functions are essentially those concerned with planning, organising, motivating and controlling, in contrast with 'doing' or 'operative' work. A self-employed person carries on the managerial as well as the operative functions of his one-man enterprise; he is both his own manager and operative.

The Industrial Revolution and the factory system divorced managerial and operative functions, authorising persons who occupied 'managerial' positions to exercise managerial functions while 'workers' performed their operational functions. Those who advocate workers' participation in management seek to bridge this gap, or even to remove it, by authorising workers to take part in managerial functions .... The participation, therefore, can be defined, in neutral terms, as 'taking part in', leaving the question whether such participation does produce a co-operative commitment to the enterprise, or involves a sharing of powers and status between the managers and the workers to be settled by evidence."

The essence of labour participation in management lies in the firm belief and confidence in the individual, in his capacity for growth and learning, in his ability to contribute significantly with his hands, head as well as his heart; and this implies discarding the narrow conventional outlook of antagonism of interests and substituting in its place a community of purpose and extending co-operation in promoting the well-being of labour and management in industry.

The principle of workers' participation in management affords a self-realisation in work and meets the psychological needs of workers at work by eliminating, to a large extent, any feeling of futility, isolation and consequent frustration that they face in a normal industrial setting. In this connection, G.D.H. Cole noted that the "Industrial democracy at the top, through nationalisation, is an inefficient condition to ensure workers' involvement in enterprises. Unlike in politics, in the case of industry, workers are connected mostly with shop floor issues. Better participation and greater responsibility in the decision-making process on the part of general workers would perhaps tend to develop in them organisational loyalty, confidence, trust, favourable attitude towards supervisors, and a sense of involvement in the organisation. The schemes of workers' participation in management, among other measures of industrial reform, are expected to democratise the industrial milieu, and ensure egalitarianism in the process."

In fine it can be said that the workers' participation as a *system of communication and consultation, either formal or informal, by which employees of an organisation are kept informed about the affairs of the undertaking and through which they express their opinion and contribute to management decisions.* It is a distribution of social power in industry so that it tends to be shared among all who are engaged in the work rather than concentrated in the hands of a minority. It is industrial democracy in action based on the principles of equity, equality and voluntarism. It gives to the employees' representatives the right to criticise, to offer constructive suggestions, and to become aware of various delicate issues involved in decision-making.

In other words:

- The participation enhances employees ability to influence, decision-making at different tiers of the organisational hierarchy with concomitant assumption of responsibility.
- The participation has to be at different levels of management: *(i)* at the shop level, *(ii)* at the department level, and *(iii)* at the board level. The decision-making at these different levels would assume different patterns in regard to policy formulation and execution.
- The participation incorporates the willing acceptance of responsibilities by the body of workers. As they become a party to decision-making, they have to commit themselves to the implementation of decisions made.
- The participation is conducted through the mechanism of forums and practices which provide for the association of workers' representatives.
- The broad goal of participation is to change basically the organisational aspect of production and transfer the management function entirely to the workers so that they can experience intricacies of "auto management."

The employer's realisation of the need for workers' participation in management was considerably influenced by the following factors:

(i) The increased use of technology in industry has necessitated the growing co-operation of workers because of the complex operations of production;

(ii) The changed view that employees are no longer servants but are equal partners with their employers in their efforts to attain the goals of the enterprise;

(iii) The growth of trade unions which safeguard the interests of workers and protect them against possible exploitation by their employers;

(iv) The growing interest of the government in the development of industries and the welfare of workers; and

(v) The need for increased and uninterrupted production which can be achieved only when there is a contented labour class.

The empirical researches undertaken by Kurt Lewin, French and others have shown that democratically managed groups, in which rank and file also get an opportunity to participate in decision-making, are healthier and more efficient than groups managed in an authoritarian way. The findings of Rensis Likert, Blake and MacGregor popularised the belief that if workers are given opportunities to participate in the management, there would be positive gains for the organisation through higher productivity, on the one hand, and reduced negative behaviour on the other.

It is quite logical to believe that if people have the right to choose their own government, the workers have the right to choose the management of the enterprise to which they belong and to whose success they contribute substantially. It rests on the fundamental premise that the worker is not a slave who has no rights at all; he is a citizen employed in an industry and has opinions of his own which, he thinks, should be taken into account when decisions are taken and policies are formulated. "The factory is not a mechanical entity which is governed by mechanical principles and economic laws, but a social system which is subject to the democratic rights of those who are involved in it."

It is no wonder that "ever since the early days of industrialisation, the demand for democracy in a worker's life has been an important feature of the many political programmes."

It may therefore, be concluded that the concept of workers' participation has its deep roots not only in political and social norms and in the ethos of our times but also in the empirical studies on human behaviour at work.

OBJECTIVES OF WORKER'S PARTICIPATION IN MANAGEMENT

The objectives of the workers' participation scheme vary from country to country, because they largely rests with their socio-economic development of country, its political philosophy, industrial relations scene, and the attitude of the working class.

Accordingly, the objectives may be democratisation of management, eliciting workers' co-operation in the attainment of corporate goals, personalisation and humanisation of the management process, and behavioural approach to the management of workers-management relations, etc.

In the words of Gosep, workers' participation may be viewed as:

(i) An instrument for improving the efficiency of enterprises, and establishing harmonious industrial relations;

(ii) A device for developing social education for the purpose of promoting solidarity among the working community and for tapping latent human

resources (by getting employees' suggestions and by improving attitudes towards work and the organisation);

(iii) *A means* for attaining industrial peace and harmony which lead to higher productivity and increased production;

(iv) *A humanitarian* act, giving the worker an acceptable status within the working community and a sense of purpose in his activity;

(v) *An ideological* point of view to develop self-management in industry.

In India, according to the Industrial Policy Resolution, 1956, the aim of the government in advocating *workers' participation in management* is "a part of its overall endeavour to create a socialist society, wherein the sharing of a part of the managerial powers by workers is considered necessary."

The purpose which workers' participation in management try to achieve, in the words of the Second Five-Year Plan, are:

(a) Increasing productivity for the general benefit of the enterprise, the employees and the community;

(b) Giving employees a better understanding of their role in the working of the industry and of the process of production; and

(c) Satisfying the workers' urge for self-expression, thus leading to industrial peace, better relations and increased co-operation.

These objectives may be achieved as a result of the consequences resulting from the process of workers' participation. These consequences are:

(i) Challenging work for workers;

(ii) Heightened sense of responsibility;

(iii) Meaningful relationship to work;

(iv) Availability of workers' ideas and suggestions to management;

(v) Realistic management decisions;

(vi) Accommodation, change, motivation and commitment to implement decisions;

(vii) Effective communication system;

(viii) Better worker-supervisor relationship.

The workers' participation in management is inevitable from the economic, psychological and sociological points of view.

Economically, it flows from the assumption that employees can contribute substantially to the progress and prosperity of the enterprise, and that they have, therefore, a legitimate right to share equitably in the gains of higher productivity. The higher productivity is achieved through the fullest co-operation between labour and management, for "poor labour-management relations do not encourage the workers to give more than the minimum necessary to retain the job; and that, in many cases, is all that he gives."

Psychologically, it implies recognition of employees' non-economic needs; the satisfaction of these needs through effective participation can help to raise the level of motivation. "Participation gives the worker a sense of importance, pride and accomplishment; it gives him freedom and opportunity for expression; a feeling of belonging to the place of work, and a sense of workmanship and creativity. It provides for the integration of his interests with those of the management by making the worker a joint partner in the enterprise."

Sociologically, the need for participation arises because modern industry is a social institution with the interest of the owner, the employer, the community and the workers equally vested in it. It aims at reducing the number of industrial disputes and creates positive conditions and an atmosphere in which industrial harmony and peace can develop. "Participation forges ties of understanding between individuals, leading to better efforts all round; and its absence leads to stagnation of minds and allows the abilities of producers to remain dormant, introduces a sullenness in behaviour which ultimately may flare up into breaches of discipline and a consequent loss in production."

FORMS OF PARTICIPATION

The form or the way in which workers can and do participate in management varies a great deal. To some extent, this variation is related to the differences in management, the issues or areas on which participation is sought, and the pattern of labour-management relations. It may also vary from organisation to organisation, depending upon the level of power or authority enjoyed by managers at different levels in different types of organisations.

The specific way in which different forms of participation may take place also varies from situation to situation. There may be formal organisational structures, such as the Works Committee, Plant Councils, Shop Councils, Production Committee, Safety Committee, Joint Management Council, Canteen Committee, P.F. Management Committee, etc. The participation may also take place through informal mechanisms and forums. A supervisor or a foreman may consult a worker before taking a particular decision in which the latter is interested, such as granting or rejecting an application for leave, allotment of work on overtime, transfer from one section to another.

If workers participate in management either through formal mechanisms or through informal procedures, it should be considered as an instance of participative management. Whatever form it may take, it is necessary, for the effective functioning, to promote the interests of both the parties — management and labour. The managements' primary interest lies in improving productivity, reducing cost, and thus improving profitability. The workers' interest lies in improving their earnings. When earnings improve through sharing gains in productivity, apparently a harmony of interests is promoted. If participation is to be effective as a process or device, it should be integrated with a scheme of improving productivity and gain-sharing.

The participation may be *ascending participation*, where workers are given an opportunity to influence managerial decisions at higher levels through their elected representatives to Work Councils or the Board of the Enterprise (*i.e., integrated participation*). In *descending participation*, they may be given more power to plan and make decisions about their own work (*delegation* and *job enrichment*). They may participate through collective bargaining (*i.e., disjunctive participation*). They may also participate informally when a manager adopts a participative style of supervision, or when workers employ unofficial restrictive practices.

The important forms in which workers can participate in management are: collective bargaining, joint administration, joint decision-making, consultation and information sharing.

The issues over which the interests of workers and management are competitive, such as employment conditions, wage rates, working hours, and the number of holidays, are the usual areas for *collective bargaining.* On the other hand, the issues over which the parties are equally concerned, such as the efficient management of provident fund money, canteen, annual sports, workers' welfare facilities, etc., may form the subject of *joint administration, joint decision-making or consultation.* The difference between joint administration, joint decision-making and consultation is important, but narrow. In joint administration, workers and management share the responsibility and power of execution. In joint decision-making, even though two groups participate in deciding the policies, execution is generally effected by the management. In the joint consultative form, the management only consults workers — their desires, opinions, ideas, suggestions; but retains to itself the authority and responsibility of making decisions and executing them.

LEVELS OF PARTICIPATION

The participation is possible at all levels of management. It depends upon the nature of functions, the strength of the workers, the attitudes of trade unions and that of management. The areas and degrees may differ very considerably at different levels of management. At one end, where the exercise of authority in decision-making is almost complete, participation will be negligible; while at the other end, where the exercise of authority is relatively small, participation will be maximum. In between these two extremes, the nature and extent of participation will vary, depending on a variety of factors, including the problems or issues, the attitudes and past experience of the management, and the development of human relations in general and labour management relations in particular. The fact is that workers' participation in management will have to be at different levels. The workers may be given an opportunity to influence or take part in managerial decisions at the higher level through their representatives on a supervisory board or on the Board of Directors, or through works councils. The participation may also be at lower levels at which workers are given some authority to plan and take decisions about their work, like job enrichment, job enlargement, delegation, etc.

Broadly speaking, there are four stages of participation. At the initial stage, participation may be *informative and associative participation*, where members have the right to receive information, discuss and give suggestions on the general economic situation of the concern, the state of the market, production and sales programmes, organisation and general running of the undertaking, circumstances affecting the economic position of the concern, methods of manufacture and work, annual balance sheet and profit and loss account and connected documents and explanations, long-term plans for expansion, redeployment, and such other matters as may be agreed to. There are the areas in which the members have the right to receive information and discuss these, and make suggestions which are binding on the management.

Consultative participation involves a higher degree of sharing of views of the members and giving them an opportunity to express their feelings. In the process, members are consulted on matters relating to welfare amenities, adoption of new technology and the problems emanating from it, safety measures, etc. Its managements' prerogative to accept the suggestions of workers given at participative forum.

Administrative participation involves a greater degree of sharing of authority and responsibility of the management functions. Here members are given a little more autonomy in the exercise of administrative and supervisory powers in respect of welfare measures and safety works, the operation of vocational training and apprenticeship schemes, the preparation of schedules of working hours and breaks and holidays, payment of reward for valuable suggestions received, and any other matter that may be agreed to by the members.

Decision participation is the highest form of participation, where sharing in the decision-making power is complete and the delegation of authority and responsibility of managerial function to such a body is maximum. In matters like economic, financial and administrative policies the decisions are mutually taken.

In short, workers' participation in management can deal with and exercise supervisory, advisory and administrative functions on matters concerning safety, welfare, etc., though the ultimate responsibility is vested in the management. However, all such matters as wages, bonus, etc., which are subjects of collective bargaining, are excluded from the purview of the workers' participation schemes. The individual grievances are also excluded from their scope. In short, the creation of new rights as between employers and workers should be outside the jurisdiction of the participation schemes.

PARTICIPATION IN ORGANISATIONS

The participation of workers in management is nothing new for India. In 1920, Mahatma Gandhi had suggested this on the ground that workers contributed labour and brains, while shareholders contributed money to an enterprise, and that both should, therefore, share in its prosperity. He observed: "Employers should not regard themselves as sole owners of mills and factories of which they may be legal owners. They should regard themselves as trustees. There should be a perfect relationship of friendship and co-operation among them." As for the unions, he said: "The aim should be to raise the moral and intellectual height of labour and thus by sheer merit, make labour master of the means of production instead of the slave that it is." He insisted that "capital and labour should supplement and help each other; they should be a great family, living in unity and harmony." The influence of Mahatma Gandhi bore fruit; and for the first time, the joint consultation model was adopted in the cotton textile industry. A few works committees were also set up in the printing presses of the government. TISCO had established joint committees in 1958 and the Delhi Cloth and General Mills Co. Ltd., accepted an elected representative on the Board of its Directors. In some railway companies and the Buckingham and Carnatak Mills of Madras, works committees were set up. The year 1920 may, therefore, be regarded as a landmark in the history of joint consultation in India.

Commenting on works committees, the Royal Commission observed that: "The results achieved have been disappointing." The Commission expressed similar views about working of joint committees on railways set up in 1923. There were several reasons for this state of affairs illiteracy of the working class, unorganised labour unions, and defective recruitment systems. The Royal Commission reported that some employers apprehended that works committees would encroach on their management rights. The opposition of the trade unions themselves was one of the reasons, for they looked upon works committees as rival institutions.

The first major step in this direction was the enactment of the Industrial Disputes Act in 1947. Further in 1957 the scheme for joint management councils was formulated following the suggestions to this effect in the Second Five-Year Plan. Prior to it, the Industrial Policy Resolution (1948) had suggested that labour should be in all matters concerning industrial production. The First-Five Year Plan had also called for the constitution of joint committees for consultation at all levels and reiterated the government's faith in works committees. It said: "Works committees for the settlement of differences on the spot between the workers and the management are the key to the system of industrial relations as conceived in this Plan."

A Study Group on Workers' Participation in Management, consisting of representatives of the government, employers and workers, was set up in 1956, which, after closely examining the systems of workers' participation in management in the UK, Sweden, France, Belgium, West Germany and Yugoslavia, favoured the system of joint management councils, and submitted its report in May 1957. It emphasised that:

(i) In India, an educational campaign should be launched so that workers and managerial supervisory staff may realise the implications of such a scheme;

(ii) The joint consultation should be 'in-built', *i.e.*, it should not be a matter of merely bringing together two parties, but there should be jointness all along the line, and technical experts and supervisors should be an organic part of the consultative scheme;

(iii) Importance should be given to reorientation of attitudes, strong self-confident trade unions, and good industrial relations for the success of any scheme of participation;

(iv) No compulsion should be applied in setting up the councils, and only permissive legislation be favoured.

The main recommendation of the Committee were:

(1) It would be advisable to have some permissive legislation empowering the government to set up joint management councils in selected undertakings.

(2) The main function of the joint management councils might include the means of communication, improvements in working and living conditions, implementation of safety measures, improvements in productivity, encouragement of suggestions and assistance in the administration of laws and agreements; alterations, in the Standing Orders; planning and execution of welfare programmes; retrenchment, rationalisation, closures, reduction in or cessation of operations; introduction of new methods of production and manufacture including re-employment of men and machinery; methods of manufacture and work operation of vocational training and apprenticeship schemes; rewards for valuable suggestions and procedures for engagement and punishment.

(3) To reduce the danger of apathy, the councils of management may be entrusted with some administrative responsibilities — the administration of welfare measures, supervision of safety measures, operation of vocational training and apprenticeship schemes, and payment of rewards for valuable suggestions.

(4) There should be a strong self-confident trade union, closely connected with the machinery of participation, which should have a reasonably clear separation of functions.

(5) The co-operation of junior managers, supervisors and foremen should be sought.

(6) There should be a single council for an undertaking as a whole, provided that it is not made of units at different places. For undertakings spread over several places, there may be separate councils at local, regional or national levels.

(7) The question of size, the existence of local demand and the state of workers' organisation and of their preparedness for participation must be taken into consideration while deciding whether the law should be applied to a particular undertaking.

These recommendations of the Study Group were accepted by the 15th Indian Labour Conference in July 1957. It appointed a 12-member sub-committee to consider further details of the scheme. The committee recommended that:

(i) The scheme should be initially tried out in 50 selected undertakings in the public and private sectors;

(ii) There should be only one single council for the undertaking as a whole;

(iii) The employees' representatives should be nominated by the trade union concerned, and not more than 25 per cent of the employees' representatives should be outsiders;

(iv) The size of the joint council should be restricted to 12 persons; and

(v) The joint council should meet during working hours.

These recommendations were discussed at a Seminar on Labour-Management Co-operation in New Delhi on January 31, and February 1, 1958. It drew up a Draft Model Agreement between management and labour for the establishment of joint management council, which was entrusted with three sets of functions: *first*, to fulfil its functions as an advisory body; *second*, to receive information on certain matters; and *third*, to fulfil administration responsibility.

SACHAR COMMITTEE ON WORKERS' PARTICIPATION

A high-powered Expert Committee on Companies and M.R.T.P. Acts was set up by the Government of India under the chairmanship of Rajinder Sachar. The terms of reference for the Committee were: "*(i)* to consider the provisions of the Companies Act and M.R.T.P. Act and *(ii)* to suggest measures by which workers' participation in the share capital and management of companies can be brought about." The committee submitted its report on August 1978.

The main recommendations of the Committee were:

(a) Regarding Representation of Workers on Board of Directors — These were:

(i) To begin with, participation shall be limited to companies which employ 1,000 or more workers (excluding *badli* workers).

(ii) The definition of workmen is given in the Industrial Dispute Act, 1947, would be appropriate for the scheme;

(iii) This participation at the Board level should be introduced if at least 51 per cent of the workers vote in a secret ballot in favour of such participation. In that event, the company will be legally bound to fall in line with their wishes. However, any company can voluntarily introduce this participation scheme.

(iv) Before fixing the proportion of Worker Directors on the Board, a more detailed consideration should be given to the issue by the Central Government.

(v) The Worker Director will be elected by all the workers at the company's premises by secret ballot with cumulative voting rights.

(vi) The Worker Director must be from amongst the workers employed by the company and not an outsider.

(vii) A pre-requisite of this scheme of participation is a programme of training designed to be in line with the business of company. It will be the responsibility of the government to organise this training programme. "An awareness of industrial relations and business techniques will certainly make the workers more aware of the actual problems faced by the companies in modern society. The training of the employees must, therefore, be immediately taken in hand."

(viii) The presence of Worker Director on the Board would not lead to any breach in the confidentiality of the information.

(ix) The committee did not favour a two-tier representation, *i.e.* a Supervisory Board and the Smaller Management Board.

(b) Regarding Workers' Participation in Share Capital: In regard to worker's participation in share capital the committee failed to evolve any formula acceptable both to workers and employers. It did not, therefore, recommend any "mandatory participation in equity by the workers." The recommendation that emerged was:

"There was, however, quite a majority in favour of the suggestion that in all future issues of shares by companies, a portion of new shares, say about 10% to 15%, should be reserved exclusively for workers, called the workers' shares. These shares, in the first instance, must be offered to the employees of the company, and failing that only should they be offered to the existing shareholders or the public. For that purpose, Section 81 of the Act should be suitably amended. Section 77 of the Act should also be amended permitting the companies to give to the employees a loan up to 12 months salary or wages not exceeding Rs. 12,000 for the purchase of the shares of the company." This scheme, however, has not found favour with Indian industries.

VARMA COMMITTEE ON WORKERS' PARTICIPATION IN INDUSTRY

The Janata Government set up a committee in September 1977 under the chairmanship of Ravindra Varma, the then Union Minister for Labour. The terms of reference of the committee were:

(i) To study the existing statutory and non-statutory schemes;

(ii) To recommend on the outlines of a comprehensive scheme of workers' participation, especially keeping in view the interests of the national economy, efficient management and workers; and

(iii) To recommend the manner in which the concept of trusteeship in industry and the participation of workers in equity can be given a practical shape in a scheme of workers' participation.

The main recommendations of the Committee, which submitted its report in 1979, are:

(i) A three-tier system of participation, *viz.,* at the shop floor, plant and corporate or board levels, should be adopted.

(ii) Legislation on workers' participation covering all undertakings employing 500 or more workers, irrespective of the fact whether it in public, private or corporate sector, should be introduced.

(iii) There should be provision for extending the scheme to units employing at least 100 workers.

(iv) The representative for the participative forms should be elected by secret ballot with a view to avoiding any possible friction between the collective bargaining agent and the representative. The committee suggested that there should be parity between the representative of employers and workers on the participation forums at shop and plant levels, but it could not agree on the number of workers' representatives at the corporate level.

(v) The issue of equity participation was recommended as optional. Not less than 10% of all new shares to be issued in future by a company should be reserved exclusively the workers' shares of the workers of that company.

The workers' representatives and some of the state government representatives favoured the participation at the corporate, plant and shop floor levels; but employers' representatives were of the view that participation should be confined only to the shop floor level.

The Sixth Plan observed: "At the enterprise level, workers' participation in management should become an integral part of the industrial relations system and serve as an effective instrument of management. It should be made a vehicle of transforming the attitudes of both employers and workers with a view to establishing a co-operative culture which may help in building a strong, self-confident and self-reliant country with a stable industrial base ....There is a wide area of relationships in an enterprise outside the domain of collective bargaining where employers and workers can work jointly for the common interest of different groups and the enterprise as a whole. Such a system of consultative and joint decision-making should ensure frictionless co-operation at various levels, provide job satisfaction, release the latent creative energy of workers, reduce their alienation and enhance the commitment of workers and the line management to the common ideal of better performance. But it is necessary to provide training facilities to workers and managerial supervisory personnel so as to motivate them in making the scheme of workers' participation a success ...."

"…. It is also necessary to strengthen the tripartite consultative machinery so that it may be possible to evolve the broad framework of labour policies and programmes and full consideration and discussion among all interests concerned — trade unions, employers and government. At the industry level, Standing Tripartite Committees could serve a useful purpose in identifying the bottlenecks and deficiencies and suggesting corrective measures."

COMPREHENSIVE SCHEME FOR EMPLOYEES' PARTICIPATION IN MANAGEMENT (1983)

Based on a review of the working of the various schemes of workers' participation in management introduced in 1975 and 1977 and the experience so gained, the government in 1983 formulated a comprehensive scheme for workers' participation in the Central public sector undertakings. The main features of the scheme are:

(i) The scheme will not have any legislative backing to begin with;

(ii) It would cover all public sector undertakings, except those specifically exempted;

(iii) All the undertakings run on departmental lines by the Central Government will be excluded;

(iv) It will operate both at the shop floor and the plant levels;

(v) The employees and employers shall have equal representation on all the participative forums; and

(vi) The functions of the participative forum would be as laid down in the scheme and can be modified with the consent of both the parties.

But a host of constraints — such as multiplicity of union, inter-union rivalry, lack of proper knowledge on the part of workers about the scheme—have acted as a stumbling block in the successful working of the scheme.

FORMS OF WORKERS' PARTICIPATION IN INDIA

In the country the workers 'participation in management scheme is is vogue in three forms, viz.

(i) The works committees (set up under the Industrial Disputes Act, 1947);

(ii) The joint management councils (set up as a result of the Labour-Management Co-operation Seminar, 1958); and

(iii) The scheme for workers' Representative on the Board of Management (under the Management and Miscellaneous Scheme, 1970) on some public and private sector enterprises, including industrial undertakings and nationalised banks.

Since July 1975, a two-tier participation model, namely, the shop council at the shop level and to joint council at the enterprise level, were introduced. On 7th January 1977, a new scheme of workers' participation in management in commercial and service organisations in public sector undertakings was launched with the setting up of unit councils. On 30th December 1983, a comprehensive scheme for workers' participation in public undertakings was introduced. It was decided that workers would be allowed to participate at the shop level, the plant level and the board level.

As the scheme of shop council and workers' representation on the board of directors were already functioning, greater emphasis was placed on the setting up of unit councils.

At present the following participative forms are prevalent in India:

(A) Works committees, suggestion schemes;

(B) Joint management councils;

(C) Joint councils;

(D) Unit councils;

(E) Plant councils;

(F) Shop councils;

(G) Workers' representative on the Board of Management;

(H) Workers' participation in share capital;

(I) Participation through quality circles;

(J) Participation through Collective Barganing.

(A) WORK COMMITTEES

The Industrial Disputes Act, 1949 provides for the setting up of works committees as a scheme of workers' participation in management which consist of representatives of employers and employees. The Act provides for these bodies in every undertaking employing 100 or more workmen. The aim of setting up of these bodies is to promote measures for maintaining harmonious relations in the work place and to sort out differences of opinion in respect of matters of common interest to employers and employees. The Bombay Industrial Relations Act, 1946 also provides for these bodies, but under the provisions of this Act they can be set up only in units which have a recognised union and they are called joint committees. The workers directly elect their representatives where there is no union.

Functions: These works committees/joint committees are consultative bodies. Their functions include discussion of conditions of work like lighting, ventilation, temperature, sanitation etc., amenities like water supply for drinking purposes, provision of canteens, medical services, safe working conditions, administration of welfare funds, educational and recreational activities, and encouragement of thrift and savings. It shall be the duty of the works committee to promote measures for securing and preserving amity and good relations between the employers and workmen and to comment upon matters of their common interest or concern and endeavour to reconcile any material difference of opinion in respect of such matters.

Structure: The works committees have, as office bearers, a President, a Vice-President, a Secretary and a Joint Secretary. The President is a nominee of the employer and the Vice-President is the Workers' representative. The tenure of these bodies is two years. The total strength of these bodies should not exceed 20. The employees' representatives have to be chosen by the employees.

These committees functioned actively in some organisations like Tata Iron and Steel Company, Indian Aluminium Works at Belur, and Hindustan Lever. In all these, the managements have evolved joint committees independently of the statutory requirements.

Suggestions scheme: allows employees to express their views and suggestions on improving productivity, reduce wastages, energy saving, safety measures. Rewards are given for accepted suggestions. This procedure enables the management, to involve workers in active cooperation on matters of mutual interests and builds a relationship.

(B) JOINT MANAGEMENT COUNCILS (JMCs)

The Second Five Year Plan recommended the setting up of joint councils of management consisting of representatives of workers and management. The Government of India deputed a study group (1957) to study the schemes of worker's participation in management in countries like U.K., France, Belgium and Yugoslavia. The report of the study group was considered by the Indian Labour Conference (ILC) in its 15th session in 1957 and it made certain recommendations:

(1) That workers' participation in management schemes should be set up in selected undertakings on a voluntary basis.

(2) A sub-committee consisting of representatives of employers, workers and government should be set up for considering the details of workers' participation in management schemes. This committee should select the undertakings where workers' participation in management schemes would be introduced in the first stage on an experimental basis.

Objectives: The objectives of Joint Management Councils are as follows:

(i) To increase the association of employers and employee thereby promoting cordial industrial relations;

(ii) To improve the operational efficiency of the workers;

(iii) To provide welfare facilities to them;

(iv) To educate workers so that they are well equipped to participate in these schemes; and

(v) To satisfy the psychological needs of workers.

A tripartite sub-committee was set up as per the recommendations of Indian Labour Conference which laid down certain criteria for selection of enterprises where the JMCs could be introduced. They are:

(i) The unit must have 500 or more employees;

(ii) It should have a fair record of industrial relations;

(iii) It should have a well organised trade union;

(iv) The management and the workers should agree to establish JMCs;

(v) Employers (in case of private sector) should be members of the leading employers' organisation; and

(vi) Trade unions should be affiliated to one of the Central federations.

It was observed by the sub-committee that if the workers and employers mutually agree they can set up JMCs even if these conditions are not met.

The sub-committee also made recommendations regarding their composition, procedure for nominating workers' representatives, the membership of JMCs etc. The details of these aspects have to be worked out by the parties themselves. A draft model was drawn up regarding the establishment of JMCs. The sub-committee was later reconstituted as the "Committee on Labour-Management Co-operation" to advise on all matters pertaining to the Scheme.

(C) JOINT COUNCILS

At every division/region/zonal level, or, as may be considered necessary in a particular branch of an organisation/service employing 100 or more people, there shall be a joint council. The main feature of the joint council shall be:

(i) Each organisation/service shall decide the number of councils to be set up for different types of services rendered by it in consultation with the recognised unions — or workers as the case may be, in the manner best suited to the local conditions.

(ii) Only such persons who are actually engaged in the organisation/service shall be members of the joint council. Each organisation/service may decide the number of members in the manner suggested in item(s) but the membership should not be unwieldy.

(iii) The tenure of the council shall be two years. If, however, a member is nominated in the mid-term of council to fill a casual vacancy, the member nominated shall continue in office for the remaining period of the council's tenure.

(iv) The chief executive of the organisation/service or of its divisional/ regional/ zonal branch, as the case may be, shall be the chairman of the joint council. There shall be a vice-chairman who will be chosen by the worker-members of the council.

(v) The joint council shall appoint one of its members as its Secretary who will prepare the agenda, record the minutes of the meetings and report on the implementation of the decisions arrived at every meeting. The management shall provide the necessary facilities within the premises of the organisation/ service for the efficient discharge of his functions by the secretary.

(vi) The joint council shall meet whenever considered necessary, but at least once in a quarter. Every meeting shall review the action taken on the decisions of earlier meetings for an effective follow-up action.

(vii) Every decision of the joint council shall be on the basis of consensus and not by a process of voting; it shall be binding on the management and workers and shall be implemented within one month, unless otherwise stated in the decision.

FUNCTIONS OF THE JOINT COUNCILS

The following shall be functions of the joint council:

(i) The settlement of matters which remain unresolved by unit level councils and arranging joint meetings for resolving inter-council problems.

(ii) Review of the working of the unit level council for improvement in the customer service and evolving for the best way of handling of goods traffic, accounts, etc.

(iii) Unit level matters which have a bearing on other branches or on the enterprise as a whole.

(iv) Development of skills of workers and adequate facilities for trading.

(v) Improvement in the general conditions of work.

(vi) Preparation of schedules of working hours and holidays.

(vii) Proper recognition and appreciation of useful suggestions received from workers through a system of rewards.

(viii) Discussion on any matter having a bearing on the improvement of performance of the organisation/service with a view to ensuring better customer service.

(D) UNIT COUNCILS

Encouraged by the success of the Joint Councils scheme in manufacturing and mining units, a new scheme of workers' participation in management in commercial and service organisations in the public sector, having large-scale public dealings, was announced on 5th January 1977. The scheme envisaged the setting-up of unit councils in units employing at least 100 persons. The organisations include hotels, restaurants, hospitals, air, sea, railway and road transport services, ports and docks, ration shops, schools, research institutions, provident fund and pension organisations, municipal and milk distribution services, trust organsations, all financial institutions, banks, insurance companies, posts and telegraph offices, the Food Corporation, State Electricity Boards, Central Warehousing, State Warehousing Corporations, State Trading Corporation, Mines and Minerals Trading Corporation, irrigation systems, tourists organisations, establishments of public amusement and training organisations of Central and state governments.

FEATURES OF THE SCHEME

The main features of the scheme are:

(i) A unit level council, consisting of representatives of workers and management of the organisation/service, employing 100 or more workers, may be formed in each unit to discuss day-to-day problems and find solutions; but, wherever necessary a composite council may be formed to serve more than one unit, or a council may be formed department-wise to suit the particular needs of an organisation/service.

(ii) Every unit council shall consist of an equal number of representatives of the management and workers. The actual number of members should be determined by the management in consultation with the recognised union, registered unions or workers in the manner best suited to the local conditions obtaining in a unit or an organisation; but their total number may not exceed 12. It would be necessary to nominate suitable and experienced workers from various departments, irrespective of their cadre, affiliation or status, and not trade union functionaries who may not be actually working in the unit.

(iii) The management's representatives should be nominated by the management and should consist of persons from the unit concerned.

(iv) The management shall, in consultation with the recognised union or the registered union or workers as the case may be, determine in the manner best suited to local conditions, the number of unit councils and the departments to be attached to each council of the organisation/service.

(v) All the decisions of a unit council shall be on the basis of consensus and not by a process of voting, provided that either party may refer the unsettled matters to the joint council for consideration.

(vi) Every decision of a unit council shall be implemented by the parties concerned within a month, unless otherwise stated in the decisions itself.

(vii) The management shall make suitable arrangements for the recording and maintenance of minutes of meetings and designate one of its representatives as a secretary for this purpose, who shall also report on the action taken on the decisions at subsequent meetings of the council.

(viii) Such decisions of a unit council as have a bearing on another unit of the organisation/service as a whole shall be referred to the joint council for consideration and decision.

(ix) A unit council once formed shall function for a period of three years. Any member nominated or elected to the council in the mid-term to fill a casual vacancy shall continue to be a member of the council for the unexpired period of the term of the council.

(x) The council shall meet as frequently as is necessary but at least once a month.

(xi) The chairman of the council shall be a nominee of the management. The worker members of the council shall elect a vice-chairman from amongst themselves.

FUNCTIONS OF UNIT COUNCIL

The main functions of the unit councils are:

(i) To create conditions for achieving optimum efficiency, better customer service in areas where there is direct and immediate contact between workers at the operational level and the consumer, higher productivity and output, including elimination of wastage and idle time, and optimum utilisation of manpower by joint involvement in improving the work system;

(ii) To identify areas of chronically bad, inadequate or inferior service and to take necessary corrective steps to eliminate the contributing factors and evolve improved methods of operation;

(iii) To study absenteeism problem and recommend steps to reduce it;

(iv) To eliminate pilferage and all forms of corruption and to institute a system of rewards for this purpose;

(v) To suggest improvements in the physical conditions of work, such as lighting, ventilation, dust, noise, cleanliness, internal layout, and the setting up of customers' service points;

(vi) To ensure a proper flow of two-way communication between management and workers, particularly about matters relating to the services to be rendered,

fixation of targets of output and the progress made in achieving these targets;

(vii) To recommend and improve safety, health and welfare measures to ensure efficient running of the unit;

(viii) To discuss any other matters which may have a bearing on the improvement of performance in the unit for ensuring better customer service.

(E) PLANT COUNCIL

The plant council is formed in pursuance of the recommendations of the second meeting of the Group on Labour at New Delhi on 23rd September 1985. The scheme is applicable to all Central public sector undertakings, except those which are given specific exemption from the operation of the scheme by the government. The main features of the scheme are:

(i) There shall be one plant council for the whole unit;

(ii) Each plant council should consist of not less than six and not more than eighteen members. There should be parity between the representatives of employees and employers. One-third of the employees representatives should come from the supervisory staff level. If the number of women employees is 15 per cent or more of the total workforce, at least one representative should be a woman employee;

(iii) Only such persons as are actually engaged in the unit should be members of the plant council;

(iv) It's tenure shall be for a period of three years;

(v) The chief executive of the unit shall be the chairman of the plant council; the vice-chairman shall be elected from among the employees;

(vi) The plant council shall appoint one of its members as secretary who will be provided with adequate facilities for the effective discharge of his duties within the premises of the undertaking/establishment;

(vii) If a person quits the council for whatsoever reason, the member who is nominated to fill the mid-term casual vacancy shall serve on the council for the unexpired period of the term of the council;

(viii) The council shall meet at least once in a quarter;

(ix) Every decision of the plant council shall be on the basis of consensus and not by voting, and shall be binding on both the employees and the employer. The decisions so arrived at shall be implemented within a month, unless otherwise stated in the decision itself. All unsettled issues shall placed before the board of directors for their decision.

FUNCTIONS OF PLANT COUNCIL

The plant council shall normally deal with the following matters:

(A) Operational Areas

(i) Determination of productivity schemes taking into consideration the local conditions;

(ii) Planning, implementation, and attainment and review of monthly targets and schedules;

(iii) Material supply and preventing its shortfall;

(iv) Housekeeping activities;

(v) Improvement in productivity in general and in critical areas in particular;

(vi) Quality and technological improvements;

(vii) Machine utilisation, knowledge and development of new products;

(viii) Operational performance figures;

(ix) Encouragement to and consideration of the suggestion system;

(x) Matters/problems not sorted out at the shop floor level or those that concern more than one shop; and

(xi) Review of the working of shop level bodies.

(B) Economic and Financial Areas

(i) Profit and loss statements, balance sheet;

(ii) Review of operating expenses, financial results, and cost of sales;

(iii) Enterprise performance in financial terms, labour and managerial cost, and market conditions, etc.

(C) Personnel Matters

(i) Matters relating to absenteeism;

(ii) Special problems of women workers; and

(iii) Initiation and administration of workers' programmes.

(D) Welfare Areas

(i) Implementation of welfare schemes, such as medical benefits, housing and transport facilities;

(ii) Safety measures;

(iii) Township administration; and

(iv) Control of the habits of gambling, drinking and indebtedness among the workers.

(E) Environmental Areas

(i) Environmental protection; and

(ii) Extension activities and community development projects.

(F) SHOP COUNCILS

MAIN FEATURES

The main features of the shop council scheme are:

(i) In every industrial unit employing 500 or more workers, the employer shall constitute a shop council for each department or shop or one council for more than one department or shop, on the basis of the number of workers employed in different departments or shops.

(ii) *(a)* Each council shall consist of an equal number of representatives of employers and workers.

(b) The employers' representatives shall be nominated by the management and must consist of persons from the unit concerned.

(c) All the representatives of workers shall be from amongst the workers actually engaged in the department of the shop concerned.

(iii) The employer shall, in consultation with the recognised union or the various registered trade unions or with workers, as the case may be determine in the manner best suited to local conditions, the number of shop councils and departments to be attached to each council of the undertaking or establishment.

(iv) The number of members of each council may be determined by the employer in consultation with the recognised union, registered unions or workers in the manner best suited to the conditions obtaining in the unit. The total number of members may not exceed 12.

(v) All the decisions of the shop council shall be on the basis of consensus and not by voting, provided that either party may refer the unsettled matter to the joint council for consideration.

(vi) Every decision of the shop council shall be implemented by the parties concerned within a period of one month unless otherwise stated in the decision itself, and a compliance report shall be submitted to the council.

(vii) Such decisions of the shop council having a bearing on another shop or department or the undertaking as a whole shall be referred to the joint council for consideration and decision.

(viii) A shop council, once formed, shall function for a period of three years. Any member nominated or elected to the council in the mid-term to fill a casual vacancy shall continue to be a member of the council for the unexpired portion of the term of the council.

(ix) The council shall meet as frequently as is necessary but at least once a month.

(x) The chairman of the shop council shall be a nominee of the management; the worker members of the council shall elect a vice-chairman from amongst themselves.

FUNCTIONS OF SHOP COUNCILS

To achieve increased production, productivity and over-all efficiency of the shop department, the shop council should attend to the following matters:

(i) to assist management in achieving monthly/yearly production targets;

(ii) to improve production, productivity and efficiency, including elimination of wastage and optimum utilisation of machine capacity and manpower;

(iii) to specially identify areas of low productivity and take the necessary corrective steps at shop level to eliminate relevant contributory factors;

(iv) to study absenteeism in the shop/department and recommend steps to reduce it;

(v) to suggest safety measures;

(vi) to assist in maintaining general discipline in the shop/department;

(vii) suggest improvements in physical conditions of working — lighting ventilation, noise, dust, etc., and reduction of fatigue;

(viii) suggest welfare and measures to be adopted for efficient running of the shop/department;

(ix) to ensure proper flow of adequate two-way communication between the management and the workers, particularly on matters relating to production schedules and progress in achieving the targets that have been set;

(x) suggest technological innovations in the shop;

(xi) to assist in the formulation and implementation of quality improvement programme;

(xii) to determine and implement the work system design;

(xiii) to formulate plans for multiple skill development programme;

(xiv) to assist in the implementation of cost reduction programme;

(xv) to supervise the group working system;

(xvi) to ensure a periodic review of the utilisation of the critical machines;

A report of the Ministry of Labour indicates that the scheme of wokers' participation in management is in operation in as many as 162 Central public sector undertakings. Some of these have claimed that participative management is "working smoothly" at the shop floor level. These undertakings include the Steel Authority of India Ltd. (SAIL), the Rourkela Steel Plant, Bharat Heavy Electricals Ltd. (BHEL), Cement Corporation of India, Mineral Exploration Corporation, Hindustan Photofilms Manufacturing Company, Bharat Gold Mines, Oil India and the National Textile Corporation.

One undertaking under the Department of Agriculture and Co-operation, five under the Department of Fertilizers, two under the Department of Atomic Energy, two under the Ministry of Commerce, two under the Department of Communications, and eight under the Department of Defence Production are reported to have claimed that they have implemented the participative management scheme either at the shop floor or plant level.

The Department of Coal has claimed that NECL, SCL, NLCL, WCL, CCL, ECL and BOCL have implemented the scheme of workers' participation in management. In the Department of Power, the National Hydro-Electrical Power Corporation and the National Thermal Power Corporation have implemented it.

The Union Ministry of Industry has put the participative management scheme into operation in five units under the Department of Chemicals and Petro-chemicals and fifteen units under the Department of Industrial Development.

The Ministry of Petroleum is also reported to be operating the participative management scheme in Madras Refinery, Oil and Natural Gas Commission and Indian Oil Blending Ltd., while the Ministry of Steel and Mines has claimed to have introduced the scheme in five companies under the Department of Mines and six under the Department of Steel.

According to the Department of Surface Transport, six companies have introduced the schemes, including the Shipping Corporation of India, Hindustan Shipyard and the Delhi Transport Corporation (DTC). The Ministries of Welfare and Science and Technology, too, have one undertaking each where the scheme is in operation.

A noteworthy achievement in this regard is that of the Textile Ministry. As many as eleven textile corporations in Andhra Pradesh, Bihar, Delhi, Gujarat, Madhya Pradesh, Maharashtra, Punjab, Tamil Nadu, Uttar Pradesh and West Bengal, and the Cotton Corporation of India have implemented the scheme of workers' participation in management.

The Department of Public Enterprises has furnished a list of nine undertakings which have adopted the participative management culture. These include BHEL, Bharat Heavy Plates and Vessels, Bharat Pumps and Compressors, Tungabhadra Steel Products, Triveni Structurals, HMT, Maruti Udyog and Burn Standard Co. Ltd.

"The Labour Ministry claims that among the 94 public enterprises which have implemented the scheme, it is working quite smoothly at least in the coal fields. But according to some other sources, this claim is far from true. The sources say that in the last 10 years, when the Coal department introduced the participation forum in collieries to begin with, the experiment ended in a fiasco."

(G) WORKER'S REPRESENTATION ON BOARD OF MANAGEMENT

On the recommendations of the Administrative Reforms Commission made in its report on public sector undertakings, the Government of India accepted, in principle, that representatives of workers should be taken on the Board of Directors of public sector enterprises. A few notable features of the scheme are:

(i) The representatives of workers on the board should be those actually working in the enterprise.

(ii) To begin with, participation should be limited to companies which employ 1,000 or more persons (excluding casual and *badli* workers).

(iii) The definition of 'workmen', as given in the Industrial Disputes Act, 1947, would be appropriate for the scheme.

(iv) The participation at the Board level should be introduced if at least 51 per cent of the workers vote in a secret ballot in favour of this participation. In that event, the company will be legally bound to fall in line with their wishes. However, any company can voluntarily introduce this participation scheme.

(v) Before fixing the proportion of Worker Directors on the Board, a more detailed consideration should be given to the issue by the Central Government.

(vi) The Worker Director will be elected by all the workers of the company through secret ballot. Each voter will have cumulative voting rights.

(vii) The pre-requisite of this scheme of participation shall be training in the business of the company. It will be the responsibility of the government to organise this training programme. An "awareness of industrial relations and of business techniques will certainly make the workers more aware of the

actual problems faced by the companies in modern society. The training of the employees must, therefore, be immediately taken in hand."

(viii) The presence of the Worker Director on the Board would not lead to any breach in the confidentiality of the information required by him.

(ix) The Reforms Commission did not favour a two-tier representation, *i.e.*, a Supervisory Board and the Smaller Management Board.

FUNCTIONS UNDER THE SCHEME

The employees' representative/Worker Director participates in all the functions of the Board. Besides this, they also review the working of shop and plant councils and takes decisions on matters not settled by the Council.

WORKING OF SCHEMES IN INDIAN INDUSTRIES

A few public undertakings in the country have introduced the scheme on a somewhat experimental basis. A great enthusiasm has been shown by the banking industry. One director on the Board of each nationalised bank is appointed by the Central Government from among the employees of that bank, who is a worker and is chosen out of a panel of three employees furnished to the government by the representative union within the prescribed period. Workers' representatives have been appointed on the Boards of Management of a few public undertakings on a trial basis — in Hindustan Antibiotics Ltd., the Hindustan Organic Chemicals Ltd., the National Coal Mines Development Corporation has always had a nominated workers' representative on the Board. In the Port Trusts, there have always been two workers' representatives as Trustees or Commissioners, while on the Dock Labour Board, the number of workers' representatives has been more. BHEL, National News Print and Papers Mills (Gujarat), National Textile Mills (South Maharashtra, West Bengal, Assam, Bihar and Orissa), and the Rashtriya Chemicals and Fertilizer Ltd., have trade union leaders on the Boards of Directors of these undertakings.

For want of extensive empirical research in the working of the scheme, not much can be said about the effectiveness of this schemes. A great deal of evaluative theoretical writing on the subject has questioned the advantage of the implementation of the scheme. It has been argued that when, in the absence of healthy labour-management relations, schemes such as the JMCs, WCs and shops councils have failed miserably it is futile to think of the scheme for the representation of workers on the Board of Management of an enterprise, which calls for a higher degree of participation. A study of the scheme in the nationalised banks conducted by the National Labour Institute has shown that it has failed in fostering a congenial relationship based on mutual trust, respect, undertstanding and co-operation. It has also been observed that it has had little impact on industrial relations or on decision-making.

(H) WORKERS' PARTICIPATION IN SHARE CAPITAL

The Sachar Committee had, in its report to the government, observed: "Quite a majority (was) in favour of the suggestion that, in all their future issues of shares, the companies should reserve a portion of their new shares, say about 10% to 15%, exclusively for the workers, called the workers shares. These shares, in the first instance, must be offered to the employees of the company; failing that, they should be offered to the existing shareholders or the public. For that purpose, Section 81 of the Act should be suitably amended. Section 77 of the Act should also be amended, permitting companies to give to the employees a loan up to 12 months' salary or wages, not exceeding Rs. 12,000, for the purchase of the shares of the company." This scheme, however, has not found favour with the industries in India.

(I) PARTICIPATION THROUGH QUALITY CIRCLES

Quality circle is an association of. employees voluntarily formed to discuss with employer representatives, matters of interest to both the workers and employer. Each of the department in the company can have a QC where members are trained in problem solving techniques. These techniques include brain storing part to analysis, quality control, cause and effect analysis and other means.

Quality circles have worked successfully in some organisations and the employer has benefited with valuable ideas and suggestions coming from the shop floor workers and directly from employees in improving methods of work, improving quality, cost savings, wastage reductions. Employees are involved in decision making which make it easier to implement accepted suggestions. These circles encourage the employees to participate and in arriving at conclusions, to be implemented at the worksite which result in improving productivity and quality.

In Indian industries there are examples of such circles working satisfactorily and in some companies they have not produced desired results. On the positive side the workers feel confident that they are being recognised and on the negative side the unions feel that QCs are means of getting more work through the employees. These are voluntary associations and hence once employees participate, they make useful suggestions. Coilective bargaining process confers on workers right to negotiate with the employers on most important matters like terms of employment contract, wage levels, gradation, working hours, welfare treasury facilities to be provided and levels of performance standards and benefits which employers can extend. In this process both the parties come together and negotiate appropriate terms including wages, leave, incentive bonus, welfare amenities (besides legal provisions) and other terms for employees. When relations with unions and workers are cordial this is an effective way of participation in creating mutual confidence and trust and understanding.

(J) PARTICIPATION THROUGH COLLECTIVE BARGAINING

Collective bargaining process confers an workers right to negotiate with the employers on most important matters like terms of employment contract, wage levels, gradation, working house, welfare measuring facilities to be provided and levels of performance standards and benefits which employees can extend. In this process, both the parties come together and negotiate appropriate terms including welfare amenities (besides legal provisions) and other terms for employer when relations with unions, and workers are cordial this is effective way of participation in creating mutual confidence and trust and understanding.

EVALUATION OF WORKERS' PARTICIPATION IN MANAGEMENT SCHEME

The progress of working of the scheme was reviewed by tripartite committee on workers' participation in management in its meeting held on September 20, 1994. It remarked that 66 "out of 236 Central public sector undertakings which have been monitored, 108 enterprises have implemented the 1983 scheme or earlier schemes of the Ministry of Labour at the shop floor and plant levels, 63 enterprises have their own participative forums, 23 enterprises could not implement the scheme due to problems regarding method of representation of workers and 24 enterprises did not consider the scheme suitable as they have non-manufacturing units and employ only a few employees. The remaining 18 enterprises were in the process of being set up. The Committee also considered the provisions of the Participation of Workers in Management Bill, 1990 and the notices received for amendments to the Bill in the context of the changes that have taken place in industrial, trade and economic policies."

In India though the concept of participative management is supported in principle by all the parties — government, employees and employers — no serious interest has been shown in it, except, of course, by the government. From time to time, the government has come out with a variety of schemes which best serve the national interest; but it is disheartening to note that all the schemes have failed miserably. This is evident from the following observations.

"The workers' representatives are more concerned with the enlargement of their amenities and facilities and with the redressal of grievances, higher wages, better conditions of work and security of service than with such larger problems as reducing the rate of absenteeism, increasing productivity, effecting economies in the operations of the enterprise and suggesting better methods for a more efficient utilisation of plant and equipment. In a majority of cases, the joint management councils are not functioning satisfactorily."

"Employers do not take the joint management councils into their confidence in regard to amendments of Standing Orders, the introduction of new and better methods of production and manufacturing processes, redeployment of men and machines, and reduction in, or cessation of, operations despite their agreement that they would do so. The communication with, or the practice of giving information to, the workers has not been adequately developed; and although the management has agreed to transfer some administrative responsibilities to joint management councils, there has been no such transfer in actual practice."

A variety of factors that have contributed to the failure of the scheme have been discussed in the following paragraphs.

1. *Ideological Differences between Employees and Employers Regarding the Degree of Participation:* There is a fundamental difference between employees and employers regarding the level of participation by workers. The employers are of the opinion that workers' participation at the Board level should be introduced gradually in stages, while the employees feel that the scheme should be simultaneously introduced at all levels. The result is that the various schemes have been accepted half-heartedly.

2. *Failure to Imbibe the Spirit of Participation by the Parties:* One of the major factors responsible for its failure is the inability of the parties to imbibe the spirit of participation. The employer looks upon bipartite bodies (the shop council, plant council and JMCs) as substitutes for trade unions, while employees regard it as their rival. This attitude has generated hostility, apathy, and at times even jealousy, among them, with the result that the spirit of participation has suffered death *ab initio.*

3. *Multiplicity of Participative Forms:* The existence of a number of joint bodies — the works committee, joint-management council, shop council, unit council, plant councils, canteen committee, safety committee, suggestion committee etc., — each with an ill-defined role and functions has often created confusion, duplication of efforts and resulted in a waste of time and energy. The resultant effect has been the improper functioning of the scheme.

4. *Lack of Strong Trade Unionism:* In comparison to strong trade unionism in such developed countries as the USA, UK, Germany, Japan, etc., the trade union movement in our country is fragmented, poorly organised, reven by intense inter-union rivalry, and coloured and by various political philosophies. In such a state of affairs, it is futile to think of effective workers' participation in management through their own elected representatives.

5. *Unhappy Industrial Relations:* At no point of time in the economic history of the country the industrial climate has been free from labour unrest. It is a pity that the government has imposed participative schemes on industries in such a climate where, for its anticipated result has been its total failure. In fact, the scheme has turned out be a fiasco from its very inception.

6. *Illiteracy of Workers:* The workers' representatives on various participative bodies are, by and large, illiterate. In the absence of adequate knowledge on their part of the concept, rationale and benefit of the participative schemes, they are unable to actively participate meaningfully in their working. The result is that either they fail to arrive at any decision or bank on outsiders for guidance who invariably persuade them not to expect that forum to solve their problems. This fact is reflected in workers' inability to accept the scheme.

7. *Non-Co-operative Attitude of the Working Class:* The litigation-minded workers' representatives on the various participative forums quite often raise those issues which are beyond the scope of those forums or bodies. This attitude tempts employers not to use the schemes while dealing with workers' problems. This fact, therefore, has had a dampering effect on the working of the scheme.

8. *Delays in the Implementation of the Decisions of Participative Bodies:* One of the major handicaps in the effective working of the participative scheme is that there are inordinate delays in the implementation of the decisions arrived at by the various participative forums. This often generates apathy or dissatisfaction and frustration among the workers — a fact which invariably leads to their waning interest in the participative scheme.

CONDITIONS NECESSARY FOR EFFECTIVE WORKING OF THE SCHEME

Although the participative culture has taken root in some enterprises in the private and public sector, however, its overall progress is not very much encouraging. Therefore, attempts should be initiated to provide necessary momentum to the scheme. Herein a few measures are listed, which needs consideration in making the scheme more meaningful.

(i) One of the important factors in the success of the scheme is that the work environment must be congenial enough to motivate workers to give whole-hearted co-operation with a view to ensuring its efficient operation. An environment of industrial conflicts flowing from bad interpersonal relations

will generate frustration and alienation among workers, which will have a dampering effect on the working of system. Therefore, attempts be made to cultivate a healthy work environment.

(ii) There must be total identity of approach on the part of both the parties to the working of schemes at different levels. There must be complete agreement on the manner in which the various participative schemes should function. Once the areas are clearly spelt out the side-tracking the main questions is avoided, the scheme can yield desirable results.

(iii) Both the workers and management must have complete faith in the efficacy of the system and should pool their talents and resources, and demonstrate their will to work for the realisation of their goals.

(iv) The concept of labour participation in management must be given a wide publicity so that the idea of participation may take root in the minds of those who are to implement the scheme. Necessary lectures, discussions, film shows, conferences, seminars and other methods of propaganda may be fruitfully employed to create enthusiasm about the scheme among the management personnel as well as the workers.

(v) The participation should be real. The issues related to major strategies, product diversification; the evaluation of costs, the development of human resources and the expansion of markets should also be brought under the jurisdiction of the participating bodies. These bodies should meet frequently and their decisions should be strictly adhered to and implemented in time.

(vi) The objectives to be achieved should not be unrealistically high, vague or ambiguous but be achieverable, clear and tought to all focal participants.

(vii) The form, coverage, extent and levels of participation should grow in response to specific environment capacity and interest of the parties concerned.

(viii) The system of participation must be complementary to the collective bargaining process.

(ix) The participative schemes should be evolutionary. Therefore, to begin with, each should be introduced at the shop floor and plant levels. Till these schemes get going the scheme of workers' involvement at the Board level should not be undertaken.

(x) The workers' participation scheme on order to be effective, must be based on mutual trust and confidence. Therefore, attempts to enforce it by law or compulsion would defeat its basic purpose.

(xi) The trade union movement should be developed on sound lines, so that the workers may enjoy real involvement in the various participative forums. The proliferation of unions in industries should be restricted by legislative means.

(xii) The programmes for training and education should be developed comprehensively. For this purpose, "labour education should be concerned with not the head alone, not the heart alone, not the hands alone, but with all the three: it should make workers think, feel and act." Labour is to be educated to enable them to think, clearly, rationally and logically; to enable them to feel deeply and emotionally; and to enable them to act in a

responsible way. The management at different levels also needs to be trained and oriented to give it a fresh thinking on the issues concerned.

(xiii) There must be a free flow of information between labour and management throughout the enterprise. This will help both labour and management to work in co-operation and not at cross-purposes and constructively, too, in the attainment of enterprise goals, for distrust and suspicion, which often puts obstacles in the effective working of the participative scheme, will go by the board.

(xiv) The decisions taken at different participatory forums must be sincerely carried out in a stipulated period of time so as to generate faith in the utility of the scheme.

(xv) The management should design a proper system so that the effectiveness of the scheme may be assessed periodically, and, if required, the necessary changes may be made to make the scheme more beneficial for all the parties.

CONCLUSION

Though the scheme of workers' participation in management has not shown satisfactory results, it should be made to work at least in the field of increasing the production and productivity of labour by giving the workers a feeling that he is an integral and important part of the organisation and so creating a climate in which he may get reasonable opportunities to show his worth in contributing his share to the production targets. Joint consultation should form a part of labour-management decisions on important issues affecting not only production but also the very working lives of the employees. Management should have a constructive attitude and should regard trade unions not as an obstacle to be overcome but as a highly valuable and powerful instrument which, if properly handled, can be of very great help in increasing production and productivity. Both employers and unions should solemnly resolve to carry on the experiment in proper spirit. The government should take responsibility for the provision of a satisfactory workers' education programme so that they may be properly equipped for their tasks. The scheme seems to have a bright future.

❑ ❑ ❑

13

Personnel Manual

We have seen in the earlier chapters the role and the responsibilities of a personnel manager in an organisation.

The personnel manager to be effective and efficient has to have before him a set policy guidelines, practices to be followed and rules which will be adhered to.

A personnel manual should be prepared by him containing philosophy of the organisation various policies, objectives, practices and procedures, programmes, the responsibilities of different individuals in the organisation, also contain the work flow chart, initiation, implementation and approving authorities. Such a manual can be given to all line and staff managers for their use and follow up.

This chapter outlines the topics that can be included in the manual. Each organisation will have to decide its strategy on the basis of which the Personnel Policy can be drafted. It should be noted that due to environmental changes the personnel policy and practices will need modification and hence these will be have to be flexible and not rigid the topics outlined here are based on standard practices followed by some successful companies.

CONTENTS OF THE PERSONNEL MANUAL

(1) Organisation goals and objectives.

(2) Personnel Policy.

(3) The role of the Personnel Department.

(4) Human Resources Planning.

(5) Job Design, Job Analysis, Job Evaluation.

(6) Recruitment and Selection

(7) Orientation, Induction and Placement.

(8) Training and Development Education.

(9) Performance Appraisal.

(10) Remuneration, Rewards, Incentives.

(11) Employee Benefits and Services including leave, leave rules.

(12) Promotions, Transfers, Separations.

(13) Employee Welfare/Employee Relations.

(14) Safety and Health, Counselling.

(15) Employee Communication, Suggestion Schemes, Quality Circles.

(16) Grievance Redressal.

(17) Discipline and Disciplinary Action including Legislative rules.

(18) Employee Participation.

(19) Industrial Relations including relations with unions.

(20) Human Resource Audit.

(21) Legal Compliance of various Labour Laws.

(22) Building Employee Commitment.

(23) Retirement and Retirement Benefits.

We give below some illustrative examples of some items:

(1) ORGANISATION GOALS AND OBJECTIVES

The goals of our organisation are:

(1) Long-term Survival.

(2) Maximum growth.

(3) Maximum earning.

(4) Reputation for Industry Leadership.

(5) Reputation as a good employer and a good place to work at.

(6) Larger share of market

(7) Others — e.g., to produce goods/provide services which will satisfy customers, customer satisfaction.

(8) Produce Quality Products.

(9) Care of Shareholders and their interest.

(10) Contribute to the national growth.

(11) Follow Fair Business Practices and others....

Each of these objectives can be further elaborated briefly in the manual.

(2) PERSONNEL POLICY

Meaning of Policy: A policy is a man made rule of pre-determined course of action that is established to guide the performance of work toward organisation's objectives, goals. Personnel Policies constitute guide to action. Policies define the strategy of the management, company policy reduces the range of individual decisions and encourages management by exception, policies furnish the general standards or basis on which decisions are reached. Their gensis lies in an organisation's values, philosophy, concepts and principles. Policy statements and (to be incorporated in the manual) areas to mentioned in the manual relate to —

(a) Employment: Fair practices in selecting the right man for the job, provide equal opportunities for career progression based on merit and performance.

(b) Training and Development: We shall offer training to all employees so that they qualify for better jobs and career progression and meet the required manpower needs like improved skills, improved performance and employee commitment.

(c) Security of Employment: It is the policy of this management to assure security of employment to employees whose performance is excellent and who work will commitment. Such employees will be rewarded by incentives and by recognition of results achieved.

(d) It is our policy to communicate with all employee through appropriate channels and this communication will be two way communication. Employee will be encouraged to give suggestions for improvement and a fair grievance redressal system is established to redress their grievances.

(4) HUMAN RESOURCE PLANNING

Policy: It is the policy of our company to forecast manpower requirements for every succeeding three/five years with a view to utilise to optimum level all human resources presently employed and to plan for future needs to fulfil the organisational objectives.

Objectives:

(1) To determine recruitment levels

(2) To forecast future new skills, functions and developments.

(3) To ensure timely recruitment of the required employees.

(4) To plan for the training schedule.

(5)

(6)

Responsibility: It is the responsibility of the Human Resource Manager and he will take following actions:

(1) To obtain manpower requirements from the departments.

(2) Draft a HR Plan and forecast considering.

(a) Actual strength of employees on the date;

(b) Separations due to — (i) Retirement, (ii) Resignation, (iii) Transfers Promotion, (iv) Offer reasons for separations, (iv) New Vacancies.

(3) Succession Planning/Career Planning

(4) The Plan should be approved by concerned authority.

(5) To implement the approved plan at appropriate times.

(6) To periodically review the plan. (annually)

(8) TRAINING DEVELOPMENT POLICY

It is the policy of our organisation:

(1) To give top priority to human resources development to enhance the skills level improve attitudes, performance and productivity through training and developmental programmes. It is understood each individual employee is equally responsible for his development:

(2) To provide training if necessary before placement.

(3) To regularly monitor performance levels and identify the training needs and provide facilities for such training for individual growth.

(4) To encourage through training activity internal promotion, career development and provide employees for company needs from time to time.

Responsibility: The Human Resource Department alongwith the support of line managers shall be responsible for training and development activity.

The Human Resource Department will asses whether suitable internal resources are available for imparting training. If such resources are not available internally the HR Dept. will average for appropriable external resources.

We give below an outline of the sub contents of some items of contents of the manual. (illustrative examples).

(9) PERFORMANCE APPRAISAL SYSTEM

Policy and Objectives

(1) Objective assessment of performance and competence of employes for the purpose of determining, their:

(a) Salaries.

(b) Increments, Rewards.

(c) Transfer, Promotion, Separation.

(d) Potential assesment and Career Planning.

(e) Training and Development needs.

Responsibility: It is the responsibility of the HR Department to initiate actions for:

(a) Devising appropriate appraisal systems and get them approved.

(b) To train the line managers to appraise their employees objectively.

(c) To devise forms and instruments for employees appraisal periodically.

(d) Use appraisal for salary rise, rewards, promotion, training and development career planning.

Methods of Appraisal: The company (has to choose) appropriate method of appraisal from the following available methods.

(1) Past-oriented methods:

(a) Rating scales.

(b) Forced choice method.

(c) Forced distribution method.

(d) Critical incident method rating.

(e) Behaviourally Anchored Rating Scales (BARS).

(f) Performance tests and observations.

(g) Annual Confidential reports.

(2) Future oriented methods:

(a) Management by objectives.

(b) Psychological appraisals.

(c) Assesment centres.

The following steps will be followed in Appraisal:

(1) Defining the job including duties, responsibilities.

(2) Appraising the performance of an employee, periodically, regularly.

(3) Providing feedback to the employee.

(4) Training the appraisers on how to appraise.

(5) Using the appraisal for decision making.

(6) Choosing the method and forms to be used.

A separate manual of job descriptions and duties and expected standards. Key performance areas is available in the personnel department. This gives guidelines as to what exactly is to be appraised.

Although this manual is primarily a guide book for Personnel department, copies of this book should be given to all departmental managers after writing in detail on each of the topics covered. This will facilitate the line managers practising fair, right personnel practices.

The manual needs to be revised from time to time to bring it up-to-date. In certain organisations a common manual is used for both blue collar and white collar workers and separate manual is prepared for Managerial staff. This manual should be used only by appropriate staff. If needed the levels of decision-making, authority available to various staff who use this manual should be described in the manual.

Specimen of Form that can be used for Performance Appraisal
(Method M.B.O.)

Name of the Company ____________________

Period for which Appraisal done year ____________________

Name of Employe __________ Age __________ Date of Entry __________

Department __________ Title __________
(Position)

Major Responsibilities ____________________

Main Duties (Key Performance Areas KPA) ____________________

Immediate Supervisor/Superior ____________________

Next Superior ____________________

Date of Appraisal __________ Names of Raters/Appraiser __________
1 __________
2 __________

(A) Performance Review Against Objective By Employee

Agreed Objectives __________ Targets Achieved __________ Ratings __________

Targets	O	VG	G	A	I
1					
2					
3					
4					
5					

O = Outstanding *VG* = Very Good, *G* = Good, *A* = Adequate, *I* = Inadequate.

(B) Performance Against Objectives (By Immediate Superior)

Outstanding V Good Good Adequate Inadequate

(C) Appraisal of Critical Attributes (By Immediate Superior)

Critical Attributes

		O	VG	G	A	I
1. Initiative	Ability to determine and initiate actions that results in improved performance on jobs without waiting to be hold.					
2. Resource fullness	Ability to muster resources to achieve the targeted results and devise ways and means of solving problems in difficult situations					

		O	VG	G	A	I
3. Inter personal	Ability to interact Relations & Team Spirit with employees at all levels to gain their support and confidence, respect to work in collaborative and participative manner.					
4. Communication	Ability to convey skills thoughts and feelings clearly through oral and written experience					

(D) Areas of Strengths and Improvements
(By Immediate Superior)

Major Strengths:

Areas of Improvement:

(E) Potential for Growth (By Immediate Superior)

Immediate

Near Future

Future

(F) Needs for Training Development (By Immediate Superior)

Incompany Training Programmes (Please check with Training and Development Section)

1. Course ______
2. Course ______
3. Course ______

External Courses (Mention course no..) ______

(1) ______ (2) ______ (3) ______

(G) Specific Development Plans and Proposed Action Programmes (Please)
Action

Job Enlargement ______

Job Rotation ______

Others ______

(H) Comments by senior superior:

(1) Specific ______ (2) General ______

(I) Recommendations for Salary Increase/Incentives or Rewards (In Keeping with Company Policy)

Previous Year	This Year
Signature ______	Signature ______

(J) For use in Personnel/HRD Department Comments by HRD Head: Agree/Disagree Others

(1) On Potential/Growth/Training Development

(2) Salary Rewards /Promotion/Transfer

(3) Profile of last three years

(4) Feedback date — Feedback to be given by

(1) Mr. ________ (2) Mr. ________

GUIDELINES FOR PREPARING PERSONNEL MANUAL

(1) The HR Manager has to study conditions obtaining in the organisation and discuss the contents with line managers.

(2) A copy of Personnel Manual can be given to the Line Managers and others who are incharge of employee or groups of employees.

(3) The manual being a guide for successful operation of the Personnel/HR Department the contents should be very carefully drafted after studying standard practices in the industry/region.

(4) The directions in the manual should be followed strictly without any deviations.

(5) It is recommended that apart from the manual which is a guide for the management and managers HR Department should prepare a "Handbook for employees." This handbook will contain information on terms, conditions of employment, rules of discipline, expectation from employees, policies relating to employment, remuneration, promotion, grievance handling, procedure, rules of discipline and other. The handbook should clearly mention everything, that employee should know about his employment conditions.

(6) This personnel manual should be updated periodically.

(7) The section on legal compliance should be clear and latest, rules & directions to be followed should be briefly mentioned.

(8) The contents of the manual can be abridged or expanded depending on the actual user's need.

(9) The manual should contain various forms which are used by personnel department, e.g., Interview guidelines, performance Appraisal, Forms relating to Health Safety, Employee information and History.

(10) While preparing the manual, the terms to be included, their description, action to be taken, persons responsible for taking actions should be clearly mentioned in it and the extent of their authority should be mentioned.

(11) The manual should contain matters relating to rules of discipline, how discriplinary actions are to be initiated and the outcome of such actions. It should clearly state the grivance handling procedure. If there is any legislation on the matters of discipline, it should be followed.

(12) In the section pertaining to Industrial/Employee Relations, the policy of the Management in relation to the Unions of Employees, Bipartite relations, functions, responsibilities of the unions in the company must be mentioned.

A specimen of some items of HRM, manual of "ABC" company is given below:

"ABC" COMPANY

HUMAN RESOURCE MANAGEMENT DEPARTMENT MANUAL

CHAPTER **CONTENTS**

1. Philosophy of "ABC"
2. Human Resource Policy of ABC
3. Human Resource Planning
4. Employment, Selection, Placement
5. Training, Development, Education
6. Organisation Design and Structure
7. Performance Appraisal System
8. Promotions Transfer, Separation
9. Salary, Wages, Administration
10. Employee Relations — Communications
11. Employee Discipline, Grievance Redressal
12. Information System

We elaborate in brief contents of a few chapters below

5. EMPLOYMENT SELECTION, PLACEMENT

(a) Policy, (b) Objective, (c) System, (d) Responsibility.

Policy (i) It is the policy of 'ABC' company to follow a sound and systematic employment, selection and placement procedure in order to place the right man on the right job at the right time at all levels in the organisation.

(ii) This is the policy of 'ABC' to employ the most suitable candidate on the basis of education, experience, aptitude, qualities, habits which will result in superior performance on the job and career progression with 'ABC'.

(iii) This the policy of 'ABC' that when a vacancy arises it may be filled by promotion, transfer of a suitable employee provided he is capable and suitable for this position.

Intent: The intent is to attract and retian employees of superior qualification, skills, aptitudes, abilities, experience and place them on jobs for which they are most suitable and deserve to pursue a career with 'ABC'.

SELECTION PROCEDURE

(a) Interview of candidates who are primarily found suitable after screening of their application.

(b) Interview by Committee Consisting of (i) HR Manager, (ii) Line Manager, (iii) Departmental head, (iv) If necessary by the CEO.

(c) Candidates for employment required to fill the company's Application form and appear for interview when called.

Responsibility	Action
(1) Line Managers	(i) Initiate requisition with authorisation for recruiting the Candidate
(2) HR Manager	
—do—	(ii) Initiate action to recruit suitable candidate by using
—do—	(i) Interval or (ii) External source
	(iii) Take action for interviewing & selecting suitable candidate if there is no suitable candidate internally available.

(d) As for as possible the decision of selection should be taken on the same day on which the candidate is called for interview or interviews (by a committee)

(e) HR Manager will use the interview/selection Form (Appendix I to this Chapter)

APPENDIX I

INTERVIEW

Interview/Selection Form of ABC company

Name of the candidate .... Position applied for ....

Date of Interview

Members of the Interview/Selection Committee:

(1) Mr.. (HR Manager)

(2) Mr.. (Manager Department)

(3) Mr .... (Departmental Head)

(4) Mr.. (CEO when necessary)

Requirement of the Job (Key Performance Areas)

Comments of the Interviewes:

(1) Meets requirement of all KPA

(a) Adequately,........................... (b) Partially.................. (c) None....................

(2) Levels of Knowledge, Skills, Experience

Knowledge —	O	VG	G	A	I
Railways					
Skills					
Experience					

O = Outstanding. VG = Very Good. G = Good. A = Adequate. I = Inadequate.

❑ ❑ ❑

14

HUMAN RESOURCE AUDIT

In the previous chapters we have noted different functions of HR Management. Howsoever carefully we may design the HR system, the implementation is an important step for successful function of HR management. It is however necessary to know, regularly and at frequent intervals, how the HR management activities are doing. This is possible by carrying out HR Audit, i.e., auditing various functions of HR department. The HR audit can be carried out by a suitably qualified person of the organisation. The HR audit is a tool for evaluating the personnal activities of an organisation. It gives feedback about how well the HR specialist and the line managers who practice HR applications are doing. It acts an overall quality control check on HR function and the evaluation reveals how these activities support the overall strategy of the organisation. The benefits that result from such an audit are:

(i) To identify the contribution of HR dependent on the organisation.

(ii) To identify and take corrective actions on the shortcomings/and or weaknesses that were noticed as a result of the audit.

(iii) To improve the performance of personnel department and the performance of line managers who practise HR management in day-to-day discharge of their duties.

(iv) It clarifies HR department's duties and repsonsibilities.

(v) To locate critical personnel problems and take necessary action to resolve them.

(v) To find out how HR department can become more effective.

SCOPE OF AUDIT

The HR Audit should cover all aspects of HR function and the scope can be understood by asking several questions like —

(1) Is personnel planning, recruitment and selection render timely help for manpower supply?

(2) Does job analysis exist for all jobs?

(3) Is the training and devleopment activity useful? What corrections are necessary in this respect?

(4) Does the remuneration and reward system, motivate employees to do their best? Are any corrective steps necessary.

(5) Does the performance appraisal system help in assing the true perforamnce of all employees an ddoe sit reflect the potential existing in the organisation.

(6) Are the employee relations cordial, are their any conflicts, is the girvance redressal rpocedure working satisfactorily?

(7) Are the communication channels working do they need any changes?

(8) Does the HRm practices respond to employee satisfaction needs.

(9) Are employee related costs within the budgeted limits.

(10) Is the percentage of employee turnover high? What are the reasons and what corrective steps are necessary.

(11) What is the level of employee motivation commitment and morale amongst- the employees.

The audit-report should be used to effect corrections and improvement in the performance of personnel function.

❑ ❑ ❑

REFERENCES

1. Jucius, M.J. *Personnel Management,* Richard D. Irwin, Illinois, Homewood, 1973.
2. Yoder, Dale. *Personnel Management and Industrial Relations,* Prentice Hall of India, New Delhi, 1972.
3. Flippo, Edwin B. *Personnel Management*, McGraw, Kogakush Ltd., 1980.
4. Wendell, French., *The Personnel Management Process*, Human Resources Administration, Houghton Mifflin Co., New York, 1974.
5. Scott W. Clothier R. and Sprigel, W.R. *"Personnel Management, Principles, Practices and Point of View*, Tata McGraw Hill Pub. Co., New Delhi, 1977.
6. Functions of Personnel Department Institute of *Personnel Management,* London, 1949.
7. North, Colt C.F. *Personnel Management: Principles and Practice.*
8. Pigors Paul and Myers Charles. *Personnel Administration,* 1973.
9. Wendell, French. *The Personnel Management Process,* 1974.
10. Koontz, Harold, and O'Donnel Cyril. *Principles of Management,* McGraw Hill Book Co. 1976.
11. Drucker, Peter. *The Practice of Management,* Harper and Brothers, New York, 1954.
12. McGregor, Douglas. The *Humanside of Enterprise,* McGraw Hill Co., New York. 1960.
13. SiKula, Andrew F. *Personnel Administration and Human Resource Management,* John Wiley and Sons, New York, 1977.
14. Rudrabasavaraj M.N. *Personnel Administration Policies in India*, V.M.N. Institute of Cooperative Management, Pune, 1969.
15. Robbins, Stephen P. *Personnel — The Management of Human Resources,* Prentice Hall Inc., New Jersey, 1978.
16. Flippo Edvin. B. *Principles of Management,* 1976.

17. I.L.O., *Job Evaluation: Studies and Report,* New Series, No. 56, Geneva.

18. I.L.O., *Wages: General Report,* 1948.

19. Beach D.S. *Personnel*, The Management of People at Work, 1977.

20. Subba Rao, P. *Essentials of Human Resource Management and Industrial Recoliar,* Himalaya Publishing House, Mumbai.